BFI SILVER

Representing the very best in critical writing on films and film-makers, these beautifully presented new editions and reissues of classic titles from BFI Publishing feature new introductions by leading film critics or scholars. They assess the unique contribution of the work in question and its author to the field of film studies and to the wider public understanding of moving image culture.

ALSO AVAILABLE:
Godard
A Long Hard Look at 'Psycho'
Mamoulian

A Mirror for England

British Movies from Austerity to Affluence

2nd Edition

Raymond Durgnat

with a foreword by Kevin Gough-Yates

palgrave
macmillan

A BFI book published by Palgrave Macmillan

This edition published in 2011 by
PALGRAVE MACMILLAN

on behalf of the

BRITISH FILM INSTITUTE
21 Stephen Street, London W1T 1LN
www.bfi.org.uk

There's more to discover about film and television through the BFI. Our world-renowned archive, cinemas, festivals, films, publications and learning resources are here to inspire you.

Palgrave Macmillan in the UK is an imprint of Macmillan Publishers Limited, registered in England, company number 785998, of Houndmills, Basingstoke, Hampshire RG21 6XS. Palgrave Macmillan in the US is a division of St Martin's Press LLC, 175 Fifth Avenue, New York, NY 10010. Palgrave Macmillan is the global academic imprint of the above companies and has companies and representatives throughout the world. Palgrave® and Macmillan® are registered trademarks in the United States, the United Kingdom, Europe and other countries.

Series cover design: keenan
Cover image: *This Sporting Life* (Lindsay Anderson, 1963), Independent Artists
Images provided by BFI Stills, Posters and Designs
Designed and set by couch
Printed in China

This book is printed on paper suitable for recycling and made from fully managed and sustained forest sources. Logging, pulping and manufacturing processes are expected to conform to the environmental regulations of the country of origin.

British Library Cataloguing-in-Publication Data
A catalogue record for this book is available from the British Library
A catalog record for this book is available from the Library of Congress
10 9 8 7 6 5 4 3 2 1
20 19 18 17 16 15 14 13 12 11

ISBN 978-1-84457-453-7 (pb)
ISBN 978-1-84457-454-4 (hb)

(previous page) *The Man in the White Suit*: Alec Guinness

Contents

Reading *A Mirror for England*

KEVIN GOUGH-YATES

A Mirror for England was first published in 1970 by Faber & Faber;[1] copies had been circulating among Raymond Durgnat's friends and colleagues in various manuscript forms for over a year as he continued to revise and modify it, in response to the developments in film studies which were part of the wider cultural shifts that were occurring in schools, art colleges and universities. The late 1960s was an exhilarating moment in film studies and the book has a sense of discovery and dash. It runs where others were treading cautiously and takes risks both in its manner of writing and in its judgements. Durgnat was fully aware that he was breaking new ground for himself and for writing on British cinema; he wanted to complicate rather than simplify our understanding of it, to reveal its complexities rather than to ignore or dismiss it as critics usually did, as not having the values or the qualities of European and American cinema. Reading *A Mirror for England* now, one has the sensation of a discursive and deliberately uncompleted work, notes for a larger book that was never written, but it is very much as he wanted, of the moment and a combative intervention into the debate on film theory.

After 40 years, writers on British cinema still kick off with *A Mirror for England*. John Hill's *Sex, Class and Realism* (1986), refers to it on its second page, if only to challenge its premise 'that conclusions about British society can be arrived at on the evidence of the films alone. Films, he suggests, can be understood as 'reflections' of the society that makes them'.[2] Although Durgnat makes no such claim, it is of no matter as there has been no skirting round *A Mirror for England* since its first appearance. The historian, Jeffrey Richards recognised its iconic significance in his *Visions of Yesterday* and quotes from it approvingly.[3] The cultural historian, Sue Harper returns to it when writing on Powell and Pressburger's *A Matter of Life and Death* (1946).[4] The film historian,

Melanie Williams, makes use of it in writing about the 'female-centred films' directed by J. Lee Thompson, as recently as 2009.[5] Citations abound; the list seems endless. Even now, it astounds by its courage and its audacity; if you think that you have an 'original' approach to a film or a director's work and check it against *A Mirror for England*, you generally discover that Raymond Durgnat has said it already. '*The Crazy Mirror* (1969)[6] and *A Mirror for England* were written very quickly.' Durgnat said later in an interview. 'They're full of inaccuracies, which I think doesn't matter, because the main point was arranging a kind of rendezvous between thinking about movies and thinking, not so much about sociology, as about the experience that people are having all the time.'[7]

Well, certainly, but *A Mirror for England* has other purposes. One is to emphasise the importance of fantasy and of imagination in the making and the study of cinema. A second is to rescue the concept of British cinema from the contempt of auteur critics who slavishly followed *Cahiers du cinéma*. And another is to rescue film criticism from the moral cant, slavish snobbery and good taste of the *Monthly Film Bulletin* and *Sight and Sound*, which took their authority simply from being official publications of the 'uniquely institutionalised' British Film Institute. If Durgnat took sides, he associated himself more closely with the magazine, *Movie*, with its emphasis on the rhetoric of cinema and the manner in which the response of the audience is affected.[8]

Cahiers had disdainfully dismissed British cinema, François Truffaut famously describing it as a non sequitur, essentially because it had no auteurs. Durgnat considered it risible to rate highly 'such Hollywood conformists' as Howard Hawks, Leo McCarey, and Raoul Walsh, on auteur theory principles, but not to do so with British directors such as Roy Ward Baker, Terence Fisher, and Michael Powell, each of whom were, he insisted, distinctive cinematic voices. Thematic considerations were often of greater importance to style than 'textual' ones. He was, he said later, interested in 'the decent truths asserted in run-of-the-mill and B movies ... the cinema needs rescuing from the film buffs who treat every identifiable director as an auteur and every auteur as a thinker and every thinker as a minor genius.'[9] He does not waste time looking for a governing principle to define a British film, he asks only how the concept of one might operate. 'Our criterion has to be rather arbitrary and subjective; is it about Britain, about British attitudes, or if not, does it feel British?'[10]

He was scathing at *Sight and Sound* for sneeringly comparing, what it described as '*The French Line*', as though there was only one, with its own 'humanism' and in which the younger English critics were described as seeing art as 'something for kicks', where violence 'on the screen is accepted as a stimulant'. 'Not surprisingly', he writes, 'they disliked this representation of themselves when all they were asking for was for more directors to be treated with critical respect and for more attention to be paid for subtleties of style.'[11] Each film creates its own frame of reference, formal considerations are not the only ways in which ideas might unfold; an artist's style is as individual as his face or his finger-prints because he tends to bring similar insights and details to every subject he treats, it is not mere visual mannerism.

The *Sight and Sound* critics, Durgnat continued, were

heirs to an upper-middle-class climate of cultural habit and opinion exemplified, at its best, by the novels of E.M. Forster, at its most mediocre, by the complacent pessimism of the remarks on the popular cinema by Palinurus in *The Unquiet Grave*,[12] and at its least pleasant, by the disdainful assumptions of superiority over, and censorious defensiveness towards 'the popular'. They brought to the task of film criticism a philosophical infrastructure which, felt rather than stated, and certainly never examined, included such axioms as that the civilized few must protect the humanism of the a minority art-culture against and unthinking and vaguely unpleasant world which was exemplified by, variously, 'the moguls', the 'mass media', the 'undiscriminating public' or an undefined *sensed* 'ruck' of inferiority.[13]

Durgnat's reputation as a contrarian is sealed at this time. He fires in two directions, despairing at British film criticism, and unable to accept the idea that a distinctive visual style was a sufficient condition for distinguished film-making. He understood the better part of 'middle-class' British cinema to be more nuanced than Truffaut and other critics appreciated. It was 'richer in tension, in honest doubt and sophisticated misgivings' than allowed for by the *Monthly Film Bulletin*. He did not engage directly with Truffaut over the ways that ideas are communicated through individual style, rather he attempted to adumbrate (a favourite word of Durgnat's) a fruitful approach to streams of British cinema to its directors who had previously received short shrift from its writers and critics. He argued that an essential strength of a film was its capacity for multiple readings and meaning. Any artistic creation emerged from a culture, a history and, perhaps, a collective vision, not from a director's inner voice and feelings. 'Before Barthes', Durgnat once said to me, 'there was Empson',[14] in a characteristic knock at the belief that, without France, there would be no theories of art and that, without *Cahiers*, there would be no film theory in England. 'It's a major cultural disaster', he later declared,

for the English speaking left-wing that *Cahiers du cinéma* caught the fashion when it did – first with the Nouvelle Vague and then again in May 1968 – and that *Positif* didn't. *Cahiers* 1960-style forced it into a kind of stylistic-auteurist-idealist cul-de-sac, then came a rigid counter-reaction, saturated with an idealism masked by an old-fashioned rationalism. Now I come to think of it, *Positif* throughout the '60s was fed by a double stream, of anarcho-Surrealism and of Marxism, that combined aspects of two alternative extremes – the hippie years as a kind of neo-anarcho-Surrealism, and the rebirth of Marxism. But English-speaking film criticism has been spinning between a right-bank aestheticism and a sort of bourgeois radicalism ... [Read] *Premier Plan* on the Nouvelle Vague. And *Positif.* They saw it as the expression of a new free-wheeling bourgeois culture, which had learned to be very mobile, which had learned to be radical in the sense that it was constantly ready to revise its own opinions and its own character, which was just anarcho-bourgeois. After all, Truffaut, Chabrol, Rivette, Rohmer are all thoroughly conservative directors now.[15]

His Catherine Wheel approach: his asides, his puns and alliterations, his digressions into imaginary scriptwriting and such, provide the kind of writing that led one leading newspaper critic and writer to find him 'unreadable' and, certainly, some passages in *A Mirror for England* are torturously augmented, although generally with a purpose. His celebrated description of *The Tales of Hoffmann* (pp. 210–11), for example, ridicules the moral posturing of the *Monthly Film Bulletin*, which dismissed the film as having

no clear sense of direction, no single purpose at all ... Powell and Pressburger's most spectacular failure ... a welter of aimless ingenuity ... the total ensemble of striving romanticism, of Offenbach, of expressionist theatrical décors by Hein Heckroth, of rich Technicolor photography, of simultaneous opera and ballet with dubbed voices issuing from the dancers as they pirouette, and of camera tricks, results more in overwhelming confusion even than incongruity.[16]

Durgnat's education, his exposure to British film industry and his post-graduate research at the Slade School of Fine Art, under the auspices of film director Thorold Dickinson, led him to disdain over-arching theories. As an undergraduate, Durgnat was influenced by the influential literary critic I.A. Richards and his pupil William Empson, who brought rationality and the close reading of texts to their fields. Durgnat was deeply influenced by Dickinson, whose films, such as *Gaslight* (1940) and *The Queen of Spades* (1949), were cornerstones in British cinema. He, along with Hitchcock, was the only British director to take seriously the rhetoric of cinema and to consider the communication process as much a part of film-making as the production itself. Dickinson, surrounded by students, would sit at a Steenbeck, running a film backwards and forwards, describing and analysing selected films, but also interrogating the interpretive process by methodically examining the responses of his students. As a method, it offered a closer reading of film than Durgnat had previously encountered. Dickinson, who had been an influential insider within the British film industry since the early 1930s, an editor and a director, was able to illustrate and describe both technique and purpose. Durgnat was finally able to relate British cinema to its audience, the nation's history and to his own background.

Durgnat was very much a creator of his family myth. The family, on his father's side was descended from refugee French Huguenots who settled in Switzerland. His great-grandfather, according to his account 'came down from a Jura Mountain village with all his worldly goods in a handkerchief on a stick of his shoulder' to settle in the Swiss canton of Vaud, where the family prospered by opening the village shop. His mother's family was 'fairly wealthy peasant bourgeoisie' from French-Switzerland, Roman Catholics 'from a sort of rural proletariat' or 'sunken middle-class', who converted to Protestantism, which he described as 'a certain kind of evolved Calvinism, to which she gave an Armenian flavouring ... simply by taking religion seriously.' His own parents moved to London during the depression of the 1920s and opened a draper's shop in Walthamstow, East London, close to the Leytonstone, where Alfred Hitchcock was brought up and in whose work he had a lifetime interest. He grew up in a family that he described as 'part petit-bourgeois, part upper working class' in which art was transmuted through religion and amateur dramatics.

At the outbreak of the Second World War, he was seven years of age and evacuated to avoid the German bombing of London. It was a searing experience to be trundled through 14 different schools in five years, where he never fitted and was sometimes tormented and it confirmed him as a permanent outsider. A beneficiary of the 1944 Education Act, he went to Grammar School and to Cambridge University where he read English but still felt isolated. By the end, he was yearning to work in the film industry and instead of accepting a proffered Junior Research Fellowship, he grasped the opportunity to join ABPC (Associated British Picture Corporation), which was unfortunately gradually shrinking to become the British end of Warner-Pathé. He received no credits, but remembered working on the romps *Girls at Sea* (Gilbert Gunn, 1958) and *Tamahine* (Philip Leacock, 1963). There were others, but he describes the experience, that many of his contemporaries envied, as like being in *L'Année dernière à Marienbad* (1961), 'but without the luxury; two people writing the same script unknown to each other, with the script-editor deciding

Girls at Sea: Guy Rolfe, Richard Coleman, David Lodge, Ronald Shiner – All classes aboard the British ship

which parts of both scripts should be pushed into a third version by yet another writer.'[17] Aware of the system, he had little nostalgia for it. Five years later, when the studio closed, he went and remained freelance.

Three years before *A Mirror for England*, he laid out his stall with a selection from already copious writing in *Films and Feelings*. 'Mon premier "hardback" – avec beaucoup d'amour – à mes très chers parents – de Raymond', he wrote in a copy intended for his parents in June 1967.[18] It is one of his most influential works which, although it barely mentions British cinema, strikes out at the state of British film criticism and etches out a number of areas that would preoccupy him for much of his life. *La politique des auteurs* is quickly bagged, ridiculed for its insistence, despite the evidence, that the work of recognised directors was, by its nature, always a profound expression of an artistic, even philosophical personality. Wiser, he considered than selecting auteurs as 'in' and others as 'out', would be to evaluate a director's films by other criteria, as 'key', 'interesting', or 'useful'. Apart from offering greater variety, it would rescue critics and film

Tamahine: Nancy Kwan – A challenge to British taboos

historians from having to watch the 'dreary, pusillanimous, or repetitive films which all [auteur status nominated] directors have perpetrated from time to time.' 1967 was early days for film theory, but Durgnat is already marking out the territory in which he would fight in the fierce debates of the 1970s.

Alfred Hitchcock is treated no differently. Hitchcock could produce and direct dross too, among it the popular *The 39 Steps* (1935) which Durgnat discounts for its 'superficiality'. Contrarily, Durgnat equates *Sabotage*, which Hitchcock made the following year and is widely considered a failure, with Fritz Lang's *Fury* (1936) and Orson Welles's *The Lady from Shanghai* (1947), as 'the profoundest film of Hitchcock's thriller period, and perhaps of his career,' in which he hits us 'as hard as in *Psycho*'.[19] Watching it in the late 1960s, Durgnat saw it as capturing a dreamlike overlap between memories of the London anarchist bombings of 1911 and the terrors of the blackouts in the forthcoming war that was widely expected. Contemporary audiences, he thought, would have seen the same things.

For Durgnat, the most significant British films were densely packed histories of Britain, especially of England. We have a clear illustration of this in another thread of his career at the University of East London where he was Visiting Professor. His seminars with students and occasionally staff, were directed towards illustrating the themes he saw as deeply embedded in them. For him, the scene in *A Matter of Life and Death*, in which Dr Reeves (Roger Livesey) opts to change the jury that is overseeing the hearing that will decide whether Peter Carter (David Niven) will live or die, relies for its effectiveness on an awareness that the British Empire was in decline. A full appreciation of the scene depends on the knowledge that mass immigration to America was part of the battle between nation states for international dominance. The internationalism of America is in the mix; all the jury members would once have been British, now they are American. *A Matter of Life and Death*, as Durgnat presented it to his students, was a rethinking of Britain's position in the world, a film conscious of national decline, without a death wish, but one that required the country to adjust to the present. It was of greater interest, he felt, to relate the Berlin–Baghdad Railway to the Alexander Korda production of *The Thief of Bagdad* (1940) than to construct the film as the inspirational creation of one of its many directors or of its producer. It would make greater sense, he

The 39 Steps: Robert Donat, Lucie Mannheim – Foreigners and Brits – 'Can I come home with you?'/'What's your game?'

thought, if the film could be shown to have spun out of the struggles of British foreign policy; after all Sir Robert Vansittart, the mandarin and adviser to the British Government, was a close associate of Korda at the time.

Durgnat was a Churchillian, but it had little to do with political values; he wasn't a Conservative voter. Politically, he disliked orthodoxy, however much as he might agree with some elements of it, he advocated a form of working-class radicalism. The working class, which he was prone to call the 'proletariat', had little to give to the State, except its labour, but had its own commandments, notably variations on stubbornness, of which the most important was, 'Thou Shall Not Be Moved'. Yet it would suspend defiant positions for a defined purpose, if that was in its interest. A favourite cartoon was Low's 'All Behind You Winston', with Churchill and members of the Wartime Coalition Government, rolling up their sleeves and leading the nation into battle. Durgnat identified the image of firemen who have lost their lives in the German bombing raids of British cities, leading a group of victims up the endless staircase to heaven in *A Matter of Life and Death*. One led to the other; it was

Sabotage: Silvia Sidney, Oscar Homolka – Cruelty unmatched until *Psycho*

embedded in the culture. Both recognised, Durgnat felt, the undemanding support that that the working class gave to the Churchill Government during the war. They indicated its willingness to advance support for a cause, but it had strings and could be withdrawn equally readily. In the end class was an inevitable requirement of creating a relevant British cinema, but it was not the only one.

We see this in his consideration of *Great Expectations* (1946), which he presents as a rethinking of Britain in relation to the past and of the class system. Accompanying his seminar discussion was his own flow chart of the British class system in which everyone has his place, if not among the gentleman farmers and prefects, then among, perhaps, the 'shabby genteel'. Pip's spectacular rise from the solid working class, namely a blacksmith's apprentice, to a gentleman who could hobnob among members of the upper strata of society, although he would never be one of them, exposed, in Durgnat's terms, both the rigidities and flexibilities of British class system in post-war Britain.

The Thief of Bagdad: The Berlin–Baghdad Carpet Express

His 'adoptive father', Joe Gargery (Bernard Miles) is a poor blacksmith. That is to say, he combines a modest independence (lower-middle-class) and manual labour (working-class). In other words, he is a generalized 'common man', a 'typical Englishman'.[20]

Pip (John Mills) nevertheless becomes a snob and 'thinks that all that is best in his life comes from the upper-middle-classes. In fact it comes from the marsh and the hulks, that is, the proletarian underworld. Merely by simplifying Dickens, the movie trembles on the brink of being a classic Marxist fable about bourgeois 'confusionism'.'

If one feels that he misses a trick with his analysis, that he doesn't consider the film in terms of the post-1945 optimism, promise, and potential disillusion that the Labour Party landslide offered, it enabled him to relate the history of Britain through the development of its class structure and to illustrate how the film challenged the myths of post-war consensus politics.

You might expect Durgnat to make much of a class ridden society where wealth is dutifully claimed by the State, like a form of taxation, but just at the

A favourite wartime cartoon and an inspirational image for *A Matter of Life and Death* (see p. 108)

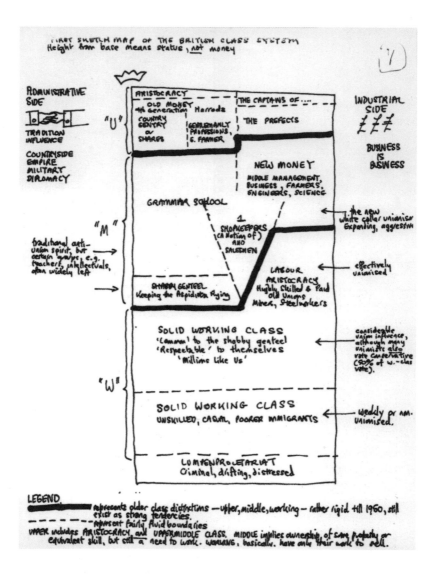

RD's flow chart for Class: Where do you think you really are?

point that he may have painted himself into a corner with a description of 'the lower orders' remaining 'consistently the realm of both nightmare-like violence – and also of strong, warm, masculine emotion,' he surprises the reader by slipping into another key and another genre. The self-immured Miss Havisham, Estella's guardian, who has brought up Estella to reek her revenge on men, is transformed. 'As Pip tears down her musty curtains, letting the sunlight in, a coal rolls from the grate, and icy Miss Havisham catches fire. It is as if she is the living dead in a mausoleum ... In a word, she is a vampire of upper-middle-class snobbery and frigidity, accepting gratitude, giving nothing'.[21] Durgnat has made his shift, to draw two threads of British cinema together: the cold misanthropic films of David Lean and the soulless Dracula films of Terence Fisher. Indeed Martita Hunt, who plays Miss Havisham also appears as the Baroness Meinster in *The Brides of Dracula* (1960). He would reply to those who pedantically wrote to point out such things as Miss Havisham's death and Pip pulling down the rotting curtains from the room in which she lived, with her rodent infested wedding cake, occur in two different scenes, generously explaining that the book was written before domestic VHS machines were available and regretting that he was obliged to rely on memory. Then again, the cinema, for Durgnat was constantly transforming itself, its meaning dependent of the changing perceptions and associations of each member of the audience. After reading Durgnat, and re-watching Miss Havisham die screaming, you have second thoughts. Pip drags the heavy table cloth from the wedding table and throws it over her body, but when the flames are damped down there appears to be nothing underneath, perhaps only a little dust, as there might be in Dracula's coffin. It may have been a slip of memory on Durgnat's part, but just as likely it wasn't. He was emphasising that two very different kinds of British cinema had more in common than they had separating them. For Durgnat, films that he repeatedly watched became 'conversations about experiences'.[22] The cinema that appealed the most was a tapestry in which class provided one thread and passion provided the other. His theme may well have been taken from E.M. Forster's preface to *Howard's End* 'Only Connect', with its emphasis on the need for society to be interlinked as a whole and for its individuals to connect its prose and its passion. He saw its expression in English cinema where the representation of the working-classes in such films as *Great Expectations*,

Outcasts of the Islands and *The Leather Boys* provide the emotional strength to an otherwise disconnected body of films.

This is articulated in his consideration of the now, almost forgotten, Roy Ward Baker adaptation of Margery Allingham's London novel, *Tiger in the Smoke* (1956). Its opening sequence of a street-band of wretched and embittered ex-servicemen tramping through London fogs 'is a superb image for a world "possessed" by the equal and complementary evils of unaware complacency and craven spite.'[23] A 'homicidal maniac' tricks its members out of their share of a 'priceless' treasure which, ironically, turns out to have no material value; it is, as Durgnat writes, 'a symbol of the spiritual values which he can never understand.' This might be enough, but typically, this explanation is made complex, by association. 'For all its melodrama, it comes, at moments nearer the fuliginous lyricism of [Georges] Bernanos[24] than the [Graham] Greene films ... the barbed force of Baker's films lies in his feeling for evil as being *both* the result of injustice *and* an impersonal force which, lurking in the nature of man, takes him over.'

Durgnat had multiple lives as a writer but the two that concern us here provide perhaps his most important contributions to film culture. The first is as a somewhat hermetic yet dedicated popular and productive writer of film history and criticism. As such, he avoids classification and perhaps applies no single method consistently, but it is worth observing that it hinged on a form of working-class scholarship: the use of public libraries and serendipity, more than on traditional academic research techniques. The second is as an influential and self-effacing teacher who encouraged his students to recognise and value their own responses to a work. His argument for a British cinema that augmented the nation's history and which could be successful in its own terms, not as versions of Hollywood or of European cinema is now established. That British cinema retains its interest and is established at all levels of academic study is in great part a consequence of the continuing influence of *A Mirror for England*.

Introduction

1. Where we come in

This book is not a popular history of the British film industry (Charles Oakley's waspishly entitled *Where We Came In* fills that bill pretty well). We offer a survey of some major recurring themes in British movies between 1945-being the end of the war and the election of the postwar Labour government – and 1958, when the success of *Room at the Top* marks the breakthrough of a new cinema. Thereafter the dominant tone is a mixture of a cynical realism about society, working class references (the 'kitchen sink'), the 'New Morality', 'Swinging London', and stronger cosmopolitan influences, particularly via a renewed influx of American finance.

Our concern therefore is with a climax period of a middle-class cinema with its intimations of controversy and its premonitions of decline. Since no artistic period stops and starts with the brisk promptitude of a calendar, the book takes in various films from before and after the period. The question of whether, on balance, a film's 'traditional' elements predominate over others is often difficult. Particularly in the later stages, when the defensive culture, realizing the new challenges, becomes more subtle, makes concessions, and agrees to deal with hitherto hidden themes. And film-makers for obvious – box office – reasons try to get the best of both worlds. The reader may enjoy brooding darkly over such questions as why this study includes Philip Leacock's *Reach for Glory* (1961) but excludes Caspar Wrede's *Private Potter* (1962), why it includes Jack Clayton's *Our Mother's House* (1967) but excludes his *The Pumpkin Eater* (1964), why it

Room at the Top: Laurence Harvey, Heather Sears – The human cast of upward social mobility includes Bryan Forbes's *Whistle Down the Wind* (1961) but excludes his *The L-Shaped Room* (1962).

And although there's a general limitation to entertainment features we have devoted a chapter to thirties' documentaries. Their thematic and stylistic programme deeply affected critical responses to the mainstream British film. A brief sub-chapter on cartoons (an appropriate subject on which to bend if not break all the laws of gravity) also allows some parallels between mainstream cinema and a genre less flippant than it seems.

Whether British films have ever had criticism as detailed as they deserved is a doubtful matter. George Orwell's remarks about our intelligentsia's inverted jingoism hold good inside our period. The 'documentary' school of critics was grinding an obvious axe in its attacks on the entertainment cinema. In any event, the relationship between these secular Sunday School teachers with their sound civic pieties, and all the fleshpots, fake, fun and fiddle of show-business too rarely was one of mutual understanding. The regular abyss between uplifter and entertainer was only apparently narrowed when, with the purposeful sobriety of the war years the public voted for characteristics hitherto associated with documentary (location photography, deglamourization, demelodramatisation, nonprofessional actors, the stiff upper lip). The post war years perpetuated the honeymoon between critics and 'quality' films, notably, filmed classics, Ealing comedies and war films. From the praise emerges only summary analysis. More is discouraged by the paper shortage, as well as by pleasure in the commercial success of bad British films, in the hope of establishing at last a financially solid film industry independent of Hollywood. But increasing critical misgivings are sharpened by the Rank Organisation's near-monopoly and its switch, after the failure of some ill-advised prestige pro-ductions, to an aggressively 'commercial' policy. A useful milestone is Richard Winnington's remark in June 1949 that *Christopher Columbus*, an expensive prestige flop, 'contrives with something like genius neither to inform, excite, entertain, titillate or engage the eye'. By 1954 critics generally are agreed that something has gone wrong, and a *Sight and Sound* writer calls even documentary 'the sulky fire'. From about 1954 the only British films to be con-sidered thoughtfully belong to the categories, or directors, whose reputations had been established before or during the 'patriotic' period. Even then, they arouse more approval than excitement, and impatience with British movies rapidly intensifies. Indeed, the pendulum swings to the other extreme. One might, for example, have expected the earlier English films of Joseph Losey to have met with some sort of acknowledgement, however qualified. But if we consult the *Monthly Film Bulletin* for August 1954, April 1956, July 1956, May 1957, March 1958, September 1959, November 1960, and May 1963, we find them considered purely as potboilers except insofar as they are dismissed as 'ludicrous-pretentious' and 'exaggeratedly hysteric'. It may seem unkind to say that the conformism of the British film industry is matched by the obtuseness of the British Film Institute Publications Department. The fact remains that the film industry did at least make the films, in which these critics saw nothing of interest whatsoever. Other middle-class films, and their changing tone are ignored, and discussion blandly assumes that *Room at the Top* somehow derives from the documentaries of Free Cinema.

There can be no doubt that, taken in bulk, the movies which concern us regularly perpetrated distortions and omissions which proved extremely galling to this writer's critical generation. These irritations are, I hope, duly emphasized in these pages. Nonetheless one duty of criticism is to give the devil his due, and the contention in these pages is that many of the middle-class movies are richer in nuance, in tension, in honest doubt and sophisticated misgiving, than they have had credit for in circles influential simply because uniquely institutionalized.

The chapters that follow differ from most British movie criticism also in concentrating less on evaluating the texture of films than on critical exegeses of certain themes, undercurrents and overtones. It is often assumed, though it has never been shown, that artworks not of the highest textural quality don't deserve thematic exegesis – that if they don't ring true to the highly sophisticated critic they can't ring true to anybody, and that what doesn't ring true can't have any meanings or subtleties. Anyone familiar with the difference between rigorous textural criticism and the actual responses of your actual spectators in your actual cinema, and in conversation, and of students in seminar, will prefer to at least entertain the proposition that less sensitized textures may work for less, or otherwise, sensitized audiences and be more subtle and challenging than critical conventions usually allow. I've argued this, albeit briefly, in *Films and Feelings*, but even those who find it a coarse, philistine and obnoxious attitude will perhaps agree that there's some point in supplementing the usual textural emphasis by a predominantly thematic one. If clearly marked personal style is one's criterion of interest, then few British films reward the concern given to such directors as, say, Dreyer, Buñuel, Franju and Renoir. But other criteria of interest exist, whereby many of the subtlest meanings behind a personal style may be related to the collective vision of a particular tradition, period, background or 'school'. It's logical and usual to consider even impersonal and anonymous artworks as expressions of a general consensus.

Even within the assumptions of auteur theory, I would suggest that it's absurd to notice such Hollywood conformists as Hawks, McCarey and Walsh, yet deny equally high honours to, say, Roy Baker, Michael Powell and Terence Fisher. It's possible only because, for some English and European intellectuals, American cliché possesses the double appeal of (*a*) a hard-edge dynamism, in contradiction to certain native traditions of soft-edge sensitivity, and (*b*) the spurious and specious exoticism of scarcely nuanced emotional and moral primitivism. It's easy enough to summarize an epoch by selecting the most distinguished films of the most distinguished directors, and concentrating thereon. But the manifest conveniences of this process have confirmed one of the principal distortions of film criticism. The impression is conveyed that run-of-the-mill movies never say anything, that vivid or insightful remarks or situations are a monopoly of a few prestigious individuals. In fact many fascinating moments occur in generally mediocre films and I've tried to offer a titillating selection here.

To cast a new light on unfashionable movies is not the archaeologists' exercise it might once have seemed. In the first place, of course, films can and often do remain in the memory for many years. In the second place, films share with pop music the serious, historical-minded allegiance of more young intellectuals than ever before. And thirdly, TV programming has placed a film archive in every home. It's high time we had a channel showing nothing but old movies from midday to midnight, over and over again. Where the audiovisual media are concerned, the past is vividly alive in the present as never before in their history. This only reinforces the extent to which this generation, like every other, has its own perspectives into the past, and needs its own criticism.

2. When is a British Film a British Film?

The question of defining a British film was a thorny one even before the recent influx of American capital. In the thirties the Hungarian Korda, the German Pommer, the Austrian Schach and M.G.M.–British loomed large on the production scene. In a 1939 *Kine Weekly*, 'Screencomber' distributed his annual awards thus:

Best Director of a British Film ... Leopold Kryshi Stockolevitch
Best Script of a British Film ... Hiram Z. Wimplepole
Best Photography of a British Film ... Ching Chang Chong
Best Acting in a British Film ... Mdlle Noktova
Best Montage in a British Film ... Zchshwwschy Owyowschchkow
Best bit of Carpenting in a British Film ... Bill Smithers, Esq.

Many a film which, being made in a British studio, is eligible for British quota, is, to all spiritual intents and purposes, indistinguishable from an American one, even to its setting, like David Greene's *The Shuttered Room* (1966). Or again, *Fahrenheit 451* (1966) is British insofar as it was made in England, stars Julie Christie and appears to be set in England in the future; but it's American insofar as it was made for an American company (Universal), from an American story (by Ray Bradbury) set in America; and French insofar as it has a French scriptwriter-director (François Truffaut). If it came within our period the balance between inclusion and exclusion would be a narrow one. Our criterion has had to be rather arbitrary and subjective; is it about Britain, about British attitudes, or, if not, does it feel British?

It's surprising, but natural, that confusions of nationality should arise in so insular, nay, xenophobic, a land. Films cost so much that the advantages of exporting, of going for the world market, occur relatively quickly to the film producer. Such expedients as co-productions, cosmopolitan topics, dual-language versions and foreign financing rapidly arise. (If a director is a film's real auteur, should we count Polanski's English films as Polish films, Losey's English films as American films, and Hitchcock's American films as English films?) Second, Britain's common language with America has exposed both her audiences and her talents to the full weight of Hollywood appeal (dumping, brain-drain, ideological conventions), while offering British producers the alluring yet elusive prospect of crashing through into the American market.

A particular problem arises from what one may call the internal insularity of British culture. It's a truism that in Britain class subdivides the nation culturally more extensively and intricately than in most countries. And in addition, middle-class ideology is at once more puritanical, more unsophisticated and less questioning than the European, but more deficient in the stylized 'life-force appeal' (sex, violence, strong simple moral issues) than the American. Thus Britain, an island situated halfway between America and France, united the spiritual disadvantages of both – being less sophisticated and less vulgar.

Class fragments Britain into islands within an island. It's a fairly reliable rule of thumb that, in a highly industrialized country, all mass media naturally tend to aim for the cultural overlap between middle and working-class attitudes. They stress common denominators, and omit, or soft pedal, or skirt tactfully round the conflicts between them. The middle-class can compensate for its numerical deficiency by the influence of censorship, criticism and, most importantly, the social ambitions and cultural values of film-makers themselves. One may note a significant contrast between the American and British consensus. American ideology admits, indeed, romanticizes, ambition, competition, conflict, tension, and moral and emotional intensity. Similarly, American films accommodate violent conflicts, while making them more melodramatic, morally more soot-and-whitewash, more escapist in topic, more sentimental in outcome, and more fixated on terms of physical violence, than the processes which they paraphrase and conceal. In British middle-class culture, most of these aspects are far less marked; the style, far from being vehement to the point of hysteria, is underplayed to the point of inertia. When American style is used as a model, it often rings false to English reactions and situations. British working-class culture is rather more hospitable than middle-class to the violent and the cynical, with the result that American movies sometimes come much nearer the actual attitudes of British audiences than most British ones. But English working-class attitudes are also more stoic and realistic than American movies (with their middle-class strain) allow: and it is this which the British film industry didn't discover until the late fifties (nor did its intellectual critics). Furthermore, most British film-makers naturally tended to exaggerate the middle-class traits which American movies didn't satisfy (such as the stiff upper lip), while being forced back into a narrower range of subjects and stereotypes (since the Americans did so many popular genres better). Thus Margaret Rutherford appears as a typical British eccentric, while Alf Garnett, even in the late sixties, is supposed by middle-class liberals to be a monster, an exotic figure. During our period British films progressively gain the favour of the British public, and begin, albeit with painful slowness, to extend their range. With *Room at the Top* it finds, at last, the appropriate strategy, which is to assert scandal and revolt against passivity and puritanism. By appealing to the working-class, the young, and a new cosmopolitanism, it spreads its roots far more deeply and widely into human nature. Not only do British stories turn the tables on Hollywood, but British films in British settings combine American life-force appeal with European realism and sophistication and find an immediate response in American spectators, just at a time when Hollywood was old, flabby and had grown chicken with respectability.

3. Meaning Cut Meaning

Like their American cousins the majority of British film-makers strenuously protest that their films have no ideological chip on their entertainment shoulder, they embody no particular message, are devoid of all preachment or indeed, personal opinion, on any important or controversial issues. Their intention is to thrill or amuse, with purely personal stories of personal perplexities or, in a pretty impartial way, to 'make people think'.

Occasionally these protestations of neutrality are undermined by the film itself. The claim to impartiality is meant to reassure the trade, and the public which has often found message films too uplifting or too depressing to be entertainment, and fears that 'message' is just another word for propaganda (and so it is, even if it's propaganda for tolerance, or irresponsibility, or impartiality!). But it is also true that every sphere of life is determined by ideologies. Our ideas about life affect not only politics and religion, but every human situation and emotion, including our life-goals (success, happiness, responsibility, contentment). They influence the simplest gestures of common courtesy and what sorts of private sex play ought to be allowed between whom, when and on what conditions. Even a film which seems uncontroversial to its makers and most of its spectators is loaded with assumption, and so, to someone else it will be a 'message' film. Thus, we all know that Hollywood exports the American way of life, and similarly British films have often hoped to spread the influence of the British way of life. Merely by being about people, their problems, and how they solve them, they're message films. Of course the majority of movies may remain, in the usual sense, non-controversial. But it's easy and natural for a substantial minority of movies to move into controversial areas. For a film, to entertain many, must echo widespread ideas and experiences, and therefore conflicts, and conflicts are nothing but internal controversies. Much depends on whether this conflict takes the centre of the stage, or not, and on how it's resolved, and on whether the personal story is related, overtly or by implication, to the more general terms. But so long as human beings have conflicts art will, of itself, tend to move into areas of controversy. That of course is why it's often in trouble. It must also be remembered that a film-maker may be interested in a story precisely because it challenges his certainties, because it chastens, disturbs and fascinates him. He thinks others may be similarly affected, and he makes the film precisely because it threatens to contradict what he believes. He may not go on to change his principles. He may simply be reminding himself, and others, to apply them with care, humility and understanding. In this case to deduce a principle from the action of the story would be wrong. Because the British generally are less quick to connect example and principle than the French, it may be misleading to interpret a British film in precisely the same way as one would interpret a French film.

Because the artist isn't concerned with logical consistency, one might expect him, quite naturally and without any feeling of hypocrisy, to make, say, a left-wing film one day and a right-wing film another day. In practice this seems to happen rarely, precisely because one's ideologies tend to connect with one's whole view of life. By and large it seems fair to say that in general film-makers, intentionally or otherwise, put more meaning in their films than spectators ever take out. Notably, a spectator who is enjoying a film (perhaps for its congenial story, or actors, or aesthetic qualities) will usually fail to reconstruct an unwelcome or unfamiliar message in it. But if he dislikes a film (if only for reasons of aesthetic crudity) he will readily attribute an objectionable message to it. Conversely, if an unwelcome 'message' has caught his eye, he'll usually persuade himself, and others, that he's objecting, not to a point of view, but to some other quality in the film. It doesn't ring true. There are exceptions, notably in the case of challenging, slap-in-the-face films like *Look Back in Anger*, which work on the spectator's internal conflicts, and which the film industry has been too frightened of making. Nor are they easy for those who don't enjoy controversy to make.

One type of meaning, rather different from the quick French way of relating the particular to the general, has a special importance in British movies. To a distinguished British film director a critic once put the then topical question, 'Would you make a movie on the Ward case, if you had the chance?' The response was a prickly glare that anyone should raise so vulgar a topic; the second, a sad, 'Oh no, I couldn't possibly ...', modulating to a wistful, 'but what a dramatic story it would make ...', leading up to a quick comeback: 'Ah, but what about Parnell?' Now *there* .... What indeed? The fighting retreat from today's bannerlines to the defused scandals of yesteryear is all too typical. The present is so vulgar, the past so romantic.

But it works the other way too. *Oscar Wilde* and *The Trials of Oscar Wilde* are also about the Wolfenden Report. Thus British films can work on atmospheric associations, on moral principles, so vague yet so strong that they require a method of approach which it is interesting to follow, as we do, more thoroughly than usual. Often one must follow, not concepts, which hardly appear, but atmosphere.

This diffuseness poses problems for a critic when he wants to underline unnoticed ambivalences in those movies which he would like to promote from the ranks of mediocrity to the status of interesting or poignant films, and even, occasionally, a minor classic. To tersely summarize atmospheric films is to seem arbitrary; to follow all the nuances of atmosphere is to become prohibitively lengthy. Our solution has been to look at a few films in some length (notably in the section entitled 'Gangrene – British style'), and summarize others with sometimes drastic brevity.

A further problem has been how far to match a film's picture of reality against other evidence as to the real nature of this reality. This affects, for example, our consideration of films about strikes. *The Angry Silence* obviously tunes in on various popular assumptions, such as that strikes are a major cause of our country's economic difficulties, and that unofficial strikes are almost always irresponsible and so have an alarming affinity with mob violence. How far these assumptions are justified is obviously relevant to the quality of the film, and to discuss them would be well within the province of film criticism, which I take to include any matters arising out of a film's treatment of its subject or theme. But the practical difficulties – including sheer length – are so enormous that I've contented myself with respecting the film's point of view while noting disagreement with it. I've occasionally allowed myself the indulgence of a few terse and testy ripostes to certain myths which seem to me to fly a little too freely in the face of a slightly soured common sense.

4. Critic: Judge or Accomplice?

Our study centres on certain moral, emotional and social themes which are often marginal to the personal story through which they are conveyed. In most cases it is the personal story which is the main focus of the film-maker's interest, and it's certainly on the personal story that the audience's interest is first focused. More often than not, neither film-maker nor spectator thinks things out further. Thus our comments may be so much at cross-purposes with a film-maker's intention, and with the spectator's immediate reaction, as to bewilder and annoy. Our justification is that, in or out of the cinema, our feelings about personal stories often depend on feelings about values, mostly justice, and conduct which we don't need to make explicit. We simply react. But what films, and people, take for granted, often reveals more about them than what they emphasize. It's not what people say to convince you that reveals them, so much as what they assume there's no need to say. When we say that a film was unpopular because of such and such an assumption, we don't of course mean that people criticized it in just the terms we use here. In other words, the personal story rubbed them up the wrong way, or prevented them from living through certain experiences related to it, so that they were only mildly amused, or felt obscurely worried, rather than being shocked and exhilarated.

A critic's is, of course, the wisdom of hindsight, that is to say, not wisdom at all. The sensible critic doesn't suppose that he's cleverer than the artist in whose work he finds flaws. But he has consumer's right to criticize, and in some cases he may have done as much work in his own way as the artist in his. Conversely, the dismissive language sometimes used of films, or of a director's work, isn't meant to apply to that man as a man. In the same way, when one finds a personality in a poet's work, one is speaking about 'a man who might have done that work', and not of the man who did, and may well have expressed only a misleading part of himself in his poems. In the same way, it's quite possible for an intelligent man to make stupid films all his life, simply by not bothering to put the best of himself into his films. No remarks here are meant in a personal sense, nor to reflect on purely professional abilities. Artists and critics are, at best, friendly enemies, and there can be mutual respect in that relationship. If many notable actors are ignored or neglected, it's because this approach has been through films and directors, rather than actors. There's no reason, other than critical customs and prejudices, why actors shouldn't also be treated as auteurs, and used as the basic images of an entire cinema's ethos.

I can't claim to have seen every British film released between 1945 and 1965, and may well have missed some gems. This work is meant to provoke discussion, not to terminate it.

The reader who finds the very idea of interpretation, of ascribing meanings to other people's work, pretentious or dogmatic, might like to remember that every sentence is preceded by invisible words like 'My feeling is ...', 'In my opinion ...', 'I have a hunch that ...', and 'It seems to me ...'. This is offered as one man's view of British films, not God's.

POSTSCRIPT

In a long delay between the completion of the book's original draft and its publication (for which the present publisher was not responsible), the climate of discussion of certain topics changed rather less than during the 1970 election run-up, while the final draft was in proof. An explanatory note may therefore be helpful.

In 1965, when the original draft got under way, the angry young men had ceased to provoke anger, the gist of their case was refined by the satirists, and various urges towards new thought and initiatives were represented by, diversely, our Common Market application, a new Labour government, and the

New Morality. Until a recent lashback, there seemed little likelihood of serious misunderstandings of the value placed, in a chapter entitled 'The Age of Acquiescence', on responsible dissent, criticism and questioning.

Now I'm not so sure. Through 1970, controversies about law and order, the permissive society, student demonstrations, and echoes of conflicts in America, France and elsewhere, have brought a sharpening of tone, exemplified by some curious imputations in *Encounter*, about my 'dialectic'.

More than ever, it seems, a certain lunatic fringe is concerned to deny that dissent is an English middle-class tradition (fortunately for democracy, it is a continuing one). Personally I find it hard to believe that all the suffragettes were agents of Chairman Mao.

I should perhaps clarify the position from which 'The Age of Acquiescence' ventures to place a high value on responsible dissent.

(*a*) Obviously any society (even an anarchist one) must command some radical loyalties from every member thereof.

(*b*) The emphasis in these films on the *danger* of dissent, and the omission of *value* or *opportunities*, seems to me to be dangerously near something like this: 'Our society is democratic, therefore it allows no real injustices, and is easily menaced. Therefore anyone whose dissent becomes obstreperous, or conspicuous, or even open, must be arrogant, or fanatical, or a traitor.'

(*c*) This argument has its insidious aspect, for it uses the democratic element in government to give added (moral) power to the erosion, by bureaucracy and other forces, of individual freedoms. It is of course a favourite argument of totalitarianisms of left and right alike. In the English case its unthinking acceptance is helped by, notably, the evolution undergone by the nonconformist conscience (Section 26) and the team spirit of (any) old boy net (Section 8).

(*d*) Given the obvious dangers to individual freedom in the structure of modern society, I would tolerate, sometimes approve of, the responsible elements in what might be called 'abrasive dissent' (on the analogy of 'abrasive competition') – that is to say, certain forms of civil disobedience, direct action, demonstrations and riots, in the Wilkite-Chartist-suffragette-conscientious objector-Hunger Marchers-Cable St.-Hornsey-Guildford tradition. As all these examples show, dissent can be abrasive without being extreme or irresponsible. It would be difficult, now, to make a film in which audience sympathy wasn't largely with the suffragettes (although naturally one would criss-cross sympathies, accommodate continuing prejudices and stereotypes, involve the sex war, etc.).

(*e*) This tolerance or approval are politically complex, and it would not be easy for me to ascertain the relative importance of (1) an in a certain sense right-wing concern with individual initiative versus 'they', (2) an in a sense left-wing dissatisfaction with (to borrow a shorthand term) 'the establishment', (3) sympathies with the principles underlying Liberal schemes for co-ownership and more positive public involvement in government, and (4) a middle-of-the-road, trimmer's, belief in at least challenging, and if possible redressing, the balance of power between the individual and the mass.

(*f*) The objection is to the number of films taking for granted a kind of love-me-love-my-warts submission to authority and the status quo, and ignoring the pressing needs for improvements. After all, *Encounter* once devoted an entire issue to the supposed *Suicide of a Nation*, i.e., Britain's.

1: The State of the Nation

5. The British Constitution

Since 1940 complacency and criticism have alternated as dominant moods in British films. In wartime, morale boosting came first, but a self-critical determination to turn over a new leaf, after Jarrow and Munich, and win the peace, appears in films from 1944. It continues under austerity and the Attlee Government. From 1951, with the Festival of Britain and the onset of affluence, a happier and shallower mood prevails. But hints of disquiet about the time of Suez (1956), lead rapidly to *Room at the Top* (1958) and *Look Back in Anger* (1958). Their success establishes another, and continuing, mood of uneasiness, of which another Labour government, and this book are expressions.

In affirmative films that evocative phrase 'the English way of life' often identifies national character, and patriotism, with the tone and attitudes of the upper-middle-class. It borrows sacredness from that constitution which, Britain being such a harmonious nation, has never needed to be written down. It's a gentleman's agreement. It's traditional, it's established, it's as wonderful as our policemen, it wasn't planned, it just came about, by the happy incidents which this island race attracts because it deserves. Dim memories of strife and rancour remain, and just enough tensions and misunderstandings remain to keep us from the complacency which is the failing of our peacefulness and niceness.

Thus this 'blest isle with matchless beauty crown'd' is, in its modest way, *The Demi-Paradise*. The Shakespearean phrase provides a contentedly ironic

The Way to the Stars: Rosamund John – Lightweight celebration of a special relationship

title for a movie directed by Anthony Asquith (1943). In honour of our temporarily gallant Russian ally, Laurence Olivier plays a Soviet engineer sent over to liaise with a traditionally British shipbuilding firm. This male Ninotchka is worried, understandably, because gentleman-tycoon Felix Aylmer enjoys leisurely dainty teas and chats about everything except work, while a dear old lady demonstrates British business-as-usual by playing the cello in the garden during an air-raid to inspire the nightingales on 'some wet bird-haunted English lawn'. All in due time, our earnest ally is dumbfounded to find the leisurely old Englishman suddenly zooming past his norms like a ritardando Stakhanovite with his rump on fire, and Russian engineering is inspired to design its revolutionary new propeller while stirring an L.N.E.R. cup of tea in a loveably dingy station buffet.

Ostensibly a bouquet to our Communist allies, this tribute to a landowner-industrialist establishment is followed by an equally narcissistic gesture towards those nice Yanks. For obvious reasons, the gesture is less gimmicky, and artistically more satisfying. Yet *The Way to the Stars* (1945), which once seemed a major movie, now looks more like a poignant lightweight whose intensest moments – the exploration of the deserted airfield, little Jean Simmons singing 'Let him go, let him tarry' – have everything to do with Asquith's feeling for place and mood and little to do with its theme, which is how initially brash American airmen come to love uppercrust young English ladies and respect the quiet sacrifices of their limey brothers. What British critics pretended to think was a tribute to Anglo-American unity is a placidly immodest tale about the Americans coming to admire everything traditionally English, i.e. 'U' (for upper-middle-class).

It's a small excuse, but some, that English films were following Hollywood precedents. Through the thirties, Hollywood, catering primarily for an America vexed by the lingering Depression into a nostalgia for cosy security, and harassed by the Legion of Decency, made the most of tales of happily solid family innocence which included such reassuring Victoriana as *David Copperfield, Little Lord Fauntleroy, Quality Street,* and so on and so forth. Hollywood's moving into English studios from 1937, and then American sympathy for Britain vis-à-vis Hitler, prolonged the theme, and from Jack

Conway's *A Yank at Oxford* (1938) through William Wyler's *Mrs. Miniver* (1942), it was *Goodbye, Mr. Chips* with everything but the kitchen sink. American generosity probably enervated the natives, who, having managed not to lose the war in 1940, went on to persuade themselves that they were primarily responsible for winning it, and that tradition needed only a few running repairs to see a splendid resurgence of the Elizabethan spirit.

The documentaries of the period flaunt no less brashly all the stock-in-trade of Ye Olde Curiositie Shoppe. Humphrey Jennings's *Words for Battle* (1941) panoplies all the cliché at which the gorges and hackles of Osborne's generation were to rise. It flourishes patriotic verse from Shakespeare, Browning, Kipling, and, of course, Blake's *Jerusalem*, wrenched out of its true meaning into a vapidly patriotic one. *London Can Take It!* (co-director, Harry Watt, 1940), felt, in its time, as an uncompromisingly realistic film, seems too clearly a morale booster. It employs an American commentator, Quentin Reynolds, to pay us our compliments, while also, of course, furthering the government's policy of appealing to American public opinion and bringing America to our rescue as fast as possible. In both films, as in *A Diary for Timothy* (1945), a scattering of faces, of observations extremely beautiful in themselves, and, to this writer, tearingly nostalgic of some intense childhood moments, are pressed into the service of a quiet near-jingoism which, altogether understandable in war, cannot achieve more than second-rate artistic status. The notion of harmonious coexistence between old ways and new informs Ealing's feature documentary *Painted Boats* (Charles Crichton, 1945), which reassures us that there is no need for hostility between picturesque horsedrawn barges and efficient steam ones, on British canals. Quite apart from nostalgia about Britain's Glorious Countryside (which we all love so much we've moved into the suburbs), what's ominous is the choice of a neglected, stagnant, and doomed industrial network, to suddenly carry so much feeling.

Less sensitive in detail than the Jennings' films, far more interesting in certain overtones, is *Went the Day Well?* (1942), directed at Ealing by Cavalcanti, from an idea by Graham Greene. In its story of German agents quietly taking over an English village, a few dissonances seem more than mere grace notes. The principal enemy agent is the bluff English squire whom the villagers mistakenly trust. The upper-class lady so nicely, so deceitfully, so foolishly, tries to keep the truth from the children ('Put it to them as a game'), but it's the hard-headed Cockney evacuee, and poacher's mate, who, by 'getting through', brings help. The killing by a peaceloving old lady of a not unkindly German soldier who reminds her of her husband is worked with a loving eye for treachery and brutality. It's an affirmative film, but the dotted lines of some peacetime tensions are there, and the collateral mood, of distrust and dissatisfaction with our paternalist betters.

Hard on a quarter of a century later, it is hard to write of the self-satisfied films without irony. Yet no one denounced them at the time, the lustily Tory Robsons apart, for, after all, in the war, the worst had not happened. Old institutions had buckled but not broken, and even those who urged a welfare state and post-war planning and all sorts of Utopian Socialist ideas accepted without demur this identification of England with her upper crust.

Things changed abruptly with the unleashing, after the wartime truce, of political controversy, of which more later. The Festival of Britain and the Coronation ushered in another bout of cinematic satisfaction with the *status quo*. A little cluster of patriotic films asserted the continuing dynamism of tradition, peaceful in theme. Hence, *Scott of the Antarctic* (Charles Frend, Ealing, 1948), a fine saga for boy scouts, *The Lady with a Lamp* (Herbert Wilcox, 1951), with Queen Victoria as Florence Nightingale, Group 3's *The Conquest of Everest* (1953), as if it mattered, and Castleton Knight's *A Queen Is Crowned* (also 1953), ushering in the era of what Malcolm Muggeridge derisively labelled 'telly monarchy'. The British attempted to intoxicate themselves into the belief that they were colourful, gay, ebullient, thrusting, swashbuckling, patriotically united, privately enterprising, New Elizabethans all, under their grey flannel faces. The effort was almost as absurd as Mussolini's revival of Ancient Rome, and dissenters found the case of *The Magic Box* (John Boulting, 1951) deliciously symptomatic. The film industry pooled its best talents for this Festival Film Production, which celebrated the achievements of the photographer Friese-Greene, alleged to have 'invented cinematography' in 1889. Raymond Spottiswoode neatly punctures such historical wishful thinking.

Friese-Greene did not originate any of the major ideas of cinematography though he was much ahead of his time in grasping the possibilities of the motion picture and in working strenuously if lamely towards their accomplishment ... In two respects he was indubitably a pioneer. He designed one of the first cameras and the projectors to use the new film ... he did shoot a film in Hyde Park in 1889 showing a man and a boy walking. Whether he succeeded in projecting it, as he claimed ... is less certain; engineers who have since examined his projector ... have detected deficiencies which, they say, would have prevented the film from being shown at the rate ... needed to give an illusion of motion ...

And Charles Oakley remarks:

Eric Ambler [the film's scenarist] must also have been disconcerted by the descent of Friese-Greene from a successful "Court Photographer" to a discard on the fringes of the trade ... Anticlimax is not usually favoured by story-tellers. Nor could the plot be linked with any outstanding developments in cinema photography because he had made virtually no contribution to them ...

To crown everything 'the film was not released until the end of 1951 when enthusiasm for the Festival of Britain had almost evaporated. The result did not appeal to the public. No other major production can have played to so many half-empty houses.'

The Magic Box and *Scott of the Antarctic* are both stories of gallant failure, as if, albeit unconsciously, the British could hardly respond to the idea of success without an aura of failure surrounding it. This in many ways mature attitude is confused by the insistence that a gallant failure is somehow a success. A moral success, maybe; but, also, failure.

Meanwhile a sense of happy continuity with the still flourishing past inspires a frivolous, but significant cycle. A scattering of old crock movies portrays Britain as a sort of Betjemenesque Ruritania in which upper-class connoisseurs can create their jolly Game Reserves for old crocks and mechanical pets. The *Painted Boats* of 1945 blaze a trail along Britain's stagnant backwaters and are followed by *The 'Maggie'* (Alexander Mackendrick for Ealing, 1954), which seems, significantly, aimed at American tourists. *Genevieve* (Henry Cornelius, 1953), nicely conjugates its automobile antiquarianism with a contemporary spirit, but sires such reactionary progeny as *The Titfield Thunderbolt* (Charles Crichton at Ealing, 1952), and, limping home, *The Iron Maiden* (Gerald Thomas, 1962). How much ground has been lost since the thirties is evidenced by comparison with that 1937 epic of the iron horse, Marcel Varnel's *Oh, Mr. Porter!*, starring Will Hay. Its picture of British railways in the days of private enterprise may be summed up by the scene where Moore Marriott affectionately pats an old steam-engine named Gladstone. 'Good for another hundred years!' he says affectionately, whereupon she, or he, or rather it, promptly blows up.

6. Good Irresolutions

If such satisfied movies had more impact then than now seems possible it was partly because they were working against an undercurrent of uneasiness. This flowed from what everybody had to admit was a long series of national ignominies at home and abroad, from Versailles through Jarrow to Munich and Dunkirk. Suddenly it wasn't good enough that the common or garden English soldier should have to go back to a life which was that not of a demi-paradise but of demi-slump and semi-slum.

Few movies could bring themselves to criticize the social structure in as wholehearted a way as the satisfied movies praised it. One group of films paraphrased social discontent in terms of moral purifications.

The Boulting Brothers' second wartime feature film, *Thunder Rock* (1942), concerns an embittered and defeatist intellectual (Michael Redgrave) who becomes a lighthouse keeper out of misanthropy, until goaded by ghosts into shouldering his social responsibilities once more. Strictly speaking it's a criticism of the ivory tower megalomania frequently attributed to intellectuals, but, illogically, it caught, in its time, a feeling against Munich-era non-interventionism. England is the lighthouse-island whose laissez-faire policies had failed it in international and domestic affairs alike. *Thunder Rock* is both a moral homily and a left-of-liberal-centre film.

Retrospective shame over pre-war muddles shaded into a more forward-looking concern with internal reform on the publication in 1942 of the Beveridge Report. Drawn up by a Liberal, it became the basis of the Labour Government's plans for the Welfare State. A lively debate over social reconstruction ensued, although in movies direct political controversy was carefully skirted. Basil Dearden's *The Halfway House* (Ealing, 1944) crosses *Thunder Rock* with the omnibus film (that forties genre whereby a motley collection of characters, of whom none is an outstanding hero, meet in a certain place, whether barrack-room, prison camp, or dance hall, and constitute a sort of group hero. It had a great deal of meaning during the war years, when mobilization brought many people into new group activities and across class barriers, often for the first time). The landlord (Mervyn Johns) of a Welsh roadside inn, and his daughter (Glynis Johns), cast no shadow, and time has mysteriously moved back a year, before incendiary bombs gutted the inn. A Mayfair couple decide not to divorce. A black marketeer (Alfred Drayton) decides he can't face his fear of arrest (the insistence on the need for sternness is noteworthy). An Irish diplomat decides to abandon his neutrality and come down on the British side. An unjustly cashiered officer (Guy Middleton) decides to forget his grudge and muck in again as a private. A saddened skipper (Tom Walls) decides to be kind but firm with his over-emotional French wife (Françoise Rosay) and stop her morbidly mourning their slaughtered son. And the orchestral conductor (Esmond Knight) who's working himself to death flying the flag of English culture in neutral countries decides to accept death and the Christian faith while humbly wiping-up for the landlord's daughter. Society's problems are paraphrased by a job lot of individual stocktakings, and none of the characters decides to do anything that isn't in the moral copybook. The wartime plea for self-sacrifice becomes a stalking-horse for the notion, not peculiar to the establishment, that the individual must always sacrifice himself to keep things going. Still, the film's sense of an esprit de corps involving voluntary sacrifice has a certain urgency and poetry, and the deaths by fire are grim, so that the film attains a stoic moral dignity.

Dearden's next film was described as a film record of the stage production of another Priestley play, *They Came to a City* (1944). In this sober fantasy, nine people are offered a chance to live in Utopia. They, almost all, turn their backs on it. Like many message films it can be understood in several mutually unconnected or incompatible senses. Charles Oakley sees it as 'advocating universal friendship', others have seen it as a rejection of life without struggle, for others again it repudiated post-war planning and the Welfare State. (Priestley perhaps meant only to repudiate a colourless uniformity.)

The indomitable old crock cycle is balanced by another minor cycle, dedicated to the theme: 'For want of a nail ...' *The Man in the Sky* (Charles Crichton, Ealing, 1956) is a test-pilot (Jack Hawkins) whose wife (Elizabeth Sellars) doesn't understand that men must work while women must weep. He keeps a damaged prototype aloft for hours so as to impress an unsuspecting American buyer. The film imbues 'export or perish' with the Dunkirk spirit and bristles with patriotic plugs for Bristol, Rolls-Royce and private enterprise. In the cycle's climactic film, Roy Baker's *A Night to Remember* (1958) the huge, proud liner *Titanic* plunges, gallantly, Blimpishly, to her doom, as little misjudgements, complacencies, and unpreparednesses, in a word, British muddling through, take their toll.

Don Chaffey's farce about nonchalantly blundering aircraft mechanics, *Nearly a Nasty Accident* (1960), waspishly spotlights the same traits on the artisan level. *Carry On Spying* (Gerald Thomas, 1964) treats Britain's security precautions with the same gleeful derision. Comedies generally indict a carelessness all but institutionalized on every level of British life.

Right-wing thinkers dwell on the complacent inefficiency of the British workman, who always forgets his tools, while left-wing thinkers stress the indolent amateurism of the ruling classes, and certainly neither has ever evolved a method of protecting itself from the shortcomings of the other, or indeed, its own.

7. Trouble at t'Mill

Other films, more probingly, tackle the question of class relationship which looms so tacitly yet so massively in this traditionally class-and caste-conscious island. The need for a reconciliatory readjustment was, by 1945, widely admitted. In general, one may take as left-wing those films which stress the need for concessions to the lower orders, and as right-wing those which stress the need for reconciliation without readjustment. Similarly, one may class as left-of-neutral those which affirm the working-class's right to little revolts (like *Waterloo Road*, of which more later), and as right-of-neutral those which insist on discipline as salvation (like *The Bells Go Down*).

Films overtly introducing the idea of class tension usually have a historical setting, so as to avoid picking up over-detailed controversies, and they tend to urge acquiescence in fairer play for the lower orders in future. A group of such films coincides with the Labour landslide of 1945. Boldest of the group is Brian Desmond Hurst's *Hungry Hill* (1946), after Daphne du Maurier. True, it opposes to its brutal English industrialist (Cecil Parker), not the English proletariat, but the Irish peasantry, who resent being dragooned into industrial rhythms. By sinning against his employees, the patriarch of the capitalist dynasty brings down a curse on his own children. His aged widow (Margaret Lockwood) must show forbearance to the mob who killed her son.

Thus the film is conciliatory to the rowdy villagers, i.e. the lower orders, i.e. those who voted Labour. On the other hand, their leader is a rabblerouser, and our primary involvement is with the upper-class family. It's *their* story, not the workers', which is ours. This is surprising, since the cinema audience is 70 per cent working-class. (The phenomenon of identification upwards is a familiar wish-fulfilment mechanism, as crucial in politics as in entertainment. The suffering and humiliated, finding their own frustrations intolerable, prefer to forget them, and to identify with their rulers, who can turn this identification into loyalty sharpened, in crisis, by finding a convenient third party on to which hatred can be projected. Peter Ustinov gives a clear picture of the process in *Billy Budd*.) The widow's fine moral attitude to what is not always far from a rabble is, in itself, carefully non-political, but it does carry political meanings. The middle-class dismissal of the workers, even in 1945, was often couched in terms like 'They don't deserve any better than slums, they'd turn Buckingham Palace itself into a slum'. And the widow has to renounce the view of the lower orders as beneath concern and, in a sense, apologize. Yet the fact that the finer moral feelings come from the upper-class characters, who provide our only continuous identification, seems to me to tilt the balance of this interestingly equivocal film to right of centre – albeit a chastened, conciliatory, right – a harbinger of Butskellism, perhaps.

A similar moral, perhaps less consciously, underlies David Lean's version of Dickens's *Great Expectations* (1946). Young Pip is grabbed and badly scared out on the marshes by a fearsome old convict, Magwitch (Finlay Currie), whom he nonetheless pities and attempts to help. Later, he is taken as companion to a haughty young girl Estella (Jean Simmons), who calls him a nasty dirty common boy. Years later, when an unknown benefactor enables him to go to London and learn to be a gentleman, he assumes him to be Estella's guardian, the morose recluse Miss Havisham (Martita Hunt). Only later does he discover that his real benefactor is none other than old Magwitch. After being recaptured, Magwitch was transported to Australia, where he made good, became rich by sheep-farming, and never forgot the boy who befriended him out on those cold and shivering marshes. He now risks life and liberty to return to the Mother Country and see 'my boy'. Betrayed, he is caught, and dies in the hulks, without realizing, in his rough simplicity, that Pip has become a snob. But his death brings Pip to his ordinary decent senses. Denouncing Miss Havisham, he wins a chastened Estella from the aristocratic suitor who abandoned her on learning that she was a convict's daughter.

Pip's adoptive father, Joe Gargery (Bernard Miles), is a poor blacksmith. That is to say, he combines a modest independence (lower-middle-class) and manual labour (working-class). In other words, he is a generalized 'common man', a 'typical Englishman'. Right at the beginning he sides with Magwitch against the soldiers, i.e. a brutal order. Miss Havisham and Estella, with their snobbish contempts and aspirations, belong to the upper-middle-classes, Magwitch, 'father' of both young people's fortunes, dies a martyr's death.

Thus Pip *thinks* that all that is best in his life comes from the upper-middle-classes. In fact it comes from the marsh and the hulks, that is, the proletarian underworld. Merely by simplifying Dickens, the movie trembles on the brink of being a classic Marxist fable about bourgeois 'confusionism'. It's drawn back from class-consciousness by a scattering of remarks stressing the moral rather than the social angles. Pip says, 'I had become a snob'. Joe Gargery pities Magwitch as a 'poor hungry miserable fellow-creature'. And, of course, it is as a self-made man that Magwitch thrives. In these respects, the film contrasts with René Clément's *Gervaise* (1956), which in some ways is its French equivalent. There the proletarian tower of strength is another blacksmith. He is imprisoned for organizing a trade union. And the attempts by Gervaise (Maria Schell) to be a self-made woman fail. She becomes a drunken wreck, and her daughter, Nana, grows up to become the curse of the aristocracy – which, oddly enough, is just what Miss Havisham wanted Estella to be.

There is another class contrast. At first, Magwitch is infinitely menacing. But, as he becomes, by turns, respect-worthy, even pitiable, the atmosphere of smouldering violence is maintained by another convict, described simply as his old enemy. Thus the lower orders remain consistently the realm of both nightmare-like violence – and also of strong, warm, masculine emotion. Miss Havisham, jilted years ago on her wedding eve, living by her rat-infested wedding-cake, bringing up Estella to be her revenge on men, and Estella herself, cold and calculating, are, between them, just what the film's last images evoke. As Pip tears down her musty curtains, letting the sunlight in, a coal rolls from the grate, and icy Miss Havisham catches fire. It's as if she is the living dead in a mausoleum, whom the sunlight burns – in a word, she's a vampire, the vampire of upper-middle-class snobbery and frigidity, accepting gratitude, giving nothing. The film says: 'However frightening the rough lower orders are, *they* are the foundation of your wealth, the warmth of your heart.'

Yet as the film ends, Magwitch is dead: Estella will give Pip a cool, chastened, grateful hand; his future is with the upper-middle-class image after all.[25]

A weak story betrays the *Hungry Hill*-type allegorization which can be read into Frank Launder's *Captain Boycott* (1947). And it's a pity, for refreshingly, it's unequivocally on the side of the rabble. It returns us to Ireland, with Cecil Parker as the English landlord, the English army playing a fascist role, and Stewart Granger saving the peasantry from a doomed uprising by inventing the boycott. If the end result is a distinctly rosy view of Anglo-Irish history, the film reveals its true meaning in terms of the upper- and middle-class fear that any affirmation by the lower orders will end in disorder and mob violence (the boycott is, after all, a paraphrase of the strike, which other directors were shortly to equate with *High Treason*). A more amiable attitude to proletarian 'anarchy' is just what one would expect from the Launder-Gilliat team, already responsible for *Millions Like Us* and *Waterloo Road*.

Other films paraphrase the same conflicts in more contemporary form. The central characters of Cavalcanti's *For Them That Trespass* (1949) is a clergyman's secretary (Stephen Murray) turned writer. When he finds his working-class mistress murdered, his moral cowardice – centred about his social status – makes him keep silence while the wrong man, a working-class type (Richard Todd), is sent to prison for many years. Again, the honest worker is wronged by his prim betters. But again, it's another worker, a stoker, who is the real brute.[26] The nice worker's rather middle-class motive ('clearing my name'), and the middle-class view of working-class behaviour 'I swear I didn't do it, guv'), short circuit a profounder theme: a sheltered youth's discovery of how the other half lives, of his own bad faith, of his creative sensitivities being at their cost. The film remains notable for its mood of diffuse guilt and for Cavalcanti's sense, quite worthy of Carné, of the sad poetry of squalid, smoky streets.

The same period sees two films about upper-class dynasties. Walter Forde's *Master of Bankdam* (1947) locates all capitalist excesses in the past; everything's all right now, i.e. don't nationalize t'mill, just subsidize us. *So Well Remembered* (1947) has an American director (Edward Dmytryk) and an American co-producer (R.K.O.-Radio). Much less deferential, it takes an unexpectedly hard-edge look at class barriers in its three-generation saga of politics in a northern town. It asserts that they're as rigid as ever, albeit in a subtler way.

Another bold treatment of class distinction had to wait for another semi-American film, John Guillermin's *Town on Trial* (1956). It bears American taste very much in mind (adapting the formula of the embittered cop) and it accentuates those aspects of Home Counties life which answer to American motifs (the bible-quoting sex maniac, his possessive mother, tennis club for country club, intervening psychiatrist). Yet the simple fact of transposing into English terms the relative American frankness about 'the wrong side of the tracks' makes it a minor breakthrough in admitting that there's a wrong side to the old school tie. One's initial feeling that John Mills isn't exactly England's Glenn Ford may lead on to the reflection that an apparent miscasting only adds to the vehemence: 'If so nice a guy is embittered, shouldn't we all be?' 'That's a Harrow tie, isn't it?' he sneers at a suspect. 'Well, er, yes, it is, as a matter of fact,' the other replies modestly, 'Which was your school?' – 'London Polytechnic.' Defiantly our hero clings to what is described as a 'typically working-class' meal of cheese and pickles, and though he is finally required to admit that his inverted snobbery is mildly neurotic (whereas uninverted snobbery isn't?), a hero's class sensitivities are aired with rare realism and relish. The movie is a straw in the wind of change as, two years later, *Room at the Top* makes plain to all.

2: Cross Sections

8. The Nine Lives of Colonel Blimp

What, in a democratic readjustment, are we to do with our betters?

The discontents behind the 1945 Labour landslide were widely felt to reflect upon an established order whose screen symbols included the idyllic tycoon of *The Demi-Paradise*, the lady of Mrs. Miniver's manor, the Mayfair playboy (Rex Harrison) of *The Rake's Progress*, and, of course, Anna Neagle and Michael Wilding in those Herbert Wilcox frolics which rejoiced in such titles as *I Live in Grosvenor Square* (1945), *Piccadilly Incident* (1946), *The Courtneys of Curzon Street* (1947), *Spring in Park Lane* (1948), *Maytime in Mayfair* (1949) and *The Lady Is a Square* (1958).

We're obviously in the presence of what is not so much a clearly defined group as a conglomeration and interfusion of groups. Once, perhaps, quite distinct, now, less so, the stratum is often described by left-wing writers as 'the establishment', by right-wing apologists like Simon Raven as that of 'the English gentleman', by Brian Inglis, writing in a liberal-nonconformist spirit about English morality, as 'um-class' ('um' standing both for upper-middle and for that interjection of supercilious vagueness), and by Nancy Mitford as 'U' people ('U' standing for upper-middle, as opposed to non-U for those below).

Disparate as its various strands may be, this group's basic social institution is the (reputable) public school. The groups who there learn to rub along may be listed as (*a*) the aristocracy, (*b*) the country gentry, (*c*) financiers and the higher professional classes, and (*d*) businessmen and industrialists.

The Battle of the Sexes: Peter Sellers – Not sexual resentment, merely a resentment of progress

Exactly how these still partly disparate groups came to integrate, and how far they integrate now, is still controversial and beyond our scope.

One popular and partly accurate myth requires some comment, underlying as it does so many movies. This is John Galsworthy's *schema*, typified in his play *The Skin Game*, which he wrote in 1920 and which Alfred Hitchcock filmed in 1931. Hillcrist, the landowning gentleman, associated, like his name, with land and moral loftiness, is challenged by Hornblower, the hard, thrusting, vulgar industrialist. Hillcrist emerges triumphant, chastened by the fact that he has stooped to methods as low as Hornblower's. The fact that he's so worried about it reassures us that he's very decent really, and their children give a little promise of some sort of reconciliation in which the best may prevail.

This distinction between a landbased gentry (linked to the aristocracy) and industrialist parvenus recurs in Ronald Neame's *The Card* (1952, after Arnold Bennett). It influences such contemporary subjects as *The Night My Number Came Up* (Leslie Norman, 1955) and *Time without Pity* (Joseph Losey, 1957). In the first film, set in a transport plane in distress, a coarse crude self-made businessman makes a bad showing against the smooth calm well-spoken senior R.A.F. officers. In Losey's film the tormented marriage of brutal, too energetic sports car manufacturer (Leo McKern), and his too fastidious, frigid wife (Ann Todd), echoes the same dichotomy.

Which isn't altogether unreal, albeit queried by the gentleman-tycoon of *The Demi-Paradise*. Another figure also gives us pause: the brutal aristocrat of *Great Expectations*, as, indeed, of all the Gainsborough costume melodramas. It's suspicious, too, that the nearest historical equivalent of a gentleman versus businessman confrontation is the Repeal of the Corn Laws, 1832. Subsequently we find middle-class characters like Mr. Chamberlain and Mr. Macmillan hobnobbing with the aristocracy on pretty equal terms. If Hillcrest and Hornblow settled the matter in about 1920, would the division still be so marked in 1955?

It's probably truer to say that Asquith's gentleman-tycoon is a late bud of the Whig merchant aristocracy which dominated England in the eighteenth century – and sooner or later invested money in the rising industrial enterprises. The brutal aristocrat typifies the upper-class backwoodsmen, the Tory country gentry, who, in the same period, ran their farms in aggressively capitalist style. It's an even bet that the Hillcrist estates were created by a grandfather even more merciless than Hornblower. The truth of the matter seems to be that, ever since the Tudors ended the Wars of the Roses, the English aristocracy has consisted largely of money, and families, fairly recently jumped up from the middle-classes (and producing also an impoverished aristocracy, and gentry). For the English gentleman, is in the best moral sense, by no means a traditional figure. His blend of evangelical (middle-class) conscience and of country gentry style (blood sports) appears during the middle of the nineteenth century and it may well be that his sense of responsibility to the lower orders owes less to residual feudalism than to (1) splits within sections of the upper-classes, jockeying for lower-middle-class support, and so stumbling on (2) the usefulness of compromise and concession for staving off working-class revolution, as well as (3) maintaining a wealth-producing Empire cheaply (i.e. by gentleman's agreements with native princes rather than by expensive suppression).

The public school facilitates extremely useful interconnections and, of course, intermarriages, between hitherto distinct Whigs, Tories and Liberals (the rising industrialist class). In movie Britain, two upper-class streams are conspicuous. First, City finance and traditional business enterprise (whence the Whig demi-paradise), and, second, the country gentry's special connections with Empire and army (whence the Tory Colonel Blimp).

Movies freely criticize the 'self-made man' (on the one hand) and Colonel Blimp (on the other), but rarely the more central characters, the happily married children of Hillcrist and Hornblower. The reason is obvious. The criticized figures represent marginal attitudes, respected by the establishment mainstream, but often resented by the opposite pole within it. Criticism of the 'mainstream' – the public-school-and-money nexus – has to wait for the angry young men and satirists of the period following ours. The establishmentarian estate agency of Clive Donner's *Nothing But the Best* (1963) might have been 'Hillcrist, Hornblower and Hornblow Ltd', while Donald Wolfit in *Room at the Top* is both a self-made industrialist and a pillar of the establishment. Mayfair was the interwar playground of this um-class idle young, and *their* son is Tony in *The Servant* (1963). He's far cooler and nicer than an old fire-eater like Blimp, but the scheme he's at one point involved with, for shifting large masses of poor foreigners about the world, promises to be, in its nonchalant way, just as paternalist and disastrous, for them, as some of the old boy's.

Created by David Low, the *Evening Standard*'s cartoonist, Colonel Blimp expressed wartime criticisms of an ineffective establishment, and did so by emphasizing its links with the country-gentry (squire-officer) spirit. That the emphasis lay here rather than on the business-finance establishment suggests that Low didn't recognize, or shrewdly preferred to be more indirect about, the extent to which Britain's troubles were due to the loss of impetus by British industry from as early as 1870. Some reputable historians have since suggested that it was slowed down by the influence, not only through the public school, but in the world of contacts and affairs, of the older, business-despising establishment groups on the more dynamic middle-class element.

Low's character nonetheless constituted an effective criticism of the establishment and its old boy net. Hence Blimp found his defenders. It's of the essence of Low's Blimp that he's not only inefficient and pompous, but mean and vicious. As played by Roger Livesey in Powell-Pressburger's *The Life and Death of Colonel Blimp* (1943) he's a forlorn old boy, touchingly gallant in his Edwardian prime, but far too gentlemanly for this modern world. He resigns, voluntarily, after being trapped in his Turkish bath by a young Home Guard amateur who, geared to Nazi trickery and total war, attacks before manoeuvres are due to start. The love (Deborah Kerr) Blimp lost to his equally gallant Prussian foe he sees again in his young A.T.S. chauffeur. And although her voice is pretty upper-crusty too, the difference in rank, and the young man's aggressive style, is a gesture towards democracy.

The same directors' *I Know Where I'm Going!* was felt at the time as a tribute to Britain's glorious countryside (for which middle-class people often liked to feel they were fighting). The film is in fact far more interesting. It asserts an antagonism between the materialistic money-based middle-class world of the heroine (Wendy Hiller) and the irrational but wise other-worldliness of Celtic myth, championed by a Scottish laird (the country gentry [and Roger Livesey] again). Wendy Hiller had portrayed the heroines of two Shaw movies (Asquith's and Gabriel Pascal's *Pygmalion*, 1938, and Pascal's *Major Barbara*, 1941), and the Powell-Pressburger movie is by way of riposte to the Shavian proposition that in our society money-making is the logical and satisfying expression of life-force. The bluestocking and brashly cash-based heroine's notions are decisively queered by wayward Celtic winds-and-waves.

She is worked upon by Celtic females (Pamela Brown, Nancy Price), whose fey wisdom is disturbing rather than reassuring. They have the glances of eagles, the laird's nose is distinctly aquiline, and an elderly, Blimp-type major is training a golden eagle which bears his name. The youngster proves that he understands the real meaning of tradition by defying an old legend, whose play on words vindicates this defiance. Clearly true Toryism must be neither money-grabbing nor supinely traditional, must recharge its ancient enterprise by defying the conventional wisdom, must be less like Blimp than the brain surgeon – also played by Roger Livesey – who features in Powell and Pressburger's next movie.

A *Matter of Life and Death* (1946) is generally taken as an extravaganza, a vague, eccentric, enjoyable contraption advocating closer ties with the U.S.A.[27] But the politics of this 'Halfway Heaven' are far more precise. They express perennial Tory criticisms of the Socialist Utopia – that is, the Welfare State.

A British bomber pilot (David Niven) narrowly escapes death in his blazing plane, and thereafter suffers from intermittent but consistent hallucinations. He believes that he is visited by a Heavenly Messenger (Marius Goring), the ghost of a witty aristocrat at the court of Louis XVI. The Briton owes his life to an almost unprecedented error in Heaven's filing system, and must now come quietly. Pilots and aircrew find Heaven a pretty depressing place, rather like a Services Depot, all red tape and unsmiling clerks handing out wings over a counter. Our pilot has become accustomed to wartime regimentation and resigns himself to being 'called up'.

However, his brain consultant (Roger Livesey), and an American girl (Kim Hunter) with whom he has fallen in love, take his hallucinations as evidence of a psychological crisis. To instil in him the will to live, they urge him to challenge Heaven's arbitrary decrees. Heavenly logic concedes him the right to a Heavenly trial. The Prosecutor (Raymond Massey) is an embittered American colonial from the War of Independence. But our pilot's case is won when the prosecutor's anti-imperialist arguments are outweighed by the modern girl's tear on a rose, symbol of her readiness to sacrifice herself for her lover by taking his place in the heavenly host.

Clearly the pilot represents Britain. His escape when he 'should' have died recalls the 'miracle' of Dunkirk. He is lured towards Death by the witty, decadent frivolity of the French (a 'false friend' becomes 'collaborationist'). But his salvation is America's and Britain's mutual love.

Critics of the time felt that Heaven must stand for Hitler's 'New Order', his arbitrary totalitarian world. The Robsons drew many parallels, even stretching their argument to claiming that Himmler means Heaven in German. But surely this heavenly city isn't bestial enough for Nazism. It isn't even malicious, merely coldly efficient. And the film's preoccupation is not with Britain's survival in war, but with her survival in peace. For the Heavenly Jury consists of people on the receiving end of imperialism, such as an Indian, a Boer, and of course, the Prosecutor, a successful rebel, and respectworthy adversary.

This Heaven is a futurist Utopia. It's a planned society. It's machine-like (one mounts to it on an inexorable escalator, whence the film's U.S. title, *Stairway to Heaven*). This stairway is flanked by the imposing, but dead-white, statues of such great idealists as Plato (whose Utopia is, of course, thoroughly totalitarian). As Tories claim planning drains colour from life, so, here, the Technicolor of earth pales to celestial monochrome. Heaven's values are those of the collectivity (as opposed to the selfless individualism of romantic love). Planned, bureaucratic, idealistic, totalitarian, colourless, theoretic – all these are the words Tories like to use of Socialism. Once again, we come to a city, and we opt out.

But it isn't only the British soul which is menaced by this fate worse than death. Gum-chewing American aircrews find Coca-Cola machines there. All modern societies are menaced by a monotonous, superficial routinization. And it's quite logical that the emissary of totalitarianism should be its apparent antithesis, an irresponsible French dandy. He got too irresponsible, decadent, in fact, and had his head cut off by the common people, in another 'democratic' revolution, for whose excesses he has mostly himself to blame.

The American colonialist also levels accusations of decadence at the British way of life, which is defined in upper-middle-class terms – notably, a toffee-voiced cricket commentator. Everyone is concerned with the decadence or otherwise of aristocratic traditions. But on the whole the modern British pilot and the modern American girl seem to be the best compromise between French flippancy, American vulgarity, and something a little too superior in the English upper-classes – represented by our hero's brain consultant ally and father-figure. For he peers at the humble villagers through his *camera obscura* and seems to be not only some sort of village doctor but some sort of village squire, caustic and slightly Godlike. With his surgical skills, his expertise at ping-pong and his ton-up motorcycling, he is surely a stout-hearted, old-new-fashioned British Tory – allied to the girl from America, where individuality and free enterprise are every ordinary decent person's birthright and philosophy.

The American right comes under friendly fire. The ex-Colonial's isolationism (usually associated with the Republican party) must cede to the ordinary (Democratic) American girl. She steps onto the escalator in the hero's place, so halting it, but her readiness for self-sacrifice suggests 'America must engage and risk herself, or at least make some sort of temporary concession to post-war planning, so as to save us, and, really, herself'.

Even the Socialist Heaven has one point in its favour. It has facilities for fair trial (provided you stick up for yourself against its bureaucracy). Its High Chief Justice (Abraham Sofaer) is a man of the greatest integrity, who allows the pilot's appeal in the name of love. So that Heaven is an, albeit icy, ideal of fairness. But if Britain's sense of fair play makes her susceptible to the appeal of Socialism, it should also operate, as fair play to the individual, to protect us from it. At any rate, the Socialist longing for admirable justice goes with a coldness of individual feeling, and a crushing of initiative, and we must side instead with our home-grown squires and the friendlier Americans.

The stress on the Squirearchy in Powell's work may spring mainly from his romanticism. Yet the notion that the countryside is somehow more truly and nobly English than the city is not always apolitical. Cities swarm with discontented Labour voters; the villages seem quieter and more feudal. In Wyler's *Mrs. Miniver*, an American film, but, alas, English by adoption, the 'Lady of the Manor', who for twenty years has always awarded herself First Prize in the village chrysanthemum show, now, in honour of the democratic war effort, awards first prize to a 'typical English housewife' (Greer Garson) who lives in a house with, if I remember, two grand pianos. Seeing this dreadful film now, it's hard to believe that at the time Mrs. M. was accepted as a national heroine whose glycerine tears and saccharine trials seemed of Boadicean proportions.

Of all the films on the aristocrat problem, Sidney Gilliat's *The Rake's Progress* (1945) comes nearest some sort of social realism. The rake (Rex Harrison) is an amiable Mayfair playboy who can't settle down, makes all sorts of fluffs and gets into all sorts of scrapes, through a nonchalant negligence which is only the diffidence of honour without a cause. He's too gentlemanly to live either up to the nastier forms of aristocratic irresponsibility, or down to the grinding middle-class industriousness which is the other half of his family tradition. On the field of battle, he makes more than amends for a life whose ineffectuality becomes an affectionate but emphatic farewell to an ethos of which he is the hapless but very likeable scion.

Jack Lee's *The Woman in the Hall* (1947) tells the tale of a decayed gentlewoman (Ursula Jeans) who takes her daughter (Jean Simmons) with her on begging trips around the grander um-class homes. By claiming to be the relative of a relative she lives parasitically, on hand-outs. The film's quiet

How I Won the War: Jack MacGowran – Surviving the war with savage, dazzle-camouflage

insistence on such connections as a parasitism leads also to the reflection that the old girl network is something of a class welfare state within a state, bailing out the black sheep, the idlers and scroungers, and no more defensible than the Labour Party's Welfare State, often belaboured by the right for featherbedding the feckless. This essentially woman's film has a cautious complement in Charles Frend's *The Loves of Joanna Godden* (Ealing, 1947), a study in upper-middle-class feminine self-reliance and energy. Miss Godden (Googie Withers) is a self-made farmer – country gentry capitalist – who survives personal tragedy and near ruin to continue her private enterprise. It fits in with Ealing's post-war interest in agrarian England and Empire, and marks a transition between the *Hungry Hill* genre and those films of the fifties which urged the middle-class Englishman to show more self-confidence and get-up-and-go.

The Labour Government's self-imposed exit, the Festival of Britain's appeal to tradition, and the Coronation of Queen Elizabeth II, go with a

The Rake's Progress: David Wallbridge, Charles Victor – It's not the Eton lads who won the war, but the long-suffering fighting man

reacceptance of the aristocracy. They bother us less than the bureaucracy, and, insofar as they can talk cheekily and effectively back to it, can seem to be on our side. A new contentedness with the *status quo* is registered by Ronald Neame's *The Card* (1952). This unbeatably anachronistic piece joyously celebrates the romantic outcome of love-hate misunderstandings between the aristocracy (Valerie Hobson) and the industrialist (Alec Guinness). situated, this time, in the Edwardian era. The burly, jolly workers look happily on. They're happy because, far from striking, all they care about is the success of their local soccer team, through supporting which the lovably crafty card gains their enthusiastic admiration. A more ingenious, albeit unstylish, variation on the same theme is provided by John Paddy Carstairs' adaptation of William Douglas Home's stage success, *The Chiltern Hundreds* (1949). Goaded by his demandingly democratic American girlfriend, the Lord of the Manor's son runs as Labour candidate and turns his attentions to the maid. Meanwhile his shocked butler runs for the Tories, backed by the same American girl. The comic twists neatly paraphrase some major paradoxes of English politics, including working-class Conservatism, whose true depth and extent the Left is usually loath to consider. After all its twists and turns this quite entertaining movie is resoundingly, and of course, propagandistically, affirmative of true blue values. The Conservative is the true democrat, because he's blithely unconscious of class. The Labour politician and the American girl are exposed as the real snobs. The maid tastes a lady's life for a day and thereupon declares that ladies work harder for no money than their domestics for £2 a week. By switching from the Lord (leaving him free to return to the Tories) to the butler (who resigns his Parliamentary seat), she keeps herself in her proper station. As you were. By the right. About turn.

A well-meaning wish for limited reform underlies the social films directed during this period by the Liberal Anthony Asquith; *The Winslow Boy* (1948), *The Final Test* (1953) and *Carrington V.C.* (1954). All these films, irrespective of their actual setting, have an Edwardian feel. And Asquith's presumable intention, to indicate that the ordinary man must insist on his rights vis-à-vis bureaucracies and networks which are dominated by establishment indifference, and bend them to some sort of law and equity, is never far from metamorphosis into the suggestion that (1) the fundamental decency of our betters regularly induces them to accommodate true democracy, and (2) virtually all the readjustments required happened in the recent past. A handful of earnestly, cautiously, and usually dully left-wing movies maintained some sort of resolution to reform. The Boulting Brothers' *The Guinea Pig* (1948) tackles the perennial public school problem in a significantly stodgy and depressed style. A bright scholarship lad (Richard Attenborough) from Walthamstow, a lower-middle-class district where he might quite possibly have sat in the desk next to mine, is jumped up to a crack public school. His starry eyes about his betters are speedily replaced by black ones, but a lame, kind master teaches him that he mustn't give in, must hold on in the face of snobberies, and, on behalf of kith and kin, change the system from within. Perhaps it's not unfair to offer the opinion that the odd guinea pig who infiltrates the system will rapidly find himself a happy and perpetual prisoner within it. In any case the upper-middle-classes infiltrated the Labour party far more effectively than Labour can hope to infiltrate the establishment, and it was all the more ironic that the Boultings had named their production company (Charter Films) after their old school (Charterhouse). Isn't Guinea Pig strategy the Trojan Horse which the um-class offer their middle-middle-class antagonists, to separate them from the lower orders?

Derek Twist's *All Over the Town* (1948) puts the Capra formula to an anti-establishment theme. When a reforming journalist (Norman Wooland) comes up with facts which the best people would rather the general public didn't know, he finds the local old boy net solidly arrayed against him. The local lady huffily withdraws her advertising. Therefore his co-editor refuses to sign his cheques. Meanwhile the businessman brazens out the enquiry. Only one man in overalls stands by the honest journalist.

This is substantially the picture presented, more fierily, by the angry young man, the New Left, *Private Eye* and the TV satirists, except that there the journalist would also be betrayed by the trade unions. Even before *Look Back in Anger* hit the boards the Boulting Brothers re-emerged from their spiritual doldrums of the early fifties with the first of their satires, *Private's Progress* (1956), followed by *Brothers in Law* (1956), *Lucky Jim* (1957), *I'm All Right Jack* (1959), *Carlton-Browne of the F.O.* (1959), *Heavens Above!* (1963) and *Rotten to the Core* (1965), none of which exempt the establishment from their general accusations of venality. In the wake of *Town on Trial*, Losey's *Blind*

Date (1959) worried its producers because an establishment-voiced detective suggests to his rougher colleague (Stanley Baker) that it's better that an innocent should perish than that scandal should taint the government of the day.

Two films written by Bryan Forbes, directed by Dearden and produced by Relph in 1960 exemplify, in a more general way, an exasperation with the establishment which is common to right-wing individualism and to left-wing egalitarianism. Leader of the *The League of Gentlemen* is an ex-army officer (Jack Hawkins). Having fallen on hard times in Civvy Street, he blackmails a whole old-boy net of ex-army comrades into joining him in an elaborate robbery. Trained for like a commando raid, it's only narrowly foiled. The theme might seem meat for every deferential working-man's chuckling admiration of the rascally Toff, who combines illogically but powerfully, traditional authority with a bluff, bureaucracy-baiting, colourful right-wing anarchism. But it's subverted by the film's ironies. These officers and gentlemen, unprepossessing as Simon Raven's fictional characters, are a press-gang of moneygrubbing or dishonest scoundrels, largely caddish, seedy and mean.

An equally disabused attitude animates what is in a sense its sequel, *Man in the Moon*. A jolly, earnest, hardworking, class-unconscious, middle-class eager-beaver (Kenneth More) is put in the space-race against another 'league of gentlemen', a set of ex-public-school trainee astronauts, who constitute a First XI of steamingly intense Empire-builders. They are absolutely confident that their lofty social status justifies their use of any and every dirty trick against our vulgar little upstart. But the – bureaucratic – headmaster has the worst offender brainwashed into a spirit of brotherly love, whereupon he loses his erstwhile stiff upper lip and persecutes the hero with assurances of friendship whose homosexual *double entendres* are worthy of *Victim* and queer the B.O.P. pitch with effective insidiousness.

9. Pigs in the Middle

If the problem of what to do with our belted earls is an anachronistic one, a more interesting division lies between the upper-middle-class, with its various sub-groups, and the middle- and lower-middle-class.

The upper and lower edges of the middle-class can't be clearly distinguished from upper- and working-classes. For our purposes, the middle-classes may be 'streamed' along the following lines. (1) Raymond Williams relates middle-class idealism to the nonconformist conscience and to the spirit of service. Its incarnation might be the poorly paid, but devoted, schoolmaster played by Laurence Olivier in Peter Glenville's *Term of Trial*. (2) Another middle-class sector retains money-making individualism from an older, harder Puritan strain (like Leo McKern in *Time without Pity*). (3) Movie figures of middle-class materialism, without benefit of religious origins, include Peter Sellers' crooked garage proprietor in *Never Let Go*, the crooked property-developer in Robert Hartford-Davis's *The Yellow Teddy Bears* (1963), the crooked councillor in Ken Annakin's *Vote for Huggett* (1948). The same cut-throat rat race thrustfulness may infest show-business (*Expresso Bongo*, 1959) and the managerial office (*The Mark*, 1960). (4) The suburban semi-detached is the castle of the quiet, modest, little man in a reasonably secure position, or of the small shopkeeper, whose competitiveness is muted, for obvious reasons, and whose individualism is quiet, passive, defensive, contented and fair-minded (as in David Lean's consistently quietly beautiful *This Happy Breed*, 1944). (5) The shabby-genteel, ruled, as George Orwell noted, by the fear of falling among the rough, common, insensitive class below, and by the humiliation of their present constraints. Such characters include the poorly paid private schoolteachers of *Mr. Perrin and Mr. Traill* (Lawrence Huntington, 1948), of the lodging house phonies in the ironically-titled *London Belongs to Me* (Sidney Gilliat, 1948), and Alec Guinness in *The Lavender Hill Mob* (Charles Crichton, 1951).

From Chaucer's time until Edwardian times, English social history has seemed to feature 'the rising middle-classes'. By 1950 there's a general feeling that some such steady rise has ceased – at last. The combination of affluence, inflation, welfare state and trade unions favours the workers' collective bargaining and undermines middle-class thrift. Simultaneously, scope for little man-type enterprise appears to have decreased. The supermarkets begin to sweep the little man clean off the High Street and leave only the thin wavy line of back-street corner-shops. Suddenly a great many more of us feel shabb-genteel, for even if we're better off than we were before, in absolute standards, we're no longer better off than all the lower-classes. And its relative position which constitutes position. This shift devalues a great many moral qualities – such as thrift, punctilious honesty, devotion to work, and so on. A not always humorous grumbling becomes the characteristic mood of the middle-class cinema.

The films of middle-class disappointment may be divided into those which blame bureaucracy; those which see inertia and apathy as a loss of morale which a new Elizabethan spirit might overcome; those which feel morally betrayed by the nation as a whole; and those which blame the system. In parallel with these disabused movies, others express a cheerful relish of affluence, which sets in from the early fifties. Some of these cheerful films flourish a happy cynicism, as if the weight of the nonconformist conscience and the spirit of service had just been lifted from people's shoulders.

It's bound to be a moot point how far screen attacks on bureaucracy are meant to imply attacks on the idea of planning, and therefore on the Labour Governments of 1945-51, or how far they express a wistful, apolitical anarchism increasingly relevant to modern life under any government. The first batch of Ealing comedies are leftwards-inclined, and offer an agreeable *revanche* to happy cooperatives formed by crossing the lower-middle-class boundaries. Thus Alexander Mackendrick's *Whisky Galore!* (1949) has almost every inhabitant of a Scottish island uniting against its English overlord, its customs authorities and its odd killjoy, to plunder a stranded cargo ship laden with Scotch. The same defiance of the licensing laws is transported to Cockneys for *Passport to Pimlico* (1949), where shop proprietor Stanley Holloway unearths an ancient treaty proving that Pimlico is part of Burgundy, and makes a monkey of Whitehall. Robert Hamer's *Kind Hearts and Coronets* (1949) suavely justifies a disowned son (Dennis Price), who uproots an entire family tree of establishmentarian Alec Guinnesses. *The Lavender Hill Mob* (Charles Crichton, 1951) has a white collar worker (Alec Guinness) finding a rascally happiness by teaming up with Stanley Holloway, incarnating the labour aristocracy. Two comedies by Alexander Mackendrick, *The Man in the White Suit* (1951), and *The Ladykillers* (1955), may be ranged as classics alongside Hamer's *Kind Hearts and Coronets* for their saturnine overtones. *The Man in the White Suit* (Alec Guinness) meets his Waterloo in the ubiquitous stagnation which is the backdrop also of *Look Back in Anger*. He's Jimmy Porter's technical-college-educated elder brother. An industrial backroom boy,

Kind Hearts and Coronets: Alec Guinness – The sinking classes

he invents an everlasting cloth, and, not surprisingly, his most effective enemies are the top-hatted textile manufacturers in their Rolls-Royces. But the moral *coup de grâce* is inflicted by the sad steely accusation of a beshawled old cotton-worker for whom the new invention promises only hardship and slump. The whole nation is a network of sectarian vested interests, in stalemate, so long as the status quo endures. In *The Ladykillers*, Alec Guinness endows his nasty master-mind with an atmosphere of sly, repressed underdog, who has earned his right to his rebellious little day. But this time his prey is dear old Katie Johnson, redolent, like Alison's father, or Archie Rice, or Sergeant Pepper, of all that was nicest in England's Edwardian prime. The to and fro of her invincibly ignorant benevolence, and his seething, impotent malice which we can't but share, gives the film a quality of moral paradox regrettably lacking in Ealing's second wave of anarchist comedies, initiated by *The Titfield Thunderbolt* (1952).

This time it is the Squire, the Bishop and other Tory backwoods worthies who raid a museum, steal an antique locomotive, and keep the local Bluebell Line running, despite bureaucratic bullying and unfair competition by a vulgar middle-class businessman. In *Barnacle Bill* (Charles Frend, 1957) Alec Guinness plays an old seadog who's never been to sea but has its salty spirit and defends his pier against tyrannical officialdom. All of which is no more anarchist than *Punch*; one hardly needs to draw the comparison with, for example, Pierre Prévert's 'omnibus' comedy, *Voyage-Surprise* (1947), or his *Adieu Léonard* (1943), which it's intriguing to imagine as an Alec Guinness vehicle.

It's no accident that while Ealing's left hand was producing 'anarchist' comedies, its right hand produced *The Blue Lamp* and other hymns of love to the perfect British bobby. Barnacle Bill might defy the Whitehall planners, but Michael Balcon told Ken Tynan he could never make a film which profoundly criticised such British institutions as the army. Such reverence is rare, even in Britain, and the ambiguity appears equally in the studio's serious films. Harry Watt's *The Overlanders* (1946) celebrates, thirstily, the simple, manly life enjoyed by the ordinary Australian cowboy. But it takes a Hollywood company (Burt Lancaster's) to put an Ealing director (Leslie Norman) to work on a subject indicating Australian social tensions (*Summer of the Seventeenth Doll*, 1959). Harry Watt invites us to sympathize with rebels in *Eureka Stockade* (1949) and *The Siege of Pinchgut* (1959), the second transposed from the American prison-break formula. The stockade gold-diggers (1854) are poor (left) but object to licences (right). The authorities are establishmentarian by speech (right) but impose licences to subsidize a well-balanced colony (state planning, i.e. left or at least left-of-Tory). Although insisting that justice to gold-rushers is incompatible with law-and-order (i.e. the authorities are not wrong) the film espouses the miners' idealism once troops replace police, their flag is up, and mob status transcended by concern for others. One might mistake the film as a transposition of the Peterloo Massacre into a justification of self-sacrificial violence on behalf of laissez faire, i.e. ultra-right, i.e., Titfield Poujadism. But Ealing de-emphasize the individualism of gold-digging and their – unique – vindication of revolution – in Australia, in the past – is intended to imply Australia, now, as land of egalitarian opportunity, where the masses, nicely blending individualism and solidarity, haven't, as at home, both right and left on their back. If the characters are a little thin, the action a little worried, for this antipodean Western, much that is poignant in wartime documentary is perpetuated in Chips Rafferty's lean grave figure and sadly firm, elegiac voice. Disappointingly less complex in thought, if more massive in impact, is the Studio's swan song, *Dunkirk* (Leslie Norman, 1958), which, impressively and unjustly puts all the blame on bureaucracy for Britain's defeats. If, after all, the day went well, it's thanks to the spontaneous free-enterprise of the boat-owning Barnacle Bills amongst whom the better-off appear to predominate.

Ealing's fortune waned as its spiritual centre of gravity shifted from lower-middle to upper-middle-class. By the mid-fifties those anti-bureaucracy movies which we may loosely describe as 'school of Ealing' had lost most of their social and moral sting. The Government's own Group 3 simperingly indulged such rustic topics as comic smuggling (*Brandy for the Parson* and *Laxdale Hall*, both 1952) and bird sanctuaries (*Conflict of Wings*, 1954). All (directed by John Eldridge) squander nice details on nothing themes. The third opposes the needs of bird sanctuaries to those of the R.A.F. and hits on the boringly obvious principle of compromise. Group 3's executive producer, John Grierson, erstwhile inspirer of the Empire Marketing Board and the G.P.O. Film Unit, was hardly the man to challenge the establishment spirit.

Innumerable other films urged meek little men to show more get up and go. In *The History of Mr. Polly* (Anthony Pélissier, 1948) a meek draper's assistant (John Mills) has a go at a lower-class bully (Finlay Currie again) and possibly intends just that class moral. Two very likeable films by Henry Cornelius plump the little Englishman into tight corners and show how, better late than never, he rises to the occasion. In *I Am a Camera* (1955) Laurence Harvey feels much better after punching a storm-trooper in pre-war Germany. In *Next to No Time!* (1958) Kenneth More finds that the nightly gain of an hour on a west-bound liner parallels the magic word 'Shazam!' and frees the timid British boffin from his inhibiting native modesty, as from his deeply ingrained cringing before a stick-in-the-mud business establishment. Charles Crichton's *The Man in the Sky* (Ealing, 1956) imparts real suspense to its episode in the export drive, while *Touch and Go* (Michael Truman, 1955) urges middle-class families to borrow money and emigrate to Australia.

Alas, national lethargy is more accurately summed up by *The Battle of the Sexes* (Charles Crichton, 1959). A highly traditionalist Scottish textile firm hires an American efficiency expert (Constance Cummings) to streamline its operations. Its meek, loyal, frightened chief clerk (Peter Sellers) fears redundancy, and sets out to murder her. The title is cannily misleading, for the real theme is not sexual resentment at all, but British resentment of progress (a highly understandable one, after all). What's being kept out is not the woman's touch, but the American way of life. The title helps the film to appeal to American anti-Momism, and nostalgia for British quaintness, without seeming too pointedly anti-American (though it's interesting to brood over a variant in which Sellers' victim has a takeover bid in his pocket and only a strike by bloody-minded shop-stewards helps keep the American invaders at bay).

Another approach to 'industrial fatigue' was engineered by the Rank Organisation. It possibly arose, involuntarily, as a result of imitating a Hollywood thirties formula. During the long eclipse of the Western, Warners' sought milieux whose rough, tough feel would justify manly melodrama. The formula was restored to everyone's awareness by Clouzot's *Le Salaire de la peur* (1953). Its adoption by Rank's resulted in, on one hand, the 'empire' cycle, of which more later, and, on the other, a small group of films about heavy industry. Most of the latter were reasonably entertaining, and imbued, quite, one suspects, deliberately, with a *Daily Express*-type up-boy-and-at-'em spirit. They include commercial salesmen (John Guillermin's *Never Let Go*, 1960), the Novia Scotia fishing industries (Philip Leacock's *High Tide at Noon*, 1957), truck drivers in *Hell Drivers* (Cy Endfield, 1957), tug-boat skippers in *Sea Fury* (Cy Endfield, 1958), and dam builders in *Campbell's Kingdom* (Ralph Thomas, 1957). The last, being set in Canada, where the natives are white, is industrial, rather than imperial, in spirit. Dirk Bogarde plays a pale English clerk with leukemia. Motivated less (of course) by naked greed than by a determination to clear his dead father's name, he takes on a brutally virile North American contractor (Stanley Baker). He drives his heavily laden trucks through the latter's road-blocks, and finally wins out, subsidized, in extremis, by two dear old English spinsters who bring out their secret hoard of gold bricks. The film presumably intends to reassure us that apparently ailing and frail English little men and old ladies can match the tough guys and not only win the girl but prove not to have leukemia after all. It's not only the Canadian setting that evokes the gospel according to Lord Beaverbrook. From a less indulgent point of view, the surprising strength of those old ladies (of Threadneedle Street?) is their past accumulations, rather than their present dynamism. Cy Endfield's films are particularly interesting, not only for their melodramatic efficacy, but because their enterprising activities are so perilously cut-throat that the films emerge, by implication, as vehement justification for all sorts of restrictive practice.

The lot of the middle-classes as pigs in the middle is admirably summarized by a sadly underestimated British movie, worthy of George Orwell, as a study of a man in the spiritual prison of his class situation. Roy Baker's *Passage Home* (1955) is set in the Slump years. Merchant skipper Peter Finch feeds his men rotten potatoes so as to take his cut from their food allowance. His characteristics establish him as public schoolboy and prudent petty bourgeois (he puts the money he saves aside and allows himself only one luxury, collecting clocks). When a sailor tips the offending potatoes overboard, he threatens to sign up an entirely new crew unless others sneak on the – sympathetic – mutineers. He drowns his guilt in the drunkenness which in its turn loses him the love of waif-stewardess Diane Cilento. He spends the rest of his life alone, and the film is told, in ironic, secretive flash-back, as, on his retirement, the company offers him a little gift for his lifetime's 'proud' service.

The film's study of a social order is cut short by an in itself admirably nightmarish storm sequence. While the captain, in drunken death-wish, skulks in his cabin, two mates, one sourly ambitious, the other a cold professional, quarrel over how to save the ship. The first has given an order which he now realises is wrong, but sees his life-chance of promotion go if he countermands it. He hesitates between manslaughter-suicide, and failure – a hesitation grimly true to life. At this point the skipper rouses himself, and the fact of his rank averts the danger of violent anarchy. Thus, in its last reel, the film softens towards the British fear of mob-anarchy and that desire for order, at whatever cost, which, in practice, gives whichever order happens to be in power a free hand in every real or pretended crisis. Nonetheless, it has desecrated 'red duster' sentimentality, depicted a nasty class war, and concerned itself, movingly, with the obliteration of a man's moral sensibilities and, therefore, authentic being, by his class position. The wreckage of his love affair is not so far, after all, from Sartre's, and Marx's, theories of alienation from society being alienation from others and from one's self.

Never Let Go marks something of a retrogression. As everybody, including Arthur Miller, knows, a salesman's life affords innumerable opportunities for depicting the nervous strain of the rat race. The problem is how to stop it being too depressing; there are various answers, an artistically more interesting one being exemplified by Jay Lewis's *Live Now Pay Later*, of which more subsequently. At any rate, John Guillermin's film is a middle-class *Bicycle Thieves*, inspirational and melodramatic. Salesman Richard Todd's car is stolen. If he doesn't find it quick he'll lose his job, his wife (Elizabeth Sellers), and what's left of his self-respect. The police can't help and he has to brave the rough tough Teddy Boys (Adam Faith) in their call. Through them he gets to Mr. Big, garage proprietor Peter Sellers, who goes into a Hitler rage whenever his little popsy leaves her hot cigarette ends on his swish radiogram. We're told, alas, that the hero lost his nerve due to wartime shell-shock (alas, because ordinary peacetime weakness of character would have been more interesting. It's significant, though, that all his inner obstacles could have sprung from middle-class meekness – fear of a public row, of self-assertion, general timidity). Clearly the film paraphrases the little man's feeling of sinking vis-à-vis the bigger capitalist and the rough lower orders. But the plot is as phoney as any sad saga of a side street grocer who's being driven out of business because Mr. Victor Value has secretly been hiring thugs to hijack the loads of groceries meant for the little man. Finally his victim braves the brutal long-distance lorry drivers and strong-arms his way into the Value warehouse, where he clobbers the Chairman of the board of directors silly by bombarding him with family-size tins of cut price instant coffee. The logical finale of *Never Let Go* would have our disillusioned hero buying a car dirt cheap, knowing it's stolen – and his hitherto scornful wife praises him for it.

Precisely this moral disenchantment inspired the films of the Boulting Brothers, with whose political evolution from Labour to Liberal it is closely bound. Those who raged at the angry young men and the TV satirists forgot these no less virulent denunciations, whose targets included the army, the legal profession, the universities, the foreign office, the unions, the Church of England, and something more general, perhaps, the entire upper-middle-classes (*Rotten to the Core*). The satires are the not-so-flip side of the almost humourlessly earnest movies which they had made from *Pastor Hall* (1940) on. Looked at in more detail later, their recurrent theme, in its diverse settings, is the progressive disillusionment of an earnest, conscientious, middle-class innocent (usually Ian Carmichael) who discovers the world's cruel unkindness to his ideals, which, indeed, earn him only universal enmity.

The same disgust is biliously expressed in Peter Glenville's *Term of Trial* (1962). A secondary modern school-teacher (Laurence Olivier) is accused of criminal assault by a pupil (Sarah Miles) whose advances he has rejected. The Judge is in the act of sentencing him when the girl confesses the truth (so much for British justice). Teacher is vindicated – but is appalled to find that his class respect him for 'having got away with it'. So does his wife (Simone Signoret), who had hitherto despised him for his moral stand as a conscientious objector. And another time-honoured authority figure, the headmaster turns out to be rotten to the core.

A little too seriously, perhaps, Glenville lyricizes one of James Barlow's liverish visions of British demoralization. Too many reminiscences of other kitchen-sink movies confuse a basically old-fashioned vision. Oh, that gratuitous beating-up (from every American picture), that brick through the windscreen (ex-*The Angry Silence*), Signoret amorous near a fuming geyser (ex-*Room at the Top*), Sarah Miles being all gawk (sort of Rita Tushingham), those love scenes with passionately thrumming trains (from any forties English picture), and that little sequence (ex-Free Cinema) of modern youth's *Nice Time*, all leather-jackets, dirty bookshops, and films with sex and violence, both qualities in which *Term of Trial* is not itself conspicuously deficient. At least Glenville seems aware of some of his hero's shortcomings, notably when, on finding an insolent pupil (Terence Stamp) looking at a sexy book, he loses all self-control and canes him viciously. Nonetheless, we seem to be expected to applaud Teacher's 'courageous' stand before all those frightening boys and girls. Even those working-class kids who have a longing for higher things remain a rabble. Sarah Miles, a woman scorned, brings her teacher to the gates of prison. And a bright young lad, unable to do his homework because his ma kicks him out of the house so as to perpetrate amorous shenanigans with her leering fancy man, takes hysterical revenge by trying to burn the latter's disgustingly lush automobile (he only burns himself).

It's fairly typical of the less generous side of middle-class thought in being both more and less than a study in middle-class contradictions. It becomes, also, an attack on the working-class for being disgusting. Certainly, it reveals that the headmaster, too, is corrupt. Still there's an overtone as if 'decency's flank has been turned', 'the citadel has been betrayed', for we have been persuaded that only a thin chalk line has been holding proletarian savagery at bay. Now it's perfectly true that many English schools are blackboard jungles. One might go on to argue that, given the imperfections of the English educational system, including various moral prejudices which permeate the curriculum and just don't fit the facts of life, particularly lower-working-class life, it's no surprise if a constant state of near-mutiny is a perfectly understandable reaction, an expression, in fact, of intuitive intellectual integrity, among other, less desirable, things.

The film itself offers two examples. One is Teacher's own ignorance as to how society actually works and thinks. The second was underlined by Franco Valobra in an Italian magazine. He pointed out that the most natural character in the film is the schoolgirl who, with a simple straightforwardness, offers herself to the man she loves. Teacher's horror at her sexuality betokens his confusion about teenagers. He can't understand that older schoolchildren are, biologically, adults. From this angle it's not in the least surprising if after being caned in public, Terence Stamp gets his cronies to help him beat up teacher. Teacher has exploited his legal ascendancy, not only to assault, but, far worse, to publicly humiliate, another adult, who retaliates, in his way, quite reasonably. In politics it's called a deterrent. The film has the considerable virtue of relating schoolroom crises to class issues, and movingly involves us in the non-conformist agony.

On the other hand, affluence, for many, cushioned the shock of disenchantment. What one may call the 'affluence cycle' of the fifties was sparked off by Henry Cornelius's delightful *Genevieve* (1953). Its nice young couple (John Gregson, Dinah Sheridan) are spruce, smart and cosily prosperous, and a spicey frankness pervades the sex-duel between Kenneth More and Kay Kendall. It's this latter pair, with their amiably dishonourable intentions, who set the tone for the highly successful *Doctor in the House* series and their innumerable locum tenens (*True as a Turtle, Upstairs and Downstairs,*

The Captain's Table). The little wish-fulfilment leap, not to Lubitsch luxury, but to lower-upper-middle-class cosiness; the air of gay, youthful, relatively modest contentment and sauciness; the pre-*Town*, pre-*Queen* feel of wardrobes and decor – no, Swinging London isn't here yet, but these comedies are certainly celebrations of dawning affluence.

Jack Lee's *The Captain's Table* (1958) gave the cycle its first slug of happy cynicism – and had the first script with the Bryan Forbes claw-marks on it. Fledgeling skipper John Gregson gradually discovers the dishonesty and amorality which has been going on all the time, and rapidly and joyously resigns himself to being no better than he ought to be. Significantly too the classy British lady (Peggy Cummins) proves herself no less provocative and knowing than her exotic vamp rival Nadia Gray. The steward as he wakes the skipper lisps chattily, 'I'm sorry I'm late, Captain, but my friend suddenly came over all queer this morning ... we live together, you know, oh, very platonic ... it's all a laugh, all a giggle, isn't it, sir?' Despite bowdlerization, enough remained of Forbes's and John Whiting's original script to make this the *I'm All Right Jack* of the expense-accounts. In fact a transposition of its theme to an *Executive Suite* level would still be worthwhile.

Forbes's script for *Only Two Can Play* (adapted from Kingsley Amis's *That Uncertain Feeling*) centres on a provincial librarian (Peter Sellers), who lives in drab furnished lodgings with a too shrilly sensitive wife (Virginia Maskell) and stag-cluttered wallpaper. He is tempted to rise in the world by accepting the favours of the Mayor's promiscuous and all the more influential wife (Mai Zetterling). But when she tries to smarten his suits and his character, his male pride reasserts itself. He may have little or no success or pleasure in life, but he won't be bossed around and improved. So he goes back to his wife and his stag-hounded dreams. Sometimes over-broad, the film accurately registers that defensive, querulous, negative middle-class pride which can react against glamour and ambition but not against nagging and guilt, which is at once contentment and masochism, modesty and fear, puritanism and meanness.

Live Now Pay Later approaches the same tangle of cynicism and affluence in a likeably relaxed way and despite plunges into a *Carry On Salesman* tone rates as a key film, a worthy harbinger of Joan Littlewood's *Sparrows Can't Sing*. Its author, Jack Trevor Story, has a sharp and understanding eye for the supposedly 'Americanized' (flashy and opportunist) streak in British middle- and working-class culture (actually quite indigenous and 'American' only in trappings). His *These Dangerous Years*, produced and directed, astonishingly, by Herbert Wilcox, was an early (1957) and spirited defence of rebellious English teenagers against national service, in the *Waterloo Road* spirit. But Story comes into his own with this gallimaufry of crooked town councillors, rapacious estate agents, gullible but unconsciously cynical clerics, available wives, and salesmen battening on one another like shark-rip-shark. If the smooth-tongued hero (Ian Hendry) loses the girl he loves it's not because he's hard and vicious (he isn't), nor even because he sets about his sharp practice with the obsessiveness of a pathological gambler, but because he can't help lying, even to his beloved. The big sell is the only form of communication,

of human relationship, he knows. In a weird paroxysm in a big store at night, he smothers his girl (June Ritchie) in consumer goods, buries her alive in them, and passionately embraces a window dummy whose disarranged wig reveals a bald skull – even his love goes to a plastic image, like the false Maria in *Metropolis*.

Against the hero's conspicuous consumption the film asserts a moral norm altogether different to that of *Term of Trial*. Family happiness is attained by a wife with five children, one of whom is another man's, and by her old-fashioned hubby who works as a railway porter but more than compensates for his small wage and tubby figure by solid old-fashioned kindness. This *Under Milk Wood* folk morality, with feckless yet reliable good nature as the *summum bonum*, justifies a nice if naughty view of our heroine soaping her titties in the bath and prefigures Barbara Windsor's sloppiness over babies and hubbies in *Sparrows Can't Sing*. But the conjunction of working-class themes and the new, or folk, or feckless morality, indicate that we have strayed over the boundary at which our survey ends.

10. Journey to the edges of the working-class

Since the working-class and below account for between 55 per cent and 70 per cent (depending on your definitions) of the population, it's surprising, on the face of it, that film-makers didn't from the beginning stake everything on intensively appealing to it by portraying its standards and customs.

On closer examination, reasons become apparent. Daydream and wish-fulfilment are satisfied with more obvious ease by 'identification upwards'. Moreover, the middle- and lower-middle-classes shade only gradually and confusingly into the upper-working-classes. Thus it's natural and easy for many working-class people to take middle-class characteristics as their ego ideal. Many British films about the 'little man' concern characters who, like the blacksmith in *Great Expectations*, or the Huggetts (Jack Warner, Kathleen Harrison, Petula Clark, Jimmy Hanley) are equivocally lower-middle- and upper-working-class.

It's doubtful though whether the rarity of non-middle-class working-class traits – those so successfully explored by such movies as *Saturday Night*

Sparrows Can't Sing: Roy Kinnear, Fanny Carby, Marjie Lawrence – Working-class themes conjoined with feckless morality *and Sunday Morning* and *The Family Way* – can be explained entirely in terms of public demand, or even of external middle-class pressures. Among exhibitors pre-war British films were notorious for a toffee-voiced prissiness to which cap-and-muffler audiences vastly preferred American toughness. After the war the stiff upper lip, with its deadpan ambiguities, proved an only too handy lowest common denominator. The less your hero gives away, the less he alienates anyone.

Even less than the old boy nets at the top can the working-class be considered as a homogeneous group. Very schematically, one may distinguish: (1) an element of sunken middle-class; (2) a 'labour aristocracy'; (3) secure, or semi-skilled, or effectively unionised, 'solid working-class'; (4) unskilled labour dockers, casual labourers with a rougher image; and so on down to the layabouts and the criminal fringe. One can also distinguish two main psychological tendencies. One is to consider oneself as middle-class and self-

Saturday Night and Sunday Morning: Albert Finney – Exploring non-middle-class working-class traits

consciously respectable (and there is, after all, usually someone below one to be middle by comparison with, and frightened of). The other, perhaps more egalitarian and robust, is to consider oneself as 'ordinary folk' or 'working-class'. Such nuances don't become very important until the late fifties, except to help explain certain ambiguities and overlaps in British movies. For example Magwitch is so nightmarish, not only because he represents, in Dickensian nightmare form, the mob, that is, the *common* people, but also to avoid angering the masses (whatever class you are, he feels like the class below you).

A middle-class cinema will tend to acknowledge the working-class only (1) insofar as they accept, or are subservient to, middle-class ideals, (2) where they shade into the feckless and criminal stream, and (3) humorously. All these approaches can be concertina'd into one. This is, indeed, an old-fashioned stereotype, nicely typified by a World War I propaganda short, *Everybody's Business,* with Gerald du Maurier and Mathieson Lang as its solid middle-class

The Family Way: Murray Head, Hywel Bennett, Hayley Mills, John Comer, Thorley Walters – Tolerant, appreciative working-class drama

citizenry. When her stalwart son brings his chum home on leave from the undaunted fighting forces, Mother worries about the household's unpatriotic waste of bread. Father chides her, but dozes off in his armchair. His dream teaches him that while the Navy 'preserves our shores inviolate' and our guns in the trenches 'pound the Hun', he too must do his part. His edict goes forth. With no more protest than a pretty pout, frivolous Miss refrains from feeding sugar to her pet dog. It's Cook and those below stairs who are last to be persuaded of their patriotic duty. Finally, however, Mother may sigh contentedly, her inspirational duty done, even via working-class adults, naughtiest of Britannia's children.

By and large this image holds good through the best remembered films of the twenties and thirties. In Monty Banks's *Shipyard Sally* (1939) Our Gracie sings the workers out of unemployment. Gracie Fields and George Formby comedies blend pert Northern personalities and sharp cheery asides with a genuine relish of only inoffensive sorts of cheekiness. Such Hitchcock movies as *The Skin Game* (1931) and *Number Seventeen* (1932) stress, perhaps ambivalently, the nervous obsequiousness of lower-class characters towards their social betters. It's something of an affirmation when *Pygmalion* (1938), under cover of Shaw's prestigious humour, declares that the working-classes would quite like the advantages of the others. To admit a gap, to allow opportunism and cynicism, is at least a step towards ventilating the problem with the fresh air of unsentimental realism.

If the respectably contented are cheerful to contemplate, the crime thriller winkles us into those picturesquely seedy areas where the lower orders shade into the criminal classes. A para-American film, *They Drive by Night* (Arthur Woods, 1938), based on a low life novel by James Curtis, has a fine feeling for proletarian locales – tea shops, dance halls, transport caffs – and it paraphrases, in thriller terms ('there-ain't-no-justice-for-the-man-on-the-run'), the bleak despair of the thirties. Its model is American Depression melodrama. It's also a preview of the Chandler/Bogart movies, and far more firmly rooted in realistic detail and social sense. Forgotten by movie historians, the film holds out hope of many more surprises in store for us among such equally neglected movies as John Baxter's *Doss House* (1933) and *The Small Man* (1935) and Brian Desmond Hurst's *On the Night of the Fire* (1939).

Certainly there's a lot that's pretty beguiling in Basil Dean and Graham Cutts's *Looking on the Bright Side* (1932), with Gracie Fields as a girl bobby who on patrol in the market isn't above snitching an apple and sixpennorth of haddock while the stall owner's looking the other way. It's slightly salty vignettes of cultural minorities have some charm – the sharp, rascally, and he needs to be, Jewish businessman, the irascible Italian hairdresser, the juvenile lead so tweely Mayfair that he says 'thet' for 'that' (and who couldn't have been brought into the plot as anything but a ladies' hairdresser). Everybody's finally reconciled in a neighbourhood party in a multi-storey tenement set which, no doubt, owes something to the populism concurrently inspiring both French and American film-makers (e.g., *Lonesome, Street Scene, Roman Scandals, Sous les toits de Paris, Prix de beauté,* and *Le Crime de Monsieur Lange*). Carol Reed's celebrated *Bank Holiday* (1938) seems, in retrospect, merely agreeable, not comparable, in dramatic dignity, to Carnés *Hotel du Nord,* and relating principally to lower-middle-class characters anyway.

After Dunkirk, the war effort's mobilization of energies broke down many class barriers, and inspired the upper-classes not only to see much good in, but actually to feel indebted to, the great unwashed. With a sense of 'Look, we have come through', the Depression years and their bitter conflicts are reviewed in Carol Reed's *The Stars Look Down* (1939) and John Baxter's *Love on the Dole* (1941). The better-remembered film's self-taught hero (Michael Redgrave) fits the overlapping middle-working-class ideal of the scholarship boy. The best commentary on it is Richard Hoggart's *The Uses of Literacy.* Pen Tennyson's *The Proud Valley* (1939) places Paul Robeson among the Welsh miners, with the sudden stress on imperialism as democratic.

Bad language is one of those traits which traditionally distinguish the middle-class, and the middle-class strain within the working-class, from the more refractory and solid working-class. It's no accident that the first naughty word to raise a blister on British screens was perpetrated in a Ministry of Information morale-booster directed by Thorold Dickinson soon after Dunkirk. Robertson Hare plays a prim middle-class clerk drafted into a munitions factory. His wife is very ashamed of his lost status and he is very apprehensive about mixing with those big, coarse, manly, Magwitch-type labourers. But as he trembles at his lathe he is clapped on the back by none other than Ernie Bevin, left-wing Minister of Labour in Churchill's wartime coalition. Our white-collar worker comes home whistling jauntily, in, oh dear, his overalls. His wife spies him from the window and calls tremblingly 'Oh, but think of the neighbours!' To which our convert bawls out cheerfully 'Bugg-ah the neighbours!' Everybody's language is nobody's business.

From 1940, the Dunkirk spirit inspired a number of films which, because they accepted the rank-and-file as worthy of their officers, seemed to many 'democratic' and reconciliatory and so perhaps were, even if they now appear a little patronising. Among such films may be numbered Dearden's *The Bells Go Down* (1943), an A.F.S. saga where the lower orders are still naughty boys who must be smartly rulered by their shot hot officers, and Noël Coward's and David Lean's *In Which We Serve* (1942), archetypal essay in the stiff upper lip, bravely bleak for its times. Easily the best of these films, Carol Reed's *The Way Ahead* (1944) ends with its cross-section-of-society patrol advancing, perhaps a little apprehensively, and none too heavily armed, into a smoke-screen. The Robsons objected to this final image as defeatist, but it had, perhaps, a slightly different meaning. It hinted at a widespread feeling that the rank and file had not been adequately equipped, that such parlous provision was not a merely military matter, and that when those who didn't die came back they might have a few awkward questions to ask of those who thus sent them forth.

The complement of this disrespect was a burgeoning pride in, not only the country as a whole, but in a particular class. This mood inspired the very titles of an admirable trio, Charles Frend's *The Foreman Went to France* (Ealing, 1942) and Frank Launder and Sidney Gilliat's *Millions Like Us* (1943) and *Waterloo Road* (1945). In *Millions Like Us* the refined middle-class girl (Anne Crawford) has trouble adapting down to the 'common' factory girls who are her new-found comrades, but is helped by a blunt no-nonsense northern foreman (Eric Portman). In *Waterloo Road*, which is, in a sense, a riposte to *The Bells Go Down*, Private John Mills decides the war can look after itself for a day or two while he goes A.W.O.L. to batter the spiv (Stewart Granger) who has been trying to seduce his wife (Joy Shelton). It's an Arthur Seaton action; indeed, it's more rebellious than anything Arthur Seaton has to do.

Once a Jolly Swagman: Bonar Colleano, Dirk Bogarde, Sidney James – Competitiveness disrupting loyalty between mates and trade unionists

After *Waterloo Road* the populist tide receded slowly, reluctantly. At first, indeed, it seemed to spread. Only gradually did it become apparent that it had become shallower as well as broader, that its impetus was spent. Robert Hamer's *It Always Rains on Sunday* (1947), a conspicuously bowdlerized version of Arthur La Bern's vivid panorama of East End life, was a last, brave attempt by Ealing to grant the working-classes the recognition they were felt to have earned during the war. Thereafter, Ealing monotonously, applied the omnibus formulae. The feeling seemed to be that only little stories were needed to illustrate the simple sentiments, the a-to-b emotional gamut, the narrow little lives, of 'ordinary people' (a phrase which all but enabled the shabby genteel and the 'respectable' working-class style to edge the ordinary working-classes out of the picture altogether). Such films as *Train of Events* (1949) and *Dance Hall* evoke the drab fatigue of austerity's shortages and 'Work or Want'

campaigns. But creative fatigue persists, with predictable characters coming to their predictable senses, or fates, as the depression lifts with Dearden's *Pool of London* (1951), *The Square Ring* (1953) and *The Rainbow Jacket* (1954). A new regime at Gainsborough begins with omnibus movies galore – the subject matter often more intimate than their Ealing counterparts, *vide* such titles as *Holiday Camp* (Ken Annakin, 1947), *Easy Money*, about pools winners (Bernard Knowles, 1947), *A Boy, a Girl and a Bike*, about cycling clubs (Ralph Smart, 1949), and *Boys in Brown* (Montgomery Tully, 1949), ahead of its time in criticizing the running of Borstals. The perspective is less constrained than Ealing's, the approach more superficial, the execution less convinced. At least such non-um-class character actors as Jack Warner, Kathleen Harrison, Thora Hird, Bill Owen, William Hartnell and others established their hold on audience affection, some rather too firmly to avoid stereotypy.

More considerable is Jack Lee's *Once a Jolly Swagman* (1948), which did for the then booming sport of motorcycle speedway what *This Sporting Life*

Millions Like Us: Patricia Roc, Megs Jenkins, Anne Crawford, Joy Shelton, Brenda Bruce, Eric Portman – Breach of class barriers

did for rugby league twenty years later. Though set among the affluent middle-classes, it is proletarian in tone, as in its anger at competitiveness disrupting that loyalty between 'mates' which, in and out of the trade unions, is a keystone of working-class culture. In its social attack it is directer, if less hallucinatory, than Anderson's film. Michael Anderson's *Waterfront* (1950), after John Brophy, shows for its dockers' family that tenderness which it is, perhaps, captious to relate to low life romanticism à la Graham Greene. Yet both these films bear, like Hamer's, that tell-tale sign of an essentially middle-class moralizing. They contrast the good, sweet, quiet, chaste girl (e.g. Patricia Plunkett, Renee Asherson) with the sensual, sexy, selfish one (e.g. Susan Shaw, Moira Lister). In Lee's film she's a fascist – the first English fascist until John Lennon in Richard Lester's *How I Won the War*, twenty years on.

Another tell-tale sign in Lee's moving and respect-worthy film is the contempt for crowds indulged in so many British films. Crowds are always

The Loneliness of the Long Distance Runner: Tom Courtenay – Sharing the hatred of workers in a crowd

frightening for outsiders, but it's likely that middle-class individualism and its cult of sensitivity gives a special flavour to this response. One expects a hatred of proletarian crowds – 'the mob', the 'rabble' – in such right-wing films as *The Citadel* and *The Angry Silence*, even in such Liberal films as *I'm All Right Jack* and *Heavens Above!* But centre left films share this hatred of the workers when they're in a crowd – even when they're only watching spectator sports, as in *Once a Jolly Swagman*, *This Sporting Life* and *The Loneliness of the Long Distance Runner*. Very few British films acknowledge the very common feeling put thus: 'Private's the best rank, because there's more of you'. *Millions Like Us* is an admirable exception, and Jennings's (all too few) shots of wartime dance halls carry the same overtone.

The gradual decline of interest in the dull working-class is, promisingly, the subject of Charles Frend's *A Run for Your Money* (1949). Two Welsh miners come up to London as guests of a national newspaper and get fobbed off onto its gardening correspondent. Alas, the film seems to have been fobbed off onto Ealing's garden suburb correspondent. One should perhaps mention Emlyn Williams's *The Last Days of Dolwyn* (1949), a saga of Welsh villagers facing eviction by the heartless bureaucracy who want to build a new dam. It might have passed for realistic on the West End stage during the thirties. Welsh working-class communities hold on to a little more middle-class respect for a variety of reasons (miners' bravery, community homogeny, the nearby countryside, chapel righteousness, and Celtic foibles). By 1953 *The Intruder* (Guy Hamilton) ventures to transpose military paternalism into civilian life. Colonel Jack Hawkins nabs a burglar who's none other than one of his own troopers. Trying to save him from a life of crime, he traces his fall to 'bad housing, lack of affection, an unfortunate love affair, a conviction for manslaughter, and a prison break'. Ah, these morally unstable working-class fellows give their betters much anguish, but we must understand rather than condemn them. Producer (Ivan Foxwell) and director have tended to concern themselves either with the officers' war (*The Colditz Story*, *The Best of Enemies*) or with upper class views of class reconciliation (*The Intruder*, *Tiara Tahiti*). Paternalist as all this may seem, and perhaps be, it has to be looked at from another angle also: a renunciation of pre-war laissez faire.

Nonetheless, it's pleasant to turn from such 'serious' films to those which, often idiotically, sometimes warmly, maintain the traditional link between farce and working-class taste. (It's significant that John Baxter, and the Launder-Gilliat team, were also farce specialists.) Baxter produced, for Group 3, David Paltenghi's *The Love Match* (1954), with Arthur Askey, which, for all the cod gags occasioned by Group 3's congenitally ingratiating nervousness, and for all the patronisability built into the farce idiom, catches, better than any film between *Waterloo Road* and the kitchen sink era, something of the drive, the bickerings, the warmth of working-class idioms. 'Are you going to have a man lodger?' asks the daughter. "Course I am,' retorts Mam, 'You don't think I want another woman in the house, do you? Besides, your dad's too young to be trusted and too old to be particular.' The line summarizes a wealth of uncomfortable non-u no-nonsense wisdom as robustly as the proverbs cited by Professor Hoggart in *The Uses of Literacy*, and Arthur Askey's performance as the husband has some charming moments. It's a minor mystery why the follow-ups were so abysmal. Gordon Parry's *Sailor Beware* (produced by Jack Clayton, 1956) is well worthy of the earlier film, built as it is around Peggy Mount's monumental tornado, Ma Hornett, champion, apotheosis and fortissimo of all possible mothers-in-law, modulating from buzz-saw to fog-horn and back, and carrying, not only her namesake's sound, but its sting. Curious that critics should have disdained this movie, and then gone to accept the far more anodyne *Coronation Street* as a breakthrough; for Ma Hornett is every bit as large as life as Arthur Seaton. Perhaps, indeed, she appears in that movie, lightly disguised as Ma Bull. At any rate, there's a significant polarity between that rough and rebellious lad and this stout working-class Mum.

Even Maurice Elvey's dingily-produced *My Wife's Lodger* (1952) has some charming henpecking scenes and an adorable shot of a returning soldier (Dominic Roche) sagging and shuffling under his kit-bag down a drab black street towards the little terrace home where, little does he know, Roger the Lodger now reigns king of this man's castle. The lodger – focal point of cramped housing, of shift-work problems, of smothered jealousies and *crimes passionnels*, of the mixed tolerance and cynicism summed by another of Professor Hoggart's proverbs: 'A slice off a cut cake ain't missed'. Indeed *This Sporting Life* is an inversion of the classic lodger story; it's the lodger who is haunted and demoralized by the dear departed's fireside boots ....

As some Laurel and Hardy moments beautifully symbolize human absurdity, so a moment from one such Adelphi comedy typifies the helpless confusion, before the bureaucracy, of the English working man. A family greet an old mate of theirs, a lavatory attendant, camping outside his public gents, in the middle of the night. 'Hi, Bill, whatcha doing here? Thought yer was on yer 'olidays.' 'Yus, I am.' '???' 'Well I wrote to the Council saying, when could I 'ave me 'olidays, and they told me I could 'ave me 'olidays at me own convenience.'[28]

Affluence is double-edged. To some extent it exposes working-class warmth to middle-class 'refainment' and to the glib and corrosive vulgarities of the worst commercial art. But at the same time it enables the working-classes to pay the piper, and call more of his tunes.

Initially, the first process is most conspicuous. Its discontents mitigated, an older working-class generation feels it has attained the middle-class security

This Sporting Life: Richard Harris, Rachel Roberts – Haunted and demoralised by the dead

which was its aim. Symbol of the reconciliation is P.C. Dixon (Jack Warner) of Dearden's *The Blue Lamp* (Ealing, 1950). Doubtless a worker's son, he has thoroughly imbibed all that is best, firmest and most sensibly liberal in middle-class attitudes. He's popular simply because he incarnates a significant process sentimentalized.

Earlier periods evidenced a mixture of admiration and animosity for the local bobby. A pre-war *Pathetone Weekly* newsreel shows veteran music-hall star Gus Elen celebrating in song the prowess of his old pal Jim: 'It took two coppers just to make 'im move along, and another six to 'old the feller dahn.' Just this violence makes the same type a tower of strength in *Dunkirk*, where retreating troops are covered by a machine-gun manned by a burly – docker? – who coolly and calmly spits in the face of death. Such men make admirable N.C.O.s – like Harry Andrews in *Ice Cold in Alex* (1958) and Nigel Green in *Zulu* (1963) – once their energies are diverted from opposing the system to upholding it. Roy Baker's *Flame in the Streets* (1961) after Ted Willis, contrasts the old, rough, tough, tradition, now, it's felt, satisfied and orderly, with the new, hysteric, nasty Teddy Boy rebellion. As a gang of youths are about to close in on a lone coloured boy, who, but a band of, it seems, dockers (!) scowl at them, whereupon they run away.

One may, of course, prefer to see the Teds and the Rockers as last outcrops of this tough ethos. Roughness which would have seemed perfectly normal in those districts where policemen only went in twos, now seems anomalous. What appears is not, yet, a battle of the generations, right across the national board, but the breakdown of a lower-working-class tough style. It comes to seem a pathological delinquency. Yet the film-makers, even as they ignore the tradition, are dimly aware of it, and appeal to it – by the very contrast between the really tough oldsters and the only apparently tough youngsters. Dixon's kindliness is one step nearer a relaxed, and, in a sense, middle-class liberalism, spreading despite violent resistance from the summary puritanism, indigenous to both middle- and working-class.

The agreeable aspects of the improvement aren't very spiritedly recorded, except through the prism of middle-class affluence, as per the *Doctor* comedies. The nearest to it is, of course, Diana Dors, 'our Di', who, almost alone, raised the standard of enjoyable affluence – this cheeky, sexy barmaidin-sequins personifies the proletarian dream of belonging to the outwardly Americanized, chromium-plated, middle-classes. With significant perversity, her one interesting characterization is in J. Lee Thompson's *Yield to the Night* (1956), most of which she spends drabbed-down and tormented in the condemned cell. But if an industry ostensibly devoted to glamour and fun hasn't a clue what to make of her, neither had those left-wing critics who delighted in her without ever noticing that she represents just that vulgar and hedonistic relish of affluence which they attributed to the commercial media's corruption of working-class frugality.

After documentary criticism of the commercial cinema for neglecting the ordinary man, the record of Group 3 is, if by no means dishonourable, disappointing. Philip Leacock's *The Brave Don't Cry* (1952) is a manly and sensitive 'platoon' type story about a group of miners trapped in a mine, but opens no new seams. Wolf Rilla's *The End of the Road* (1954), is a dignified, stiff tale of an elderly worker (Finlay Currie) forcibly retired and unwanted by his own family. A gimmicky ending (only the old man knows a bee's nest is gumming up the factory chimney) helps it fall between two stools. *The Angel who Pawned her Harp* (1953, directed by Alan Bromly, produced by Sidney Cole) is an agreeable, penny-plain fantasy about the old East End – a nostalgia embellished, in tuppence-coloured style, by Wolf Mankowitz for Carol Reed's *A Kid for Two Farthings* (1954). This is sufficiently up-to-date to make a pleased discovery of neon lights, of brassy blondes (our Di), of glistening wrestlers and their cheerfully brutal hokum, and – first glimpse of what later became a favourite *temps-mort* in trendy *Nouvelle Vague* pictures – a passing airliner's ruby-and-emerald navigation lights winking. A pity, perhaps, that the child's fantasies irrupt into what might have been a topical, three-cornered tussle between the traditional English upper-middle-class (Celia Johnson and son), traditional East End Jewish (David Kossoff) and the happy rendezvous of old vulgarity and new affluence (Diana Dors).

Otherwise, questions of cultural old and new seemed to have less interest for film-makers than they might have had for film-goers, and it wasn't until the so-called 'Swinging Sixties' that anything new touched the imagination of anyone other than a large teenage group whose spending power had yet to affirm itself against the family audience to which the cinema circuits were still jealously geared. As juke-boxes brightened the espresso bars, Group 3 showed a Victorian angel coming alive in a junk shop.

Rank's seem to have sensed that a proletarian wind was blowing. But Roy Baker's *Jacqueline* (1956), George Pollock's *Rooney* (1958), Julian Amyes's *Miracle in Soho* (1957) and J. Lee Thompson's *Tiger Bay* (1959), are all attempts in this vein. But the regulation charm of the Oirish, of children, of Sohovians, whimsify everything into nothing, the last film retaining the dignity of sensitive melodrama.

The overlappings of traditional middle-class, and new found working-class, satisfactions were accommodated by no film-maker more popularly than by Ted Willis who, as co-scriptwriter of *The Blue Lamp*, went on to resurrect P.C. Dixon from his untimely, if initially necessary, martyr's fate, and sentence Saturday night telly to twenty years' hard copperolatry.

A firm Labour supporter, a pillar of the Unity Theatre, and subsequently speech-writer for Harold Wilson during two successful election campaigns, Ted Willis became, ironically, a *bête noire* of the New Left, appealing as he clearly does to the embourgeoisement of the proletariat. But he should also be seen as concerned with using middle-class small-l-liberalism to weaken traditional small-c-conservative working-class simplicities. It may be that to do so is to portray a kind of never-never England, of all possible virtues. And here we come across an ambiguity which bedevils film criticism as it bedevils film-making, and, indeed, all artistic activity, all rhetoric. It is natural, when seeking to influence people, to offer an attractive example of the desirable state of affairs, to demonstrate, in dramatic form, the benefits of its working. Yet to show an exemplary world is, in a sense, to assert its actuality; and many will deduce that this happy state of affairs already prevails. Conversely films which never affirm without first criticizing may be felt as nihilistic; indeed, they may sometimes intensify an amorality and apathy altogether opposed to their creator's hope that a robust and bracing pessimism could lead to more thoughtful and efficacious action. The interlocking problems can be solved, but if we all solved them the same way art would be very monotonous. Because we solve them in different ways, misunderstandings are the order of the day, as the divergent responses to such formidable creators as Losey, Brecht and Osborne testify.

Such problems underly the profound, and doubtless significant, ambiguity of such a film as *It's Great to Be Young!* (1956). Directed by Cyril Frankel, its script is by Ted Willis, who may reasonably be postulated as the real auteur of a film which it is this writer's unreflective response to dislike intensely. His biggest hit after *The Blue Lamp*, it concerns a strike (working-class theme) by the clean-faced boys and girls of a grammar school (middle-class theme), after the music master (John Mills) and his plans for a school orchestra are crossed by a well-meaning but too traditionally authoritarian headmaster (Cecil Parker). Eventually mutual concessions are made, the principle of submission to authority *per se* is duly preached, and harmony reigns. It's worth insisting that this compromise does go both ways, that it's not a capitulation, even though it's hardly the dictatorship of the proletariat either. Prophetic parallels with Hornsey and Guildford 1968 remind one that Willis would have done well to stress the capacity of the authorities for cynical deception and gratuitous vindictiveness. For all that, the film does stand up, against strong traditional prejudices, for co-education, for all this modern leniency in schools, for healthy anarchy, for strikes. Galling as the film undoubtedly is to those who assume that the only justification of a movie is its rendition of life as is, the fact remains that as an agreeably assimilable mixture of liberal reformist pill and entertainment jam it may plausibly be supposed to have had a progressive effect. Of course one may still have preferred a more radical topic – for example, the dirty-faced boys of a bad secondary modern school revolt, with a bit less song and dance as well; *Term of Trial* with Terence Stamp as its hero. Why not, after all, a secondary modern *If....?*

Equally, if Willis's brand-image goads one beyond endurance, one may wish to write off *Woman in a Dressing Gown* (1957) as the *Brief Encounter* of the council houses. Or one may play on it reputedly being written as a reaction to critical enthusiasm about Paddy Chayefsky, to show that others could manipulate the same formula no less effectively. Even if one postulates a case of flattery by ambivalent imitation, it nonetheless goaded Willis to his most uncompromising film. A good formula constitutes a genre, within which each artist can legitimately create his own moods, meanings, tone and vision.

Its sequel is a more ambitious subject, based on Willis's stage play, *No Trees in the Street*, and directed, again by J. Lee Thompson. Artistically, and, I suspect, commercially, only a mitigated success, it is not merely a labour of love, but, in a sense, its director's Last Will and Testament before, spiritually, leaving English subjects for Hollywood cosmopolitanism. Cop Ronald Howard wrests a flick-knife from a soft teenage tough and tells him about the bad old days of the grim thirties, when there were rats under the beds, bugs in the walls and no trees in the street. Implication, 'Then, at least, resort to violence as a way out was understandable. But even then the only fellow in my wife's family who resorted to it was poor little Melvyn Hayes. When he tried to be a big shot, waved a gun around, and killed a poor old lady, he only proved what a hysteric weakling he was, and had to pay the price. For, even then, toughness was for the weak and the wicked; the strong and the decent stuck it out. It's true, alas, that my wife (Sylvia Syms) was tempted into a prostitution-like marriage to ruthless gangster Herbert Lom, who humiliated her cruelly. But – here we are, in our snug tower block apartment, with trees in the nicely landscaped spaces below. So don't you be taken in, today, by a myth that never was, in this brave new Welfare State, young fellow-me-lad. You should be happy, orderly, grateful, and always ask the nice policeman to help you across the road of life to the pension at the other side. Think it over, son, and be a good lad, I'm sure you will.'

Of course this quick history lesson ignores the effects of a still continuing, if less obtrusive, poverty, and of subtler, but no less crushing, pressures (ten years' continuous contempt in the schoolroom, for example). It's easy to relate this little copper-vicar's sermonette to the widespread British inability to take psychology, sociology and, indeed, anything but knockdown fundamentalist notions of responsibility, seriously, so that while the Americans can make *Rebel without a Cause* this falls back on the obvious untruth that 'most thugs are blubbering cowards really' and its equally unconvincing liberal counterpart ('even bad boys can have a sensitive streak beneath').

Possibly the violence theme was only a too-intrusive peg on which to hang a reminder of the good old days. But what, then, was the right way to strike out for self-respect? Here the film runs into trouble. 'Be a self-made man' is too materialistic. A useful alternative – 'improve yourself through education and become a Labour councillor/M.P.' – is a little dated (smacking of *The Stars Look Down*), a little too earnest (compare *Term of Trial*), and politically much too controversial. 'Win the Duke of Edinburgh's Award?' 'Be a copper like me?' Not even. The film suggests only an inert, aimless contentment and gratitude for what the older generation did.

In fairness, the plea for gormless conformism is not the only point of the film's retrospective form. It's a traditional working- and middle-class view that in Britain the way to affluence lay through determined self-restraint from unconstitutional methods, through a kind of orderly respectability and solidarity which is, in a way, a sort of self-policing. This film has to ensure that its policeman hero represents Us and not Them. And indeed it inserts a strong implication that the firm good cop is a Labour supporter. For his belief in his wife-to-be's, and probably his own, class, is contrasted with the hard-faced Tory type inspector's clipped remark to the effect that you can't expect much from the scum that lives in Kennedy Street.

Yet one doesn't have to be a psychoanalyst, or even to believe in the war of the generations, to feel the inadequacy of the policeman's well-meant homily. He offers the lad only a humiliatingly passive role vis-à-vis a generation whose standards, and satisfactions, he can no more make his own than his grandfather could feel raptures of delight over living in a snug brick slum instead of a mud hut. The standards of comparison of the young are properly with others, now. The screenplay's standards are ominously retrospective, and, though typical of the middle-aged, flaccidly so.

If the thinking behind the screenplay had followed itself through, then to give the modern hero an aim would end in one of two possibilities. Either the youth has nothing much to improve on, so he's a rebel without a cause, and that's a serious social problem. Or else there are things he can improve, and the, perhaps subtler and less obvious, equivalents of treeless streets still exist. If, in fact, we substitute a Labour M.P. for the cop, then the film comes very near *The Fame Is the Spur* or possibly *No Love for Johnnie*. He's out of touch, complacent, and forces the kid into excessive, self-sabotaging protest.

Instead there's a curious circularity. Melvyn Hayes is a fifties hysteric back dated to the thirties. Doubled up like this, the film's moral is so heavily loaded it defeats itself. Having your tough guy a sort of failed, male, thickear Lolita proves, not that crime doesn't pay, since we all know it may, but that hysteric nitwits should choose some less exacting profession. If poverty really gave some sort of plausibility to violence, then your violent character needed to be, *neither* a looney non-starter like this little tich, *nor* a perennial crook like suave cold Herbert Lom, but someone such more like a prepossessing, tough, sullen ordinary guy like, in fact, one of my forties' favourites, Maxwell Reed. The stock gangster might well have been rethought on the analogy of Jack Spot, who began by leading Jewish youths against Mosley's Fascist marchers, realized he had a gift for violence, and applied it, not altogether unrewardingly, to crime. And why not put the blame for seducing Sylvia Syms not on everybody's *bête noire*, the opulent gangster, but on a representative of middle-class money and respectability, seducing her, with no need at all to sink, or rise, to crime, no need, indeed, to do anything but congratulate himself on not being a snob, on kindly lifting this girl to his level?

Details also creak. Like too many of old Ted's working-class characters, these, when they want to emphasize something, tack 'I tell you!' on the end of their sentence. Again, friendly old Ted sets up a degrading environment, but can't bear to think that the solid decent Briton could ever be degraded. So Stanley Holloway gets amiably drunk over winkles and sings jolly old music-hall songs. Embittered old Mum is ever so guilty about having to be so hard. And if Sylvia Syms was born and bred in Kennedy Street, then Diana Dors is the Queen Mother's aunt. (Too many of Ted's nice people are just visiting from the middle-class.) Another dud image is the old blind uncle who sits there, sad and acute, like everybody's conscience, or better self, as if they needed one.

Yet, spasmodically, the film settles into itself, the individuals become a family, a collectivity, at once a cause and a trap, like fate, and the moment they do, an emotional current flashes through it, and the film which should have been crystallizes, miraculously, in our hearts, and even in our eyes. A grubby ragged little girl, scabs round her mouth, sits on the tenement steps, nursing a dolly on her lap and shushes a passer-by. 'Is she asleep?' 'No, she's dead.' Sylvia Syms, trapped by the collective ideal, and its guilts, settles down to stay in the slum, her middle-class hopes gone, and wearily getting herself as drunk as her mother. Awkward as is the pair formed by Melvyn Hayes and Sylvia Syms, who seem to exist on completely different wavelengths, the scenes between primly correct sister and infantile brother, have the poignancy of desperate maladjustment, a perverse heroism – complementary, somehow, in their dual virginity to the screams of their elder sister (Lana Morris) as she's carried off

by her drunken and bestial husband to another bout of beating, rape, copulation. Flawed in every direction and on every layer, this passionately interesting film has at least the immense merit of suggesting what it fails to be: an epic of the English working-classes, a cross between *The Grapes of Wrath* and *Gervaise*, and its beauty of intention shines through.

The tragic-comic irony is that all the problems of the period setting disappear if the film is, quite simply, demelodramatized, and given a present-day setting – the setting of *Up the Junction*, of *Poor Cow*. If only Ted had looked *around* in anger – not simply *back* ...

Which he thereupon tries to do, in Roy Baker's *Flame in the Streets* (1961). Here he crosses union troubles (perhaps by way of riposte to *The Angry Silence*) with Notting Hill race riots (perhaps by way of follow up to *Sapphire*). Grandad (Wilfrid Brambell) founded the local union branch, of which Dad (John Mills) is chairman. The works lads don't want a Jamaican (Earl

Poor Cow: John Bindon, Carol White – Problems of construction resolved when demelodramatised

Cameron) to become foreman until Dad talks them round in a moving set piece speech. But when he comes home, his daughter (Sylvia Syms), apple of his eye and upped to Teachers' Training College, has got engaged to another coloured fellow, and then, oh brother, it's shame and scandal in the family. Mum (Brenda De Banzie) spills out a prejudice which is not just 'what'll the neighbours say?' but violently sexual, and as daughter and mother scream hammer and tongs at each other, poor old Dad realizes just how little of a man at home he is, thanks to his dedication to lads who weren't so decent as he thought and to principles which now his own flesh and blood rebels against. In a parallel plot, shamefaced Cockney Judy (Ann Lynn) screams at her spade hubby for tearing instead of cutting the bread and stammers a vague, baffled, inarticulate apology for her nerves, scraped raw by the squalid rooms to which mixed marriage condemns her for life. Dad finally comes round when he sees a thug push his coloured foreman into a Guy Fawkes bonfire. And Mum follows suit.

Flame in the Streets: The Notting Hill riots – A carefully unidealistic, unsatisfying film

It's unjust that so honest, so devoted, so carefully unidealistic a film should fail to satisfy us. Perhaps it's a matter of construction. It hesitates between being a family drama (which would require concentrating all the issues into one situation) and a works drama (which would require concentrating all the issues into another) and a social canvas which Relph-Dearden's detective format fitted better. Of course we're all against thugs pushing people into bonfires; but the case for Liberalism is lost if it has to equate race prejudice with this. Yet all these contortions can be seen as an intuitive feeling that if we allow the issues to accumulate, whether in the family circle or on the factory floor, too many nice people in the audience are going to shift to the wrong side. Maybe the best hope was to go for broke, to lash out like *The Angry Silence*, and clear the air that way. Understandably, this script doesn't.

Cannily, courageously, it shoots its moral quills in every direction. And yet, and yet ... As John Mills tells his men: 'If you don't let spades into the union, all you'll do is create a pool of cheap, non-union labour'. And what's the answer to that? If you didn't think of it immediately, Enoch Powell approximated it for you.

The build-up of racial feeling under the mass media's solid, devoted and militant liberalism has an element of tragic poetic justice about it. Merely to rehearse the sins of omission and commission in liberal propaganda gives one twinges, but the problem of such a film is to provoke, and then trump, the fact that, underneath all, unrestricted immigration was allowed for so long as it was for two main reasons. From the employers' point of view it provided a pool of less skilled labour for jobs which the British worker no longer wanted to do. From the latter's point of view, it helped his upgrading to middle-class status. Colour conveniently criss-crosses class antagonisms, and the immigrants arouse *both* a middle-class contempt – and its working-class echo – of the great unwashed of Kennedy Street *and* lower working-class fear of a sudden great influx of competition for jobs, for housing. This isn't to assign an unimportant role for non-economic favours like cultural differences and sexual fantasies. The film needs a tone as cynical, as tough, as all these misgivings, maybe using (but not taking refuge in) melodrama.

If only by way of illustrative exercise it's entertaining to consider the advantages and the pitfalls of a parallel story. For purely academic reasons let's begin by turning our three West Indian men into one, and then make consequential changes. Daughter's a secretary at Dad's factory, improving herself by evening classes. There she falls in love with a coloured boy whom at the factory she didn't bother to notice. Mum's steamroller prejudices about babies (only), and Dad's weakness (at home), goaded her to break off relations with them and get (hastily?) married. The audience as well as Mum feel the daughter's stiffly inverted-prim in this. A weird triangle operates at work, between father, daughter and son-in-law, sharpening tensions within the couple, in their squalid rooms. Mum can't bring herself to go to the christening party. Dad secretly does and finds himself alone amongst West Indians. They're friendly and that's a problem in itself so he has to go and sit on the stairs outside, feeling rather lost. There he sees a coloured and a white housewife stupidly ignoring each other but struggling weakly, because alone, with shared tenement squalor. Living in the next flat is his son-in-law's sister. She has several illegitimate babies by the same man, whom she regularly throws out, and readmits again. Different ideas about bringing up babies spark further difficulties between husband and wife. The white girl with her middle-class notions is a bit upset by the extended family spirit, and also by her husband's readiness to help discipline along with the belt. Dad, far from being a scorching idealist, doesn't really want a coloured foreman either, but his daughter needs the money, and she shames him into finding arguments which he then realizes do actually apply. The disappointed candidate for the foreman's job is also the boyfriend the daughter jilted and though he's drunk and spiteful we can still feel pretty sorry for the poor guy when he gets briefly thuggish, though thuggery is the least of everyone's worries. It's when the poison pen brigade and a graffiti artist lash out, that Mum, who will *not* be bullied, comes round to see the baby at last, and, after many a swallow, manages to point out the ways in which the baby looks like her and takes after his father – hilariously, she never mentions the different colour. But these are the only grandchildren she'll have, and the realization that she's hated her own flesh makes her cry, and the fact that this has happened to her makes her cry again, but now she has to make the best of it, whereupon she cries again, and the family closes up a little, whereupon she cries again. At work things won't be too bad so long as the factory doesn't have to lay off men. There's no dedicated liberal in the story, the nearest to a liberal line being a cheeky guy who says, apropos immigration, 'You wanted an empire, mate, you've got it'. My point is the pitfall – provocation without release.

Dearden and Relph's *Sapphire* (1959) is situated in those extensive regions where the shabby genteel strive to differentiate themselves from the 'rough' people. As, later, with *Victim*, a murder hunt by detectives leads us through a cross-section of social types and strata, thus combining the essential of the omnibus formula with a strong overall dynamic. Inspector Nigel Patrick, investigating the murder of the coloured student who gives the film its title explores this subcity of spades, from seedy criminals to the white-despising African Prince. It slices into a massive job lot of prejudices, from sexual psychopathology to landladies barring coloureds because the other gentlemen wouldn't like it. As in *Victim* it admits there are prejudiced policemen (though easily cowed, apparently). While repudiating that Uncle Tomism which would turn a blind eye to coloured thuggery, prostitution and thievery, it isn't itself devoid of a certain vengefulness (an apparently blonde girl in a sleazy club betrays her coloured blood by lasciviously squirming in her seat with rhythm). The tone about miscegenation struck me as distinctly sinister rather than sympathetic, and is reinforced by the suggestion that Sapphire is not only a student, but, unbeknown to her innocent English fiancé, a debauchee. 'You never really know where you are with them, do you? Oh, I dare say most of them are all right, but as they're so different it's best to steer clear of them, isn't it?'

Sapphire's murderer is, in the end, the sad English housewife (Yvonne Mitchell) whose motive was to save her son. The sympathy for, even in condemnation of, prejudice, establishes the film's inspiration as stemming from the conservative wing of a position which is not so much liberal as insistent on conduct not prejudicial to good order and civilian discipline. No accident that the movie ends on a reverent shot of a police car moving smoothly away down a shabby street, its pacifying mission made all the more difficult by an explosive racial mixture. But if London's now a racial jungle, the intention probably isn't alarmist; for according to the Dearden-Relph line, established later, all characters who drop their aitches need to have their lives sorted out for them, or their heads knocked together, by the British bobby and his social superiors.

Sapphire: Nigel Patrick – A murder victim constructed as fantasy

First and last film to try a roaring old denunciation of the rabble is Glenville's *Term of Trial,* and it dares try it only because the approach has dropped, for obvious reasons, out of political currency altogether. We all respect the workers today; it's the strikers we're indignant at. *Term of Trial* brings us back to the good old days of the thirties and forties. 'They're feckless, they breed like rabbits, they use bad language, they spend all their money on drink, or cheap make-up, they're insolent instead of polite, they'd knock you down as soon as look at you. Class conscious? Us? Nonsense. But these people, by heredity, or by deeply ingrained character, are semi-animals, or at least of very limited intelligence. What do you think would happen if these feckless rowdies ever got the upper hand? What can one feel but a nauseated pity for these Yahoos? Best thing to do with lads like these is draft 'em all into the army where they can be taught self-respect by licking my boots.'

The middle-class traditions can get us to the fringes of the working-classes, but the journey to the centre is the prerogative of the so-called kitchen sink school, and reactions to and continuations of it which take one beyond the confines of our subject.

11. Odds and Bods

A cinema which only touched the fringes of its nation's majority culture couldn't be expected to do more than glance at other subsections, except insofar as they're trouble-makers or problems. The heroine of *Sapphire* exists only in relation to colour prejudice; the heroine of *Tiger Bay,* an in some ways atmospheric film, turns out to be not Shirley Bassey, but, almost pointedly, a white, underage, well-spoken choir-girl (Hayley Mills). If the jazz club isn't the antechamber to Hell (*vide* Herbert Wilcox's *My Teenage Daughter* [1955]) the jazz world is a noisy, lively but formularized omnibus called *Jazz Boat* (Ken Hughes, 1959). Leaving aside the too tidy and lukewarm nostalgia films, Jewish colour peeps into some sharply anxious scenes in Val Guest's *Expresso Bongo* (1959), which still leaves out the musical's best song, 'Nothing is for nothing', and Ken Hughes' sometimes lacerating *The Small World of Sammy Lee* (1962), with Newley's authentic bitterness. There are some vivid Jewish showbusiness faces in the otherwise execrable *Charley Moon* (Guy Hamilton, 1955). Teenage delinquents get a chapter to themselves, and a dismal one it is.

One has throughout the feeling of peep-holes, rather than of a frank, friendly, interested gaze, and given the variety of cultures in London, and the fact that mergings and clashings and miscegenations, spiritual and physical, are going to be on everyone's agenda for the next hundred years or so the main reason for this withdrawal is presumably that the feelings involved are still too hot to handle. Yet it's just those conspicuous taboos which can become a dominant motif a few years later. As recently as 1947 the publicity campaign for Ealing's *Frieda* (Dearden) asked, with bated breath, questions like 'Would you want your son to marry a German woman?' *Abie's Irish Rose* had its day in immigrant New York; any moment now we'll have *Panchali's Cockney Spade.*[29]

3: Points of View

12. Left, Right and Centre

For obvious reasons establishment and patriotic imagery overlap. Any Labour government has a further problem which Conservative opponents haven't. It can only serve its supporters by disturbing the system on which they depend for what affluence they enjoy. No Labour government has yet steered for long between the Scylla of not doing enough for its supporters, and so angering them, and the Charybdis of provoking upsets and kickbacks, which its supporters have the least reserves to meet. Either it seems lukewarm, the Tory's lackey, or it seems fanatical and dogmatic.

The Boultings were first to condemn the Attlee administration. Their *Fame Is the Spur* (1947) traced the rise and moral fall of a Labour Prime Minister (Michael Redgrave), and shows that his principal motivation was not even the substance of power, but its emptier shadow. If the story caught the mood of disappointment and discontent which, despite the introduction of the Welfare State, attended austerity, this tardy broadside against Ramsay MacDonald seems an inappropriate form for what was more like a failure of nerve and imagination, or simple weariness in running a system against its grain.

A friendlier approach to Labour's problems is made, rather late in the day, in Robert Hamer's *His Excellency* (1951), one of Ealing's thematically more audacious movies. It transposes to the Malta Dockyards (foreigners, maybe, but, more freshly then, Malta G.C.), an affectionate but violent hostility between Labour leader Eric Portman and the mob. Skipping smartly between

Miracle in Soho: Belinda Lee, John Gregson – Inordinant prayers and Catholic influences

their brickbats, he explains that strikes are bad for the country, and therefore their wages, and finally wins their hearts by (1) his fellow-interest in football (shades of *The Card*) and (2) frank and fearless dialogue like 'You're no more fit to govern yourselves than a lot of blue-nosed baboons!' (The origins of the English workman's streak of political masochism vis-à-vis his betters is beyond our scope here, but the film was probably right to sense his awareness of his own incapacities and bitter respect for the establishment's closed shop and special skills.) Our fire-brand demagogue justifies the Left to establishment figure Cecil Parker (again) and all's well that ends well. The lads rally to Labour, who stay in power. So this is, appealingly, that rarity, a Labour film.

Not until 1961 does another film brood over Labour's problems; and this is that kettle of very queer fish, Ralph Thomas's *No Love for Johnnie*, based on a posthumously published novel by Labour M.P. Wilfred Feinburgh. The film follows the novel's plot closely. Under a hypothetical Labour government, Johnnie Byrne, M.P. (Peter Finch) realizes that he is sick unto death of the pettiness, stupidity and greed of his constituency faithful. His ideals are further challenged by the contradictory values represented by his frigid Communist wife and the nice upper-middle-class girl (Mary Peach) with whom he has an almost idyllic affair. Although the Labour P.M. (Geoffrey Keen) is a man of integrity, and a staunch, stalwart working-class-Labour streak is represented by Stanley Holloway, Byrne's ideals are given the *coup de grâce* by the inevitable cynicism of political calculation. There seems no way forward for his ideals, only room at the top for one.

Much in this accurately sums up some of the Labour Party's internal problems. It's curious though that the hero's ideals are represented by his upper-middle-class mistress and her doctor father, who, one guesses, would vote Liberal. More than this: the point is made of her moving happily in the world of conspicuous consumption. She's a fashion model (although a vignette of a gay photographer (Dennis Price) suggests that even the well-spoken can sometimes be corrupt – in a jaunty way, of course). On the other hand, the working-class are unpleasant or ludicrous almost *in toto* – from the constituency workers who represent the hero's conscience, to the charwoman who answers his phone. The station master is a pompous ass – because of his pretentious top hat? or as a symbol of a nationalized industry?

It's just possible that this caricaturization of the working-class is simply a carry over from middle-class traditions. But the political context inevitably changes its meaning to the proposition that spiritual grace and gracious living are one. The pay-off is reserved for the last scene. The two parties confront each other in the House of Commons. While our newly corrupt hero and his equally cynical Postmaster-General put their feet up, smugly indifferent to the issue of the debate, delighted with their personal pre-eminence – on the other side of the House a Conservative M.P., with urgent sincerity, concerns himself with the welfare of the common fisherman (Labour's voters!). At this point the film has ceased to concern itself, either with Johnnie Byrne's soul, or with politics as such being a dirty game. It shows two cynical Labour ministers, while the Conservatives are passionately devoted to absolutely everybody.

One may feel there's something too sharp to be nice about taking a novel which was a laceratingly honest self-criticism by a Labour M.P. (who died in harness, and certainly never crossed the floor of the House!), and transforming it into pro-Conservative propaganda. Yet, on reflection, the Box-Thomas duo are entitled to bend the novel to their own purposes, just as the critic must show that what is ostensibly 'mere entertainment' is political propaganda. Indeed one purpose of this section is to suggest how much more ideology invests British films than critics (certainly) and film-makers (probably) have realized.

If the question of power is part of Labour's problems, that of strikes and labour relations is another. We've already glanced at *Shipyard Sally, His Excellency* and *It's Great to Be Young!*; and one can't but reminisce fondly over that grittily intimate awareness of restrictive practices as the very stuff of life, which inspires *Oh, Mr. Porter!* (1937). Will Hay's first day as station master of Buggleskelly Station classically exemplifies the breaking-in of new brooms by recalcitrant employees (Graham Moffatt, Moore Marriott). And there's a classic little demarcation dispute between station master and engine driver: 'You take your hand off my train!' – 'Then you take your feet off my platform!'

First movie to tackle the topic head-on is Bernard Miles's *A Chance of a Lifetime* (1950). Queered as was its pitch by the circuits' refusal to play it except under government pressures, still, the disappointing public response seems testimony to an authentic distaste for the topic, which the treatment was not quite able to overcome. Not that it's a left-wing film. In complete contradistinction to Labour's nationalization programme, it advocates Liberal co-ownership policies – although the very idea of meddling with private ownership in any way doubtless struck many as being a sinister extremism. Fast deteriorating labour relationships in a small family firm goad its decent if irascible boss (Basil Radford) into his equivalent of a strike – he'll just give up until they ask him back. A group of workers, headed by Bernard Miles, take over and transform the ailing works, to the boss's eventual satisfaction. It's an English, conciliatory, counterpart to Jean Renoir's Popular Front-era *Le Crime de Monsieur Lange*. It bravely depicts the mutual hostilities of workers and managements. Unfortunately it does so in such terms as the boss being shocked into uncontrollable rage by four letter words in the suggestions box, or the revelation that the workers' leader, who has mortgaged his house to finance the enterprise, hasn't an inkling of how to draft a business letter. Yet workers do manage to run trade union branches, friendly clubs, and so on. For all its goodwill, the film, I suspect, made the working-class spectator feel doubly incompetent, nor did, or do, the workers, perhaps alas, want added responsibility to imperil their not always superabundant resources. A brave, infinitely sympathetic film, it is hot on the track of, yet is, perhaps, insufficiently bloody-minded, is too quickly too kindly, to achieve that delicate balance of misgiving and triumph needed to tackle a topic so fraught with the weights of everyday humiliations, defeatism and resignation. Bernard Miles had already made *Tawny Pipit. A Chance of a Lifetime*, adding social to rural concerns, puts him in something like the William Cobbett tradition.

Roy Boulting's *High Treason* (1951) is its paranoid counterpart. Exactly what is the connection between the Cold War and any Communist Party schemes to sabotage British industry via unofficial strikes isn't a simple issue, but it was extremist to think that such strikes found their unique or principal inspiration in the thoughts of Comrade Stalin. The Boultings, fresh from belabouring the Labour government for its lukewarmness, now smartly about face and attribute our troubles to the swarms of cold-faced left-wing fanatics who are about to take over. Almost McCarthyite in its witch-hunt, and no doubt heartily regretted, now, by its perpetrators, it's something of a collector's piece, weirdly testifying to a hysteric current of its time. Several power-stations will be seized by an organization whose personnel includes (1) a pacifist (too punctilious about justice), (2) a cat-loving bachelor (i.e. a sublimated queer), so concerned with pussy's welfare that he threatens to castrate him if he doesn't drink his nice milk (welfare state despotism), (3) two lovers of new-fangled modern music in a dingy hall (arty cranks), (4) a sleek caddish M.P. lawyer with a collection of rare vases (the intellectual upper-class Labour left), (5) assorted burly doctors, (6) three printers printing leaflets for a Trafalgar Square rally, (7) the Principal of a Tutorial College (workers' educational movements), (8) various bespectacled duffle-coated characters who read books obsessively but are too impractical to handle guns, and (9) the ordinary, soft, mild, treacherous brother (Kenneth Griffith) of a tough stern one. This ragbag army will bring the country to a standstill simultaneously with an invasion (naming no names, but from the East) of Europe (one or two American statesmen have since remarked that the fear of Russian invasion never loomed large in their minds). But the thin blue line has it all in hand: 'Check up on every bar he's leant on, every bed he's ever slept in.' Every decent simple worker jumps to, instantly, gladly, at every hint by any plain clothes cop. As all Ted Willis characters say, sooner or later: 'Pull the other leg, mate, it's got bells on'.

Some years then passed before the Boultings found two middle ways between a little too much goodwill and a little too much ill will. *I'm All Right Jack* (1959) is scathing, but, helped by its humour, more commonsensical. It was resented by the Left, though its anti-union bias has to be balanced by (*a*) the context of the series, which lambasted everybody in turn, (*b*) an opening sequence raking industrial obsolescence and dishonest salesmen, (*c*) two rascally bosses (Richard Attenborough, Dennis Price) and (*d*) an epilogue in which a judge becomes as unjust as the unions. Still, the bosses smack of broad caricature, and are outright crooks, as if the Boultings certainly don't trust the capitalist classes but don't quite know what to satirize seriously about them. The trouble-stirring intellectual fanatic reappears as Comrade Kite, the shop-steward (Peter Sellers), who – and here there's a strange and interesting shift of tone – is also something of a Communist Don Quixote. There's something sadly sympathetic about his pig-headed notions of the Soviet Union as a Workers' Paradise; about his patient disappointment at his daughter's frivolous love of trashy pop-songs; and the doggedly dutiful way in which he manipulates his unidealistic rank-and-file for, as he really believes, their own good. It's more than a plot-convenience if our earnest Liberal hero (Ian Carmichael) becomes his lodger. Kite has singled him out as a 'serious educated' person *like himself*. They have a real affinity as well as an antagonism.

The film ends with the indignant innocent courageously revealing the truth about the union during a TV show. Result; a myopic J.P. fines him for disturbing the peace. The contrast between *High Treason* and *I'm All Right Jack* is an encouraging one: the former humourless, prim, stereotyped, the latter hilarious, coarse and rich in freshly observed nuance. Admirably trenchant in its satire, it's probably a key British movie of the period, and an indispensable corrective to the vague, pitying, patronizing, wrong-end-of-the-peephole view of the poor abused (or alternatively warm and heroic) workers which inspired the collateral lyricisms of Free Cinema.

Bryan Forbes's script for *The Angry Silence* (Guy Green, 1959), which was almost as great a popular success, produced even angrier reactions. In pattern it's similar to *I'm All Right Jack*. Its hero (Richard Attenborough) refuses to join in an unofficial strike, is persecuted by his mates, and then betrayed by his employers. The strike is engineered out of nothing by a sneaky shop-steward (Bernard Lee), obedient in his turn to the orders of a steely fanatic who makes mysterious phone calls and is surely a Kremlin nuncio. Ian Carmichael was animated by the spirit of service, but this blackleg needs no justification, other than that he's a 'little man' who (*a*) wants the money for his home and family and (*b*) won't be pushed around. To the collective spirit of the working class, he opposes an individualism which is ambiguously working- and middle-class. On the other hand, the strikers are apathetic, ignorant, irresponsible, easily driven, infested with thugs and on the point of degenerating into a yelling mob. Not only that, but the blackleg's son is smeared in the school and dubbed with tar by the other children, while Teddy Boys horribly beat the hero up.

Certainly, the hero's mate (Michael Craig), after weak vacillations, rightly batters the nasty Ted, but this saturnine view of working-class psychology is poorly balanced by the implication that the factory bears no blame for its bad labour relations, that its one fault is not supporting the

The Angry Silence: Pier Angeli, Richard Attenborough, Michael Craig – An individualism that denies the collective spirit

blackleg against the strikers, and that only one member of the Board of Directors shows anything but eager and alert efficiency.

One can make innumerable common-sense criticisms of the film's view of the why and the wherefore of unofficial strikes. If, for example, a strike can be whipped up over too little toilet paper in the loo, when all the strikers stand to lose quite as much as our hero, then the labour relationships must be at explosion-point already. It's true that the film carefully picks an *unofficial* strike, which ends with the union leadership being booed as they exhort the men to return to work, but we do seem to be in the presence of a right-wing denunciation of the collective spirit as equivalent to sheep-like acquiescence in mob violence. A French critic, Michel Mardore, even speaks of a 'polemic against the right to strike ... despite the author's cunning alibis (the offending strike has not been approved by the Unions' Central Federation), the reactionary nature of this melodrama is completely unambiguous'.

Paradoxically, though, the film was almost as successful with the audiences it insulted as *I'm All Right Jack,* and the reasons why shed another light on its meanings. First, of course, there is the moral masochism mentioned earlier, 'As we all know,' remarks David Riesman in *The Lonely Crowd,* 'the businessmen and advertisers themselves flock to plays and movies that tell them what miserable sinners they are.' The workers aren't so thick that they can't enjoy the same self-inculpation.

Second, the screen workers' yobbery and slobbery distances them from the workers in the cinema stalls, for whom these characters become, very clearly, 'them', not 'me'. The attitudes are familiar, the events outrageous – thus a kind of emotive release is accompanied by an indirect, a *nuanced* self-criticism. (Hence the 'melodramatic insult' may confuse and depress less than a too-kind criticism of likeable behaviour, à la *Chance of a Lifetime.*)

In the same way, the intervention of the Teddy Boys, the hero's loss of an eye, amount to saying, not, 'This is what keeps happening in unofficial strikes,' but 'Once you, the ordinary, morally mediocre fellow, become apathetic and abdicate your responsibility, then those things are in the direct line of possibility.' The film follows the so-called Hitchcockian principle (far older than Hitchcock) of leading the spectator from the everyday to an extreme situation in which everyday undercurrents, by becoming exceptional climaxes, reveal themselves.

Again, although the hero is only one against everybody, with his vacillating mate between, the picture of the working classes isn't felt as 'statistical'. The hero's prominence, and one's identification with him, make him the working-class norm, after all. From this point of view it's important that the factory owners are relatively blameless, at the beginning, and that the strike is manipulated from outside – for otherwise his individualism would become simply the creepy egoism of a scab.

Since the owners, to placate the strikers, lock our hero out, they too become 'strikers' the moment it suits them. Only idiots stand by their bosses. By and large, of course, the film conforms to the general practice of the mass media in this country in religiously quoting the management's figures of export orders lost or delayed while hardly bothering with the men's side of the case. All this as well as the intrinsic negative aspects of the strike weapon, helps to make things much easier for this black view of strikes and strikers, and more difficult for a more constructive film like *Chance of a Lifetime*.

Yet it's probably true to say of *The Angry Silence* that no critic has 'seen' it until he's seen it, on its home ground, among the working-class audiences whom it attacks, and seen its parade of discontents compelling from them their turbulent, shocked, exhilarated approval. It shouldn't be impossible for an equally *insolent* left-wing riposte to enjoy the same success.

More general political issues are rarely handled, notable exceptions being Halas and Batchelor's *Animal Farm* (1954), Michael Anderson's *1984* (1955) and Anthony Asquith's *The Millionairess* (1960). All exemplify the magic power of English earnestness to lovingly smother its critics and rebels. George Orwell, who was always a man of the Left (or should one say of *a* left?) wouldn't have obtained the celebrity he did if he hadn't boldly exposed the pro-Stalinist sentimentalities of his fellow travellers and in so doing written two anti-Stalinist allegories which could be understood as attacks on regimentation, bureaucracy and, of course, planning. *Animal Farm* is probably his slightest book; one can't expect too much from an allegory in which the masses are represented by animals and their betters by man. The cartoon is competently handled, but tells us nothing that we don't know already: Freedom, good, Stalinism, bad. The *1984* film completely misses Orwell's point, which is that this nightmare Utopia is not uniquely a Communist one at all. It represents the state to which he believed all societies were tending, one way or another, and is fraught with the atmosphere of public school conformism and the 'cells of fear' which was how he described the shabby genteel home in pre-war capitalist England. To treat the novel in terms of s.f. Commissars is to miss the point, which is that it should all feel nightmarish, yes, but as familiar as *It Always Rains on Sunday*. The tone is more nearly caught in Kevin Brownlow's and Andrew Mollo's *It Happened Here*, with its semi-documentary treatment of London under the Nazis.

Another radical, smothered in admiration, is George Bernard Shaw. Not that Shaw's commitment to Fabian Socialism is unambiguous. As few left-wing idealists can bear to do, he gave egoism, ambition, power and therefore riches, their due. If they corrupt our idealism, it is only because they are so marvellously satisfying to our souls. If checks on capitalism are necessary, it is only because capitalist greed is so direct, jolly and ebullient an expression of the life-force. His happily ruthless rationalism, and frankness about the amoral egoism of the establishment, annoyed the right-wing, with its careful emphasis on reverence, tradition, paternalist authority, and so on. Equally, it annoyed the puritan idealist streak in left-wing thought. His limitations are those of his rationalist stress on calculated self-interest. This leads to his underestimation of passions and irrationalities, or any non-egoistic expression of instinct – hence the cold fish lovers and cool saints of his plays – and to his concomitant assumption that everybody in the world would in the end turn to be as reassuringly reasonable as the English middle-classes. His historical plays reduce everyone to, at worst, petulant Tory types, more often humorous business-minds (like Caesar with Cleopatra), and sometimes enlightened liberals frustrated mainly by the recalcitrance of their benighted subjects. Moreover he usually localizes power in one magnificent individual (all at odds with the facts of power in any, especially industrial, society, where real power is spread between mutually limiting networks and counter-networks of establishments, committees, boards, pressure-groups, and so on). In its stress on the exceptional individual who runs society, Shaw's thought is essentially romantic-aristocratic, and it's easy to see how he could have been seduced by Mussolini's picture of 'Socialistic Fascism' – Socialism imposed on people by a philanthropic, ruthless, civilized Superman.

The Millionairess transposes his 1936 play into contemporary terms. Sophia Loren incarnates Epifania, the Superwoman and millionairess twice over (once by inheritance, once self-made) and Peter Sellers the Egyptian (changed to Indian) doctor who has his own kind of indomitability. In the original play, the stress lay on his Mohammedan fatalism, but here it is shifted slightly to post-Gandhi feelings of self-effacing kindness and charity. The story becomes a yin and yang tussle between Epifania (the amoral, egoistic life-force) and the doctor's brand of Fabian Socialism. A third force consists of various bumptious parasites who represent the English upper-middle-classes – a play-about husband (George Cole), an unproductive lawyer (Alastair Sim), a psychiatrist (Dennis Price). Epifania grandly takes over a small sweatshop-owner (Vittorio De Sica) representing another sector of small-scale capitalism.

The main shift in the film is that the parasites no longer add up to an establishment, as their counterparts in Shaw's play did. They remain, simply, assorted unpleasant individuals. Thus the film loses Shaw's point that the um-class, far from consisting of a meritocracy, must at best be a mediocracy, and, probably, a parasitocracy. Second, the film's updating has Epifania seeking to please her philanthropic doctor, setting up a huge, impersonal free medical clinic, contrasting with his poky little private practice surgery. The free clinic must, of course, suggest the National Health Service, and the fact that it all becomes huge and soulless and bureaucratic puts the film, maybe involuntarily, on the Conservative side of the line. Most important of all, Sophia is so unremittingly sumptuous, and the Sellers character, in extremis, so defeatist and confused (wasting his chance on a feckless colleague) that there's no doubt at all who'll wear the trousers. Maybe he saves the millionairess from the megalomaniac mysticism which is her imperious, empty parody of his humble, likeable charity. But the Conservative-Socialist dance becomes, not so much a Liberal co-ownership, as a female Mammon kindly condescending, because she's so sensitive, to uplift the Welfare State to her level and decide how much pocket money it can be allowed to play with. 'Let's put our trust in tycoon-and-takeover-bid capitalism, which will lift us all up to its roof top prosperity, so benefiting even our left-wing idealists whose moral principles seem so human and attractive at first but who, in practice, turn out to be sad, dim, drab, and inept.'

Since Britannia is no longer Superwoman, we can guess why the real N.H.S. is under- rather than over-financed, and why a pie-in-the-sky mysticism is the least of all our temptations. The sense of the sweatshop episode, however, is not what, logically speaking, it might seem to be – that low pay and long hours in unhealthy basements are preferable to Epifania-style automation, affluence and good wages. On the contrary; the advantages of the latter are so obvious that the film can lament the other rhetorically, to make the point that automation, when it comes, won't solve those problems of alienation to which the Left has more lately turned its attention. Nor is the insistence on an Indian doctor giving charity to slum Londoners without an edge. In this bright, gaudy, very likeable film, which concludes with idealism and amorality, Socialism and competitiveness, Eastern mysticism and Western greed, Eastern passivity and Western egoism, mother-obeying male and father-emulating female, repenting of their excesses and joining in a joyous dance under a heavenly blue sky, Asquith has very fairly expressed the middle-of-the-road Conservative-Liberalism which is the mainstream British assumption about politics – including the overwhelming majority of Labour voters. The conformist reasons for Shaw's continuing popularity are also made unusually clear. Shaw, by criticizing the opposites, also condones both. What he doubtless meant as an exposition of hypocrisy becomes a vindication of the compromises which went into the *status quo,* and therefore of the *status quo.* Shaw, now, is merely 'mischievous', as reactionary as, even in their time, Gilbert and Sullivan.

One wouldn't know, from Asquith's films, that he was a pillar of the A.C.T.T., for his *The V.I.P.s* (1963) is a romantic fairytale with a capitalist moral. Self-made but tender-hearted tycoon Richard Burton selflessly signs the cheque that gives go-ahead Australian super-tractor manufacturer Rod Taylor control of his own firm. Hard-boiled disreputable film genius Orson Welles signs the cheque that saves dear old dithering but plucky Duchess Margaret Rutherford's stately home from passing out of the family line. 'Here's to 1973,' says Richard Burton, 'when top people will be up there not because they're born there but because they deserve to be' – a nice thought quite irrelevant to the film, which implies only that our aristocracy ought to be supplemented by smarter businessmen and bigger American cheques. The film's producer, Anatole de Grunwald, and its script writer, Terence Rattigan, had been associated with Asquith in several of his 'traditionally British' films, and their shift of tone, here, might be an emblem of things to come. Film production isn't our only industry to become a sidekick of those cheque-signing Americans.

13. And so, as the sun sets slowly, we bid adieu

Pre-war attitudes to Empire were pleasantly uncomplicated. The nicest thing about us firm and kindly British is our readiness to say, 'You're a better man than I am, Gunga Din'. The white man's dividends are fair returns for the White Man's burden, and in due time the Pax Britannica will redeem the cannibal nigs from their heathen ways.

Hollywood agreed. Errol Flynn won the North-West Frontier for us, just as Greer Garson braved the blitz on our behalf. At home, Alexander Korda's sumptuous line in exhilarating imperialist-militarist epics (and you could be worse than militarist, in the era of appeasement), like *The Drum* (1938) and *The Four Feathers* (1939) are confirmed in their moral idyllism by such commerce-encouraging documentaries as *The Song of Ceylon* (Basil Wright, 1934) and the post-war *Three Dawns to Sydney* (John Eldridge, 1949).

Hints of real politics appear. *Sanders of the River*, directed, like the Korda productions above, by Zoltan Korda (1935), wobbles deliciously between Sanders' line 'The job of a ruler is not to be feared, but to be loved', and a plot which proves the exact opposite. Indeed the natives, with childish wisdom, observe, 'We realize that we must live in peace and love one another for if we do not O white master you will punish us most cruelly'. Michael Balcon's production of *Rhodes of Africa* (directed by Berthold Viertel, 1936) is rare in being neither idealistic nor cynical, but a picture of power politics *as such*.

The problems besetting a more complex approach are illustrated by Thorold Dickinson's *Men of Two Worlds* (1946), from a story by Joyce Cary. A coloured concert pianist, sent back to his tribe on a friendship mission, finds himself succumbing to the spells of a malevolent witch doctor. Any overtone of spiritual paternalism is overridden by our identification with the pianist, and Dickinson's hallucinogenic direction bulldozes us into admitting the irrational unconscious in ourselves also. Brothers under the skin, we're edged even deeper into that grey matter where libidinal nightmares skulk in wait for all.

The penalty of this salutary transposition is that a classical pianist with a tribal background is doubly remote from the public's experience and aspirations. Thirties Hollywood had made some compassionate movies about the noble savage (mainly South Sea islanders). But African tribes labour under unfriendlier myths. In the sixties such a film might well opt for a picture of tribal life which would accommodate some Western nostalgias – about manliness, pain, eroticism, belonging – and indeed anthropological documentaries like *The Sky Above, the Mud Below* have become popular, though with European, West End and sensation-house audiences rather than ordinary English audiences. But the forties were more prim and parochial and if this movie is a little thin for its scope it's because of its too straightforward identification of the Western with the likeable, disinterested, rational and uncomplicatedly progressive. Ironically, its nightmares remain spell-binders even for those of us who think we're rationalists, and if white frailties had been fed back into the story-line it could have been a masterpiece.

There's no doubt that, from the fifties, the general public was not just surprised but dazed into numbness by the way in which even the Conservatives were prepared to give away the Empire. After all, no one had ever told them that the Empire was not run primarily for philanthropy, nor even for the patriotic glory of painting the map of the world as red as possible, but to secure trade and profit. The slogan 'trade follows the flag' puts the flag in its place, second. After 1945, profit was clearly better safeguarded by trade agreements with politically independent but economically dependant nations than by military operations which come expensive and halt production. The way in which, in Kenya, Jomo Kenyatta switched from being a 'bestial terrorist' to a staunch friend of Britain, is one of the paradoxes which might have made interesting dramatic material.

Aside from the continuing idyllic films of Empire, three productions exemplify treatments of the conflicts. Harry Watt followed his game-reservation 'Western' (*Where No Vultures Fly*, Ealing, 1951) with *West of Zanzibar* (1954). Far from inaccurate in its account of a local situation, it's significant that this situation should have been chosen, rather than others, for it can be taken as a vindication of British administrations versus independence movements generally.

Anthony Steel plays a District Commissioner whose African protégés are lured into ivory smuggling by an unscrupulous Arab, on whom they finally turn, after he has killed their courageous old Chief. On the other hand, the English hero has no economic considerations to weigh in the balance against the best interests of these proud, childlike African tribesmen, who are too primitive to rule themselves for many, many years (as their chief obligingly keeps repeating). But Indian traders are put in a very unfavourable light. The film also stresses that a mean and sneaky Indian lawyer is an intellectual, with a chip on his shoulder about the hero's (in fact non-existent) colour prejudice. Moreover, he finishes up as a pitiable coward, begging the Englishman to protect him from the righteous (but likely to be barbaric) wrath of his African dupes. The English gentleman does, but also relieves his feelings by knocking his tiny prisoner flat with a cracking right to the jaw.

So much for African nationalism. It's not African in the first place, it's purely intellectual in the second place, it's paranoid in the third place, it's a hypocritical cover for exploitation of the natives in the fourth place, it's in cahoots with Arab robber-industries in the fifth place, and it's snivelling and gutless in the sixth place. Capitalist exploitation is a non-European monopoly. The problem of white settlers edging African farmers off the best land doesn't exist, the threat to the rural-tribal system is the immaturity of the natives, not the socio-economic forces generated by the cities which are there because of white intervention.

Within its sphere, the film's case is a strong one. The Arab role in Africa has often been destructive, the sense of responsibility of many Colonial Office personnel is real and admirable (in fact a good film could have been made about differences between pre-war and post-war personnel). Yet the film encourages a complete ignorance about actual colonial problems, and therefore about both the reactionary and progressive elements in British policy, and the very real difficulties either way.

Both mean and silly is Ken Annakin's *Nor the Moon by Night* (1958). Here it's not the Arabs who set the natives poaching on game warden Patrick McGoohan's preserves but a brutal Pole (Eric Pohlmann) who spends his rare leisure moments chasing his sweet English rose of a daughter round the house with a horsewhip. One suspects that the film wanted to have a less-than-perfect white settler, but couldn't bear for him to be a Briton, so made him a bloody foreigner instead. It's true that in a rather dotty prologue Belinda Lee's sexually frustrated spinster sister accuses her of poisoning their mother, which proves that there are juju-minded natives in Britain's countryside too, though that's nothing to do with any problems of Empire, of course (more probably an encouragement to the young spectator to emigrate). It's this film which has that action-packed moment when Eric Pohlmann is being attacked by one lion while, miles away, Patrick McGoohan is attacked by three, and, climbing up a tree to get away, meets a rhinoceros coming down. It also has the intercutting with wet, bare, black, bouncing African bubbies, of Belinda Lee's no less glorious orbs, softly straining at wet linen.

Ronald Neame's *Windom's Way* (1957), adapted by Jill Craigie, goes as far as connecting problems of Empire with economic affairs. In a remote district in a Far Eastern country (which may have a white or a native government, and which in the former case might as well be Indonesia as England), Asiatic employees who want to grow their own rice rather than buy the company store's unjustly high prices, go on strike. Their action is clumsily handled by two company officials. 'We're the only white men in the district,' one persuades the other. 'We must work together as white men. The only thing they respect is strength.' The dignified village headsman is arrested and accidentally killed by a brutal (native) cop. The strike becomes a riot. The sensitive-eyed natives storm the jail, kill the cop and devastate the plantation. Then not even selfless and much-loved Doctor Windom (Peter Finch) can stop them from being tricked, and then dragooned, into fighting for the nasty terrorists. Because it accepts the possibility of negative elements in imperialism, because it repudiates simple-minded anti-Communism, and because it outlines the existence, and problems, of a third world, this is one of the maturer films of Empire.

It has a tormented parallel in John Guillermin's *Guns at Batasi* (1964) which, in its strong, simple, old sweat's way, makes no bones about its opposite sympathies. Native one-party rule is going to be the sort of dictatorship that'll take a very nasty revenge on all those native N.C.O.s who were decently loyal to the Queen. Any end-of-Empire policy which will hand them over to such villains is enough to make the simple Bible Englishman's gorge rise. Just one such gorge belongs to brass-throated, brass-lunged, copper-bottomed R.S.M. Lauderdale (Richard Attenborough), goaded, at last, to hurl a glass at the mess portrait of the Queen, before, uncomprehendingly submitting, he straightens his shoulders and marches off to his home posting. Intellectuals like the schoolie and the bossy Labour M.P. (Flora Robson) don't come out of it too well. One may not share the R.S.M.'s attitude, which is also the film's, and feel one understands why the establishment characters (Governor and C.O.) are prepared to turn bolshy and retreat with the rebels; it's all to do with the balance of payments and military bases, old chap. But one can feel for this military predecessor of Alf Garnett; and who indeed are we to patronize him? for who isn't confused, outraged, paralysed, by the Machiavellian tactics of politicians? Even if the film is visually flat (under-budgeted?) it's very far from inconsiderable, for it's accurate account of army attitudes, and for the richest anthology of army idioms outside *The Long and the Short and the Tall*.

A more elegiac farewell to Empire is J. Lee Thompson's *North West Frontier* (1959). Captain Kenneth More, aided by his Indian engine driver (I. S. Johar), and subject to caustic anti-imperialist comments by American governness Lauren Bacall, protects our friendly Indian Prince on a long train journey across the Indian plain. The Eton boating song floats out to the hot dry foothills. If the Hindus and Moslems massacre one another horribly, it is largely the fault of Herbert Lom, who's embittered into half-insanity, probably because he's a half-caste. Insane isn't an altogether unfair epithet for Hindu-Moslem massacres, and, as Miss Bacall has to accept, it's easy for idealist outsiders to criticize administrators. Yet the film has an intriguing little backlash to it. The English officer, contemplating the mutilated corpses, accepts, in turn, that, having elected to run the country, he has some responsibility if such things go on. The film touches briefly on the cynicism of political maturity. The princeling assures his escort 'My father says that when I grow up, I shall have to kill the British to get them out of my country'. True, he's a foreigner, and he's wrong. But he's only wrong because we renounced our Empire.

Equivocal in a less amiable way, for possibly purely commercial reasons, rather than for conviction, is Cy Endfield's *Zulu* (1963). Equally Empire-building Zulu warriors surround a party of British troops, led by Stanley Baker and Michael Caine, and can't overrun them. They generously salute their enemy's courage before moving off. The film may seem 'progressive', given its up-from-the-ranks Baker edging upper-crust Michael Caine out of command, and the unflattering picture of a drunken and cowardly missionary (Jack Hawkins) and his fine-looking but null daughter (Ulla Jacobsson). Second thoughts are less reassuring. The missionary has made a point of attending native ceremonies in a friendly spirit, in contrast to the whites and Zulus who gallantly go their separate ways. Real understanding is attained through – apartheid, might one say? – whereas those meddling clergymen ... like Father Huddleston, perhaps ... Rapidly the film settles down to one long, splendid, Kordaesque battle-scene which makes Walsh, Sturges and the be-auteured Americans look like also-rans at the action game.

It takes the erstwhile exponent of B.O.P. drums-and-topi imperialism to demystify and deglamourize, to brood with neo-realistic sombreness over the tragedies of *apartheid*. Zoltan Korda's *Cry, the Beloved Country* (1951) opens with a crabbing shot from the window of a train speeding from the African countryside through, first, shack-riddled countryside, then ugly suburbs, then spewing factory chimneys and lastly the centre of Johannesburg, revealing the ugly dislocations of a split society in, literal, cross-section. The shedding of exoticism is the beginning of wisdom.

14. Tunes of Bogey

Accusations of war-mongering are often flung by middle-class puritan, and some left-wing, critics, against the British cinema. Certainly the popularity of war films from 1950 for some years after requires explanation.

After World War I, a similar pattern applied. A five-year moratorium of war films was followed by a cinematic evocation of those experiences, which is what one would expect – a rest, followed by 'recollection in tranquility'.

The Cold War gave a further twist to things. World War is again on the agenda immediately. The ignominies of pre-war appeasement seemed to carry an obvious moral with respect to Stalin. But the prospect of World War III was so unappetizing, that anxieties could agreeably be fed back into movies about World War II, which was undoubtedly justified, and over, and won.

Third, the general trend in post-war film-going has been towards action movies. The Western, for example, has enjoyed previously unprecedented popularity among middle-class audiences. The war film is the European Western. All three factors working together explain the post-war 'hump' of war films.

Initially, war films retained the no-heroics, stiff-upper-lip feel of wartime war films. Until about 1955, British film critics were at one with industry and public in admiring this tone. It's as critics' anxiety about screen violence grew that they gradually came to feel English understatement as a method, quite as insidious as American braggadocio, of making war seem routine, manly and easy. From the mid-fifties came a tendency to object to the very qualities so admired a few years earlier. This was quite understandable, but equally so was the public's clinging to a tone which, after all, hadn't become altogether untrue simply through repetition.

Just as there are shades of grey, the stiff upper lip allows a variety of tones. Michael Anderson's *The Dam Busters* (1955) orchestrates the prolonged anxieties of lonely research, barrack-room jollities, and the grim satisfactions of derring-do, to lead up to the gruelling losses of the return flight. Lewis Gilbert, probably the most diligent applicant of the tone, reduces Douglas Bader in *Reach for the Sky* (1956) and Violette Szabo in *Carve Her Name with Pride* (1958) to austere metallic icons of heroism, brass rubbings, as it were. Jack Lee's *A Town Like Alice* (1956) is slightly less reticent, sustainedly more moving. Charles Frend's *The Cruel Sea* (Ealing, 1952) even allows a flashpoint of revulsion and insubordination. To sink a U-boat which may be there (and isn't) destroyer skipper Jack Hawkins drops a depth charge among British matelots struggling in the sea, killing the lot. 'Murderer!' shrieks an angry sailor, which is unfair, but – but: the film goes on to a long, deliberately anti-climatic second half which eases us through dull routine to a sober satisfaction. The film's prevailing tone is so sombre that it's surprising to find a Hampstead pub named after book or film; maybe testifying to the extent to which people accept that it is precisely the horrors of war which give heroism its meaning.

One may fairly exclude from the charge of militarism those films which want the unity, comradeship and moral purpose of war to be carried over into peace, and regretted its passing, much as Dearden and Relph's *The Ship That Died of Shame* (1955), when put to post-war smuggling. For nostalgias for these moods are common to most servicemen, who would nonetheless find conscription and futility too high a price to pay.

By the late fifties the stiff upper lip style was exhausted, and films moved in three directions. One is the reversion to bright battle-painting epics like Powell and Pressburger's *The Battle of the River Plate* (1956). Even further out is an aggressively militaristic genre, cooked up as much for American as for English palates, like Terence Young's *The Red Beret* (1953) and John Gilling's *High Flight* (1957). Third is a small, sour group of movies which, if not precisely anti-war, are pretty discouraging about it.

A few films lay a special emphasis on a mood of near-defeat, as if to paraphrase the war's grimmest and most humiliating eighteen months (from Dunkirk to Pearl Harbor). Wartime documentaries already stress Britain's capabilities of passive endurance, indeed, their apparent diffidence as to whether she could dish it out as well as take it worried some neutral nations (and the Robsons). From *London Can Take It!* through *San Demetrio London* (Charles Frend for Ealing, 1943) and *In Which We Serve* to *Western Approaches* (Pat Jackson, 1944), the British, with dire honesty, represent themselves as on the ropes. Although aggressive films weren't unknown the last shot of *The Way Ahead* was characteristically subdued.

This passivity remains in some post-war movies of which the flagship is undoubtedly *Dunkirk* (1958). Its pride plunges into something much darker as the lines of troops queuing and praying scatter, scream and grovel under the Stukas. In Lewis Gilbert's *Sink the Bismarck!* (1960), the sinking of H.M.S. *Hood*, which sent a horrid shudder down the nation's spine, is carefully planted. 'The *Hood*'ll get her!' say the matelots confidently, and the one-shot sinking of the nation's pride is emphasized by the drowning with her of civilian dockyard workers caught on board when she raced out of port. Since it takes entire fleets and squadrons to sink one Nazi ship, one might feel it needs all its emphasis on the German Captain's arrogance to stop us sympathizing with an outnumbered underdog. More probably, the British sense of fair play is less dogmatic than it's usually supposed to be; the ship isn't an underdog, or even a fox or a stag, but a bear being baited by bulldogs. And war is war.

Similarly, Michael Anderson's *Yangtse Incident* (1956), based on the *Amethyst* action in Korea, stars Richard Todd as the Commander whose ship, contrary to all the rules, is fired on and trapped by Chinese shore batteries. Tough negotiations proceed between the British Commander and a Commissar, played Fu Manchu style by Akim Tamiroff. Eventually the British ship slyly slips anchor and fights her way downriver to freedom. The film's ambivalence lies in its long middle section, when the Chinese, seeking a diplomatic victory rather than a naval one, not only refrain from sinking a sitting duck, but supply their British semi-prisoners with fruit, eggs and fuel-oil. It's hard to imagine an American film acknowledging the existence of, let alone celebrating a victory over, so helpful an enemy. The two films seems to represent a not altogether easy, but an emphatic, abandonment of simpler, gallanter notions about war and fair play for something more humiliated and realistic.

If we extend the term 'anti-war' from a strictly pacifist connotation to mean something like a feeling that its debasements inevitably tarnish victory and outweigh glory, then anti-war films are far more frequent than those critics who attacked the industry as war-mongering care to remember. Among them Peter Ustinov and Michael Anderson's *Private Angelo* (1949) of which more later, and Philip Leacock's *Escapade* (1955), from a play by pacifist playwright Roger Macdougall. A sixteen-year-old schoolboy, who we never see, is inspired by his pacifist father (John Mills) to strike a blow against cold war tensions by flying a light plane over the Iron Curtain, to Vienna. His first name is Icarus and the film might be sub-titled, *Reach for the Sky*, with which it shares the same producer (there's no contradiction between that and this lonely harbinger of student C.N.D. direct action). But the sharpest repudiation of the Dulles image of the Cold War is Anthony Asquith's *The Young Lovers* (1954). An employee in the American Embassy in London (David Knight) and the daughter of an East European diplomat (Odile Versois) are the Romeo and Juliet who cry 'A plague on both your houses', elope, and find happiness in flight – or death?

Anthony Asquith is sometimes claimed as a pacifist, largely on the strength of *Tell England* (co-directed with Geoffrey Barkas, 1931), though it's no more pacifist than *The Cruel Sea*. And there's an admirable repudiation of pacifism in his *Guns of Darkness* (1962), in which two English citizens (David

Niven, Leslie Caron) come to see the necessity for armed revolt, by guerrillas, against, not simply a right-wing dictator, but domination by foreign capital. This is a rare example of a British film advocating the overthrow of any *status quo*, and it takes, in principle, a pro-Castro line. Even if its stylistic wings are clipped by under-budgeting, its human sensitivity puts it in the same high class as the same director's more celebrated *Orders to Kill* (1957), a bitter tragedy about a patriotic Frenchman mistakenly murdered by an American officer (David Knight). He cringes with disgust as those who had required him to strangle his victim with his bare hands now require him to decorate, and condole the widow. The film may seem sentimental in synopsis (since tragic mistakes are part and parcel of war), and some French critics concluded that the film's pacifism was an insult to the Resistance. Yet there's nothing illogical in the position that war, even if inevitable, remains revolting and tragic. A similar nausea inspires Jack Lee's *Circle of Deception* (1960). This time it is the British Secret Service who arrange for one of their own men to be tortured past his breaking point so that the Gestapo will credit the – false – information entrusted to him. He ends a broken man, and the film is a bitter cry of rage against that Machiavellian logic which, here, makes the British the accomplices of the Gestapo.

An interesting case is David Lean's *The Bridge on the River Kwai* (1957). To sustain the morale of his fellow P.O.W.s, Colonel Nicholson (Alec Guinness) insists they make a good job of constructing a strategic bridge, as ordered by their brutal Japanese captor (Sessue Hayakawa). Gradually he comes to believe that his big, beautiful, peaceful bridge is of more spiritual importance than losing the war, and tries to prevent a raiding party (led by Jack Hawkins and guided by William Holden) from destroying it. He shows such courage and idealism that some spectators take his side, heedless, apparently, whether the railway enables the Japanese Army to put the entire British Army in prison-camps. After all, our side maintains what really matters, our self-respect, our pride – we whistle while we work ... But Petain is Colonel Nicholson's middle name.

This might have been a pacifist film if Hawkins and Holden had blown up the bridge while all the British prisoners were lined up on it, and even that wouldn't have proved anything, for the analogous depth-charge episode in

The Cruel Sea doesn't lead to a pacifist reaction. You can't make an omelette without breaking eggs and you can't make war without scrambling a few guts. In America, even better class audiences, it appears, shriek 'Kill Him! kill him!' as Nicholson tries to save his bridge. Industrial hall audiences here don't shriek, and they fell sorry for him, but – he's got to go. For the anti-Nicholson audience, the doctor's cry – 'Madness! madness!' – refers to Nicholson's actions. For the pro-Nicholson audience, it condemns the destructiveness of war. For those who feel with both sides, even if they know that Nicholson must die, it underlies the tragic criss-cross of heroisms of which the greatest has gone wrong, in a convulsive and challenging way. Nicholson's own evolution is not particularised. Is the bridge, for him, a symbol of the unconquerable quality which he, and his men, can show? Is it an emblem of honour, beyond all question of usefulness? Or do its associations with engineering relate it to the long utilitarian-liberal-middle-class tradition with its pacifist leanings (the merchant skipper of *Billy Budd* is an earlier champion of the same creed)!

Some critics took the peculiar line that the film is specious, since it pretends to be pacifist, but isn't. It's certainly effective in introducing a certain, probably healthy, unease into everyone's thinking about war, and this is probably because we are surprised to find ourselves, in a situation which demands for or against engagements, split four ways with respect to the gentlemanly code. There, perhaps, is the film's real theme. Guinness is the too brave Briton, upheld by an idealism which, in the end, blinds him to the world. He's Blimp-Chamberlain-Christ. Jack Hawkins, in peacetime a don, is intellectually sharper, and therefore more commonsensical. He stands for the values of the mind, but the pools of blood give us second thoughts about just how far those values take us. William Holden is the initially thoroughly selfish American who escapes from the P.O.W. camp with only self-preservation in mind and slowly, to his own surprise, finds himself succumbing to moral principles and returning to the jungle hell. Sessue Hayakawa incarnates the dingo Oriental gentleman whose ill-treatment of the prisoners seems bestial and malevolent but is, in fact, accepted under his code, which he observes. Having four different heroes, all our assumptions about war come under complicated strain.

Blow-Up: David Hemmings –
Something in the detail

Tiger in the Smoke: Donald
Sinden … against something
in the fog …

Great Expectations: John Mills, Finlay Currie, Valerie Hobson, John Mills

The convict's scowl, or the vampire's promise …

The Browning Version: Michael Redgrave, Wilfrid Hyde White, Bill Travers, Ivan Samson
Torments and guilt of the Establishment

For Them That Trespass: Robert Harris, Valentine Dyall, Stephen Murray

Time without Pity: Michael Redgrave, Leo McKern
Myths and models of the middle-class conscience

Reach for Glory: Harry Andrews, Michael Anderson Jr

A Matter of Life and Death
Reluctantly towards a drab Utopia – and the deathly fiestas of affluence
Live Now Pay Later: Ian Hendry, June Ritchie

Passage Home: Michael Craig, Glyn Houston, Geoffrey Keen, Bryan Forbes
Red dusters, Red Flags …

I'm All Right Jack: Peter Sellers, Irene Handl, Ian Carmichael, Liz Fraser

I Believe in You: Celia Johnson, Joan Collins

Illusions of class and caste

The Millionairess: Sophia Loren, Peter Sellers

The Man in the White Suit: Michael Gough, Alec Guinness, Cecil Parker, Desmond Roberts, Howard Marion Crawford, Ernest Thesiger

Inventors and Plutocrats, or, Whatever Happened to Private Enterprise? Artists and Bureaucrats, or Building Big Brother's New Jerusalem

The Damned: Viveca Lindfors

Carl Foreman reputedly made a *sub rosa* contribution to the script of *The Bridge on the River Kwai*. Three films which he produced exemplify some of the difficulties involved in anti-war movies (a main difficulty lying in the obvious moral polarities set up by Nazi Germany). The heroine of *The Key* (directed by Carol Reed, 1958) is a beautiful woman (Sophia Loren) who, like some consolatory angel of death, gives herself to one tug-boat skipper after another just before the mines or U-boats get him. The males, cowed by convention, suspect that she's mystically bringing them death instead of offering them a chance to throw off their death wish. The film drifts in and out of its sombre action climaxes, converting them into anti-climaxes, meaningless crescendoes of ineluctable pain. Even the love affair feels none too real, and this film is more deeply broken-hearted than at first it seems.

The Guns of Navarone (1961), an ironic epic of heroism, was turned back into an ordinary epic by J. Lee Thompson's emphasis on energy. After these experiences Foreman produced, wrote and directed *The Victors* (1963), a star-studded *Paisà* also relating war and women. Managing to be unequivocally anti-war, it was immediately scolded by English critics for being over-obvious, while American women's clubs resented it as an insult to their saintly and chaste doughboys. You just can't win.

Colonel Nicholson's perplexities act as starting-gun for a trio of movies about British military tradition, in peace and war: Ronald Neame's *Tunes of Glory* (1960, also with Alec Guinness), Michael Powell's *The Queen's Guards* (1961) and Philip Leacock's *Reach for Glory* (1961).

Behind them there lies, it seems, a realignment of traditional attitudes. During the greater part of the nineteenth century, the army was the preserve of the country gentry (as officers) and of the riff-raff (as rankers). As *Great Expectations* suggests, it was disliked by middle- and lower-classes alike, as a potential weapon of repression (unlike the Navy). Imperialism, and the German threat, slowly restored the army to general acceptance. Two world wars, with conscription, made it much more familiar, albeit in a highly ambivalent way. Post-war conscription closed the gap between army and general public, and the armed forces became one of the few social experiences which the adult male half of the nation had in common. The upper-middle-classes took in the public school cadet corps as part of their common style with the gentry, though below the um-class line people were usually even more indifferent to regimental tradition than they were to Empire Day. But one way or another people had been sensitized to officers and their attitudes – and the officer class in its turn had had to make concessions towards (in wartime) a 'democratic' army, and (in peacetime) the limitations of National Service. The whole area was very intriguing.

In *Tunes of Glory*, Alec Guinness plays a plebeian and demagogic Regimental C.O., a gruff, rude, red haired animal who has shot up from the ranks and still shocks his gentlemanly subordinates with peppery squaddie lingo like 'That man's got tabs for titties.' 'That man' is his successor and rival, the new Colonel (John Mills), scion of a traditionally military family, a stickler for the book of rules, but remote from actual fighting experience. His Achilles heel is proneness to rigidity and rage, Blimp-like characteristics (unconvincingly) excused by some story about his having been subjected to torture during the war. His rival senses his weakness, works on it, and inadvertently drives him, not to resignation but to suicide. Seized with remorse, he treats his erstwhile comrade and foe to an enormous, full dress, ceremonial funeral, that is, he assents at last to the aristocratic tradition.

If this film moved me less deeply than it might it is no doubt because the splendid full dress funeral evoked something like a squaddie's nightmare of rehearsal, bull, jankers and cancelled leave. Nor does the fall of the once mighty, that traditional tragic motif, instill me with that awe which the film seems at times to assume rather than create. It remains poignant, fascinating, and, in the best sense, strange. It catches something of the old womanishness of army life. It paraphrases the gradual erosion of the relatively 'democratic' wartime army by peacetime relaxation. Young Blimp's son, here, dies, no doubt, but he has, at last, infected the earthier, stronger man, with his code. And even that ex-squaddie is ready to smash the mere ranker who dares date, now, his precious daughter. It's a more contemporary Skin Game, sharpened by another upper-class character, a cool, snide, treacherous adjutant (Dennis Price), who will be as lickspittle as they like until his time comes. Does he represent another style, less easily despicable than we'd like to think? At any rate, one is at perfect liberty to reverse the apparently intended moral, whereby the funeral is the swansong of the grand old tradition, and see it instead as a sad case of Blimp's son posthumously converting today's parvenus to his way of thinking.

Michael Powell's *The Queen's Guards* shows army officers maintaining their fine aristocratic traditions in peace as in war. Like many 'quality' British films (Neame's), it aims at American art-houses. Philip Leacock's *Reach for Glory* shared with *A Chance of a Lifetime* what is almost an accolade in itself: warm, lively, familiar, it was sufficiently radical to disconcert the circuits' bookers, and found only the most sporadic release. Its hero, wartime evacuee John Curlew, becomes a member of an upper-class set in whom the cruelty normal enough in boys has been hyperstimulated, rather than discouraged, by such educational ingredients as the country gentry code (cadet corps and blood sports), class snobberies (a running feud with 'slum kids'), anti-Semitism, xenophobia and wartime propaganda. The film's opening scene is a trenchant piece of mock-heroic parody. Whooping kids on bicycles peddle furiously after a terrified cat, whom they drive over a cliff edge. The hunt leader's speech is largely composed of patriotic cliché: 'When men are dying every day for their country, can we have tears for a cat?' John's more thoughtful side is brought out by his friendship with Mark Stein, a refugee from Nazism, ostracized by John's friends as being both a German and a Jew ('If you don't like it why don't you go back to where you came from, and see how they treat you there?'). John is able to bring him into the gang. But when Mark, unhappy at unfair play, betrays an ambush set for the 'yobs', they decide to play act out the military code whereby the wartime punishment for cowardice in the face of the enemy is death. While the town turns out to honour its young V.C., they stage their little mock-execution. And the accidents that are part of child's play cast a disturbing light on the inculcation, by adults, of children with notions of military disciplines as a social norm. 'This term your games periods will be given over to cadet training. War is the greatest game of all.'

The moral is not simply underlined, but counterpointed, by a subplot which contrasts John's daydreams of heroism with his guilty secret. His elder brother is a conscientious objector. (The gang beat up another boy: 'There's one thing we can never forgive and that's somebody's who's yellow. His brother's a conchie and while other people are fighting for their country he's having a good time in London as an air raid warden'.) John's family is riven by bitter quarrels between his elder brother and his father, a disappointed ex-officer. In a purely superficial sense, the film's impetus and impact are possibly mitigated by its multiplicity of topics and issues. Yet, in a deeper sense, this is precisely how it comes to transcend its nominal theme, the effect of wartime propaganda on immature minds. It shows society as a network of little wars: the 'yobs' versus the 'girls' (class), WASPS versus Jews (race), pupils versus teachers, brother split between brother and peer group, a whole criss-cross of hardly admitted animosities. The pomp surrounding a local V.C. is contrasted with the spotting of an M.C. in a junk shop window. Its mere presence there has reminded us of those bitter inter-war stories about war heroes reduced to selling their medals in a supposedly grateful country. Now shopkeeper and starry-eyed partisan of the hero cult swop sob stories to bargain over it, thus reducing heroism to the exploitative ploys of a remorselessly money-based system. It's just as well the film is about children, for on an adult level it would be hardly less savage than *How I Won the War*, without that film's − as it happened ineffectual − dazzle-camouflage of zany humour.

In detail *Reach for Glory* has the rare quality of being at once calmly accurate (in the teacher's confusion between cadet corps and O.T.C.), and devoid of misanthropy (apart from the climax, all the torments are the familiar stuff of everyday experience). Its script is exceptionally deft in switching between these various themes, even if the price of its speed, in combination with Leacock's restraint, is a certain lightness of tragic blocking-in. It has another kind of impressiveness, that of everyday experience suddenly clarified by unexpected patterns. It might have carried, as ironic sub-title, the title of Losey's subsequent *King & Country*.

15. Gangrene − British style

So far we have summarized some of the political and social overtones and attitudes in movies with a briskness which, while necessary in covering one-sixth of a century's movies, many of which have had little detailed reviewing, let alone criticism, must sometimes have smacked of heartlessness. Let us now slow down briefly and look into, or rather feel through, three movies, by different studios and directors, on a common, challenging theme. Our forces, in defiance of the Geneva Convention, torture enemy prisoners.

Val Guest's *Yesterday's Enemy* (1959), for Hammer, based on a TV play by Peter R. Newman, was followed by Leslie Norman's *The Long and the Short and the Tall* (1960), for Michael Balcon–Associated British, based on the Royal Court play by Willis Hall, who also wrote that for Roy Baker's *The Valiant* (1961), an Anglo-Italian co-production, that is, a joint effort by torturers and victims.

The first two deal with atrocities committed by British patrols against Japanese prisoners in Burma. The audience will of course remember the reputation of Japanese armies, who hadn't signed the Geneva Convention, and feel that one atrocity, by desperate men, can't compare with the enemy's widespread efforts, in the context of which a little retaliation becomes, at least, understandable. A second excuse, less convincing, and hinting at a bad conscience over the first, is that the patrol possesses vital information which may change the course of the war.

Norman's film tells, in a stagey, but effective, style, how a 'bolshy' bully (Laurence Harvey) vainly tries to stop his patrol, under Sergeant Richard Todd and Lance Corporal Ronald Fraser, from shooting an innocent Japanese prisoner, simply because of their hysteric belief that he was personally responsible for killing British prisoners. As if in retribution by fate, the patrol are hunted down and killed, one by one.

Guest's film lacks the saltily idiomatic dialogue of the other, but its argument is more complex. A patrol, led by Stanley Baker, leaves its own wounded behind for the Japanese to bayonet. It shoots Burmese civilians to obtain information about Japanese plans. It shoots burdensome prisoners. It fails, so their atrocities were pointless, and we won the war anyway, so their information probably wasn't so vital. The Japanese capture them, and, by their own logic, shoot them too.

But the British troops accept death in the same spirit as they inflict it. 'There's only one way to fight a war – with the gloves off!' Each set of executioners respects its victims' courage. A new, international Bushido, expecting torture, seems to apply. The 'hard' anti-torture line is represented, vociferously and powerfully, by the patrol's complement of 'intellectual' odds-and-bods: a padre, a doctor, a newspaper man (Leo McKern). The last, a cynical agnostic, possibly of dissenter stock, is far more outspoken and resolute than the Church of England man.

The inner division of attitudes is reflected by a clear contrast between the original TV play and Guest's adaptation. The body of the film follows the play closely, even to the author's deliberate challenging of the audience's assumption that the British fought fair until Japanese atrocities provoked them. For the Japanese officer remarks that the Europeans made the rules, to suit themselves, in fighting the Sudanese, the Africans, the Boers. 'Guns against swords! You made the "rules"! But when you meet an enemy who is your match, you suddenly take refuge behind your "rules"!' And, of course, immediately break them. One of the most chilling scenes from any British film, in its very casualness, is that where the fatherly, decent Sergeant (Gordon Jackson) says to an aged, bewildered Burmese, 'Come on, dad, over here' – and gently leads him in front of the firing squad.

The film concludes on a shot of a War Memorial honouring Our Glorious Dead (i.e. this atrocity-committing patrol), while a momentous voice exhorts us not to forget their sacrifices. Without that last shot that patrol's failure would have seemed a judgement on it. But its inclusion sends us off in other directions. It asks us *either* to forgive their atrocities, as those of all-too-human heroes under strain, but heroes nonetheless, *or* to 'forget' their misdeeds, as official rhetoric always forgets uncomfortable facts, *or* to honour even their commission of atrocities, as a duty which required them courageously to defy their own squeamishness. And it underscores, in sanctimonious language, an astonishing line which in the play must have seemed a shudder of horror at the endlessness of war: 'Every generation must honour its own dead'. That is, every generation can expect its own world war, history is, ineluctably, corpses piled on corpses, a hecatomb of atrocities must be faced with stoic acquiescence – and preparation. It would be nice to be able to dismiss this point of view.

Roy Baker's *The Valiant* selects another situation in which torture seems both reasonable and understandable. Two courageous and sympathetic Italian midget submariners plant a limpet-mine on the hull of a British battleship, whose sinking could lose the Allies command of the Mediterranean. Captured, the men, strictly in accordance with the Geneva Convention, refuse to reveal the mine's whereabouts to the British captain (John Mills).

The torture he applies is a 'passive' one. He keeps the men aboard the threatened ship, and refuses medical care (at first, even morphine, though on this point he later relents) to a man who is in great pain and gravely injured. This man holds out and it is his comrade who eventually, out of humanity, speaks – too late. The mine goes off. The ship is seriously damaged, but, by improvising an elaborate bluff with counter-marching Marine brass bands, the British conceal the truth from Italian reconnaissance planes, and win the war.

This time the victims of torture are not the brutal Japanese, but the amiable Italians. They win some sort of moral victory over their captor – the tortured man by his courage, the other by his humanity. Nor are the Captain's motives altogether disinterested. We are allowed to sense something very personal, almost selfish, in his identification with his ship. Lastly, the torture proves to have been unnecessary, for when the mine blows up, an alternative way, a very clean way, of saving the situation, is found: 'the bluff of British tradition'.

Perhaps afraid that the audience would refuse sympathy to a 'cold' torturer, the Captain's pangs of conscience are heavily stressed, his tortures negative and alleviated. The Italians are flatly characterized – as simply 'having a wife and a child at home' – and the Captain's action is elaborately established as being without his superior's ambiguous connivance, let alone consent. As in *Yesterday's Enemy*, the final shots of traditional rhetoric may be felt as a vindication of the Captain's initiative. And of course our concern over the ethics of torture is counter-pointed, not to say mitigated, by our concern for the ship, inclining us to suspect that a little mild torture like this could be justified, especially if it succeeds quickly.

Like so many British films, these are 'open-ended'. They accommodate condemnation and condonation alike, whether as alternatives or mixed in various proportions, depending on the spectator's own response and values. Presumably Italian audiences took *The Valiant* not as an accusation of the British, but as a study of one of war's moral, and not altogether dishonourable, dilemmas.

Yet it would be unfair to dismiss these films as *merely* ambiguous. They explore their situation with a keen sense of anguish and paradox, they disturb audience complacency (which would tend to: 'The British are gallant and decent, they never torture, but when they do, they're absolutely justified by the dastardliness of the enemy, and even when they're not, war's war.'). And they raise some of the perennial issues to which moralists' answers have been contradictory or (either way) not altogether convincing.

Circle of Deception approaches the same theme and in David Lean's *Lawrence of Arabia* (1962) Lawrence indulges his mysterious, patriotic, yet inexcusable bloodlust at the expense of Arab prisoners. There is a curious foretaste of that scene in Harry Watt's *Nine Men* (1943), a visually stylish saga in the so-called documentary style. Its gloating contempt for the gutless but malicious Eyetie reaches a climax when an Italian P.O.W. tries to escape and gets a bullet in the back from one of our nine heroes, who tersely comments, 'The stinker'. How far the film expects its audience to condemn or to condone, is a matter of conjecture, and it's probably just as well, given the film's emphasis on the Italians as slimy wop no-goods who outnumber the British (but *Sink the Bismarck!?*). True, our boys are in a tight corner, but the film seems a relatively complacent intimation of the fact that war unleashes the worst, even in us.

Since these movies were made, news from French Algeria and South Vietnam has made us all more conscious of the extent to which friendly and civilized countries have resorted to torture and similar atrocities. It could be argued that the ventilation of this topic signifies an unhealthy deterioration of public morality, or a healthy move towards a more realistic attitude, or an honest insistence that it's not so easy to remain true to the best in Britishness, or a general feeling that modern war being as indiscriminate as it is in its onslaught on women and children, it's absurd to bother too much over the treatment of male combatants. It's another question whether such films constitute subversive muck-slinging by irresponsible artists, or whether even if such things go on the best way to minimize them is to pretend they don't, or whether all's fair in war, like employing torture and then keeping it secret, so that we can reap the advantages of both the fine ideal and the foul deed. Luckily all these matters are beyond our brief. At any rate, it's worth remarking that apart from Godard's *Le Petit Soldat* (also in 1960) no movies have come as near as these British ones to a stern self-incrimination over the whole terrifying problem of atrocity in war. No doubt the influence of the non-conformist conscience is responsible. It's an honourable irony that the films most worried with the third degree and *la gangrene* should come from a nation more concerned with minimum force than the American, French or German.

16. Standing up for Jesus

Generally speaking, cinema-going Britain is distinct from church-going Britain. As a cleric remarked, 'The Church of England never lost the masses of our industrial cities, for the simple reason that she never had them.'[30] On the other hand, the British, even when only nominally Christian, tend to be sympathetic towards Christianity insofar as it represents an absolute affirmation of morality and goodwill as linked with some power for good, independent of man, in the universe. Otherwise, Christianity is not the easiest of philosophies to square with the range of experiences preferred by cinemagoers, particularly given the restrictions imposed by the pseudo-reverence of 'good taste'. The British censor, possibly taking his cue from America's Hays Code, long maintained a policy of blandly and totally banning any seriously critical portrayal of any Christian church or its clerics.

Fortunately, the censor is, like the law, an ass, and some authentic and seriously-held popular attitudes found some sort of expression in farce. Robertson Hare's clergymen (or distraught householders or scallywags disguised as clergymen), typify a fairly common suspicion that 'Christianity as she is spoke' involves prissy, fussy, hypocrisies and emasculations. In *Sailor Beware* an energetic working-class Mum keeps addressing the Reverend Purefoy as 'Mr. Pureboy' and the joke's not just on her but on him too.

The most popular religious films are those whose strong human interest is reinforced by religious attitudes which are at once absolute, amiable and exotic. Such films include Powell and Pressburger's *Black Narcissus* (1947), in which a Himalayan convent of Anglican nuns has, at last, to admit defeat by familiar human passions and eerie Oriental forces, and Ralph Thomas's *Conspiracy of Hearts* (1960), where Catholic nuns save Jewish orphans from the Gestapo. Philip Leacock's *Hand in Hand* (1960), with a Jewish and a Catholic child defying parental prejudices, is less successful – probably because sectarianism is less militant here than elsewhere, and its transcendence less inspiring. In Dearden's *Life for Ruth* (1962), a Jehovah's Witness refuses to allow his child to have blood transfusions. His attitude is perhaps too extreme, and too depressing.

A feature of the late fifties is its plethora of Rank films with religious motifs or scenes. A critic had already remarked that Lord Rank moved into cinema with a mission to make more films with the uplift of *The Great Mr. Handel* (1942) and recouped his losses by making more films with the cleavage of *The Wicked Lady* (1945). One may prefer the latter film to the former, but it would seem that Rank subsequently set out to make some sort of amends for his more profitable wild oats.

Already in 1953 Philip Leacock's *The Kidnappers* sensitively criticizes the puritanical harshness of a Novia Scotia family, which leads two children to kidnap a baby as something on which to lavish their love. If the religious style criticized is almost as rare, now, as that of *Life for Ruth*, the interaction of a sentimental subject and a sober style is a touching one. In 1958 the same director's *Innocent Sinners* (after Rumer Godden) has a neglected, abandoned London teenager (June Archer) and a street-gang leader (Christopher Hay) who befriends her, stealing earth, then statues, then money from a church to adorn their private garden on a blitz site. It's a likeable, albeit notably cautious, variation on René Clément's *Les Jeux interdits*, wherein two orphans, rendered gently callous by war, obsessively collect animals' corpses to give them decent burial. In Brian Desmond Hurst's *Dangerous Exile* (1957), an Orczy-era swashbuckler, Belinda Lee teaches a little refugee boy to say his prayers. All these films, like *Conspiracy of Hearts*, maintain the tradition of relating religious themes to childhood innocence, partly because of the evangelical notion that children are unusually innocent and close to God, partly because children readily believe what they are told, without asking awkward questions, and so create, via our identification with them, an atmosphere of belief.

But other films relate religious beliefs to adult loyalties. In Lewis Gilbert's *Carve Her Name with Pride* secret agent Virginia McKenna spends a long time praying before an altar at Notre Dame. But when she says 'God bless you' to fellow spy Paul Scofield, he pauses significantly before replying, agnostically, 'Good luck'. In Roy Baker's *Tiger in the Smoke* (1956) the heroine's father, an Anglican clergyman, is stabbed in his church by the psychopathic incarnation of evil, more sympathetically personified in the same director's *The Singer Not the Song* (1960), analysed in more detail later. In Julian Amyes's *Miracle in Soho* (1957), Belinda Lee, as an Italian girl in London, prays and prays and prays at a statue of St. Anthony until what audience there was at my lower-middle-class Odeon contributed long loud yawns and eventually catcalls. Even Cy Endfield's *Hell Drivers* (1957) had their heavenly overdrive, for Herbert Lom, an Italian truck driver in England, prays and prays at a statue of the Virgin Mary – only to die of burns received in an accident (murder?), still believing that floozy Peggy Cummins loved him, where in reality she loved his best friend, Stanley Baker. Thus Christianity, sensitive as it is, expresses only wish-fulfilment delusions, in this hard world. A similarly infidel attitude is evinced in the same director's *Sea Fury* (1958), when the walls constantly sprout crucifixes as if to stress the complete irrelevance of faith to sea-dog behaviour, except that the former, if taken seriously, would rule out scrapping and love-making, i.e. the latter's robust and consoling pleasures. An attack on religious sentimentality is doubtless a contributory inspiration in *Zulu*.

It's hard to explain this little 'religious cycle' in terms of commercial calculation, or of producers' middle-class nostalgias. For no evidence suggested that Britain was experiencing any great wave of revivalism. Indeed, despite Dr. Billy Graham's exhortations to clean up the embraces, proceeding, horribly, in Hyde Park by sunlight, Britain was half on the way to the new morality. Moreover, religious asides appeared even in tearaway melodrama, where one would least expect producers to lumber themselves with so ethereal an ingredient.

Hence it's reasonable to suppose that this cycle constituted a deliberate attempt to use the cinema evangelically, and that any mitigation of box-office returns, though to be avoided wherever possible, would be accepted philosophically. Even those films which criticized the negative aspects of Christianity would assert the presence, the relevance, of our Christian heritage, and, by implication, distinguish what religion ought to be from what it too often was. The propaganda approach was not a childish one. Simple-minded affirmations were avoided, and no attempt at polemic made.

So far so good. But Rank's bid for the international market gave the cycle a further twist. It's curious how many of these films deal with Roman Catholics, or with Anglicans so high they might look Roman Catholic after dubbing. *Miracle in Soho* even goes so far as to jeer at the pokey old (i.e. ultra-Protestant) Salvation Army while glorifying glamorous, miraculous Roman Catholicism. Again, it's true that some um-class English, as well as latter day aesthetes, are apt to go gaga over candles and madonnas, mainly because they have only a tourists'-eye-view of Catholic practice and mistakenly persuade themselves that as well as possessing its own cosiness it shares the Anglican virtues of tolerance and gentleness. But the flurry of Roman Catholic subjects from a Methodist organization suggests a different calculation. British religious sentiment has long been relatively ecumenical whereas Catholicism, during this pre-Pope John era, still frowned upon films which honoured Protestants and other heretics. Hollywood had long taken into its calculations the fact that even in WASP-dominated America Catholic pressures on the mass media were vastly more directed and effective than Protestant. This was particularly relevant in the cases of *Hell Drivers* and *Miracle in Soho*. Their Italians in England were presumably aimed at the lucrative Italian market, in which the Roman Catholic Church not only exerts enormous influence but owns a substantial number of cinemas.

In such ways, British films, far from flying a flag for the British way of life overseas, ensured that it was kept off British screens at home as well.

Meanwhile two British Lion films responded to genuine movements in British mood and thought, thus combining prestige success with commercial popularity. Bryan Forbes's *Whistle Down the Wind* (1961), with its tale of children mistaking an escaped murderer for Christ come again, catches a current British mood, or mixture of moods, about religion. On the one hand, there is a deep respect, almost a nostalgia, for faith, together with a mechanical, rather than childlike, acceptance of the conventional formulae of piety. On the other hand, there is a regretful, but firm, agnosticism. 'It's not true! God lets animals die!' But God's absence must be met with stoicism, with the same purity and resolution as if He were present ...

And so neither we, nor the oldest of these children (Hayley Mills), can tell whether she has lost her faith or not, as she watches the police handcuff and carry off her Jesus. The children's mistake is that of their uncompromising faith in faith 'I was on the lam and ye comforted me:' Like Elizabeth Fry, they see Christ in convicts. The film's contempt for established Christianity is unmistakable. Laden with scathing accuracy is the scene where the Vicar sees the girl out of the corner of his eye, and though he knows she desperately wants to talk to him, pretends not to see her, because he's more interested in reading a detective paperback. When she answers him directly, he answers with immediate warmth – and gets her name wrong.

The film is more radical than such denunciations of Christian corruption as *The Bishop's Candlesticks* and *The Passing of the Third Floor Back*. On a skyline, the murderer between two detectives becomes Christ between two robbers. The three children are the three Kings (one brings an Arabian bracelet). The ingenuities of Christian theology in establishing articles of faith about angels and the Virgin Birth are suggested when the murderer reads the children a story called *Ruth Lawrence – Air Hostess*, which they are convinced must be a parable, even though they have to admit they didn't quite understand its meaning yet.

Not that the film settles for the agreeable intellectual exercise of finding modern dress for ancient stories. The irony of these parallels is an agnostic one. Forbes studiously avoids the sort of moral switch-on-a-switch one would expect from a writer asserting faith against disillusionment, i.e. the children's very mistake could have turned the criminal into Christ *for them*. Here, the murderer drops the little text, *The Hope of the World*, which the girl has handed him, as an affirmation of her faith, and the detective sneers, 'You'll need more than that where you're going.' Whether or not the girl retains her faith we don't know; maybe it's her generous innocence which is the hope of the world. But the younger brother's scepticism turns out to be justified. 'Why did you let me cat die?', he demands of Jesus, inconsolably sobbing. The accusation carries humanity's perennial accusation of God – the problem of evil, which in the end, is that of useless suffering.

In no sense is the film merely a satire. Its blend of tender and bitter pain involves even the murderer and the playground 'Judas' who becomes so vicious because he's been excluded from the secret. Why has he been excluded from the secret? Because of his vicious ways. We touch on the cruel mystery of predestination. A sinner is doubly damned for rejecting what he rejects because he's damned ...

Satire is the mood of the Boultings' *Heavens Above!* (1963), which establishes, with macabre glee, the uselessness, in this lewd, greedy, hypocritical world, with its closed shop of vested interests, of trying to put Christian precepts into practice. Our idealist young clergyman does his best, with a success rivalling that of *Nazarin* in Buñuel's film. His attempts to practice the Christian Communism of the primitive church eventually consign him to a space capsule, in which he is left warbling hymns in orbit in a way which suggests he is now as dotty in his mystical way as the world in its cynical one. Only disappointed idealism would dare, and know how, to parody the obstinate illusions of idealism with such sober inventiveness and such sympathetic venom.

A quieter, more traditional form of agnosticism is expressed by Paul Scofield's 'Good luck'. But a belief in luck is, also, a kind of religion, often deepened by stoicism and fatalism, as in *The Key*. *The Night My Number Came Up* is a significant title – even in its understated irony (for your number coming up, usually lucky, here means death). Death itself becomes part of that impersonal, routine-and-rota system which is the public schoolboy's *real* father-figure.

17. Bloody Foreigners

1. The French. Oo-la-la, and see under *A Matter of Life and Death* (p. 33) and The *Greengage Summer* (p. 240). Ealing had a little wartime line in Françoise Rosay characters, who stood up for the French moral backbone, variously aristocrat, bourgeois or peasant. She was slightly inclined to morbidity (given the unhappy endings of French movies, and the 1940 debacle) (cf. *Johnny Frenchman*, *The Halfway House*).

2. Swedish girls are sexy and played by Mylène Demongeot because French girls are so sexy.

3. The Italians – ludicrous or contemptible during the war, loveably natural and human after it. Because the men are merely human they're losers (*Hell Drivers*). Italian au pair girls are so sexy (Claudia Cardinale in *Upstairs and Downstairs*).

4. The Germans. The brutal wartime German has to accommodate friendlier attitudes from our past: (1) the gallant Prussian officer, (2) the self-

disciplined virtuous Protestant nation, (3) the nation of musicians and cultured thinkers, and (4) the merry Rhein wine-and-beer drinkers. Come two World Wars and they all have to be rendered subservient to hysterically efficient, brutal Huns and Nazis. Whence the typical German officer with (1) sabre scar, (2) courteous hiss, (3) sitting at the grand piano and (4) raising his wine glass, but (5) finally bursting out with a maniacal high pitched shriek.

But he's a tough nut to crack. In Michael Powell's *49th Parallel* (1941), the crew of a sunken U-boat evade capture as they cross Canada and menace its unsuspecting citizens as they try to escape the still neutral U.S.A. The film is an obvious nudge to American public opinion and was apparently patronized by the Ministry of Information. Charles Oakley reports that the film 'brought out the resource and courage of the Nazi commander so powerfully ... many feared that the picture had unintentionally become better propaganda for the enemy than for ourselves'.

Throughout the Edwardian sequences of *The Life and Death of Colonel Blimp* (1943), Blimp's fumbling is contrasted not, as one might expect, with an ordinary Briton, but with the direct, efficacious, and manlier gallantry of his Prussian counterpart (Anton Walbrook). This apparent sympathy for German tradition got Powell and Pressburger in trouble with the Robsons and James Agate too. *Ill Met by Moonlight* (1957) concludes with the German general (Marius Goring) acknowledging the skill of Britain's 'amateur' soldiers. The matching of a professional aristocratic caste by democratic improvisation is felt to be a very reassuring one.

Wartime controversies give this line its meaning. Powell and Pressburger simply continue a traditional respect for the German, who is not only blonder than us, but has so many Protestant-public school virtues: discipline, hard and honest work, manly strength. Until 1940 many right-wing people felt that Hitler, although so vulgar, and regrettably expansionist, had done Germany a lot of good, especially in taking a firm hand with everybody. Others, disguised by the overwrought 'Hate the Hun' propaganda of 1914-18, refused to credit tales of Nazi atrocities until late in the war. It wasn't until 1940 that Churchill decided to direct propaganda against the Germans, and not just the Nazis, whereupon Goebbels heaved a sigh of relief. Indeed, if (to quote *Nothing But the Best*) what's wrong with our aristocracy is that it's too middle-class by half,

then what's right with the Prussian, for all his faults, is that he's managed to get the feudal-aristocratic code to prevail over the middle-class spirit. He's more military, more manly, less nervous, less mediocre.

The feeling of inferiority is fully worked out in J. Lee Thompson's *Ice Cold in Alex* (1958), set during the eventual fall of Tobruk (as sore a point as the sinking of the *Hood*). A battle-fatigued officer (John Mills), Sergeant-Major (Harry Andrews) and two nurses drive an ambulance back to Alexandria. On the way they pick up a Dutch South African officer (Anthony Quayle) who does everything brilliantly. He's pointedly tougher and more sensible than the suicidally, and manslaughterously, hysteric Captain. He's pointedly stronger than the strong Sergeant-Major, and he's also, it seems, a brilliant diplomat (twice persuading ugly-looking panzers who've captured them to release

Nothing But the Best: Alan Bates, Avice Landon, Millicent Martin, Harry Andrews – An admirable incarnation of a Graham Greene hero?

them). Even when they've found out that he's a German spy, they reckon he's a decent chap in himself as well as having saved their lives several times over. So they save his, by pretending he wasn't in Allied uniform when they caught him. The capability ranking is unmistakable: Germans or colonial top: loyal N.C.O. next: English officer, last.

The *49th Parallel* pattern is reiterated in Roy Baker's *The One That Got Away* (1957). Hardy Kruger plays the Luftwaffe air ace whose escapes from a prison camp give him a clear personal superiority over the bumbling Anglo-Saxon. Romantic respect for our once fiendish enemy reached a climax around 1960, when Rank imported Horst Buchholz, Curt Jurgens and Hardy Kruger to appeal to the German market. Consequently the bright, eager, masculine, domineering, amiable young male asserted his German virility everywhere from Oxbridge (*Bachelor of Hearts*, Wolf Rilla, 1958) to Hong Kong (*Ferry To*, Lewis Gilbert, 1959), on the grounds, either that the British were more awed by the Germans than the Germans by the British, or that the British were more inclined to sportingly *love* a gallant foe.

Changing views of national character seem to have inspired an Anglo-German co-production, *On Friday at Eleven* (1961). American crook Rod Steiger, German crook Peter Van Eyck, French crook Jean Servais, British crook Ian Bannen, and Franco-German crook Nadja Tiller, hijack a U.S. army payroll. In this criminals' N.A.T.O.-cum-Common Market, each character aptly symbolizes his nation's toughness-rating. Their leader comes from the land of gangsters and I.C.B.M.s. But he is constantly being challenged by the more calmly tough (cold and disciplined) German. A scene where Steiger, weakened by wounds, bluffs it out, may just possibly paraphrase a feeling that German ruthlessness could uncover unsuspected weaknesses in America (witness folk-lore rumour over American reactions to the panzers' Ardennes offensive). The Frenchman is a brilliant craftsman but he drinks, gets the D.T.s and sees snakes (the French are super-intelligent but have internal troubles, they are over-imaginative, and they die early on – the 1917 mutinies, the 1940 debacle). The gang's co-leader is Franco-German (the main Common Market axis), and she's a highly emancipated girl in leather (like Honor Blackman, i.e. she's the near future). And the Briton? Well, he's a slightly off centre sort of Briton, a Scot, to soften the blow a little, but – at first he promises to be a strong character – fussy, flinty, tetchy, perhaps even the team's dour conscience. Halfway through, however, he lets himself be pressurized into trying to finish off a brave, trapped, wounded guard – who kills him instead. And it's poetic justice. For what the British have to offer is their sense of fair play, their Colonel Nicholson-ism – and when they abandon that, they come one notch below the French.[31]

5. If the Germans are disturbingly near superior, most races, fortunately for us, are rather inferior, and some are actively despicable in themselves, like the Cypriots, according to Ralph Thomas's *The High Bright Sun* (1964). The Cyprus war pitted law, truth, decency, courage and kindness (all-Bogarde, all-British) against the sneaky, fanatical inhuman Cypriot terrorists. The few decent Cypriots end up dead or scared or both, and are very passive and hesitant, which, considering how clear-cut the moral conflict, is pretty scummy of them. 'A sweaty, sneaky little man!' and 'Poor old sod!' are phrases used of two Cypriots who have nothing to do with terrorism at all. Bogarde seems to think it's the entire population's bounden duty to come to the aid of the occupying army; and a neutral American of Greek extraction (Susan Strasberg) must feel morally compelled to take the British side against her own family.

The film could have been anti-terrorist without being anti-Cypriot even if one concedes that nothing makes the nicest army hate an entire population more effectively than hit-and-run tactics by a maquis in mufti whom the locals shield and support. Oddly enough, though, the film's 'Grivas' (Gregoire Aslan) turns out to be less unsympathetic than any other Cypriot. Whether this is out of some affinity for the military qualities, or for any and every authority figure, or for right-wing extremism, or all three, there's no telling. Ironically, Michael Papas's *The Private Right* (1967), a Cypriot-angled film, made in London, about the war and its aftermath, makes every friendly gesture towards the British, following the general rule that vis-à-vis foreigners the English are mean, whereas foreigners are generous to the English.[32]

6. The war against Nazism made race prejudice infra dig for a while, especially as Indians, Gurkhas and Empire races had rallied to our side against Germans and Japs. Zoltan Korda's *Sahara* (his Hollywood equivalent of *Nine Men*, also 1943) has the coloured N.C.O. overpower the representative of the

herrenvolk in fair fight. It's to the credit of Dearden that, while the English were congratulating themselves on their infinite fair-mindedness, he showed, in *Pool of London* (1950), a coloured seaman (Earl Cameron) who feels victim of race prejudice. After *Sapphire*, their *All Night Long* (1962) tries to show us how the coloured outsider feels. This jazz world transposition of *Othello* is probably reassuring for the white Englishman, in showing that not all coloured men are unstoppable big black bucks, and have psychosexual frailties too. Yet one can't help wishing for the story in 'negative', since sexual paranoia seems more characteristic of the British. Hence some spectators felt that the coloured man's role as victim dodged the crunch and wished upon the blacks a white insanity, *as well*.

4: Our Glorious Heritage

18. History is Bunk

Until about 1940 or so, British films occasionally deal with British history in a sombre, stoic and fairly realistic way. One thinks of such admirable productions of Michael Balcon's as *Tudor Rose* (Robert Stevenson, 1936) and *Rhodes of Africa* (Berthold Viertel, 1936), of Thorold Dickinson's *The Prime Minister* (1941). They don't suppose that the past is any more reassuring or inspiring than the present. They see history as political cut-and-thrust, as conflicts of interest, not infrequently cynical. The last film actually introduces the notion of social class, and shows the imperialist Tories dishing the industrialist Liberals by appealing to the lower-classes.

The rot sets in with the follow-up to Dickinson's film. Carol Reed's *The Young Mr. Pitt* (1942) sacrifices everything for the equation: Pitt (Robert Donat) = Churchill, Fox = the shilly-shallying Neville Chamberlain, Napoleon (pride of our French ally!) = Hitler. In other words it butchers the past to fit the present. If the mood of national unity with which it ends reflects 1940 it is also, of course, compatible with the establishment-favouring notion that in our island story all is always for the best. Not a word to the effect that Pitt was one of the most redoubtable enemies of British freedom of speech, that he used the Napoleonic threat as a pretext to suppress the traditional liberties of the Press, of meetings, and of speech, in his own party's interests, that he was more bitterly hated than any Prime Minister in history, and that, in the words of Professor G. M. Trevelyan, 'If Fox ... had gone over to Pitt ... the progress of British politics in the nineteenth century would very probably have been by

armed revolution and reaction instead of by Parliamentary Reform'. So much for the young Mr. Pitt.

This bias appears even in Robert S. Baker's and Monty Berman's *The Hellfire Club* (1960). It may seem strange to link this costume melodrama with anything so serious as history. But this very disimilarity underlines the point.

Jimmy Sangster and Leon Griffith's screenplay has the good legitimate brother (Keith Michell) being cheated out of his inheritance by the bad bastard (Peter Arne). He is consigned to prison and snatched there from by the gypsies, his childhood friends. He finally breaks into a Hellfire Club orgy, and exposes his wicked brother.

In the historical Hellfire Club one of the prominent 'Monks of Medmenham' was John Wilkes, Whig M.P. for Aylesbury. At this time, when Parliament was so corrupt that bribes had brought, or rather bought, it, under the control of George III, Wilkes defied the King, and was acknowledged as the champion, not only of free speech, but of the parliamentary principle, of the middle-classes, of the City of London, and of the common people. He was, indeed, the main focus of countervailing power to royal despotism. Prosecuted for obscenity, he was expelled from the House of Commons, and arrested. The public demonstrated outside his jail and the military shot six demonstrators. Even in prison, Wilkes's purse and connections enabled him to maintain his riotous life, while being three times re-elected to Parliament and three times re-expelled. He then became the first politician to hit on the technique of stumping the country to whip up support, and he succeeded in inflaming not only the British Isles but also the American colonies (so that he's a godfather to American independence). He became Lord Mayor of London in 1774, and won his case, in that the King's control of Parliament gradually wilted. His own democratic movement was split and broken in its turn when in 1780 he had to order troops to fire on anti-Catholic rioters. But his own example of personal courage and integrity was influential and lasting.

It is not my suggestion that all films about the Hellfire Club ought to be about Wilkes. It is that if Wilkes, as a defender of British liberties, had been as well known as he ought to be, then stories about the Hellfire Club would immediately take on a morally and socially more lively and complex approach.

Momma Don't Allow: Wood Green Jazz Club – Significant aesthetic limitations

What with jolly gypsies storming prisons on behalf of a dispossessed Lords' son, some vague idea of Wilkite agitation seems to be in Sangster's mind. But their role is a vigilante one of restoring a traditional hierarchy and morality: they're anti-Wilkes! Sangster's other films have relished moral ambivalence, as we shall see. But here he seems to have been paralysed by the weight and bias of school-room history, which consistently presents exactly the same distortion of history as this and *The Young Mr. Pitt*. The authoritarian forces are whitewashed, democratic forces blackwashed or forgotten.

The succeeding monarch was the subject of some criticism in Cavalcanti's *The First Gentleman* (1948), with its pointedly irreverent picture of George IV. The film industry, unwisely, as it turned out, selected it for a Royal Command Film Performance. Some people, it seems, were not at all amused. Any criticism of any English monarch who ever was could be felt as *lèse-majesté*. Yet so homely a volume as *Pears Cyclopaedia* comments on George IV's notoriety and unpopularity, and G. M. Trevelyan observes, 'The subjects of the land were in some doubt as to the Queen's character' (itself not above reproach), 'but in none at all about the King's. The fact that he was actually married to two women at once was not then generally known, though much suspected ...' As usual, the first casualty of respectability is truth, and simple, sturdy, bulldog common sense had lost a great many teeth since Korda's *The Private Life of Henry VIII* in 1933 gave Laughton's rascally Henry some spiritual affinities with James Cagney in *Public Enemy* the year before.

The treatment of the Irish question is even more outrageous. From Relph and Dearden's *The Gentle Gunman* (1952) via Michael Anderson's *Shake Hands with the Devil* (1959) through to Tay Garnett's *A Terrible Beauty* (1959), Eire's attainment of independence is presented exclusively in terms of the Irish struggling against their own tendency to violence. All three films contrast the I.R.A. fanatic who goes on killing sprees or allies himself with the Nazis, with the reasonable sort of fellow whose manly kindness ends in his opting out of resistance altogether. The Black and Tans are conspicuous by their absence – except insofar as English officers tend to be nastily stern rather than firmly stern – and of course there's silence about those historical facts which weighed so heavily on the English conscience that this country was split wide open on the Home Rule issue.

The earlier films see conflict and cynicism as part of history, as of the present. The late films, corresponding to the fifties apogee of the middle-class vision, concur with it in worshipping tradition (i.e. what, of the old order, survived) so as to forget history (what *happened*). Change is seen as coming from *within* the tradition; those who, from the outside, forced it to change are vilified or forgotten.

A sense of the past as unjust and bad returns with Richardson's *Tom Jones*. Molly Seagrim's cottage isn't a pretty thatched affair suitable for an Antique Shoppe tea-cosy.

19. The Impotence of Being Earnest

Art, being another aspect of prestige, dissolves in the same pea-souper. Charles Oakley neatly summarizes an important reason for the British industry's difficulty in maintaining its home market. 'Following Beerbohm Tree's example – and suitably enticed no doubt by high fees – many prominent players of the Edwardian theatre acted for the pictures. This now seems ill-advised. What, one wonders, did audiences in the industrial halls make of Sir Johnstone Forbes-Robertson and Sir Frank Benson in potted silent versions of Shakespeare's plays? ... Stock melodramas, *East Lynne*, *Maria Marten* and *The Lights of London* would have been more to the taste of the bulk of the picture-goers of those times. But the British cinema – or at least a considerable proportion of it – was set on rising socially.'

Within our period, Laurence Olivier's *Henry V* (1944) is a case in point. Its *raisons d'être* are the prestige of Shakespeare, a big battle, a rousing jingoism and a shaky parallel to contemporary events. Henry V invades France as Eisenhower was about to invade *Festung Europa*. Afterwards he marries a French Princess in a 'United Europe' spirit, although whether France here = France our ally, to whom Churchill had in 1940 impulsively proposed 'marriage', or Germany our enemy whom we musn't hate for ever, is quite ambiguous.

As the more thoughtful critics of the time pointed out, *Henry V* is the fourth and last play of a series which concerns the aftermath of the Wars of the Roses. Its worries are (*a*) the Tudors' legal and or moral right to the throne, (*b*) civil war, and (*c*) the challenge to medieval morality (e.g. Hotspur's chivalry) by a new realism (e.g. Henry's Machiavellian tricks on the battlefield). *Henry V* is Shakespeare's affirmation of Tudor claims, but the affirmation depends on constantly uneasy overtones about Henry's amoral realism – e.g. his real or apparent cynicism about his father's authority, about Falstaff, about international law, about the church, about his duty to his own subjects. The last play offers an answer to these moral misgivings. The new code, also, has its conscience (instead of civil war, patriotism; instead of chivalry, concern for one's soldiers; instead of ecclesiastical authority, friendship with France). Cut it loose from the preceding plays, and it becomes simply a series of rhetorical affirmations.

On the most obvious level, we have Falstaff's death scene – with almost nothing else of Falstaff. Equally strange is the scene in which Henry decides to invade France while cynically shrugging off all legal and moral rights and wrongs. It presumably shocked, but jingoistically delighted, Elizabethan audiences. In 1944 it seems to paraphrase the tough young man's tricking of Blimp, and to assert, on behalf of British tradition, a life-force matching Nazi Germany's. Giving, in so doing, the jingoism moral licence. This is how Hitler might have talked to Roman Catholic bishops. In any case, the English *lost* France.

With immense instinct, resource and intelligence, Olivier compensates for the play's shattered structure by a Pirandellian one. First we are shown the play opening in an Elizabethan theatre. A few scenes later, we are switched to 'exteriors' which set the actors against back-cloths modelled on medieval perspective. The very cinematic battle scene is altogether realistic. Bold and inventive as it is, such *Hellzapoppin*ry tempts one to a *reductio ad absurdum*. The film could have begun with a platoon of Poor Bloomin' Infantry recruits being shown the movie in a training camp. Then we move through the movie they're watching to the studio where the sets are being built. Then Sir Larry enters and plays a scene before a camera from behind which he emerges to shake hands with the actor who is playing Shakespeare sitting down to write the play, and informs him that his part has been cut out of the movie. For the film isn't about the historical Henry V, or even about Shakespeare's idea of Henry V. It's about *The Demi-Paradise*, Britain as happy home of poets and warriors alike. It remains interesting as a series of visual and verbal set pieces.

A very nice old gentleman once told me how successfully it brought Shakespeare to the masses. At the Marble Arch Pavilion, into which teachers crocodiled their pupils for morning matinees, the film regularly had to be stopped after the first fifteen minutes. He would tell the children to quieten down and pay attention, and explain to them what a very great privilege it was for them to be able to hear great verse magnificently rendered. Even if they couldn't appreciate it, maybe the person behind them was trying to, so why didn't they play the game and make the most of this marvellous opportunity? They always quietened down after that, and they really enjoyed the battle scenes.

Hamlet (1948) is faithful to Shakespeare's form, and, in its academic way has some very powerful atmospherics. It's a fascinating *version* of Shakespeare. But Jean Renoir's comment pinpoints its limitations. 'You feel dizzy when you look down from a great height. So what? What has that to do with Shakespeare?' We might have felt less dizzy if the film hadn't tried so hard to turn Hamlet into a Douglas Fairbanks hero who temporarily just can't make up his mind. But since *Hamlet* isn't a modern liberal, he considers none of the liberal problems, and the film shunts itself into a cultural limbo again. The nearest to the liberal *Hamlet* is Dickinson's *Secret People*.

The style of *Richard III* (1955) was admirably summarized by two Cockney lads studying the poster: 'Cor, look! Four Sirs in one picture!' Distinguished actors speak Shakespeare's least distinguished verse with great style and at great length. Olivier-Richard confides in, and winks at, the audience like Groucho in *Animal Crackers* parodying Eugene O'Neill's *Strange Interlude*. The soliloquies are never an easy nut for films to crack (though Welles's erratic *Macbeth* triumphs here), but this solution seems to suggest that the whole thing's a great high camp gag, along with the hump back and nose; the addition of a ukelele would turn Richard III into a medieval Tiny Tim. Claire Bloom alone gives her character any psychological solidity (possibly because, not yet being Dame Claire Bloom, she can't afford to coast along quite so easily). A nice, bright battle scene is weakened by its syntactical confusion, and, all in all, it lacks the atmospheric qualities of its predecessors.

And yet, when one's irreverence has wreaked its worst upon Olivier's Shakespeare, from a quarter of a century's distance, another interpretation of their hollownesses begins to appear, which may one day vindicate them. Their lack of conviction results, not only from Olivier's acquiescence in the spirit of their age, but from a scepticism which is not quite aware of itself. For what Olivier treats with unconscious criticism is both the film medium, and the plays. The shifting stylizations of *Henry V* oddly prefigure Godard's use of the non-realistic, the non-conviction of life seen through the filter of an art which distorts (the medieval perspectives). The theme Olivier saw in *Hamlet* is a Godardian one – '*Hamlet* is the story of a man who cannot make up his mind' – and its surface conventionality is belied by something in Olivier's screen personality, something hard, stony, resentful, something that rebels, from within, against Hamlet's sensitivity, because it sees through it, as a Commissar or a Castro might have seen through it. If Richard III confides to the audience, it is because Olivier has gone half way to converting him from villain to hero; only a little more cynicism would have been needed for Machiavellian realpolitik to have cut through the whole iridescent spider-web of Tudor propaganda. Behind all these plays looms the shadowy figure of – *The Entertainer*. Which helps to explain why these strange films, with their interpenetration of energies and hollows, make so much more impact than the far more correct Castellani version of *Romeo and Juliet* (1954), with its warm Renaissance interiors, or the stylistic puffs and curls of Shakespeare à la Zeffirelli.

Another kind of muddle presides over Peter Brook's *The Beggar's Opera* (1953). One can see what sold Herbert Wilcox on the project. All the ingredients abound for a glorious gallimaufry of Gainsborough melodrama (highwaymen, hangings, tarts and sluts), *Oklahoma* gaiety, and cultural prestige. It promises something for everybody, for the cap and muffler trade, the carriage trade, the distaff side, the highbrow and the lowbrow, not to mention the yeomen and the bowmen.

John Gay's play was the smash hit of its time (1728). It ran to forty performances (the usual run being one, two or rarely three). Its picture of underworld life was realistic (Peachum is based on Jonathan Wild, MacHeath on Jack Shepherd). It was full of tough underworld terms ('bamboozled', 'the jade is tipsy') which was the argot of its day and put its fascinated audience

The Entertainer: Laurence Olivier – The interpenetration of energies behind his many roles

bang to rights about underworld slang. It's also full of political allusions which the audience understood so clearly that its sequel, *Polly* (1729), was banned. MacHeath is Marlborough, Churchill's ancestor, then Prime Minister, and Peachum, who makes so much of his careful accounting, personifies the trading middle-classes for whom Gay had a typical Tory disdain. As William Empson shows, the constant similarities between statesmen and crooks, between the underworld and high office, make this an extremely cynical satire. To make a highwayman a hero was as shocking as to romanticize a razor-slasher would have been in 1952 – it was this play which made highwaymen romantic. Yet it is as cynical as a play which showed Westminster politics as arrangements between the Kray twins and the Richardson gang. It debunks society (Man is the only beast of prey that is a sociable animal'). It debunks bourgeois morality (when Polly's parents accuse her of being an undutiful daughter because she loves a criminal, she replies that she is 'honourably' out to get his money). It debunks love, which is either lust ('I must have women!' cries MacHeath) or a morbid thrill ('women think every man handsome who goes either to the camp or to the gallows'). In sum, the play suggests, thieves are more honourable than respectable folk, because they are less hypocritical. In spirit, Gay's piece is far nearer Brecht's adaptation of it (*The Three-Ha'penny Opera*) than a romantic piece like *West Side Story* (which it resembles in being a musical about a violence-ridden capital).

The movie bowdlerizes all this into a Gilbert and Sullivan romp. One has the impression of distinguished people from the West End theatre condescending (*a*) to make a film, and (*b*) to be light-hearted, while, (*c*) in passing, showing everybody how easy it is to be both cultural and popular. Result? elementary errors abound. The burlesque is allowed to kill the straight excitement. The acting tries to be both spirited and sensitive; but the spiritedness becomes stagey over-playing, the sensitivity turns fidgety, especially as the actors have to mime operetta singing while pretending to be realistically acting. Much of the acting engenders in this spectator a sense of physical discomfort. Whimsical prettification afflicts Christopher Fry's and Denis Cannan's dialogue, which, striving for Elizabethan gusto, just sounds twee. The actors fence as if banging hockey sticks, and the director's style has quotes from all the Best Films. Yet Kurt Weill's songs (*Mack the Knife*) suggest a really filmic key: a quiet, smooth under-played 'cabaret' style. The combination of the sardonic and the humorous recalls also, the deadpan of *The Big Sleep*. The Gainsborough elements needed a certain dramatic tension: jollification sabotages not only the dramatic interest, but the humour too. Behind the jollification is a fatal assumption of cultural superiority.

Various film versions of Wilde find a simpler and happier style. If Asquith's *The Importance of Being Earnest* has the lightest, deftest, suavest acting, the Hyde Park Corner 'overture' of Alexander Korda's *An Ideal Husband* (1947), is a supremely lavish expression of that Victorian High Summer. The styles and hypocrisies which are Wilde's butts are now, of course, extinct, and the films contrive to be gently nostalgic for older styles and graces. Nostalgia, too, progressively weakens the adaptations from Dickens. *Great Expectations*, clearly rich in nostalgic elements, balances them by its brutalities, and is undoubtedly a great movie. Its successor, *Oliver Twist* (1948), begins impressively, with its harrowing opening and the grimly atmospheric workhouse decor. Thereafter a thousand little softenings and jollifications impel the film on its downward curve, from jolly Bumble to jolly Fagin and, almost, jolly Bill Sykes.

But the apotheosis, or nadir, of jollification is plumbed by Ronald Neame's *The Horse's Mouth* (1959), after Joyce Cary's novel. Not that its account of an artistic life is devoid of sincerity. John Bratby, 'ghost' for the painter who is the film's hero, remarked 'There is the producer. He is with us. He was one of us once and still is ... Then there is the director. I never really found out whether he is with us; difficult to tell ...' Alas, *The Horse's Mouth* gets the wrong end of the horse.

Alec Guinness, who also wrote the script, portrays Gulley Jimson as a sort of thin, male Margaret Rutherford. Instead of meeting defeat and death with racy stoicism, like Cary's, the film's simperingly dotty Gully goes drifting downriver like Barnacle Bill, more eccentric suburban Sunday sea-dog than heir of William Blake. In a few brief scenes between Gulley and Coker the patient nobility, the humiliated tender strength of the woman, is movingly caught. Cary's deft literary equivalent for an artist's eye ('sun like an orange in a fried fish shop') is altogether lost in this banally bright England with its jolly art students throwing stones at the uncouth workmen. Ah, youth, and its sweetly idealistic lost causes. It's no accident that its one imaginative moment is reactionary in spirit – Gulley, about to paint an empty wall, wraps himself in a pink eiderdown and suddenly looks like a Cardinal. Though the film will have nothing to do with anything so sordid as jostling over frypans in dosshouses it's quick with a gratuitous image of traditional 'prestige'. It collapses, really, because all concerned are terrified of being too solemn about art. But one is never solemn where one is serious; and this facetiousness is only earnestness inverted, and just as impotent.

After Laurence Olivier and Peter Brook, Peter Ustinov completes a trio of theatrical talent which, for all its undoubted sensitivity and intelligence, has yet to do itself justice on film. In Ustinov's case it's less surprising, since he constantly argues that the cinema isn't an art form at all. After an engaging and observant comedy about boffins (*School for Secrets*, 1946), his *Vice Versa* (1947) is a high camp adaptation of F. W. Anstey's Edwardian farce about heavy fathers, flagellomanic headmasters, blustering imperialism, and all the rest of the nineteenth-century *olla podrida*. But it isn't very daring, in 1947, to satirize the Boer War. If the brilliant opening sequences have the seed of goonery, the rest is stony ground. By 1945, the educational tone has completely shifted away from the thunderous and paranoiad authoritarianism of a Grimsdyke, and there's far more relevance to the sweetly blind complacencies which are the butt of real satirical observation in Launder and Gilliat's *The Happiest Days of Your Life* (1950). Indeed, *Vice Versa* marks a blunting of irreverence, compared to pre-war movies. The satire on imperialism is no more virulent than in *Old Bones of the River* (Marcel Varnel, 1938) and the notion of a Victorian paterfamilias having to see junior's point of view is treated more simply and effectively in Will Hay's first feature, *Those Were the Days* (Thomas Bentley, 1934), itself a version of Pinero's *The Magistrate*. Here the switching mechanism is not a stone but a night at the music hall, and pater, a J.P., has to share the code of men of the world with the adopted son whom he wanted to keep a perpetual child.

Ustinov's next film is an anti-war tragicomedy, *Private Angelo* (co-directed with Michael Anderson, 1949), after Eric Linklater's novel. Ustinov plays Angelo as a reluctant Italian anti-hero with a cuddlesome, hapless affability, meekly yet obstinately civilized in the face of all war's ironies and insults. An American director might have handled it in a sharper, blacker vein, somewhere between Sturges's *Hail the Conquering Hero* and Wilder's *Stalag 17*. Twenty years later, many a man of the London theatre would have struggled for a Brechtian irony. Ustinov's softer handling is as appropriate, but is also more tentative. The film is wistful, quite sensitive, yet forgettable, the shifts and shades of mood on the pallid side. Maybe two directors cancelled out; maybe a search for something as light as the Lubitsch touch ended in listlessness. Certainly it seems uncertainly caught as between neo-realism and Anglicized Italianness (that trickiest of conventions). Eventually it settles for sentimental clichés about peasant simplicities, while Italy's unwarlike gifts to the world are symbolized by shots of church towers (as if Jesus were an Italian, or as if the Roman Catholic Church played strenuously pacifist roles during wars, or as if either had any special relevance to the loveable cravenness of human nature).

Ustinov, amiably at home everywhere, cosmopolitan and convivial, chameleonic yet unalienated, seems, in his films and other entertainments, to be making very friendly and likeable little forays, often satiric, never unkind, into the skins and minds of those trapped, as he is not, within their station, situation, or mental convention. Privileged by his sensitive benevolence, he attenuates into wistfulness the real shock and jolt of constriction and rebellion. If a common theme seems to link all his films, it is the moral triumph of weakness over strength, of the mediocre man over the forces around him, including, even, the forces of mediocrity. More strongly worked, this amiably anti-Nietzschean proposition might have been yin to the yang of another immune and versatile outsider, Orson Welles. Yet Ustinov confronts the film medium without the experiential pressure, the fixations and visions, which make an auteur. On internal evidence of style, any of his films could be attributed to any of many sensible British directors.

His nearest to an individual touch would be dialogue which is witty without ceasing to be gentle. It's a writer's quality rather than a director's, and one may be reminded of another director, whose work was, at its best, inspired by, and, more often, indulgent to, a wistfulness about things French – a wistfulness a little too pale, dry and sensible (sceptical?) to be a romanticism. Robert Hamer's *Kind Hearts and Coronets* recalls at once Oscar Wilde and Sacha Guitry, and, in its suave, sharp insolence, is the most brilliant, and the least typical, of Ealing comedies. That English admiration for suave amorality, labelled 'typically French', appears also in *The Spider and the Fly* (1949), where a sophisticated French policeman pursues a sophisticated French thief. In Hamer's adaptation of G. K. Chesterton's *Father Brown* (1954), the bland and wily priest (Alec Guinness) pursues the slightly less bland and wily jewel thief through France to his childhood home. The mixture of English detective story and French Catholic novel is quite agreeable. In *To Paris with Love* (1954), Alec Guinness gets all tangled up in tennis nets in an adorable pastiche of slow-motion slapstick *à la* Tati. The aristocratic French provide the background also for his version of Daphne du Maurier's *The Scapegoat* (1958). Though the British climate bowdlerised Arthur La Bern's novel, *It Always Rains on Sunday*, Hamer conferred on it a sensitive melancholy reminiscent of French populism, while the pastel melancholy of *The Long Memory* (1952) is at least a pale afterglow of *Le Quai des brumes*.

20. The Doctored Documentary

The documentaries of the thirties raised the banners of reality and 'social consciousness' which they opposed, with good reason, to the trashy glamour of the commercial fiction film.

But what is reality? and what constitutes an accurate awareness of society?

The merits and limitations of the documentary movement are aptly summarized by William Empson's remarks on *Drifters* (directed by John Grierson, founding father and major impresario of the British documentary, in 1929). 'The Englishman who seems to me nearest a proletarian artist (of those I know anything about) is Grierson the film producer. *Drifters* gave very vividly the feeling of actually living on a herring trawler and (by the beauty of shapes of water and net and fish, and subtleties of timing and so forth) what I should call a pastoral feeling about the dignity of that form of labour ... But ... for all its government-commercial claim to solid usefulness it is a "high-brow" picture (that blasting word shows an involuntary falseness in the thing): Grierson's influence, strong and healthy as it is, has something skimpy about it ... a pastoral feeling ... in an English artist, whatever his personal sincerity ... seems dogged by humbug, and has done now for a long time.'

In other words, perhaps, Grierson makes herring trawling *idyllic*: bracing, no doubt, and dangerous, but in the sense that mountaineering is bracing and dangerous. One might imagine films which saw the herring industry in the terms of, say, Céline's *Journey to the End of the Night*; or Robert Tressell's *The Ragged Trousered Philanthropists*: or the whole range of attitudes between these two poles. The humbug Empson scents is, I suspect, a specifically British middle-class variety. *Drifters* has been to sea, but on a first mate's ticket; or not even that; for it is also a public relations job; it's been to sea as a canny and original advertising copy-writer has been to sea. It imbues your breakfast kipper with that extra added attractive ingredient: Romance, without even the pessimism of that schoolroom classic, *Caller Herrin'*.

It's not in *Drifters*, in Flaherty's *Industrial Britain* (1931) or *Man of Aran* (1934), in Basil Wright's *The Song of Ceylon* (1934), in Harry Watt's *Night Mail* (1936) or Michael Powell's *The Edge of the World* (1937) that any echo of the grim thirties is to be found. On the contrary. They are romantic tone poems about the beauty of work and industry, strenuously conformist to their 'establishment' sponsors (usually the G.P.O. or the Empire Marketing Board). *Industrial Britain* includes the notorious commentary: 'So you see things are not as black as they seem ... behind the smoke beautiful things are being made ... truly beautiful things like these aerodrome lenses ... they stand for the tradition of English craftsmanship and skill ... experts say it will take other countries many generations to catch up ... dress these men in Italian costumes and you might take them for Venetian glassworkers of the sixteenth century ...' This, in full Depression!

This hear-no-evil, speak-no-evil, see-no-evil idyll is parodied almost word for word in Jacques Prévert's script for *Les Amants de Vérone* (1948), where Serge Reggiani as a Venetian glassworker of the twentieth century, who knows the work is gradually destroying his lungs, cynically mutters the patter of a tourists' guide: '*ces modestes ouvriers qui semblent venir droit d'un tableau d'Uccelle ...*'

Doubtless hamstrung by their sponsors, doubtless hoping that to sing the dignity of work might strengthen the pride and therefore the bloody-mindedness of the workers, our documentarists nonetheless made film after film parading the picturesque beauties of industry: the austere beauty of black chimneys and white smoke, the noble, toil worn hands of the old craftsmen (already anachronisms in a mass production era), happy workmen enjoying their cuppa char, steam locomotives shovelling white smoke over their shoulder ...

Industrial Britain, at least, strives to remind one of the men within the machine. It even has one sweaty, even, briefly, angry-looking worker, and it is on his face (though not at its most protesting) that it ends. But to take the craftsmanship of the old men as typical in the era of mass production and repetition; to take the highest rungs of the 'labour aristocracy' as typical of the working man; to ignore every tension of industrial psychology; to dose everything with lashings of proud, stirring 'Sons of the Sea'-type music and to lace it with a commentary whose mincingly brisk accent, and words, imply the values, of a Greek scholar-cum-brigadier, sitting on his shooting stick and squinting through a view-finder to get the right shine of sun on cloud, and occasionally peeping at his loyal lads through the wrong end of his opera-glasses; to perpetrate such editorial comment is deliberately to edulcorate the handful of mining shots which endow the dignity of labour with the degradations of toil and to blunt the nimble fluidity with which Flaherty anticipates by thirty years, the hand-held camera.

Night Mail can easily be read as: 'Railway Wonders of the World: The Daily Miracle Of How You Receive Your Morning Post.' The sub-title of *Industrial Britain* is: 'Romance of Modern Industry: Medieval Spirit Endures in Midst of Progress.' *The Song of Ceylon* is pure *National Geographic Magazine*: 'Sacred Isle's Harmony of Ancient Faith and Modern Bustle.' By shaping itself around a commentary written in 1680, the last film suggests that imperialism brings no disturbances to traditional cultures, introduces no new problems; it is, quite simply, an imperialist pastorale.

Far from being progressive, these films are, in spirit, just what they were intended to be: literally speaking, commercials, for the E.M.B., or the G.P.O., or any other part of the Establishment, and, therefore, for the *status quo* of – of all periods – the thirties. True, more complacent films might have been made; but that's hardly a very positive recommendation. Grierson affected to despise, and probably did, aesthetes and intellectuals, and congratulated himself on having fooled them. Empson, at least, had his number right away; and it's for their purely aesthetic qualities that only the very best documentaries will abide.

All the more honour then to those rare documentaries which forgo the emphasis on work as part of a harmonious social system and see it as a human experience for those engaged. In Cavalcanti's *Coal Face,* formal devices which, on paper, sound dreadfully pretentious work perfectly, at least for a highbrow audience. A choir chants statistics, facts, simple statements, wails in the style of a Greek tragic chorus as a lump of coal crumbles under the pick, asserts the cost of all this in human anguish. More direct still is Arthur Elton's and Edgar Anstey's *Housing Problems* (1935). Its sponsors, the Gas Board, wanting to sell more gas fires and stoves, had a vested interest in raising the slums and building better houses. The film-makers' documentary technique, inspired perhaps by Mass Observation, anticipates much that is best in cinéma vérité and touches the personal suffering and family intimacies of the proletariat.[33]

There are other such films – Anstey's *Enough to Eat?* (1936), Ralph Bond and Ruby Grierson's *Today and Tomorrow* (1937). They are few, and the

Coal Face: Potentially pretentious formal devices working perfectly together

Housing Problems: The dreadful fascination of a killjoy caretaker; inspired by Mass Observation and touching personal suffering

documentarists and critics of the time (and they are often the same people) surely emphasized the ideological contradictions. It was enough for these people that a film was *about* society – whether it was conformist or critical didn't matter in the least. All that mattered was that the audience should be taught something, if only the austere beauty of smogscapes. This is the attitude of a schoolmaster who doesn't mind what opinion his pupils hold so long as their heads are stuffed with facts. But if *Night Mail* is social consciousness, then *Railway Wonders of the World* is social consciousness. From a social point of view, *Song of Ceylon* is as superficial as a geography text-book with a lot of pretty photographs. It is a beautifully made film, and to say that its beauty is that of the most complacent middle-class romanticism is not to dismiss it. There is, after all, some overlap between such an attitude and real life. But let us be clear exactly what the film's qualities are; and that these qualities typify the underlying urge of thirties documentaries.

The documentary's one and only period of genuine public popularity coincided with the stiffened human pride, and the national solidarity, inspired by World War II. *London Can Take It!* (Humphrey Jennings and Harry Watt, 1940), with its poignant blitz images and its jingoistic commentary, may seem 'conformist' now. But this combination of attitudes was highly relevant and necessary then. Even so, as often with documentaries, we have to accept that its 'documentary' purpose is secondary to propaganda, i.e. inspiring half-truths, almost, fiction. At this time English fiction films were even less sober in tone, although they, too, may have learned sobriety from real life as well as from, or rather than from, a documentary film influence.

At any rate *London Can Take It!*, and a stream of successors, *Target for To-night* (Harry Watt, 1941), *Coastal Command* (J. B. Holmes, 1942), *Desert Victory* (Roy Boulting, 1943), *Fires Were Started* (Humphrey Jennings, 1943), *San Demetrio London* (Charles Frend, 1943), *Western Approaches* (Pat Jackson, 1944), *The True Glory* (Carol Reed, 1945), *Theirs Is the Glory* (Brian Desmond Hurst, 1946), and *Burma Victory* (Roy Boulting, 1945), mirrored authentic public attitudes and established the stiff-upper-lip-war-is-an-ugly-job-which-just-has-to-be-done tradition which was at first the backbone, and then the straitjacket of the British war film until 1959. Seen in the late sixties, the early films surpass their post-war counterparts primarily in newsreel authenticity. A certain laconicism, or the use of real people instead of character actors, to much the same purpose, or the simpleness of action and sentiment, is often effective. But they don't eclipse *The Cruel Sea*, or *The Dam Busters*, or *Dunkirk*, or those war films with moral problems.

The 'asceticism' represented by documentaries reached its peak during the dark years 1940-3. From 1944 on private emotions took first place again, in films as diverse as Korda's *Perfect Strangers* (1945) and Gilliat's *Waterloo Road* (1945). With the interest in post-war reconstruction, the documentary movement seemed destined to flourish. Carol Reed's *The Way Ahead* (1944) exemplifies a popular and admirable marriage of documentary integrity and of fictional warmth. The Ministry of Information's wartime trailers range from cartoons like *Dustbin Parade* to the cameos of daily woes by Richard Massingham, each ten times as funny and twenty times as true as their American equivalent, the one-reel Joe McDoakes comedies. The white hope of the movement was Humphrey Jennings, who put aside his activities as surrealist poet and musician to direct such fresh and touching films as *Listen to Britain*, *Words for Battle*, *Fires Were Started* and *A Diary for Timothy*.

Yet documentary was the big disappointment of the post-war period. Its apologists have blamed everyone else (the sponsors, the monopolies, the public, the Labour Government, the Conservative Government), and in our short survey it is impossible to consider all the possible reasons or permutations of reasons – why, for example, an offer by a documentarists' co-operative, formed before the war ended, to provide programmes for the circuits, was rejected. Nor is it possible to consider films which were never in fact produced – for they would all have been masterpieces.

Certainly post-war problems (austerity, Work or Want, bread and fuel rationing) queered the documentarists' pitch. But the documentarists themselves disappointed their warmest admirers. *Sequence* criticized Humphrey Jennings's *The Cumberland Story* (1948) and Jill Craigie's *Blue Scar* (two pictures of miners' work-problems and lives), as dreary and stilted. Perhaps, after all, Jennings's warmly sharp glance is a matter of the lyrical vignette, of a response to faces and moods, which isn't extended through structures of lives and relationships, or even ordinary dramatic modulations. He seems more at ease with the gentle upper-middle-class liberalism of *A Diary for Timothy,* for which venerable Edwardian novelist E. M. Forster contributed an astoundingly Mrs. Miniverish commentary, or with the schoolroom rhetoric of *Words for Battle.* A classical music concert becomes the centre-piece of *Listen to Britain* whereas vulgar cultural things like dance halls deserve only three or four shots. A Tory cultural vision like James Agate's could have been more populist. To make these points is not to contest Jennings's genius; merely to say that its perspective is upper-middle-class-middlebrow. That it marks, by concentrating on people, an advance on Griersonism goes without saying.

Perennially, of course, the establishment's tame romantics pumped away. Ralph Keene's *A String of Beads* (1947), John Eldridge's *Three Dawns to Sydney* (1949), Basil Wright and Bill Launder's *Waters of Time* (1951) all dissolve whatever dramatic (let alone social) impact they might have had in their sub-Fordian celebration of airlines and Empire, filtered clouds and noble peasants. They are so uplifting as to be wearying, as picturesque as empty. *Cyprus Is an Island* (Ralph Keene, 1946) is far more inelegant and introduces a social problem. It is also a little dull, and suggests that no development out of the British documentary spirit would ever have produced neo-realism.

A new approach pokes tentatively out in a tiny group of films, notably Jack Lee's *Children on Trial* (1946), Paul Dickson's *The Undefeated* (1950) and *David* (1951), and Philip Leacock's *Out of True* (1951). They find their inspiration not in schoolmasterish beautifying of superficialities, but in sociology; charting new attitudes to crime, to nursing, to mental illness, to a Welsh miner's renunciation of his poetic vocation for the sake of his wife and child. Here was a more fertile soil, both for the redemption of documentary, and for its merging with fiction traditions. Such tasks could have led to a responsible questioning of the consensus, to richer treatments of social issues, and their relationship to human experience in its fullest depth. But the new school, however, hardly shakes itself free from the view of the common man as oakenhearted in his pious simplicities. There is a significant contrast, not only with the sense of *temptation* in the ordinary fiction feature, but with most people's awareness of human weakness, meanness and nastiness.

The documentarists are interested in people only insofar as they are well adjusted citizens. Documentary banishes, or piously deprecates, rather than satisfyingly plunging into, the vulgar, or morally ugly, like conflicts of ill-feeling, let alone such *infra dig* topics as sexuality, violence, vulgarity; in short, the soul. It must fail when it comes to contacting the experiences and preferences of the common man whom it fondly imagines it reveres.

There lies a major, perhaps even a sufficient, reason, for the strange curse lying on our documentarists' ventures into fiction. Roy Boulting, Anthony Asquith and Carol Reed had made fiction films before turning to the wartime documentary, and quit documentary as soon, it seems, as they could. Ian Dalrymple, executive producer at the Crown Film Unit during the war years, had previously worked with Korda; he makes the bravest attempt at applying the documentary spirit of responsibility to post-war problems. John Grierson, while executive producer of Group 3 (1950–5), offered mainly sub-Ealing comedies so timid as to be positively ingratiating, and Group 3's best movies with their modest virtues break no new ground. Paul Rotha's one memorable feature, *No Resting Place* (1950) brings a sharply neo-realistic tone to the romantic shroud which usually envelopes Gaelic peasants. Among B features of limited resources his *The Life of Adolf Hitler* shockedly informs us that Horst Wessel was a homosexual. So what? What does that prove about Nazism? Given this moralising, this rhetoric, it's obvious why the film is so incoherent in its social perspectives, alongside, say Erwin Leiser's *Mein Kampf*. Ralph Keene's and Ralph Smart's *A Boy, a Girl and a Bike* (1949) is a run-of-the-mill cross-section of a cycling club. Pat Jackson returned from a long Hollywood limbo to make *White Corridors* (1951), which has, indeed, a feeling of potential tragedy rare in hospital films. But by 1961 he could do little but inject a sensitive melancholy into a few scenes in an antediluvian farce, *What a Carve Up*. Paul Dickson rapidly plummeted to sub-zero science-fiction like *Satellite in the Sky* (1956). Almost the only documentary-formed directors to pursue successful careers in ordinary feature fiction were Jack Lee, who followed several films for Dalrymple at Wessex with *Circle of Deception* and *The Captain's Table*, and Philip Leacock, who capped his series of restrained children's subjects with *Reach for Glory* and essayed a 'slice of life' subject, theatrically, in Hollywood (*Let No Man Write My Epitaph*).

The other prong of documentary influence is, of course, into Ealing Studios. Such films as Harry Watt's *Nine Men* (1942) and *The Overlanders* (1946), and Charles Frend's *San Demetrio London* (1943) and *The Cruel Sea*

(1952), typify various mixtures of documentary and fiction elements. The omnibus films owe something to the documentarists' sense of society as a network of individuals, and the location settings, of which contemporary critics made too much fuss, derive from documentary precepts. Yet it's possible to see the formula's rapid fossilization as due to the documentary ingredient. The stiff upper lip is one thing, but lockjaw is another. The omnibus movies allow their characters to draw only regulation breaths. As Agee spotted, Ealing man is mini-man.

It may well be that Balcon's great period will eventually be seen to be, not the Ealing years, but his pre-war career. The earlier films accept quite naturally that society is not just a system where there's a place for everyone and everyone in his place, but a series of collisions between private wills and destinies. Paul Stein's *Poison Pen* (1939), a bleak story prefiguring Clouzot's *Le Corbeau* (1943) exemplifies the range of feeling excluded by Ealing. An admirably integrated omnibus story (each family has its own dirty linen), it sees society as a network of individuals whose souls must be hidden from society, and whose common interests are spiritually none too meaningful. It's a sad irony that the more critical atmosphere of the late fifties restored a sense of tension to Ealing's view of society and prompted such films as *Dunkirk* and *The Long and the Short and the Tall* – suggesting that Ealing is a phase in, rather than a climax of, Balcon's distinguished career.[34]

The most interesting attempt to turn the documentary spirit to the serious study of social and personal tensions, critically ignored then, and virtually forgotten now, was that of Ian Dalrymple's Wessex Films (still that pastoral title goads one to ask: why not Lambeth Films?). Apart from films already mentioned, like *Once a Jolly Swagman*, *All Over the Town* and *The Woman in the Hall*, Ian Dalrymple and Peter Proud's *Esther Waters* (1948) from George Moore's Zolaesque novel, might have been an English *Gervaise*. The fifties see Wessex retreat to more conventional subjects, encouraged by the box-office success of Jack Lee's *The Wooden Horse* (1950). But Julian Amyes's *A Hill in Korea* (1956 – two years too late for maximum box-office impact) gets as far as admitting, briefly, the possibility, of squaddies being uneasy about their leaders.

Yet, why is it that, in terms of immediate, lively, bold involvement, Ealing's pro-gentry *The Titfield Thunderbolt* eclipses Wessex's anti-gentry *All*

Over the Town, Two Cities' *Hungry Hill* eclipses *Esther Waters,* a costume subject like *Great Expectations* eclipses the more contemporary 'parasite' subject, *The Woman in the Hall,* the mischievous melancholy of Alec Guinness eclipses Wessex's more serious study of middle-class depression, *Dear Mr. Prohack,* and the American *Champion* and *The Set-Up* eclipse *Once a Jolly Swagman?*

A film's moral, social attitudes and themes are only part of a film's full meaning, and they are reached through the thrills, fun and inventiveness expressed in the overt, personal story. If on this level the escapist-conformist movies are more sensitive, or more expansive, than their Wessex equivalents, it's because they can shift and swing with the tide of everybody's easy assumptions. The Wessex movies, cutting a little nearer the quick, and against the middle-class grain, smuggle in challenges as if they were modifications, reduce them to doubts and suspicions, deny themselves the bold defiance that makes even the unhappy story exhilarating, the scandal through which the life-force can express itself against convention, the robust bang and swing of outrage and counter-outrage, all the energy needed if norms are to be called entertainingly into question. Wessex movies are nice but not naughty, a little too earnest, a little too glum, a little cowed by conscience. A little too solemn to scoop up handfuls of libido and hurl them against the way things are, a little too commercial to rival *Bicycle Thieves,* they lack the depth, the bloody-mindedness, the cathartic power, of the European cinema's four bold melodramas of honest toil: Dmytryk's *Give Us This Day* (made in England, but, by our definition, hardly an English film, with its American theme, setting and artists), De Santis's *Bitter Rice,* Clouzot's *Le Salaire de la peur* and Clément's *Gervaise.*[35]

The question imposes itself, how far the Free Cinema documentaries of the fifties represent a first breakthrough by a newer cinema, and how far they represent a last, late flowering of the Grierson spirit – an effort at renewal, creditable, useful, yet, in itself, doomed to failure, and beneficiary of, rather than contributory to, a renewal which would have occurred equally well without it.

Just as Grierson's gifts as polemicist and PR man in critic's clothing earned sponsored documentaries their rarely merited reputation for gritty integrity, so the interpenetration of Free Cinema with the British Film Institute network has created an aura of importance ludicrously at variance with the realities. Young French critics in particular imagine that Free Cinema acted as some sort of catalyst on British feature film production, and that the heavy bombers of major British features were led to the target by the Mosquito pathfinders of Reisz, Anderson and (of all things!) the British Film Institute Experimental Film Fund.

'Free' implies an aspiration towards a cinema whose tone is neither 'commercial' nor 'sponsored'. Even before Free Cinema Anthony Simmons's *Sunday by the Sea* (1953) and *Bow Bells* (1954) had anticipated cinéma vérité in taking what the camera saw as basis, and so breaking from the laboriously pre-conceived story-lines of the Grierson era. The obvious development, left, in the event, to the French and the American, lay in adopting the techniques and idioms of TV documentaries so as to produce cinéma vérité (definable as a film whose exact theme, story-line and continuity are developed from what the camera has revealed rather than what the camera has been intended to reveal). Why, given their programme, the champions of Free Cinema never adopted these methods, but preferred to devote themselves to TV commercials, has never been clarified for us. It's easy to think of reasons which artistically and personally are both honourable and pressing, particularly in view of its leaders' later artistic achievements. The present writer has not, however, succeeded in thinking of a reason which doesn't make the moral and critical aura surrounding Free Cinema look silly. Certainly its achievement is minimal by contrast with the vigour and sophistication of parallel movements in France and the U.S.A. (Rouch and Anger had already shown the way; Chris Marker and Richard Leacock triumphantly followed it). Lindsay Anderson's *Every Day Except Christmas* (1957) is a subaltern's view of Covent Garden porters, 'rough diamonds, you know, but jolly good fellows, and damned hard working.' It could have been entitled *In Which We Serve*. One almost expected the sponsors to appear in Noël Coward uniform and shake hands with each of their extras as they filed past. The film looks at working-class faces with respect – as did *Industrial Britain* twenty years earlier – and the emphasis is shifted from work as a process to work as – fulfilment it would seem, even, vocation. The English common man is integrated with his work as smoothly as a John Ford cavalryman with the 7th Cavalry. This is another pastoral – 'Song of W.C.2.'

Karel Reisz's *We Are the Lambeth Boys* is a little less beautiful and this isn't to use the word ironically; only limitatively. Here the lyricism is subtler, the approval more reserved. Where capital punishment is concerned, the boys' opinions are decidedly at the Alf Garnett end of the spectrum. But this only shows how culturally deprived they are. And if they're a bit rowdy late at night, well, we were teenagers at their age, weren't we?, and their sex lives pose no challenge to the sweet nothings of nice people. An apt sub-title might be: *The Young and the Guilty* (a Ted Willis script of which more later). The film touches, like *Momma Don't Allow*, on two significant topics: the boredom of work, and class chasms (when the lads play the public school at cricket).

Such a pity the simple-minded masses are being corrupted by all that popular entertainment that's foisted on them. Popular entertainment, horror films, trashy music – now there's a popular scapegoat of middle-class pressure-groups. Let's show how frank and fearless we are and denounce sexy movies, loud music, fun fairs and amusement arcades (Anderson's *O Dreamland*, 1953, and *Nice Time*).

Momma Don't Allow (Karel Reisz and Tony Richardson) creates the impression that the jazz revival was widely popular among working-class teenagers and was a working-class phenomenon. In point of fact the vast majority of working-class teenagers preferred pops, and, later, rock'n'roll. When, later, 'trad.' reached the hit parade, it was only in watered-down forms. The jazz revival was at least as much, if not primarily, a middle-class movement. The film reminds us, at least, of the inter-class gulf; the upper-class hoorays who beam patronizingly at everyone don't dance as well as the lower-class lads and lasses.

As for presenting the people as they are, none of these films really improves on the series of short street interviews which *Pathé News* featured around 1950, when they tried to compete with television's candid cameras on their own grounds and to be the *Daily Mirror* of the screen. As social protest the Free Cinema films have little to offer, by comparison with, say, Michael Ingrams's *Sewermen* (1956), *Street Cleaners* (1956) and *Tramps* (1956). These three films – and the finale of the last-named, with a disfigured beggar busking a love-song, with hatred in his eyes, occupies middle ground between Orwell

Thursday's Children: Sensitive exploration in the margin of society

and Buñuel – make it amply clear, once and for all, that Free Cinema manages nothing that hadn't been done earlier and better *within* the commercial framework. Certainly it confers on candid camera techniques an academic gloss, and it accompanies its efforts with self-conscious manifestos. Thus Ingram's superb films are passed over in silence, those of Reisz and Anderson given, in retrospect, a totally false uniqueness.

It's apparent that the anonymous young men of that much-despised mass medium, television, showed more of the people to more people than Free Cinema, which achieved a kind of middle-class left-wing sentimentality within the purlieus of the art cinema and the film society. Similarly, while Reisz equivocates about petting in *We Are the Lambeth Boys*, it is the commercial boys of TV whose relative frankness over sexual topics tears the first great breach in popular taboos. Free Cinema is an excrescence, a highly self-conscious part of an inevitable and massive trend.

The aesthetic limitations of *Momma Don't Allow* are significant. It's badly cut, badly shot, with no feelings for jazz, for dancing, for bodies, for

clothes, or for place. The directors have even less feeling for rhythm than the hoorays at whom they laugh so heartily, for at one point all the couples are dancing a slow blues to an up-tempo jazz number. You wouldn't guess from this film that the actual jazz club had a red lamp placed strategically low so that the thighs of unwary girls would be very prettily silhouetted through their dresses. It's not just that *Momma Don't Allow* that sort of joke in here: she just doesn't wish to know that thank you very much.

The best Free Cinema films concern margins of society; Guy Brenton and Lindsay Anderson's *Thursday's Children*, Lorenza Mazzetti's *Together*, Robert Vas's *Refuge England*, and *March to Aldermaston*, a 'collective' film whose guiding hand is reputedly Lindsay Anderson. They concern, respectively, handicapped children, tramps, refugees and C.N.D. Their common theme is minority groups with problems of communication. They are, in one way or another, sensitive and beautiful films, and with *Every Day Except Christmas* and *We Are the Lambeth Boys* can be welcomed into the Jennings class.

A more contemporary approach is evidenced by John Schlesinger's *Terminus*, with its more 'televisual' style.

If we look at the development of the newer style in features, we find the trailblazer is Jack Clayton's *Room at the Top*, based on a best-selling novel. It wasn't *Momma Don't Allow* that brought Tony Richardson into the directorial chair of *Look Back in Anger*; it was the fact that he had directed the play on the London stage. While the partisans of Free Cinema were directing stage plays and TV commercials, the new wave arose from response to the work of artists in other media. Far from originating in a new documentary approach, the impulse came from the plays of John Osborne, Keith Waterhouse and Willis Hall, Wolf Mankowitz and Shelagh Delaney, novels by John Braine and Alan Sillitoe, Stan Barstow and David Storey, and a new generation of actors, like Albert Finney, Rita Tushingham, Rachel Roberts, Tom Courtenay, Richard Harris and Ronald Fraser. The films are based on proven successes in other media, their production stimulated by the influence of new talents on commercial producers. The producer of *Room at the Top* had already produced expensive Technicolor features with stars of the calibre of Humphrey Bogart. Its director had produced *Sailor Beware*, an Aldwych type farce, and its scriptwriter had written films about children for Philip Leacock. The producer of *Look Back in Anger* subsequently produced the James Bond movies. Once a whole younger generation of British talents had pointed the way, American finance kept the ball rolling, for a while. In other words the British cinema renewed itself, tardily no doubt, by orthodox commercial procedures.

5: The Age of Acquiescence

21. System as Stalemate

Many intellectual critics admire the Wild Western poker-face, while repudiating dull stiff upper lip. Ultimately, of course, the American convention is at least as sentimental as the British. But one difference is that the poker-face exists in a context of struggle, of independent individuality, whereas the stiff upper lip implies, at best, a dutiful stoicism, at worst, a docile acceptance of one's role as cog in a machine. At best, it honours selflessness and sacrifice; at worst, it glorifies facelessness. And yet Clouzot's *La Salaire de la peur* illustrates how the 'tough' cinema can involve panic and cynicism and be all the tougher.

A quiet, grey, subdued style reaches an extreme in the services films of Lewis Gilbert. *Albert, R.N.* (1953) is a dummy which the British P.O.W.s hike out on parade to fool their German captors. They could have fooled me too. In Michael Anderson's *The Dam Busters* (1955) the style is enlivened by the scenario's bold, original architecture of disappointments, destruction and loss. In Jack Lee's *A Town Like Alice* (1956) stoic understatement had the quiet intensity needed to counterpoint its extreme situation and be felt as the *tour de force it* is. This tale of pain almost without hope, as women and children are herded under Japanese guard on jungle forced marches, re-endows familiar English types with meaning, and easily banal phrases ('It isn't nice, dear') acquire the stiff, frugal radiance of candles on a frame. In Lewis Gilbert's *Carve Her Name with Pride* (1958), Virginia McKenna's clear niceness constitutes the key signature of its style; cold grey lighting imbues each image with the flat

---

H.M.S. Defiant: Dirk Bogarde, Alec Guinness – Moral corruption among the highest in the land

pathos of a bas-relief. The destruction of a German ammunition train is merely indicated. If the stiff upper lip can make heroism seem easy, it can also strip it of all but moral satisfaction.

The style's limitations may be indicated by contrasting Fred Zinnemann's *The Men* (1950), which introduced Marlon Brando as a paraplegic war hero, with Lewis Gilbert's *Reach for the Sky* (1956), based on the autobiography of Douglas Bader, V.C. The American hero is neurotic, resentful and unreconciled; indeed, it is only through this unrelenting aggression that we sense his underlying terror and pain. His emotional energy may seem almost too well attuned to American cliché about aggressiveness. One may suspect that the neurosis is a pretext for an emotional violence which will keep paraplegia from becoming too depressing for the box-office.

In *Reach for the Sky* the emphasis falls on the hero's cheerful concealment of stress. His foolhardy keenness as cadet and officer all but reconciles individuality and role-satisfaction. Bitterness and despair are very briefly established, as passing stages, but no more. As he struggles with pain on his hospital bed, his is a grey motionless face on a grey pillow – and the camera tracks reverently back. The degree of stylization, even within stiff upper lip terms, is indicated by contrast with the rehabilitation sequence of Humphrey Jennings's *Listen to Britain*. But how different the treatment of pain in the Clouzot, in any Sam Fuller movie!

At one point the film strikes a cool humour that turns casual toughness into spiritual challenge. It plays for laughs a scene where Bader, teetering on his artificial limbs, falls over four times trying to hit a golf ball. It substitutes social embarrassment for the dynamic stoicism of Kirk Douglas's thumb amputation in Hawks's *The Big Sky*.

Created as almost a national saga, the English film reputedly met a disappointing reception in the U.S.A., presumably because the treatment was too distant, the hero, apparently, too passive and meek, to come alive for a nation of aggression-cherishing individualists.

Whereas American war movies see military discipline as an arena for sharp conflicts between authority and individual, British movies of the fifties stress the soothing effect of singleness of purpose and the firmness of military discipline. Only a few films touch on its inner tensions (for what is discipline if not tension?). *A Hill in Korea* treats a minor problem a little heavily; regulars' feelings that servicemen are inexperienced arouses no basic issues. *The Steel Bayonet*, however, has the ordinarily (rather than melodramatically) bad officer which the first film first suggests then denies. How different the general stress from American films, in which authority has constantly to justify itself (*vide The Caine Mutiny, The Dirty Dozen*).

The end of laissez-faire facilitates the transposition of this paternalism into Civvy Street. Guy Hamilton's *The Intruder* is complemented by two films by Val Guest. Each focuses on emergencies which mobilize all the resources of civilized society and must be faced by many individuals, in the course of filling their everyday social roles. During the blitz, 'Business as usual' was, after all, a triumphant assertion. The functional equivalent of the blitz in *80,000 Suspects* (1963) is a typhoid epidemic, its story-line the search for the disease carrier. The title, impugning guilt to every man jack of us, is significant.

A doctor (Richard Johnson) hopes to save his marriage by a second honeymoon with his wife (Claire Bloom). When the epidemic strikes she refuses to go. Marriage or no marriage, duty calls. Certainly, her decision is *also* callousness towards him, just as his anger is less disappointed love than amorous selfishness. Angrily, he too stays to do his duty, and he earns his reward; their marriage is repaired. But its firmer basis needs a spiritual purification. She catches the disease; will she be disfigured? He faces the possibility, and still loves her; she isn't. A friendly Catholic priest (Cyril Cusack) helps them with advice, agnostics though they are. They appreciate his tolerant, socially cohesive goodwill; but they mend their marriage on purely human, stoic grounds. When Guest inserts a near-nude shot of Claire Bloom it is in a characteristically 'anti-passionate' moment, just before she dons protective clothing in a sterilizing shower.

The emotional asides (including discussions on the morality of civilized adultery and the husband's right to revenge) are far from irrelevant to the deeper theme. For private emotions are part of the whole structure of morals and morale. If *80,000 Suspects* never escapes the gravitational pull of the 'just-doing-my-duty-sir' convention, it does verge, as in the mass-inoculation scenes, on the quality of a Mass Observation survey. It has that sense of society as an organism in which individuals are specialized cells. Cells with free will, certainly; but to use it anti-socially is to become a cancer. The only solution to the tension between tyranny and anarchy is a decency stern enough to offer a modest, but overriding, dignity in helping all one's neighbours, known and unknown.

In Guest's *The Day the Earth Caught Fire* (1961) a newspaper reporter (Edward Judd) and his editor (Arthur Christiansen, Guest's erstwhile boss on the *Daily Express*) reveal the hideous truths concealed, well-meaningly, by officialdom. While the world hots up, the British people behave with, on the whole, exemplary responsibility. Bright young Chelsea things hose one another down with precious water, in a criminal orgy, but the too-subdued tone of the rest may well explain why, on release, the film proved less successful than its initial takings suggested. By 1961 we were used to rougher fare, and Guest, really, belongs to an older generation. Co-written by Wolf Mankowitz, the film is untypical of Guest in putting the authorities in the dock, but the director's stress on individual responsibility still turns it into the spiritual antithesis of *The War Game*; whatever the threat, discipline and self-discipline will prevail. Similarly, Guest's *Yesterday's Enemy* and *The Camp on Blood Island* assert the maintenance of morale in military groups facing almost certain death.

The suggestion, however, is not that this good order will inevitably prevail. It must, or else ... Guest is a hard sentimentalist; the system's moral claim to the individual's sacrifices is a categorical imperative. If duty, decency and conscience are society's spiritual bricks and mortar, irresponsibility and pleasure are a major threat. In *Jigsaw* (1961), a murder hunt leading through very routine enquiries (and a correct but, alas, boring, cross-section of society), detective Jack Warner dispenses little moral homilies to foolish members of the public, and comes down like a ton of platitudes on the lying, cowardly, vacuum-cleaner salesman who seduces one lonely housewife after another. In *80,000 Suspects* typhoid is spread, half-symbolically, by the *femme fatale* (Yolande Donlan) who threatened the doctor's marriage *before* duty did, and was the root cause of duty seeming to do so.

The contrast of system and individual is most sharply presented in *They Can't Hang Me* (1955). A civil servant (Andre Morell) passes secrets to a foreign power in the megalomanic belief that he's indispensible to Britain. We hang him. Typical of Guest's, and of a very British, vision, is the passing acknowledgement of the ubiquity of very nasty individual impulses.

'If you ask me, I think she wants her husband to hang.'

'She won't be the first wife who's felt that way.'

So what keeps us decent? Duty, and guilt, backed by a system which, through its very impersonality, becomes altruistic, are our salvation, not only from our wives, but from ourselves. It can hang anybody, even you, and you, and, dear audience, you, and that's just why it deserves your adhesion. Authority's little spats of excessive anger, like 'tec Stanley Baker in *Hell Is a City* (1959), are forgivable outbursts of generous human indignation. Here the thug brutalized a dumb girl who couldn't call for help (the social theme). But authority's brutality is less than that of the individual, precisely because its power is overwhelming, and discipline its second nature.

When 'they' can be criticized, it is in connection with science. It's no accident that Guest's science fiction fantasies are as grey-toned as all his films. *The Quatermass Experiment* (1955) contrasts detective Jack Warner who, in his 'simple Bible way', suspects scientific meddling with nature, and the hubris of ruthless scientist Brian Donlevy whose daring projects bring evil Outer Space fungus to earth. The threat is destroyed in a characteristically 'collectivist' way. It has holed out in Westminster Abbey (again, religion is an indifferent value), is about to hurl its millions of spores into the air and take over all our bodies and brains. In Nigel Kneale's original play the scientist appealed to the 'man within' the evil mass to make a supreme effort and will his own, and its, destruction. Val Guest lacks any such faith in metaphysical conscience. Into the scaffolding on which the squatting horror quivers is poured juice from every power station in London (a million homes are blacked out, as in the blitz). It howls and wails as it chars. Not that 'they' are infallible. Quatermass, being an American, resolves to risk once more the eerie danger of outer space. In *Quatermass 2*, alien minds lurk behind the suddenly icier faces of scientists, cabinet ministers and commissioners. Or the earth burns because of disastrously synchronized H-bomb tests by Russians and Americans. And then it is the little man who saves us. In the first Quatermass film it is the police whose routine tactics track the thing. In the second, a brashly trouble-stirring M.P. (Leo McKern) and scoop-famished journalist (Sidney James) raise the alarm. In *The Day the Earth Caught Fire* the *Daily Express* embodies a responsible anarchism by no means incompatible with the self-discipline of the populace. *Yesterday's Enemy's* reporter (Leo McKern) keeps an intransigent conscience.

Indeed, in Guest's essentially lower-middle-class vision of society as order and of the individual conscience as necessarily devoted to order before all, one can discern the connection, perhaps underestimated by historians, between the nonconformist conscience (more or less secularized), and conformism. The puritan conscience is turned *against* puritan individualism. Certainly the puritan strain prevails when Guest touches on the affluent, hedonistic sub-society show business. In *Expresso Bongo* (1959) and *The Beauty Jungle* (1964), Laurence Harvey and Janette Scott respectively are tempted into get-rich-quick nastiness. Their moral survival depends on whether they're prepared to renounce its lures and withdraw into decent, modest obscurity. And their success by moral weakness could be brief or illusory – for vice must be punished, since virtue is only its own reward.

Chris Wicking has contrasted two journalists turned writer-producer-director: Val Guest and Samuel Fuller. Fuller's work asserts an explosive American ambivalence between every individual's right to something like amorality (even madness), and the claims on him of a decency which is, perilously, expressed only as patriotism. Fuller, more challenging than Guest, asserts both claims at their most intense, whereas Guest soft pedals the claims of, and loses the variety of nuance within, the individual. Nor – disappointingly, for a journalist – does he show much of the seaminess, slovenliness and irresponsibility existing within and around the establishment and the 'decent' people, as everywhere else. Within its limits, however, *80,000 Suspects* has a moral dignity and social sense very close to the documentary ethos and no less interesting. On its non-U levels, his calm, quiet pace and tone parallel C. P. Snow's. The ethos is screwed to its grimmest in Charles Saunders's *The Golden Link* (1954). A senior police officer (Andre Morell), a tired functionary, is so completely part of the police machine that when the evidence persuades him that his own daughter is guilty of murder, he imperturbably continues procuring her conviction. It's true he glooms somewhat, but the restraint saps the profound conflict between love and duty which one would have found in Racine or Corneille, and which Hitchcock accommodates in *Blackmail* (1929).

Blackmail: Anny Ondra – Examining the profound conflict between love and duty

If such films are agnostic-fundamentalist in their simple severity, Ealing's more 'Anglican' tone has a softer spot for gentle eccentricities, and a more nuanced tolerance of the individual. Yet Pat Jackson's *The Feminine Touch* (1956) not only makes this nursing life look like a girl's public school dorm but preaches that, however poor the pay, excessive the work, and iniquitous the despotism of Matron Blimp's discipline, the – P.B.N., for Poor Bleedin' Nurse? – must do her duty and buckle uncomplainingly to, compensating, by unrewarded devotion, for the indifference of the hierarchy and the community. Its mixture of jollity, disillusionment and supineness, its acquiescence in the way the Florence Nightingale tradition is traded on to expedite deliberate meanness, is quite abject. It's sensitive enough to have, somewhere, a bad conscience, which makes it all the more infuriating. It's significant that though the nurse's life is subsequently treated sentimentally (*No Time for Tears*) and humorously (*Carry On Nurse*) it has never been treated, as it cries out to be, in such a way as to provide an 'angry young woman' with a positive, human, altogether non-political opportunity for constructive direct action.

Underneath fifties affluence, under the evangelical strain, a far dourer British tradition persists: that of Calvinism agnosticized, with 'the system' as God. 'The system is only apparently to blame. For if it is to blame, it's inevitable that a system will make mistakes, so one can't blame it. To blame it is to strengthen the only real alternative, the horrors of anarchy'. It is curious, and no doubt significant, that any need for, or even possibility of, substantial improvement, hardly even comes to mind. 'Since order must be accepted, with all its faults, blame can pertain only to individuals whom the system, with the slowness of British fairness – like the mills of God – will eventually track down and crush.' One makes a bid for freedom mainly in crime, in comedy, or at the point of death (*Last Holiday, Campbell's Kingdom*).

Of this civic Calvinism, the guardian angels are, of course, the boys in blue. Hagiography becomes copperolatry. In pre-war movies attitudes to the police are more combative. The upper-class attitude of the police as one's dimwitted servants shelters proletarian tongue-poking. Ivor Montagu's *Bluebottles* (1928) mocks the bobbies none too affectionately, and Walter Forde's 1943 Tommy Handley comedy *It's That Man Again* has its delirious moment when a ferocious army sergeant ties three or four rozzers up in knots of writhing limbs and leaves them hanging on coat hooks to squirm. If police were respected, it was with considerable ambivalence.

The enthusiastic post-war respect for the police may well reflect a sudden consensus between the classes. By 1950 affluence induced a substantial segment of the working-classes to feel at one with the social order. They felt middle-class. The middle-classes are always the most passionately attached to the police, as their defenders against the rougher classes and their disrespect for property. And the upper-middle-class exempted the police from their general criticisms of bureaucracy and of authority's interference, probably because police paternalism towards the public is congenial to their own traditions. Less superior than in the thirties, they feel much more subject.

1950 was the year of *The Blue Lamp* (Dearden for Ealing). Kindly P.C. Dixon (Jack Warner) is brutally shot dead by a hysteric teenage thug (Dirk Bogarde) who wanted to be tough. Thereafter, the cop-delinquent confrontation became obsessive. It's as if the reconciled sector (and age-group) of the working-class were living in newly middle-class disapproval of (or secretly repudiating in itself elements of) older, rougher, unreconciled traditions (now located in the young, always the least settled and most belligerent working-class group).

Any consonance of widespread middle- and working-class attitudes is likely to be filmed obsessively. Not until 1963 does a British film centre on the possibility of a policeman defying letter and spirit of the law, and then it's Ken Annakin's reasonable defence of a detective (Nigel Patrick) 'ruthless' enough to defy his kid glove superiors and resort to *The Informers* (the ban on which was short-lived).

While Hollywood produces studies of juvenile delinquency as thoughtful as *The Young Stranger*, *Blackboard Jungle*, *The Wild One*, *Rebel without a Cause* and *The Young Savages*, the British movie response to a far smaller problem is a little explosion of hysteria. Token references are made to 'complexes' (between gritted teeth) and to bad housing, but less obvious social and cultural problems are not even intuitively sensed. The issue is felt as one of being 'tough' or being 'soft'. Lewis Gilbert's hard-line *Cosh Boy* (1952), which expressed agonised disbelief in authority's kid glove, and saw salvation in A Good Old-fashioned Taste Of Dad's Belt. Leslie Norman's soft line *Spare the Rod* (1961) is likeable in that its reformist teacher (Max Bygraves) has nothing special to offer his lads, only decent respect – yet it ends by supposing that if excessive caning were abolished all the hard cases would take to singing carols around the Christmas tree. In John Lemont's *And Women Shall Weep* (1959) a staunch and sturdy working-class Mum (Ruth Dunning) realizes her Teddy Boy son is a cowardly murderer, disarms him by hurling a cup of good old English tea in his face, and hands him over to the police with none of your indulgent argey-bargey, while her younger son blubbers on her breast about his idol's fall.

Basil Dearden and Michael Relph attempt to get beyond the popular reduction of the issue to sex and violence. Aside from a clutter of boring cameos, *I Believe in You* (1951) relates probation officers Cecil Parker and Celia Johnson with juvenile delinquents Harry Fowler and Joan Collins. Though nearly sucked down into the underworld, they find salvation in the probation service and each other. Some relevant criticism of authority follows from Cecil Parker's probation officer who attends to his charges like some visiting Bishop. If he didn't actually wear gaiters, in my mind's eye he does. He descends upon backsliders from a great height, and gives the sullen young lover murderously pious advice. In the end, he learns humility, reverence, and respect for his social and moral inferiors. A paternalism more marked than any in the probation service itself subsists in the supposition that what lads need is a relationship with firm and responsible father- and mother-figures from the upper-classes. More recently, of course, sociologists have pointed out what common sense about 'bad company' suggests. Much delinquency isn't the product of personal misfits at all but of emotionally quite normal attachments to a sub-society poorly integrated with the other sub-society from which the judiciary springs. The sullen, electric presence of young Joan Collins dominates the whole film precisely because her grace, vigour and insolent *savoir-vivre* validate her character's subversive attitudes as the result, not of being 'misled', as the script imagines, but of a culture, of truths and experiences, from which the film is insulated. Nonetheless, the warmth and weight of four strongly-presented actors gives the film life, and English do-gooders come movingly alive on the screen.

Violent Playground (1958) summarizes the delinquency problems of pre-Beatles Liverpool. This time the good influence does come from the boys' own background; but what the film gives with one hand it takes away with the other. He's a tough policeman (Stanley Baker), and even less disassociated from the official line than good real life probation officers so often are. Its documentary-style location photography made a great impression on critics at the time, but its study of delinquency is infinitely cruder than the earlier film's. Delinquent David McCallum's sister is clearly much more sensible than he is, from the moment that she speaks with an ever so much nicer accent, while the priest and the headmaster radiate their respective kinds of benevolence. True, we see a young schoolmistress desert her infant's class just when they need her most, but this is presumably because by 1958, some young school-teachers were trying to employ methods more unconventional and thoughtful than the traditional. Inevitably, youthful idealism and inexperience are not always successful, so provoking the traditionalist equation: lack of firmness = lack of firmness with oneself = panicky unreliability. Our would-be tough-cookie takes a whole class of kids as hostages, and brandishes a machine-gun with which to mow the coppers down, but still winds up as a blubbering little boy. This reversion to the notion that 'all bullies are cowards' which was ludicrous thirty years earlier (in *Scarface*) is all the sadder in that an early scene, set at an evening institute art class, evokes Margareta Berger-Hamerschlag's reminiscences of teaching in a working-class district, *Journey into a Fog*. Published in the mid-fifties, this had already brought to the wider public the fact that juvenile delinquency related to cultural under-privilege and to a whole texture of life. In an interesting moment the gang forces a trapped 'tec to join in with them in their evil orgiastic dances – none other than the depraved rock 'n' roll, which, via the Cavern, not only helped mitigate Liverpool's violence problem but set a generation's style. It's perfectly true that the rock 'n' roll as performed, in its early days, by delin-quents, really was different in mood from what it became, and this scene could have been the product of direct, sensitive observation. But there's something oddly apposite in the film's vilification of anything which the younger generation had the insolence to choose for itself.

A welcome shaft of new insight occurs in Edmond T. Gréville's *Beat Girl* (1959). Adam Faith plays the guitar-picking leather-jacketed mixed-up kid who seems cultural worlds apart from David Farrar as the flat-designing architect, i.e. the idealistic-practical older generation. Gréville's notion of a gulf-cum-affinity between them, of an inexplicable lack of opportunity for youth, shows a heart in the right place. In a curious, gawky scene, Adam Faith merely remonstrates mildly with the thugs who try to get him to fight like a man and kick his precious guitar along the gutter. In other words, Gréville, and his scriptwriters, have spotted the birth of the cool style, even of flower power, as its happening. But then Gréville is a Frenchman (on one of his periodic visits), and capable even then of interesting himself in today's reality rather than yesterday's myths.

In twenty-five years of obsession with juvenile delinquency in one form or other, the number of consistently interesting British features centring on the topic is, precisely, three. Sidney Furie's *The Boys* and *The Leather Boys*, with Clive Donner's *Some People*, fall, narrowly, outside our period, while the documentary movement can summon up two sympathetic if simple pieces: *Children on Trial* (Jack Lee, 1946), and *We Are the Lambeth Boys* (Karel Reisz, 1959) which relates to the theme, obliquely, by insisting that not all working-class 'gangs' are delinquent. That this needs saying illustrates the crudity of a widespread public mood.

22. Dance to your Daddy

The feeling for military-style paternalism, for the system and for the police, are special forms of a general acquiescence to father-figures of a quietly heavy kind.[36]

Anthony Asquith's *Tell England* (1931) evokes, delicately, the beauties of the Edwardian order. One day pater invites his son into his study, and offers him a drink. This formal gesture marks childhood's end and accession to man's estate. The intense feeling between the two is hardly expressed, but both know it. This scene could be the model for senior-junior relationships in doldrums-era movies about World War II. How often haven't we seen the junior officer enter his C.O.'s office or tent-study, be given a difficult order, hesitate decently ('the men are at the end of their tether, sir'), be sternly assured of the vital importance of this operation, and obey. Thereupon the older man drops his guard for a moment, and reveals his fatherly feelings towards his men (with the officer as favourite son), before resuming his impersonality and dismissing him. The common herd, in turn, may grumble loud and long, but always knuckle stoutly to.

The same relationship prevails in Civvy Street. In Wendy Toye's *True as a Turtle* (1957) a pompous and impossible company director (Cecil Parker) insists that favoured employee John Gregson and new bride June Thorburn weekend with himself and his wife (Avice Landon) on his ocean-going yacht. The twist, only too foreseeable by British movie addicts, is that Gregson fits in with his boss's every whim and tells his bride not to be so ridiculously sensitive when the old bully bawls her out too. Indeed, the young man never asserts himself successfully against the old one. When Admiral Blimp's attempts at navigation prove inadequate in a thick fog, he sensibly resigns, whereupon promoted youth navigates the yacht straight into a town lido. If the film fell short by the standards of the *Doctor* formula which it resembled, it was, surely, because the hero is too conspicuously submissive, too sure of entering into his inheritance, too upper-crust, to tune into the normal, natural and healthy disloyalty of both middle-class individualism and the trade union spirit. A few American movies experiment with realistically supine attitudes (notably *Woman's World*), but even a Republican movie like *The Man in the Gray Flannel Suit* criticizes the organization man ethos whereby a man's private life is his employer's property. Here the Englishman's castle becomes a glass-house, a prison without privacy.

The contrasting attitudes to authority in British and American films parallel attitudes established by Martha Wolfenstein and Nathan Leites in their *Movies: A Psychological Study*. They summarize the divergent emphasis of American, British and French films in terms of three stills. One depicts Burt Lancaster scowling at pleading Edward G. Robinson in *All My Sons*, and carries the comment: 'America – son judges father.' Godfrey Tearle looking sternly at musing Rex Harrison in *The Rake's Progress* bears the caption: 'Britain – father judges son.' A scene with Raimu and Pierre Fresnay looking sharply across a table into each other's eyes in *Marius* illustrates: 'France – son will resemble father whom he now fights.'

These situations roughly parallel the general social history of each country. American history is a matter of change, expansion, optimism. Each generation expects to do better than its stick-in-the-mud (or un-American immigrant) father. Since 1880 or so, British social history is a matter of maintaining an established patrimony – of a contracting tradition. French history is characterized by sharp conflicts and reconciliations, complicated infighting and alliances, and a morally embittered realism, all within a volatile, continuing situation. *Plus ça change* ....

Clearly obedience and manliness, loyalty and maturity are perfectly compatible. But the British stress on obedience, on self-effacement of oneself before an on-going authority, probably helps determine two prominent English screen types: on the one hand, the 'eternal cadet' and on the other, the cad-bully, that is, the heavy anti-father.

The keen cadet is a hardy perennial, but more marked in English than in foreign literature and movies. His sub-species range from that beautiful celebration of the public school ethos, Asquith's *Tell England*, to the entertainingly nutty *Q Planes* (Tim Whelan, 1938) with Laurence Olivier and Ralph Richardson as two men-about-town who nonchalantly badinage their way through their adventures like an all-male *Avengers* duo.

In the fifties the cadet sweeps all before him as principal identification figure. America offers the surly, cynical independence, not only of Bogart (since, of course, a highbrows' cult too), but of Robert Mitchum (whose popularity was vastly enhanced by a prison sentence for a marihuana rap – another portent of intellectual cults), and of Burt Lancaster. Even in an organization man like James Coburn, a certain experience and cynicism seems held in reserve. By comparison, the English stars of the fifties – John Mills, Richard Attenborough, John Gregson, Dirk Bogarde, Donald Sinden, Denholm Elliott – are grown-up boys, trusting, vulnerable, decently worried and ready aye ready. Mills and Attenborough also played the more sensitive kinds of working-class character, though to my mind there always seems something middle-class in the former's style.

The son-type (as our principal identification) has his necessary complement in the father-type. A characteristic pair is formed by Jack Hawkins – officer-father – and Kenneth More – officer-son, both in their prime. And these keen, uncomplicated lads are paralleled by the conspicuously rich line in effective fathers – notably Roger Livesey, James Robertson Justice, Cecil Parker, Jack Warner. They share star billing with, and often outshine, the cadets. Equally formidable too is the British cinema's battery of obstructive,

They Made Me a Fugitive: Trevor Howard, Griffith Jones – Addiction to the excitement that only war brings

testy employers, officials and other ogres – one can name only a few: Michael Hordern, Wilfrid Hyde White, Raymond Huntley, William Hartnell, Richard Wattis.

By contrast the American cinema was exceptionally poor in 'star' father-figures. They were semi-sinister (like Edward G. Robinson) or absurdly sentimentalized (like S. Z. 'Cuddles' Sakall). Since, perennially youthful mature men have proliferated – Anthony Quinn, James Stewart, John Wayne – of whom only the first has had many interesting roles over the last two decades.

An interesting male figure is the heavy cad, who brow-beats heroines throughout the forties. A study of the villainy and violence traditionally smouldering (or thought to smoulder) beneath the cool surface of British conformity is beyond the scope of this book, but it's interesting that wartime

escapist movies led James Mason, Stewart Granger and Robert Newton to fame as the splendid, terrifying bullies of costume subjects. Mason became the nation's number one heart-throb after beating Margaret Lockwood to death in *The Man in Grey* (1943). In *The Wicked Lady* (1945) he rapes Margaret Lockwood, after half-strangling her to give her a taste of the scaffold from which he has just been prematurely cut down, and in *The Seventh Veil* (1945) he drives concert pianist Ann Todd into a mental breakdown by smashing his cane across her knuckles whenever she tries to live her own life. After she's cured by hypnosis it's to him she returns.

Misogynistic as these scenes are, they have another meaning, linked to the brutality of batterings between men which alarmed critics of the period. The British cinema easily matched Hollywood's increasing brutalities. David MacDonald's *The Brothers* (1947) uses L. A. G. Strong's novel of a feud between Scottish fishing families over Patricia Roc to provide fresh and thoroughly native correspondences to (and not derivatives from) the Western's setting, code and melodrama. Cavalcanti's *They Made Me a Fugitive* (1947) hasn't the Bogart-Bacall duo, but can trade punch for punch and grim jest for grim jest with Howard Hawks's *The Big Sleep* (1946), and score a win on points. It also has Cavalcanti's European feeling for night slumscapes. Indeed the British cinema has swung in a curious way between the brutal and the effete – the former relating both to gentry and proletarian traditions, the latter to a middle-class decorousness. The West End theatre's anyone-for-tennis juvenile lead was, the public pest number one of British movies throughout the pre-war years. John Mills illustrates his evolution, under the impact of the war years, into the keen cadet. A more interesting variation of the refined, middle-class male is the serious sensitivity of Leslie Howard – who has no real successor.

It's the cad who dominates the forties. But the second generation cads (David Farrar, Michael Rennie) weren't quite vintage, lacking, probably, the subjacent warmth of Mason and Granger. And the fifties belong to the cadets. Among the exceptions, Peter Finch possessed a blend of warmth, strength and mature sensitivity. Trevor Howard maintained a rebellious raffishness, while Stanley Baker increasingly expressed a bitter toughness nearer the Bogart-Mitchum-Lancaster mood (and a hitherto excluded range of British proletarian attitudes). Fellow Welshman – Richard Burton – returned from Hollywood to incarnate the classic anti-cadet. Jimmy Porter revives the woman-bashing hero-villain, expresses an angry proletarian cynicism, and adds quick flashes of vulnerable sensitivity comparable to Leslie Howard's. Since then the across-the-board masculinity-sensitivity of British actors has given them an edge over their American contemporaries.

Maleness and brutality revive together. The year before *Look Back in Anger*, Hammer movies began to penetrate the American market more successfully than any British genre since the Gainsborough films.[37]

The British do bullying stories very well, for reasons suggested by Wolfenstein and Leites in their analysis of *Dear Murderer*, cited later. And just as the Gainsborough movies announced the Labour Government of 1945, so the Hammer horrors synchronized with the angry young men. It seems to take something like a large-scale social disillusionment to allow the reintegration of the male ideal as against its fragmentation by a sentimentalized middle-class idea of a gentleman's agreement. While the Gainsborough hero-villains are both brutal and passionate, referring back to Romanticism, and Emily Brontë's *Wuthering Heights*, the Hammer movies centre on icy, dandy masterminds – as if male self-sufficiency remains fascinating and forbidden, although sexuality has slipped out of taboo. Gainsborough relates to 'hot' patriarchal, old-fashioned styles, Hammer requires aberration and 'cool'.

In the late fifties, another bridge between cad and cadet was provided by the manly German officer. Another transition figure, prevalent from the end of the cad cycle through to the mid-fifties, was the 'running man' (the 1963 Carol Reed film of that title is last of the line.) A sensitive man commits a crime of violence, and is hunted down for it; to this theme we can relate Carol Reed's *Odd Man Out* (1947), its masterpiece, and Lawrence Huntington's *The Upturned Glass* (1947), both with James Mason, Roy Baker's *The October Man*, and Robert Hamer's *The Long Memory*, both with John Mills, and Charles Crichton's *Hunted*, with Dirk Bogarde. Insofar as the 'running man' is violent, he's a cad, insofar as he's basically decent, he's a cadet. In *They Made Me a Fugitive*, where he's played by Trevor Howard, he's an ex-officer who turned to the black market because he'd become addicted, in war, to excitement.[38]

Only six years or so separate the cadet age-group from the child heroes who abound during the period. Ealing child movies kick off with Charles Crichton's *Hue and Cry* (1946), a fresh and delightful variation on the *Emil and the Detectives* motif. A gang of Cockney tuppeny-blood addicts discover spivs inserting messages into the text of their favourite serial, and harass its author (Alastair Sim), bookish, fastidious, puerophile, into joining the chase. Several films, notably Carol Reed's *The Fallen Idol* (1948), Philip Leacock's *The Spanish Gardener* (1956), Leslie Norman's *The Shiralee* (1957), and Alexander Mackendrick's *Sammy Going South* (1963), the last two Michael Balcon productions, all deal with a child's search for a satisfactory father-figure. The first fancy domestic servants (butler Ralph Richardson, gardener Dirk Bogarde). Losey's *The Servant*, being butler Dirk Bogarde, is a combination of the two. The last two fix on tramps with wanderlust (Edward G. Robinson, Peter Finch), hinting, again, that the rascally provides a human warmth and complicity missing in the remote respectable paterfamilias.

Curiously, *The Servant* relates by more than its title to the genre. A butler played by Dirk Bogarde, turns out to be a rascal, and seduces a young cadet (James Fox) from his supposed family traditions. Robin Maugham's novel on which *The Servant* is based, specifically relates his downfall to the relationship between the sons of master and servants – not butlers, but nannies; and Bogarde's Barrett is curiously fussy and motherly, indeed, constantly on the point of turning from a butler into a nanny, and mothering Tony as well as fathering him.

If Reed's film vividly catches moments of a cold and lonely childhood, Norman's is the dramatically most solid and the warmest evocation of a father-child bond. Aussie sheep-shearer Peter Finch reluctantly totes his little daughter round flat, dreary, thirsty landscapes. His neglect has turned the child's mother (Elizabeth Sellars) into a bit of a bitch. Through her pain the film turns English misogyny against itself, condemning the limitations of the rowdy, beery, all-man ideal. A pity that (*a*) a too-nice girl, (*b*) the expiatory-and-reconciliatory beating-up obligatory in British movies, and (*c*) easy suspense over whether the child has been injured in an accident due to her father's neglect, disrupt the finer psychological theme and imply that parental responsibility entails the semi-detached suburban style of life. Its follow-up,

Sammy Going South, reproduced all the most picturesque, and least interesting, aspects of the earlier picture, which takes many sensitive asides in its loping stride and has an honest harshness to it.

Poignant Ealing films on isolated children include Alexander Mackendrick's *Mandy* (1952), about a deaf and dumb child and her parents, and Charles Crichton's *The Divided Heart* (1954), about a displaced person torn between his real mother (Yvonne Mitchell), who is a stranger to him, and his foster-mother (Cornell Borchers), who is constrained to give him up.

Several Carol Reed's films feature the theme of a child's disillusionment with reality. Quite apart from *The Fallen Idol* and *A Kid for Two Farthings*, the camera in *Outcast of the Islands* (1951) repeatedly flips away to a little Malay boy. His trusting smile persecutes Trevor Howard who already knows himself to be a fallen idol. In Reed's powerful movies child and adult themes tend to interrupt each other, establishing a pattern rather than exploring a process, which is followed out with rather more depth in four films by Philip Leacock, British specialist in child stories, which one can almost treat as a quartet: *The Kidnappers* (1953), *Escapade* (1955), *Innocent Sinners* (1958) and *Reach for Glory* (1961).

Reach for Glory apart, these greyly sensitive, gently bleak, poignant films criticize adult coldness and incomprehension of childish vulnerability and idealism. If a certain restraint limits the films, by comparison with say Duvivier's *Poil de Carotte*, it intensifies an authentic melancholy. Not only is childhood gone; it happened in another country .... The remoteness appears in another form: the quiet solitudes of the adult world in which the children seek, diligently, vainly for warmth. Less immediate in impact than Reed's films, Leacock's are composed in shades of grey sadness. As moving as the innocent sinners is the spinster (Flora Robson) imprisoned within her middle-class loneliness, the restauranteur (David Kossoff) with delusions of middle-class clientele, the uncomprehending young administrators of a charity. Even if one regrets the film's Lady Bountiful's view of society, and its happy end, its qualities are sufficient to render the film's very limitations a part of its softly demoralizing quietness. Theories of childish innocence deteriorate into sentimentality with the children-and-animals formula. *A Kid for Two Farthings* has (boringly) a boy and goat. Maurice Cloche and Ralph Smart's *Never Take*

No for an Answer (1951) has a boy and a donkey (which he takes to see the Pope). Kevin McClory's *The Boy and the Bridge* (1959) has a boy and a seagull. At least we've been spared a moving story of a boy who nurses a lame reindeer and takes him to Santa Claus to replace his missing antler, but Disney would have treated it with a drastic speed and humour sadly absent in these solemn nostalgias. The idea that children tend to be sweet, trusting, inoffensively anarchistic, filled with innocent wonder, and, in a touchingly defenceless way, close to God, is really a romantic and/or evangelical reaction against puritanism. Vigorously relevant at the time of Blake and Wordsworth, it is now an absorbed, safe, spiritually defused, nostalgia (fetchingly evoked in Rumer Godden), and rarely yields as much tension and insight as the common sense and Freudian views that children are, in different ways, and often in the same ways, morally and spiritually just as complex as adults.

With *The Happiest Days of Your Life*, and its regrettably less nuanced St. Trinian's follow-ups, Frank Launder and Sidney Gilliat take the 'black' view of childish, and therefore human, nature, and under cover of black humour, are anarchistically indulgent towards it. It's interesting that pre-war Narkover is followed by a girls' school. It is as if a pre-war cynicism about middle-class pretensions has disappeared. But girls don't quite fit the public school spirit, they're marginal, slightly free, and therefore, sinister. Indeed, the St. Trinian's girls, as they grew up, adjusted to the classlessness of 'swinging London' a little more easily than their male escorts. As so often in British movies, independence and innovation are equated, even in humour, with violence. Launder and Gilliat have a sneaking sympathy for the devil's party, however.

23. Stresses and Strains

If the screen cadet is immature, it's not because the values he asserts are meaningless. Far from it. Our criticism concerns the skimped or mechanical presentation of the other values against which all heroism is an often tragic struggle. Without this sense of struggle, the cadet code is as different from the reality as a recruiting poster from a war.

One or two films allow doubts, assert some sort of counter ideal. *The Cruel Sea* is followed by Robert Parrish's version of H. E. Bates's *The Purple Plain* (1954). Its American director bestows on regulation stoicism a new key, of Technicolor physicality, and the soft full female warmth and strength of Burmese actress Win Min Than. Indeed the film, with its British producer and script and American director and star (Gregory Peck), is a subtle compromise between British and American codes. Quietly but firmly un-English is its vindication of individualism within the system. The crashed aviator who survives the Burma jungle is unsociable and undisciplined, breaks most of the rules and keeps going not by sheer plod but by fixing his mind, in extremis, on a jewel (never mind that it turns out to be a fake – for the real jewel is his life-force, longing for a woman, using any sort of pretext to assert itself, and drive him on). The American's English companion (Maurice Denham) is a stickler for regulations, as well as querulous and afraid. He dies early.

David Lean's *The Bridge on the River Kwai* (1957) and *Lawrence of Arabia* (1962) venture into the psychological complex lurking unobtrusively behind regulation idealism. Both assert the link between devotion and masochism. Both are, basically, American productions, the former also based on a French novel.

The one all-English contribution to responsible criticism of the cadet-and-gentleman ethos is Ronald Neame's *Tunes of Glory* (1960) which admits that officers' mess life has frictions over and above the call of duty.

A not dissimilar pattern underlines Peter Glenville's *Becket* (1964). Jean Anouilh's play pits the crafty, idealistic, native Saxon Saint (Richard Burton) against the rascally, human, Norman King (Peter O'Toole). Under the canny eye of its American producer, Hal Wallis, the film transposes into terms of medieval history that perennial Flagg-and-Quirt motif which Hawks has described as 'a love story between two men'. It does something like justice to Anouilh's paradoxes of loyalty and treachery being, not even yin and yang, but just heads and tails, of the same action. Whichever turns up, the flip side lies in wait. And if the worldly King has finally to submit to a sound flogging from his old friend's monks, his 'penitence' is a Machiavellian matter of political jujitsu, of yielding to conquer. Conversely, of course, the devotion of Becket is also pride. He can 'love nothing but the best', and sacrifices, coldly, it seems, for his God no more than he had already sacrificed for his King. He is first a Quisling, a collaborator, with the Norman conquerors, against his fellow Anglo-Saxons; certain overtones of this motif can be appreciated by considering the analogy with the French and Germans in 1940. Anouilh's popularity is, no doubt, enhanced by the rare tact with which he spikes prestige settings with a suave and complacent cynicism. However, the film's prestige values smother the full force of its power politics, and, at least in retrospect, it's liable to be confused with less interesting successors, like *A Man for All Seasons* and *The Lion in Winter*. One remembers a beautiful film rather than a Machiavellian one. Yet it goes some way towards the political realism of *Tudor Rose*, and relates to the same cycle as the David Lean movies, with their similar vein of honest doubt about purity and cynicism, achievement and failure. They move a little deeper into the internal tensions, psychological and Machiavellian, beneath that front of single-minded devotion which any establishment – or anti-establishment – cannot but try to present to the world.

Other films take a more saturnine look at the system as a going concern. The English pride themselves on losing every battle except the last, and the shame and guilt lurking behind this boast became conspicuous in two films produced in 1958, Leslie Norman's *Dunkirk* and Roy Baker's *A Night to Remember*. Not only the *Titanic* in 1912, but Britain's titanic complacency is holed below the water line. Both these films possess real moral tragedy and beauty, precisely because they admit some cynicism is justified. Roy Baker's blacker, more philosophic piece pays full tribute to the virtues of Captain and senior officers, but there is no glossing over the way one little complacency after another leads to the sinking of the unsinkable, nor over that callous indifference to the steerage passengers which finally drives them to a revolt which is not only panic but righteous wrath.

Indeed, something of this stoicism infuses the hideously botched, but interesting, *The Day of the Triffids* (1962). For all its superficial absurdities, there's a hideous poetic resonance about its shots of Londoners, blinded by an errant comet, dragging themselves quietly about London squares, waiting trustingly in station booking-halls for helpful policemen who won't come because they're blind too, or the blind air hostess calming the passengers with soothing lies – until they realize the pilot's flying blind, and reading the instruments with his fingertips through smashed glass; whereupon the blind turn on the blind, and tear them to pieces.

Meanwhile such films as the Boultings' satires and Joseph Losey's *Blind Date*, adumbrate the angry young men's view that the system's inefficiencies and obscurantism are part of its machinery for keeping the lower orders at bay. Some sort of establishment, without being calculatingly evil, also uses the system to preserve its own interest against everyone else's, and if pressed is quite ready to outrage its own agreements and rules so as to obviate any disturbance of its comfortable slumbers. Once the angry young men horn in on the screen the British cinema moves rapidly towards an attitude as critical as that of a pre-war, virtually American, movie, and right-wing anarchist at that. King Vidor's *The Citadel* (1938) first suggests to its audience that those who suffer from neglect by the powers-that-be can, and should, aggressively turn and fight the system, by direct action, student-style. Two young doctors (Robert Donat, Ralph Richardson) in a Welsh mining town stock up on dynamite and wreck the typhoid-carrying sewer which is a serious menace to

The Citadel: Kynaston Reeves, Mary Clare, Robert Donat – An authenticity of emotional excess

the miners' health and about which the local authorities have shown typical British phlegm. Here, there are not 80,000 Suspects – but one: the inert and callous complacency of a pre-war establishment which all decent citizens want to kick all the way up the stairway to heaven.

24. My Famous Last Word is my Bond

Inevitably this resurgent capacity for national self-criticism has its antithesis. It's a moot point whether the James Bond series belongs, basically, to the period within our brief (given its jingoistic, establishmentarian attachments), or to the subsequent period (given its swinging and kinky sexuality). No doubt the novels' success is due to their blend of American and English daydreams. In affluence and discipline, the public school ethos adapts itself to the *Playboy* era, the bluff English gentleman to the spirit of espionage appropriate for our centralized, bureaucratic, psychologizing, alienating society.

At any rate, there's a deathly hush in the close tonight – Bond J. is the last man in of the British Empire Superman's XI. Holmes, Hannay, Drummond, Conquest, Templar *et al* have all succumbed to the demon bowlers of the twentieth century, while The Winds of Change make every ball a googlie.

Whatever Brand X critics may have written, Bond isn't just an Organization Man, but a rigid jingoist, almost loveably archaic. If you have forelocks, prepare to touch them now, in fond farewell to the Edwardiana in modern drag lovingly panoplied forth in the first half of *Dr. No* (1962) as Bond glides along the Establishment's Old Boy Net. The British Raj, reduced to its Caribbean enclave, lords it benevolently over jovial and trusting West Indians and faithful coloured police-sergeants, the Uncle Toms of Dock Green. We might almost be back with Captain Kenneth More on the North-West Frontier. Meanwhile out on Crab Key lurks Dr. No, last of the war lords, whose 'chigro' minions ('I'm not racially prejudiced, but miscegenates tend to be untrustworthy and mixed-up'), blend of the Yellow Peril and the Mau-Mau, battle it out with his English co-anachronism.

Bond is also the Mike Hammer of the toffs, and the shift from Queensbury rules to neo-thuggery is a response to fear – the fear that Great Britain is no longer so strong that she can afford to lose all but the last battles on the playing fields of Eton. She is required to think in the realpolitik terms once left to all those lesser breeds without the Law. James Bond is England's 'para' and if duty called he'd clamp the electrodes to Milady's tender titties quicker than you can say 'Victoria Regina'. From another angle, he is the English lord with nary a dash, jigger or twinge of the middle-class conscience, and we all know from reading Simon Raven's *The English Gentleman* how Neanderthal that can be when its hackles are raised. Here, Bond shoots a disarmed man, out of temper.

Having said this, it's worth remembering that while pulps and politics interpenetrate and illuminate one another, they aren't after all tautologous; and to the burning question, 'Is Bond a bad influence on the youth of today?' we return the glossy answer that any man with a drop of claret in his veins prefers a rowdy young blood to a wan lay preacher. Making allowance for the fact that Bond is not a historical personage, it's only natural to like Ian Fleming's naughty hero better than the male nannies of sweetness-and-light who deprecate him. One of the things to be surreptitiously trumpeted in favour of the gentry, God save our little forelocks, is that it maintains a healthy anarchic vigour, a proper admiration for guts, grit and attack as virtues in themselves, against the drizzling moralizing that mildews so much left-wing thought from the foundations up. One's principal criticisms of Terence Young's *Dr. No* are to the effect that it is too decorous, too prosaic and too unconvincing. Fleming's novels deliciously mish-mash touches of Balchin-type verisimilitude with a streamlined, air-conditioned Gothic grotesque. And it's a pity that the latter has scared the producers off. Thus Honey (Ursula Andress), Bond's ironically scientific Girl Friday, a knife-girt Venus rising from the sea, lacks the smashed nose so lovingly detailed in the novel, even some cosmetic equivalent thereof. If the movie Bond carries a lighter-calibre revolver than he should, it is not because he loves Thy Servant A Gun as a schoolboy loves his pie, but because he is a kindly soul who would rather run an unnecessary risk than unnecessarily kill. The deaths and torments aren't half bizarre enough (what happened to the – filmed – scene where carnivorous crustacea creepy-crawl over Honey's staked out body?). Maybe the producers were right to suppress the giant squid (although only because it would have reminded me of *The Thief of Bagdad*, which framed a beauty) but Dr. No's death (in the reactor) can't hold a candle to the gloriously inglorious fate which the novel held in store for him. The facetious credits look like a 'Buy Your Kia-Ora Now' ad and destroy the 'Three Blind Mice' opener, potentially as poetic as that of *Tiger in the Smoke*. The colours are ugly, and the film plods along until we set sail for Crab Key. Thereupon, the battle against the 'dragon', Quarrel's horrible death, and the decontamination sequence, are first-rate, and here the film's intensity briefly attains the novel's poetry. Needless to say the film fails to do justice to Beau Bond. The requisite style would have the glacial elegance of the pistol which was 'A Woman's Ammunition' in the Yardley's ad, or, failing that, a sumptuousness, with cruelty.

In a TV interview, Ian Fleming maintained that Bond wasn't an Englishman at all. He had a Scots father and a Swiss mother, both his parents were killed in an Alpine accident, which he saw, while he was still a child. He was then sent to Eton for one half and after a precocious performance with one of the maids, expelled and demoted, traumatically, to a school of lesser renown. The confluence of Calvinist traditions (is Bond the Ahab of the secret service?), the Oedipal accident on the slopes of F6, the perverse yoking of status and sexuality – it's a pity Fleming never wrote this story, for I'd not only believe it, I might even buy it.

Presumably the film's producers have calculated that Flemingismus neat would alienate the middle-class and family trade, that with his reputation for violence their films' audience will accept the spectacular death as an enjoyable shock, and that maximum box-office receipts are thus to be obtained by taking Fleming lightly and strengthening, in actual context, other B.O. aspects – gaudiness, gadgetry, spectacle and send-up humour. In Young's *From Russia with Love* (1963) and Guy Hamilton's *Goldfinger* (1964) only a handful of ideas (SPECTRE's training-camp island, Lotte Lenya's Rosa Klebb, Robert Shaw's quiet hard assassin), suggest how Michael Powell in *Peeping Tom* mood could have brought to the films the true mixture of exuberance, kink, jingoism and romanticism. For Powell's romanticism, like Fleming's diagnosis, reminds us that inside every Insider there's an Outsider struggling to merge with those around him and fade away altogether.

The air of knowing, cynical and necessary double-cross with which the Bond films preen themselves suggest a renovated view, by the British, of their system. In this imperious patriotism is something brazenly amoral, rather than stoic. The villains are always nasty persons, partly because we all believe that there was never anything finer than the Pax britannica, so that anyone who doesn't accept it must be a rotten swine, and partly to divert us from Fleming's, and our, awareness that enemy agents are just foreign Bonds doing their job. In other words, patriotism is veering uncomfortably near a sense of its own arbitrariness, and putting forth all its plumage by way of counter-dazzle. Bond, essentially, is a one-man Suez task force. He's a curious, archaic counterpart of the angry young men: half-cadet, half-cad, half-freelance, half-civil servant. Oh, lucky Jim, how we envy him – and like that rebel's erstwhile author, continue him.

Bond's exceptional prowess enables him to pluck the choicest fruit from the system's expense accounts. For the rest of us, the 79,999 other suspects, he's one of the last semi-demi-semi affirmations of the top people's network as an idyllic equilibrium of virtues ancient and modern.

25. God Bless Captain Vere

If *Mutiny on the Bounty*, albeit a Royal Naval saga, was never filmed by the British, but twice by the Americans, it's presumably because it concerns a successful mutiny. But while M.G.M. were preparing the recent remake, two British movies concerned themselves with similar settings and problems: Lewis Gilbert's *H.M.S. Defiant* (1962) and Peter Ustinov's *Billy Budd* (1962). Both are studies of the Royal Navy at the time of the mutinies at Spithead and the Nore in 1797.

Lewis Gilbert's film refers only to one particular ship, blessed with a good, kind Captain (Alec Guinness) and cursed with a bad, sadistic second-in-command (Dirk Bogarde). The latter is a bastard in all possible senses. He's ambitious, and a lunatic about efficiency, and has powerful connections at home. When the Captain forces him to mitigate his floggings, he gets his cronies to keep caning the Captain's young son, too fine a lad to sneak. The anguished Captain is reluctant to interfere, for the bullies, technically, are within their rights, but eventually overrides them by threatening the un-impartial use of his own rights. Meanwhile, the men, led by sturdy, decent N.C.O.-type Anthony Quayle, have been fomenting mutiny against bad treatment and the Captain concedes the moral justice of their cause. When

Bogarde threatens to break him he is knifed by a (bad, impatient) mutineer. The newly impartial Captain is not in the least grateful, but the French providentially appear. Quayle is killed in the fighting, and the mutiny will be overlooked.

In many ways the film is conciliatory towards the notion of mutiny. Press-gang scenes establish the navy as an oppressive system. A senior Admiral tolerates all brutalities. Bogarde's bastardy and snide influence assert moral corruption among the highest in the land. Guinness understands the mutiny. But other elements counter these. First, our main identification is with the Captain, an ideal figure, a noble aristocrat with a nonconformist conscience. Second, the main victim of the brutalities is his son, who's another. Third, the villain, so far as the establishment is concerned, is an outsider – fruit of a sexual irregularity (of course) and with all the attitudes of the self-made man. *Most* officers, we feel, are like punctilious, incorruptible Alec Guinness. Therefore a mutiny, however understandable, can only be a tragic mistake. Indeed it will only discredit our (conciliatory) hero, so it is vital that it shan't happen. Fourth, Bogarde is killed by an evil mutineer, not a good one, and even the good one has to die, to expiate the other's crime, and, one suspects, his own mutiny. In brief, a mutiny is quite justifiable, so long as you don't actually mutiny, but just grumble.

The film doesn't claim to be an accurate picture of any particular event, but the historical events of which it is a reminiscence are worth recalling. The mutinies of the Spithead and Nore fleets (not single ships) were led by those officers who cared about their men. The system of brutalities wasn't invented by under-officers, but was systematic and official. Not only were men publicly flogged to death for trivial offences, but their quartermasters systematically cheated them of their pay. Far from spontaneously breaking off to fight the French, the mutineers blockaded London and left the country at Napoleon's mercy. In consequence, the Admiralty surrendered to the Nore mutineers. Those at Spithead hoped to act as catalysts for the rebellious ferment which existed throughout the country as a whole, but overplayed their hand. The story of either mutiny could make an epic of *Battleship Potemkin* calibre, and Gilbert's film reminiscently shows officers forcing men to eat cheese visibly squirming with plump maggots.

But it no more challenges constituted authority than those public school stories about a good house-master and brutal prefects. *H.M.S. Defiant* is simply an adults' version of Dean Farrar's flagellomanic public school novel, *St. Winifred's*. For simple fidelity to historical fact would have aligned the film with Eisenstein's or Kubrick's *Paths of Glory*. We would have worried in case Quayle lacked the nerve to knife Bogarde. His ability to do so would have been the final proof that he deserved to be the men's leader. The Captain would have been held responsible for the abuses proceeding under his command. Other senior officers would have made him their scapegoat, because of his decency. Spithead dreams of a national rebellion against those 'dark Satanic mills', against the obliteration of freedom of speech, and the eviction of the 'little man' by arbitrary squires and J.P.s, would have seemed sympathetic to us, even if, sadly, confused, like a mixture of William Blake and Morgan.

Billy Budd begins with Captain Vere (Peter Ustinov) despatching a boarding party to a merchantman, to press its crew members. Its Captain, very much a sturdy British seadog too, warns the boarding party that his men know about the Nore mutiny, and are likely to spread the word. Accordingly the boarding party take only one man, the good and selfless Billy Budd (Terence Stamp), who promises to say nothing. Docile as he is, Billy, being in some subtle way his own master, is hated by the brutal first mate Claggart (Robert Ryan), and tells the Captain (though not till asked) some of the truth about Claggart's brutalities. Claggart smilingly resolves to destroy a man whose sheer goodness threatens his whole conception of the world. His *agent provocateur* fails to lure the saintly Billy into an attempt on Claggart's life. Claggart, furious, frames him anyway, until Billy, in an outburst of righteous indignation strikes him, accidentally killing him. Although the Captain is well aware of Billy's real innocence, and discusses it at length with his junior officers, he resolves to take refuge behind the letter (and the spirit) of the law and hang him, as an example to the disaffected sailors. Billy, understandingly seeing the other man's point of view, and concerned that not even the suspicion of injustice shall exist to risk sparking off a mutiny, cries, with his last breath, 'God bless Captain Vere!' The men, though understandably bewildered, are no more convinced than we are, but the French fleet providentially appears on the horizon. The mutineers' leader cries, 'Come on lads, let's punish the French for what Claggart's done to us.' The opening of the engagement is shown, but not the result (lest defeat depresses us, and victory reconciles us to Vere's judicial murder?).

The providential appearance of French ships in both films isn't accidental, for the ideas spread by the French revolution might have sparked off a British revolution, if the nation hadn't first been disgusted by the Terror and then felt threatened by Napoleon.

Here again potentially conformist elements are quite evident – in our sympathy for manly and heroic Billy, in the playing of Captain Vere by likeable Peter Ustinov, in Claggart's being his junior, in the final unity against the French. Indeed, Herman Melville's story is a consciously paradoxical and profound study of good overcoming evil by submitting to it. But Ustinov, precisely by neglecting the metaphysical aspect of the story, gives Billy's story a sharper social relevance. The Captain of the British cargo vessel denounces British tyranny far more responsibly than the tavern-fodder of *H.M.S. Defiant*, and we believe his furious cry that the Royal Navy is a bigger threat to honest Englishmen, on land with its press-gangs, and abroad with its blockades, than the French. Because Billy is a saint, his submissive attitude isn't ours (indeed, only a 'tough and villainous' actor like Terence Stamp could have earned our respect for him), while it increases our indignation against the final injustice. The Captain's decision to hang a man whom he knows to be un-swervingly loyal makes him just as much a murderer as Claggart, albeit for Machiavellian rather than evil reasons. The warning is plain; treat responsible loveable officers just as suspiciously as nasty ones. It's a very direct attack on precisely the 'fatherly captain' of *H.M.S. Defiant*. The mutineers' cry, about releasing on the French, the rage felt against their own ruling class, is a savage and penetrating insight on the psychology of jingoism and the way in which war abroad is used to solve tensions at home. If Ustinov can end his film with the issue of the final battle unresolved it is because Billy's death is the tragic climax after which we should feel no enthusiasm.

26. Hard Conscience and Nonconformity
We've suggested that one characteristic of British culture is the intensity with which a nonconformist conscience has turned into a conformist conscience.

How and how far this happened is a matter for social history, but it leads to a question of which everyone is currently more aware. To what extent can the innermost recesses of our thought be manipulated by those in influence over us, in such a way as to further their own best interests, maybe at our expense? How legitimate, in a society which claims to respect the freedom of the individual, are the inter-relationships between internal and external authority? Yet how could society hold together without them?

The question can be taken at a more intimate, personal level than that of *80,000 Suspects*. And in two films Dearden and Relph attempt to do so. *The Mind Benders* (1962), like Guest's films, associates a questioning of the authorities with a science-fiction theme. Dirk Bogarde plays a young scientist who learns that his old boss, who has since died, is suspected of having sold secrets to the Russians. To clear his name, he will prove that his actions were due to being of unsound mind, after having been brainwashed while in a mentally unstable condition brought on by courageously being his own guinea-pig in testing the psychological effects of total sensory deprivation. To demonstrate the effects of the experiments, the young man repeats them on himself. The sceptical MI5 Major then implants in him the belief that his wife (Mary Ure) has been unfaithful. The otherwise rational young scientist believes it, until the act of delivering his own child clears his mind.

As usual, the hero, when torn between boss and wife, cleaves unto the former, even though he's dead and his wife is pregnant – all expressed in the rat-a-tat-terms of regulation stoicism: 'You're going to leave me?' 'Yes, I must.' But on the other hand, only his wife can rescue him from the madness which his masochistic loyalty, and authority's necessarily brutal testing, have brought on him. The spell put on him by his incarceration in rubber, water, darkness soundlessness and isolation (an impersonal, maddening womb) is lifted by the most intimate possible contact with his wife's flesh (delivering their child). The physical theme is continued via the personage of a young tart-cum-student (Wendy Craig) whose clothes are sexily skin-tight. Authority has to defend itself against many apparently well-founded charges of ruthless destructiveness, and though the Major does so, they survive in the film's final impression.

All the same, a final scene implausibly tries to shift the main weight of blame away from the security officer to an immature-seeming young scientist.

It's not authority that is to blame, it's these anti-traditional scientists. They seem, alas, to be indispensible to officialdom these days, but they, not it, are responsible for continually inventing things which trespass on the liberty of the individual. To disagree with officialdom is suspect: the film goes out of its way to suggest a connection between C.N.D. and treachery. Bogarde is authority's eager accomplice in destroying himself. It asks no more than he is anxious to give. He provokes it into accepting his unnatural sacrifice, not vice versa. And a telling symptom of his post-hypnotic madness is his refusal to immediately believe authority when it informs him that his wife hasn't been unfaithful to him after all and that though it was lying then it isn't lying now (it's never lying now).

The same team's *Life for Ruth* (1962) centres on a Jehovah's Witness (Michael Craig) whose principles forbid his little daughter having a blood transfusion. She dies. The father's crude certainties, and helplessness, are well sensed, and the film refuses to make him the moral scapegoat by pointed asides about Jewish solicitors, Catholic doctors, arrogant agnostics and red-haired typists. Nor is the attack on nonconformism as such. His sin lies not in sticking to his principles but in hoping for a miracle which would spare him their consequences. In an age which wants the pleasures but not the responsibilities, of freedom, can't we respect his willingness to bear the responsibility of his daughter's destiny, rather than leave her to 'them'? Nonetheless, he should have been more resigned before God's will. And, though the film criticizes the complacency of the humanitarian, liberal consensus, it does so by pleading for a double paternalism (God's, and fathers').

Eventually, Michael Relph and Bryan Forbes's script for *Man in the Moon* amiably turns the tables on its director-producers, and criticizes not just the scientists but the bureaucrats and the league of gentlemen for all the things which exasperate the rest of us.

Towards a severe confrontation of conscience Peter Glenville's *The Prisoner* (1955) cautiously advances. In an iron curtain country, a Cardinal (Alec Guinness) is to be broken down by an interrogator (Jack Hawkins). One supposes that the playwright, Bridget Boland, intended an anti-Communist piece which would suggest an explanation for the successes of brainwashing (still so hard to understand, despite Arthur Koestler's *Darkness at Noon*). This, more thoughtfully than usual, would show it as a human process applied by humans, who might have ideals just as some Christian inquisitors did, and who might just as often be sensitive men. The spirit recalls Graham Greene in making every concession to cynical materialism, while somehow maintaining the Christian possibility. The inquisitor, here, is played by English gentleman, Jack Hawkins. He foregoes truth drugs and torture, and even the threat thereof, insists to his sidekick on the need to understand, respect and love one's – victim? convert? – and works on the unconscious guilts which will undermine his beliefs.

He succeeds only to be brought, by sudden disgust with himself, to doubt his own agnosticism. Will Saul become Paul? Thus humanized, the Communist becomes a blend of kindly English headmaster (not altogether against a little gentle punishment ...), a kindly English psychiatrist, and a kindly English father-confessor. Involuntarily, no doubt, the film begins to move round to Orwell's own meaning of *1984*, and to criticize English techniques of brainwashing potential rebels. As in *Circle of Deception* and *Orders to Kill*, such a system breaks the individual under the brunt of a guilt which the system which imposes it on him does not feel.

A bluff, gruff warder makes a remark to the effect that people who think too deeply soon crack up, and on balance the film seems to agree with him. Cardinals are probably saved by dogma, but artists and intellectuals pose problems for conformist fundamentalism. Their special skills disturb its peace, not only of mind, but of soul, and sometimes have amazing influence on the establishment, which ought to be their reassuring antithesis. They query, they question, they reason why, they undermine.

It's true, alas, that the intellectual role, or façade, can attract peculiar temperaments, or accentuate the peculiarities of otherwise normal ones, especially in view of the leery looks they get from simpler souls. Nor would this writer's defence of English intellectuals *en bloc* be any more wholehearted than Orwell's. It's disheartening, though, that British movies generally have given artists and intellectuals a far worse press than Hollywood, where Minnelli and Richard Brooks regularly defend them.

A nonconformist-conformist attitude to scientists is exemplified, not only by *The Mind Benders* and *The Quatermass Experiment* (where they carry the can for officialdom), but by *Rockets Galore* (Relph-Dearden, 1958), where simple staunch old Scottish islanders resist the Air Ministry's attempts to convert their cottages into a rocket range. The villain of the piece is a humourless German scientist, not, of course, the R.A.F.'s top Brass.

The position of the Boulting Brothers is particularly interesting, but so closely connected with their whole moral standpoint that it's easier to establish it later. Meanwhile, an obvious, minor example may act as signpost. Their *Suspect* (1960) is an interesting inversion of *The Mind Benders*. Scientist Peter Cushing, arrogant with thoughtless idealism, wants to publish details of a vaccine that could save millions of lives. The humble sensible bureaucrats remind him that ruthless foreign powers might put it to evil use. This rather stymies him, whereupon the plot emphasis shifts to another intellectual, a mutilated and embittered concert pianist who tries to betray the secret via a high-brow cultural front organization. He is foiled by an apparently hopelessly stupid, doddering 'shabby genteel' security agent, who out-thinks the clever fellows, i.e. both the Snow and Leavis cultures.[39]

Students, particularly medical, may be mischievous, but only in hearty, traditional ways (the Dodo Society in *Bachelor of Hearts*). In *The Mind Benders* the semi-tart semi-student is shown to be useless in a crisis (which is a fair bit of observation), but the context suggests an ulterior anti-intellectuality. The same holds true of the in itself very exact and shrewd portrayal of the gullible, stiff young student who, in *Sapphire,* has become engaged to another semi-student semi-tart. 'Students are young, and tend to be unconventional, so they must be foolish, though it's excusable because they're immature. Indeed, education is a dangerous thing. Even the adult scientist may start by thinking that he's better than the average decent middle-class sort of chap, despise the wise authorities, and then what is there but to fall for all the foreign agents that infest C.N.D. and classical concerts, or become a pseudo-intellectual tarty bitch?' (this being the English gentleman's interpretation of the New Morality).

Such criticisms aren't always undeserved; they are sometimes plausible, in their highly selective way. Yet one regrets that they allow no value, no social role, and indeed only a grudging tolerance, to an activity which is, at least, one of the reasons for our civilization's free spirit. However Boultings take *Lucky Jim's* side against the academic section of the establishment.

Surprisingly, it's the first two *Carry On* films which assert the changing image of the intellectual. In *Carry On Sergeant* the sharp tongued intellectual in a friendly and patient way gives the squad dunce extra coaching. In *Carry On Nurse* he sticks up for himself, and therefore everybody else, against the battle-axe Matron. After Jimmy Porter, intellect can be detached from its connection with idealism and snobbery.

British qualms about the grinding effect of puritanical submission to the system are often expressed in two ways: their veneration for the eccentrics, and their much-touted sense of humour. Essential safety-valves these no doubt are. But the eccentrics glorified usually turn out to be *either* Margaret Rutherford *or* Alastair Sim (the twin souls of *The Happiest Days of Your Life*). At any rate, they're usually upper-class in origins and either of independent means or firmly ensconced in authority (the bishop and squire of *The Titfield Thunderbolt*, James Robertson Justice's irascible surgeons). They're usually variations on old-fashioned father and aunt figures and the eccentricity isn't eccentricity at all, but the old upper-class way of speaking out boldly and rudely. A softer variation is Katie Johnson's indomitably sentimental old lady in *The Ladykillers*. Similarly, most of the 'subversive' Ealing comedies follow foreign precedents. Robert Hamer's brilliant *Kind Hearts and Coronets* owes something to Oscar Wilde's stylistic borrowings from the French, to Sacha Guitry and to *Monsieur Verdoux*, while Alexander Mackendrick's *The Ladykillers* has an American predecessor, *Arsenic and Old Lace*. *Passport to Pimlico* may owe something to G. K. Chesterton's *The Napoleon of Notting Hill*. Comedies of murder, smut and drag, of which more later, have proved bastions of healthy bad taste unquashable even by the iron maidens of British prudery.

An inconspicuous British speciality, in intriguing counterpart to the stiff upper lip, is the film based on the exasperations of minor social conflicts and everyday routines. *Locus classicus* of a topic with universal appeal, but which the British work more boldly than anyone else, is the scene in Ralph Thomas's *Upstairs and Downstairs* (1959), where our cadet-type hero (Michael Craig) gets himself locked in a train lavatory. In Wendy Toye's *Raising a Riot* (1955) Kenneth More, and in Jay Lewis's *The Baby and the Battleship* (1956), such mere males as John Mills and Richard Attenborough grapple with all sorts of housewifely and mothercare tasks. In the *Doctor* and *Carry On* series, a discontinuous story-line enables the script to become a succession of professional and social embarrassments. In Sidney Gilliat's *Only Two Can Play* the hero's half-crippled friend (Kenneth Griffith) limps after a bus whose conductor deliberately and cruelly gives the starting signal just as he reaches for it. Ronald Neame's *The Million Pound Note* (1953) is built entirely on tailors', waiters' and other minor functionaries' response to the note which gets its lucky possessor (Gregory Peck) everything free. The style differs from American situation comedy in precisely its heavier, more considered, more dramatic, less fantasticated sense of embarrassments bravely borne. The same susceptibility underlies the U-non-U and oneupmanship theme elaborated with not always amiable obsessiveness by Nancy Mitford, Stephen Potter, and all. Robert Hamer's *School for Scoundrels* (1959), a broad but likeable piece, puts Potter's ideas in screen comedy form. Professor Alastair Sim (long-time headmistress of St. Trinian's) presides over an academy which teaches its adult pupils how to upstage, over-awe, bruise, crush, obliterate and expunge, with apparently impeccable politeness, the egos of all rivals in the universal rat race. This lumbering film has its moments. Its cardinal sin, among others, is its own lack of snob appeal. But then its producer is an American. At least it indicates the heavy crudity of middle-class ploys, while establishing that exacerbated dread of hostile judgement, that terrorized and often unjustified, certainty of every betrayal of non-stock emotion being silently noted, possibly to be noncommittally held against one, which renders the Englishman so constrained, and gives the stiff upper lip its roots, not only in stoicism, but in fear. Outside our period, *Nothing But the Best* endows a similar theme with the more sophisticated treatment it deserves.

27. The Glum and the Guilty

Just as intellectuals are usually idealistic greenhorns or moral megalomaniacs, so problems which can't plausibly be reduced to fundamentalist formulae tend to be paraphrased in terms of violence. The Irish problem? Fanatical Irish violence. The teenager problem? Teenage violence. All problems are reduced to minority-group violence versus law and order.

However, the notion of violence as endemic and irreducible is not divorced from a sense of life's everyday intimacies. The murderers who traditionally fascinate the English imagination are those who lived ordinary, respectable lives. By critical identification with the murderer, the British gratify a derivative of Calvinistic self-criticism. Liberal idealism is slightly exotic compared with the more sullen, silent, pervasive application of cynicism to the 80,000 suspects who constitute an identikit of oneself.

An observation by Martha Wolfenstein and Nathan Leites is significant in this respect. Analysing movies released in New York between 1945 and 1949, they remark, 'The tendency of British movies to intensify rather that to reduce the intimacy between a prospective murderer and his victim is illustrated in *Dear Murderer* (Arthur Crabtree, 1947). 'While characteristic of the quality of the relation between murderer and victim, this film is atypical in that it shows a man murdering a male rival in love. The hero (Eric Portman), who has been out of the country on business, learns that his flirtatious wife (Greta Gynt), with whom he is desperately in love, has been having an affair in his absence. He pays a visit to the other man, introduces himself and persuades the man to write a letter breaking off all relations with the wife. There is an interlude of gentlemanly talk between the two men; they have a drink together, and there is the expressed feeling that, under different circumstances they might have been friends. The husband then interrupts the writing of a farewell letter (which the other is writing at his dictation) at a point where it will sound like a suicide note, produces a gun, orders his victim to lie down on the couch, ties his hands and feet, climbs on top of him, tells him ragingly how much he has suffered from his wife's infidelity, and announces he is going to murder him. The victim, with whom he had been talking a moment ago in a friendly way, the live young man who will so soon be dead, protests and is gagged. The murderer then proceeds to carry out the carefully planned murder which will look like suicide. This scene presents a contrast to the characteristic murder in American films. Here the victim is purposely humanized, instead of being dehumanized, before he is murdered; a positive relation, at least as a potentiality, between murderer and victim is evoked ... the scene is thus weighted with intense emotions of suffering and destroying.' The same pattern, of affection discovered just before death, can be seen in *The Bridge on the River Kwai*. Alec Guinness discovers that Sessue Hayakawa is, in his way, an 'honourable man', and Alec Guinness himself reveals his sympathetic idealism at length before Jack Hawkins's commandos arrive and kill him. 'American films tend to drain murder of such emotion. The murderer becomes an impersonal dangerous force or the victim an impersonal obstructive being, or both, while physical and emotional contact between the two is reduced to a minimum. Another impersonalizing device frequently in American films is to have killings occur in a context of rapid and confusing action, which excludes an awareness of emotional relations.'

Another permutation of the British formula is exemplified by Edward Dmytryk's *Obsession* (1949). Here mad doctor Robert Newton keeps his wife's lover fettered in a blitzed house until such time as he has been able to fill its bathtub with nitric acid, which he brings every day in a hot water bottle. The choice of container – everyday, intimate, absurd – is a neatly nasty frisson, and, again, the men have long, conversational negotiations and bargainings, on an everyday basis.

Subsequently, of course, American films, reacting against their own cliché, turn to questions of personal motivation and guilt, after the style of such films as *Kiss the Blood Off My Hands* (Norman Foster, 1949), though usually with reference to the idea of mental sickness (shell-shock, amnesia, complexes, and so forth). British critics, significantly, got very irritated by these excuses. For we are all suspects, all potential murderers. Once 'excuses' are allowed, anyone might grab hold of the nearest poker and start battering his nearest and dearest to death. This neo-Calvinist pessimism and guilt militate against 'liberal' and reformist ideas in criminology and other fields. If American films were pervaded by a simplistic (because too optimistic) psychology, here only Anthony Kimmins's *Mine Own Executioner* (1947) and Joseph Losey's *The Sleeping Tiger* (1954) suggest that psychoanalysis has anything that isn't trite to say. Often the liberal riposte to hard-liners is to doubt everyone's guilt, by appealing to our duty not to behave barbarously towards the criminal. This riposte is of limited effectiveness against the punitive streak in puritanism, exemplified by British fascination with the condemned cell. Indeed, retentionists may enjoy abolitionist films like J. Lee Thompson's *Yield to the Night* (1956), with a horrified, fascinated awe very near the classical definition of the tragic feeling – an identification involving pity, terror, and shared guilt. The ambivalence connected with capital punishment is betrayed in two thrillers in which the (long 'hereditary') post of public hangman is associated with inherited insanity. Eric Portman's *Wanted for Murder* is the son of the public hangman. In *Daybreak* (Compton Bennett, 1948), Eric Portman, this time, the public hangman himself who leads a dual life as a hairdresser, frames his wife's lover (Maxwell Reed) for murdering his 'other' self and hangs him. This gruelling melodrama, piling guilt upon guilt, in gloomy plots whose contortions are near-expressionist, has a weird power lacking in more sensible movies about the suffering of the condemned man's family (*The Last Man to Hang?*, *Tall Headlines*). It is probably because Lee Thompson's film exists at a kind of junction of liberalism and severity that it combines something of the strength of both.

Concomitant with this vision of the ubiquity of repressed violence goes that identification with suffering passivity which contrasts strongly with the assertiveness of the typical American hero. The contrast is exemplified, on one level, by the styles of *The Men* and *Reach for the Sky*. The plethora of P.O.W. stories express it on another: the best variation on their theme brings it home to H.M. Prisons (*The Pot Carriers*, 1962). Passivity's apogee is reached in Roy Baker's *Tiger in the Smoke* (1956). Its young hero (Donald Sinden) spends most of the film tied up and gagged in a bath chair. The fight against the killer and his gang is led by his fiancée (Muriel Pavlow) and her clergyman father (Laurence Naismith). *Ice Cold in Alex* expresses the same complex of feelings in another mode (the humiliation of hysteric uselessness) yet retains a tenderly forgiving camaraderie which makes this film so moving. If the mood is insistent, to balance Hollywood's dogmatic dynamism, it expresses tenacity in adversity rather than defeatism; and it springs from a mature sense of the individual's limitations.

Baker's and Lee Thompson's heroes are already anti-heroes, accepted without the futile publicity which attended the discovery of the concept in intellectual circles. Such movies touch on a self-criticism, a stress on life as basic frustration, deeper and older than Munich and Dunkirk. The characteristic mood of English movies is sombre, stoic, slightly depressed. Their complacencies are those of relief rather than happiness, and, as such, more cynical and pessimistic, by implication, than, at first, appears. The mood seems almost independent of the particular story, and seems to arise not so much from the evolution of the plots (as it does in French films), but to precede it, or to be superimposed on it, like the – often falser – drive and eupepsia of American movies. It also dulls the pain and protest that one finds in comparable French movies. It's perhaps significant that *Le Salaire de la peur* and *Gervaise* are approached only by the first and the last films in the British cycle – *Odd Man Out* and *A Night to Remember.*

The flattish, lightish tones of Lewis Gilbert and Philip Leacock, like a bas relief in grey metal, catch the studiedly superficial equivocation of stoicism. Their nearest American equivalents in this respect, Jack Arnold and Anthony Mann, carry a heavier violence and sadness. But the most imposing British pessimist is, of course, Carol Reed. His masterpiece, *Odd Man Out* (1947), tracks wounded I.R.A. leader (James Mason) through his dying hours with a pessimistic intensity often compared to *Le Quai des brumes.* In Reed's film Civil War exposes man's radical solitude with less hope than Sartre's films allow.

Reed's stylistic *tour de force* is his version of Joseph Conrad's *Outcast of the Islands* (1951). Through visual continuities whose deft intricacy rivals Pabst's, he traces the hectic succession of gloatings and grovellings through which a mean and desperate trader (Trevor Howard) lurches to his doom. Deep focus vignettes circumscribe the action with the ironic innocence of Malayan village-life. Innocence rather than life-force – the substitution indicates the dilution of the Symbolist novelist's sumptuous lyricism. Conrad stands outside Willems, to judge him, but also remains within him, to suffer with him, fully, so fully, that every description of jungle foliage is laden with lyrical energy, temptation and pain. Reed remains outside Willems, Trevor Howard's vehement wretchedness is more coolly framed.

An analogous split weakens Reed's version of Graham Greene's *The Fallen Idol*. Its plush visuals offer neither a common denominator nor a bridge between the mind of the hero-worshipping child (Bobby Henrey) and the adult realm, in which his butler-hero (Ralph Richardson) escapes from his bitchy wife (Sonia Dresdel) to a brief encounter with Michèle Morgan. The film seems to glance down at a child peeping up, rather than recreating his emotional perspectives. The two stories, only lightly linked, leave an overriding impression of – embassy staircases. The over-celebrated *The Third Man* (1949) is an admirable mood-piece, sensitively characterized, although a second viewing reveals the conventionality of its themes. The celebrated tilted shots are anticipated in Duvivier's *Un carnet de bal* (1937) or James Whale's *Bride of Frankenstein* (1935). Effective, certainly, the celebrated zither, the neat reversal of the Western fade-out (the *girl, walking,* past the waiting *hero, towards* us), and that masochistic Nietzscheanism which the film's co-producer, David Selznick, had endowed with more fire and poetry in *Duel in the Sun* (1946), while the post-war Vienna locations unite the documentary and the expressionist in a way that a mythical Texas doesn't. Certainly Welles has the diabolic reek Peck hadn't (and was no less complex for lacking). Certainly Valli's Garboesque melancholy is classier than Jennifer Jones's splendidly tigerish Pearl Chavez. But is a *coup de grâce* by an old school chum in the sewers ipso facto profounder than a *coup de grâce* by a half-breed girl in the desert? Is the sinister stereotypy of Greene's minor villains more interesting than the older generation sub-plot in the King

Odd Man Out: James Mason, Kathleen Ryan – A pessimism that exposes man's radical solitude

Vidor film? Isn't there, in the end, no less to the gaudy baroque of the American film than the faultless rhetoric of the British?

Less striking, but, in terms of personality, as solid, is the less celebrated follow-up, *The Man Between* (1953), thanks to the presence of Mason, Claire Bloom and Hildegarde Neff. After *A Kid for Two Farthings* (1954), a rather indecisive experiment in populist local colour, and the standard Hollywoodiana of *Trapeze* (1956), Reed returned to a more personal mood in *The Key* (1958) and to Greene in *Our Man in Havana* (1959). Their relatively listless style is appropriate, though helped by black-and-white CinemaScope, worst of all possible visual formats. Yet the – ironic resignation? – that allows the inner-outer splits in *The Fallen Idol* and *Outcast of the Islands* results, here, in a soft-pedalling, almost, a loss, of the magic, the drive, of fantasy lives (Guinness's vision of spy networks, his daughter's materialistic eye for smart cars, Burl Ives's obsession with his Prussian uniform). How simply Buñuel could have made so much of such fetishes. The film softens the mood of Greene's novel from pain to drabness implying pain. It loses not only the energy but the 'passing tones' that gave Reed's earlier style its vivacity. One says this regretfully, for this is the only script in which Greene matches the sensitivity of his novels. The story is built on strong spiritual polarities; between, for example, Guinness, summa of humbled British mediocrity, and his daughter, with her fourfold arrogance (she's young, she's conventional, she's Catholic, and she's American); or between this girl and the film's purest character (a coloured nun who while under age was raped by the brutal police-chief). Indeed, the broad mockery of the English establishment and of English Intelligence is the least interesting aspect of this lukewarm, yet interesting, film. Reed has faced the same problem as his French counterpart in poetic pessimism, Julien Duvivier: one's pessimism saps, at last, the vigour of one's vision. The subject behind Reed's subjects is loneliness, which also lies behind the disjunctions of the two child films. We are all odd men out, third men, running. Only the mad artist peers, pitilessly, into our dying eyes.

Other directors essayed Greene's melancholy with, usually, less success. Trevor Howard and Maria Schell imbue George More O'Ferrall's *The Heart of the Matter* (1953) with seething spats of the Greenian vision of the everyday as hell. Edward Dmytryk allows a spiritually lax sweetness to imbue the 'anti-miracles' of *The End of the Affair* (1954), apart from a low-angle wide-angle shot of a seedy room lit by a bare bulb. The décor in the Boultings's *Brighton Rock* (1947) catches the obsessional, empty harshness of Sadistic asceticism. The extreme bleakness, curiously, banishes the Greenian blend of beauty, life-force, and fear. Ken Annakin's *Across the Bridge* (1957), an ironic morality about a millionaire (Rod Steiger) reduced to gratitude for a dog's companion-ship, misses its potential existentialism in a too obvious schema.

Greene's strength – and maybe genius isn't too strong a word – lies in his combining a journalist's knowledge of how the world works, with an intense poetic-philosophic vision of familiar urban reality. This poetic world was the big city as Auden's, Spender's, MacNeice's, Day Lewis's, rarely was. His greatest gift is a manipulation of stream-of-consciousness techniques, supple, deft, and incisive enough to counterpoint several mental layers, past and present, thought and mood, and take in its stride a strongly dramatic – sometimes even melodramatic – story-line. Unexpectedly, perhaps, internal psychological complexity and evolution tend to a tertiary role.

It's no accident that *It's a Battlefield* must owe more, in its construction, to Eisenstein's practice of intellectual montage than any other English novel. The failure of Greene's characters to change is part of their pathos; hence his plays tend to seem constructions, while, if his conversion novels are unconvincing, it's because the conversions and miracles are as external to the characters as the melodrama of *This Gun for Sale*. One has, perhaps, unjustly, a feeling of borrowing. As *This Gun for Sale* borrows from Hollywood gangster movies, so his religious novels parallel, but more palely, Bernanos and Mauriac.

Greene's widespread reputation as a 'filmic' writer depends on his intelligent and slick use of melodrama, and on the vividness of his visual detail. But this last is very much more a matter of literary imagery than of a camera eye. And most of what Greene takes from the cinema is far from rare in the cinema. Simply to translate this back to the screen is to settle for the already familiar. Greene's own script for *The Third Man* doesn't miss a trick, but on the finer points, it's further from Greene than *Odd Man Out*. The directors who could bring Greene the poet to the screen are those whose fast, fluid lyrical eye for physical detail goes with a powerful sense of symbolic detail and visual lyricism. Pabst's *Der Dreigroschenoper*, Sternberg's *The Blue Angel*, Clouzot's

Quai des Orfèvres are more deeply Greenian than any film derived from Greene. Pabst's affinity with Greene's sceptical aspects (perhaps his profoundest) is indicated by Siegfried Kracauer's account, in *From Caligari to Hitler*, of a moment from *The Loves of Jeanne Ney* (1927). It 'opens with a scene characterizing the scoundrel Khalibiev: from the tips of his shoes the camera glides along his legs to scattered newspapers, records, cigarette stubs on the table, follows his hand as it selects one stub, scrutinizes his face, and finally encompasses part of the dirty hotel room with Khalibiev lying on the sofa ... Pabst features objects because they make up the kind of reality he wants to explore. In a decaying or transitional world, whose elements fall asunder, the objects rush out of their hiding places and take on a life of their own ... the iron wash basin in the room that shelters Jeanne and Andreas for a few nocturnal hours testifies to the tristesse emanating from this background for futile sex adventures ....' As it is, the sharpest crystallizations of the Greene world in British movies are the scapegraces so sensitively sketched by Denholm Elliott in *The High Bright Sun* and (lying outside our period) *Nothing But the Best* — both admirable incarnations of the hero of *England Made Me*. Reminiscent of the Greenian world is the spirit of *The Prisoner*, where, by a double disgust, decency continues its flickering existence in man. With Carol Reed lost to Hollywood, his mantle has fallen on Jack Clayton. Apart from the seediness of *Room at the Top* (1958), both *The Bespoke Overcoat* (1955) and *The Innocents* (1961) venture into metaphysics. The first involves grim Jewish whimsy, the second parallels the Greenian theme of childhood and evil. Though only an Ophulsesque intricacy of lighting and tracking could transpose into visual terms the sinuous complexity of Henry James's prose style, Clayton has kept the full force of James's attack on the complacency of sweet puritanism. Its champion is Deborah Kerr, brimming over with delicate courage as she tries to exorcise in the boy the spirit of the evil male gamekeeper (whose sins recall Gainsborough's sex-and-bullying barnstormers). It is her faith in the power of good which drives her to challenge evil, through the boy. And when she loses, she is guilty, through hubris, of killing, and damning, him.

Considered as a story-line, *The Turn of the Screw*, on which *The Innocents* is based has dated. Its equation of precocious sexual passion with evil is rather more 'Victorian', in the worst sense, than, say, Emily Brontë's

Wuthering Heights. After Freud, and Spock, we all know that sexual precocity is a common or kindergarten matter, and has nothing at all to do with being pawns of the devil. In any case, the film would have explored its supernatural theme more thoroughly if (*a*) it had stressed the children's *internal* fight against their supernatural possessors, rather than the governess's *external* viewpoint, and (*b*) if it had counter-pointed its simple morality by our instinctive sympathy for the life-force throbbing through the Heathcliffian dead. Second, the ghost story, in its traditional forms, has been killed, probably not, as James predicted, and as McLuhan would agree, by electric light, but by the decay of our belief in ghosts. One of the reasons why vampires are flying again, in the cinema, in, precisely, the electric darkness, is that their sins are exotic and physical, they're not dependent on a theological atmosphere, but on their physical attack.

Once related to Greene, *The Pumpkin Eater* (1964) and *Our Mother's House* (1967) seem less agnostic. The second, indeed, answers all the objections to the James story sketched above. A brood of infants afraid, with reason, that the authorities will break up their family refuse to deliver their mother's corpse to the authorities, pretend she's alive, stick together and contact her by spirit seances. Their tribal infantilism fails to defend them against the morbid severities of the immature superego, from which they are saved, but simultaneously exposed to adult corruption, by the arrival of a charming scapegrace (Dirk Bogarde) although he, in the end, becomes their victim also. This very rich story-line has the one defect of its innumerable qualities of detail; it goes off in so many directions (home versus 'they', innocence about corpses but fear of spirits, *Seance on a Wet Afternoon, Lord of the Flies, The Servant*), that its themes interrupt one another. It should, perhaps, have gone the whole hog, varied its moods more, expanded to Cinerama envelopment, and become a three-hour film. *The Pumpkin Eater* is an inversion of the same theme, mother's corpse. The attack on the heroine's fertility by her husband and the world, is an attack on her physical essence as surely as a knife in the heart. The abortion and miscarriages so insistent in the kitchen sink films whose arrival marks the closure of our period, seem to express not only misgivings about the new morality, but something defeatist and destructive of life in the British spirit. In *The Pumpkin Eater* its victim is an American woman. In *The L-Shaped Room* it's a French girl. But in *Look Back in Anger*, it is Alison herself who so nearly accepts the best of her traditional family and her rebellious lover.

28. Laugh and Lie Down

The British sense of humour tends to strengthen peace of mind against self-reproach for passivity and apathy. Nonetheless Ealing made sporadic attempts to revive the gusto of the old-time music-hall, first, in Cavalcanti's *Champagne Charlie* (1944), and, even though its overt setting is contemporary, Michael Relph's *Davy* (1957). Though Tommy Trinder is an authentic, Cavalcanti's well-washed, cheerful, determinedly innocent film misses the heat and friction to which the old star's plumminess, or grittiness, or crispness, were a proudly dapper response, and which had to be caught in any period reconstruction if the songs were to recapture their third dimension. Cheerfulness is not gusto, and a sense of rugged life is far more present in the tavern sing-songs of *Oliver Twist*.

Throughout the thirties, the vintage, the unforgettable, Will Hay, with his dour, crafty, suffering face, his disreputable combination of Dickensian fruitiness and Greenian seediness, his stern yet apprehensive smirk, topped by the pince-nez and mortar-board of desperate pretention, best puts on the screen an amoral and weary indomitability which is at once truly proletarian and truly shabby genteel. Doubtless he lacked the fantasy and range of W. C. Fields, as the Crazy Gang lacked the poetic stylization of the Marx Brothers. Yet the English comedians have a homely, hot-oven intimacy whose artistic quality becomes more apparent as time passes. Sid Field's own sketches in *London Town* (Wesley Ruggles, 1946) are as scintillating as his later, more 'filmic' material, is execrable. Golden passages there are too in the British industry's bottom drawer productions like the Old Mother Riley series, and it's here that the old-time music hall puts out its last rich, knobbly, stalks and stems.

Otherwise, the comedy in British movies is keyed to various compromises between thirties variety, cheery optimism, and borrowings from Hollywood. Comedians like Tommy Trinder, Jack Warner and Max Bygraves are hoicked directly into friendly, serious roles. These comedy movies invent nothing which the stars don't bring with them or which it doesn't more or less aptly borrow from Hollywood. The only successor to the dignified cheerfulness of George Formby and Gracie Fields is Norman Wisdom, whose get-up marks him as half-worker, half-child. The strands of ingratiating eagerness and inoffensive shyness are at opposite poles to the sourer, dourer, suspicious rascality of Will Hay. But even if Norman's too much the cadet and too little the cad, his oscillations between eager co-operativeness, accident proneness, and petulant retaliation, catch something of the ambivalence within the apparent reconciliation of the classes. One's only regret is that he hadn't a Preston Sturges to invent a style and a world for him. As it is, many sequences deserve anthologizing. Rather more saucy and tigerish is monstrous little Charlie Drake, who may not have an Edwardian ripeness, but substitutes a sixties one; his somewhat sardonic cry, 'Hullo, my darlings', is about as innocent as Bugs Bunny's 'What's up, doc?', and this peculiar mixture of Tweety Pie, Fatty Arbuckle, Baby Face Nelson and Alf Garnett has had curate's egg scripts rather than the tearaway affair he deserves.

The difficulty both comics face is the absence of a middle range of sophistication in British films. Bob Hope and Jerry Lewis often play for expressionistic childishness, but their sphere of reference includes the adult world (Hope the salesman, Lewis the hypochondriac), with its cynicism and disillusionment. The scripts of their British equivalents see them as lumpy kids, or, occasionally, as clowns, long spiritually obsolete figures of pathos. It took satire to demonstrate, not simply that satire itself is quite within the reach of the masses, but that it was possible to be funny, seriously, about adult attitudes.

A more hopeful approach to farce is begun by the *Carry On* series, with a cast of old faithfuls which the first two films suggested might one day become worthy of the Crazy Gang. Amongst the realms of discussion as to their vulgarity, which most serious critics seemed to think was a new development in British culture, one point was missed. The genesis of *Carry On Nurse* is significant. The script is, simply, the best anecdotes gathered by the scriptwriter's wife during her nursing days. The film isn't quite so far from reality as one might assume, near enough to relate it to the venerable genre of scurrilous comic realism. There are nostalgic moments for old sweats also in *Carry On Sergeant*. Subsequently the series resorts to the systematic parody of genres, at best hilarious (as in *Carry On Spying*), but efforts to maintain the reference to real life collapse as ignominiously as *Carry On Regardless*, which is as bad as old quota quickies. Dismissed by critics during its first, and most promising, phase, the series has subsequently been idealized with equal lack of discrimination. One of the best scenes in Pat Jackson's *What a Carve Up!*, with Sidney James and his mate sitting down to a fish-and-chip meal in their dingy lodging-house, exemplifies the comic melancholy missing from even the best of the *Carry On* series, and which they would need, in some form or other, before they could rank alongside the mellow grotesquerie of the Crazy Gang.

A quartet of middle-class comedians is formed by Richard Massingham, Tony Hancock, Alec Guinness and Peter Sellers, with Alastair Sim as a kind of eccentric fifth wheel. Massingham, forties 'star' of Ministry of Information commercials, already has Hancock's worried look, although that worried look is everywhere, for this, not gusto, is the real, and therefore the creative, tone of a nation that takes its pleasures sadly and greets its disasters with something like relief. Hancock remains the master of minute humiliation, whether, as in *The Punch and Judy Man* (1962), completely mystified by the obscure, yet, one can be sure, platitudinous, parables of a B.B.C. religious uplifter, or, as in *The Rebel* (1960), doing as in Rome and asking the waiter at Maxim's for 'snails, egg and chips'. Alas, the earlier film eventually, though only gradually, loses his gifts in high life fantasy, while the later needed a less tired subject than the treacherously easy put-down of seaside municipalities.

If Alec Guinness is the figurehead of fifties comedy, the sixties are under the sign of Sellers. Both are mediocre Everyman, both play many roles in every film, some of their roles could be interchanged. Guinness's home key is a sad, gentle, passive wistfulness, Sellers's is more sardonic, playful, and outgoing. Guinness is a mouse darting about behind his role, Sellers a cat smoothly patting it. However fierce and forceful, Guinness's Colonels are somehow somewhere self-denying and thoughtful. Sellers's militarists are melancholy, yet too burlesqued to be self-aware. Guinness is a comedian of pathos, Sellers's comedy of self-destruction is a stage on the way to satire. Where Guinness has flexibility in depth, in straight roles, Sellers, there, is oddly blank. Something in Guinness accepts self-sacrifice as necessary to life; Sellers's exact mimicry reduces the code to pastiche and parody. Even when playing the Rabelaisian Gulley Jimson, church-mouse Guinness looks like Cardinal Heenan with an unctuously roguish smile. Sellers is Jewish-cosmopolitan, chasing a worldly satisfaction which eludes him. Guinness is earnest or shabby genteel, even in scoundrelry he's a worm turning or a shy sly mastermind who, like a recluse, has bided his time. Sellers is 'American', i.e. all but classless. Guinness's portrait gallery evokes brass rubbings, Sellers's, a colour supplement. If Guinness played a lover, it would be love's scruples, timidities and thoughtfulness he'd catch. Sellers could not resist lechery for a moment, and strive for cool attack, even if he kept tripping over his thumbs. Guinness is weightless, hinting at depth behind his candle-face. Sellers played a heavy in *Never Let Go*, with immaculate technical perfection, and made us all laugh. Guinness has a masochistic core, Sellers has no core. Guinness is Ealing's England, Sellers foretells Frost Over England. Each, one suspects, has the other's home key as lining. American comedy is keyed, characteristically, to the nervously brash salesman setting his cap at both success and the glamorous young mother figure. French comedy has evolved from the comedy of character à la Fernandel, to that of the nervous tic, à la Louis de Funès, as if life were taking on an American nerviness there. The home key of English comedy is that of the man who's withdrawn into himself, into semi-defeat, before, slyly, or dutifully, he rouses himself, almost reluctantly, for hopes are dupes, and has a go, ladies, he has a go. To the whimsy of Ealing's later upper-middle-class style one may well prefer more solid and conventional pieces like Mario Zampi's *Laughter in Paradise* (1951), *Top Secret* (1952) and *The Naked Truth* (1957). The last is the first British film to loosen its upper lip and show a satirical fang, with Peter Sellers's portrait of a loveable homey quiz master really devoured by contempt for the doddering old folk to whom he awards his prizes.

The difficulty in establishing a middle-range between facetiousness and seriousness probably explains why the British cinema never developed its own style of sophisticated comedy, as Hollywood and France both enjoyed. Hopes were raised when the actor Clive Brook who had worked the Hollywood of the 1930s, took over the direction of *On Approval* (1944), the one British film to be compared with the expertise of Lubitsch and the Hollywood school. Jeffrey Dell, with *Don't Take It to Heart!* (1944) and *It's Hard to Be Good* (1948), seemed to have caught a spark of the Sturges spirit. Both begin with happy malice, but trail off into facetiousness, like *Vice Versa*, while Dell continues by co-writing scripts with the Boultings. Rank's experiments in the sophisticated comedy of affluence seem concocted out of theories of matching Hollywood on its home ground and scarcely connect with British experience. The nearest English success, *Genevieve*, has a more modest spirit. It may be that Hollywood comedies, like Feydeau's farces, possess a materialistic, optimistic drive which alone enables their scintillating mixture of stylisation, speed and plausibility. Simultaneously, and paradoxically, the childishness of farce is exaggerated, accelerated, to a delirium of self-derision in the first Goon film. *The Case of the Mukkinese Battle-horn* (1955) subjects the myth of the sharp-as-a-knife Scotland Yard 'tec (Peter Sellers) to Goonatic desecrations. *Toute proportion gardée*, the recipe isn't unworthy of comparison with Jarry, whose Père Ubu, that two-legged, pot-bellied pantechnicon of megalomania, paranoia, cunning, stupidity and cowardice is Eccles, Bloodnok and Bluebottle rolled into one. The British trio add natural innocence only to condemn it. It's also entertaining to 'compare and contrast' (as they say in examination questions; and now that films are becoming culturally respectable one must have a question on 'crazy comedy) the respective roles of the three Marx Brothers and the three Goons, taking Sellers as Groucho (Jewish front man), Spike Milligan as Harpo (inspired child-idiot) and Harry Secombe as Chico (innocent, rather than properly cagey). The film has worn well enough for its quota quickie tattiness to become part of the joke, which is that brew of *super-naif/faux naif* which attacks conventional meanings from above and below. It's an early expression of the nonchalant nihilism underlying the deadpan parody/self-parody of the best pop art. In the same line, Richard Lester's *The Running Jumping & Standing Still Film* (1959) replaces Titfield-type nostalgia by an indefinable quality of rage, at betrayal by the smug inadequacy of one's cultural patrimony. In their stiffly Euclidean way, its pinmen exhibit mental processes and behaviour patterns which have degenerated into ritual closed systems unconnected with reality. The points implied in this protectively abstract-facetious style are later paralleled by satirists in terms of direct reference to topical personalities, events and attitudes. Bruce Lacey and John Sewell made a neat short movie, regrettably off our beat, called *Everybody's Nobody* (1966), where a proud exporter demonstrates his robot machine, called the 'Mobile Absurd Nonentity' – MAN for short. The joke applies neatly to Guinness and Sellers, as to Norman Wisdom, Benny Hill and Charlie Drake, all of whom delight in multiple roles – Here Comes Everybody being also Along Went

Nobody. Other stars have been men of a thousand faces but the English today show a special obsession with, and gift for, chameleon impersonations, people who are everybody and nobody, anonymous and two-, po-, pie- or x-faced, mere samples of types whose only differences are accidents of accent, status, sex, clothes or ludicrous mannerism, making each of us a lonely crowd, alienated, fragmented, replaceable, and pointless. If American equivalents are cuter, cruder and more perfunctory, it's possibly because they reflect a more mechanically optimistic ideal of man.

29. Love in a Damp Climate

The interaction of puritan sincerity and narrowness, of utilitarian grimness, and of the gentlemanly code, which exalts obligation and loyalty over inner feeling and spontaneity, is an intricate tangle. It's beyond our scope to unravel here this and all the other factors which combine to produce the inhibition, shyness, melancholy and pessimism so long characteristic of the British cinema's way with erotic emotion.

The fairly easy and unchallenging daydream of near-perfect love which one may call 'romance' (as distinct from the serious force implicit in Romanticism), is of course a hardy perennial, as is a profound respect for a deep and loyal friendship within the institution of marriage.

Marriage tends to be seen as a transcendent loyalty rather than as an expression of the erotic – the latter tending to appear as, at best, a luckily irresistible bait, sometimes, a danger, and, more often, an aspiration which makes men heartbroken and women ridiculous.

Insofar as man-woman relationships differ from ordinary social relationships, it is because of their permeation by sexual instincts which, by their nature, separate the couple from the rest of society. The tension between sexual and social feeling is a constant undertone (even though an alternative, post-Freudian, view stresses the similarities, rather than the tensions, between erotic love and such sublimations as the friendly and moral emotions). The older view sees extra-marital sexuality as a threat to the social fabric, or as doomed by its lack of solid social status. Even the family unit can pose a threat to social responsibility, for the man whose loyalty is overridingly to his family may well, in economic and social affairs, be an irresponsible individualist.

The tensions between (on the one hand) the system and the authority-figures within it, and, on the other, wife and family, are expressed in such movies as *The Mind Benders* and *80,000 Suspects*. What, seen from one angle, is a faintly masochistic conformism, is not at all easy to separate, is, perhaps inseparable from the relative absence of corruption which (though not unique) is a real and proud feature of British moral culture.

The theme of cleaving unto one's boss rather than one's wife links with a revealing, and realistic, exchange in Ralph Thomas's *The Wind Cannot Read* (1958). Intelligence officer Dirk Bogarde has a wartime love affair with Japanese teacher Yoko Tani. A nasty brother officer sneaks to the Brigadier. This hitherto friendly character abruptly turns hard and stern and demands that Bogarde give up this woman, with or without good reason. When Bogarde promptly submits, his senior lends the lovers his luxurious quarters as their rendezvous. What's unusual is the need to prove that Bogarde's devotion is unconditional and, in a curious sense, personal.

The absence of feminine characters in Philip Leacock's *The Spanish Gardener* also suggests the primacy of male allegiance in the public school spirit. A stiff self-righteous academic (Michael Hordern) tries to compensate for his failures by monopolizing the love of his young son, who, however, turns for a hero to a simple, gentle, manly peasant (Dirk Bogarde). Father has to swallow down his jealousy, and face the truth about himself. It's a pity that a too simple plot – will father believe the good or the bad servant? – replaces the complex and delicate psychological piece for which director and actors were admirably suited. The theme bids fair to be movingly ambivalent. On the one hand, it is the theme of the heavy father resigning his authority – a theme currently prominent throughout Western culture – and on the other hand, a perpetuation, by the elimination of women, of the all-male club – an impression underlined by Bogarde's dreamily English style, even though he's supposed to be a Spanish gardener. The feeling of growing up as something that goes on between boys and men, not involving, or only very elliptically, a feminine presence, has sufficient anthropological precedent to be defensible as absolutely normal, and not, as it's latterly fashionable to allege, homosexual. But there is an interesting contrast between the dominant themes of British and American films. Whereas American films of the fifties stress father-son conflicts, and deal with too-possessive mothers and sons, their British counterparts stress father-son friendships, and the sad but noble 'letting go' by mothers of sons. The father-son pattern is that of the system (whose inner conflicts tend to be minimized); mother is a respected outsider, either sad or embarrassing.

This point allows of numerous exceptions, and intriguing asymmetries appear. In European movies, father-son conflicts are more common than daughter-mother conflicts, which appear most markedly in American movies of the forties (e.g. *Mildred Pearce*). The latter theme perhaps relates to the 'matriarchal' aspect of Momism, and it may be that in American movies, the exclusion of women (as in the Western) has a quality of escapism, of defiance. A film like *The Spanish Gardener*, taking it quietly for granted, seems particularly the product of the public school code, which simply leaves women out of the picture. It remains, one suspects, a little too public school in spirit for the middle-class and mass public, who are more family-oriented in such matters than upper-middle-class tradition.

The animosities between romantic love and the system inspire Dearden's *Saraband for Dead Lovers* (1948). Ealing's version of the Gainsborough period melodrama is pointedly more refined, and (despite a valiant cast, including Joan Greenwood, whose suavely plummy voice enriched so many comedies with its ironies and its mockingly sexual gravity, is here tragic in intent) less brimming with life-force. It tells the love-story of Koenigsmark and Sophie-Dorothea, neglected first wife of George-Louis, the Hanoverian princeling who later became the brutal and dissolute George I of England. A quiet cynicism about the dignity of history is a welcome recall of *Tudor Rose*, and there are satisfying, if moralistic, complexities in the casting of Flora Robson as an irresistible *femme fatale* who's just a little too old to mesmerize Stewart Granger. But the most fascinating character is Françoise Rosay, as George Louis's mother. She suffers her son's turpitude with stoic resignation, with noble hypocrisy she won't hear a word of criticism against him, and she sternly sermonizes the heroine for daring to admit to an emotion, even in private. 'We have no more right to inequalities of temper than the town hall clock to irregularities of time. The people must be able to set their lives by us.' Later, when accused by her Machiavellian rival, La Robson, of sitting in pious righteousness, and then hypocritically profiting from others' intrigues, she frigidly replies, 'God may use unworthy people to bring about his ends.' Dearden's indignation that a corrupt system should trample over the individual's happiness seems matched by mesmerized acquiescence in the nobility of self-sacrifice even to a corrupt system, and by the tragic necessity of having, as Sartre would say, *'les mains sales'* – *not* to change the system, however, but to preserve order. The images, dominated by harsh flickering firelight reds and black shadow-locked spaces, by low, heavy ceilings and hard walls, evoke a stifling oppressiveness, all-too-briefly disrupted by outbursts of frantic cutting (the drunken carnival, the fireworks ironically celebrating a bestial honeymoon). If the task of maintaining a rigid, formal, encasing style without dampening emotional intensity remains difficult, the film hits on some admirable compositions – sometimes in passing, on the way to yet another regulation mid-shot, as if Dearden didn't quite dare trust the public to respond to their stiff, hard, melancholy, and poignant long-shots.

More representative of the range of middle-class loyalties is David Lean's *Brief Encounter* (1945). To see it again twenty years on, at the Baker Street Classic, is to see another film entirely. Not that it no longer rings true. But the lovers in the drab Milford Junction buffet seem so strained, guilty, cowed, and therefore cold, that in 1965 the audience in this usually polite and certainly middle-class hall couldn't restrain its derision and repeatedly burst into angry exasperated laughter. Infected by such reaction one could, with them, see how dismally Trevor Howard's cringing 'Please, please, I humbly beg you ...' suggested a little boy's shame about anything so physical, while Celia Johnson's cold, pat, yap-yapping correctness, taken at the time as the reactions of the nice Englishwoman, seemed to shriek the tensions of frigidity. The erstwhile ordinary housewife seemed another Bette Davis, with exotic-neurotic dark-ringed eyes, brittle voice and moral hypochondria. Not since *The Entertainer* on its general release have I known an audience so convulsed by loathing of a film. Even the name of the town enraged a well-spoken young lady who finally cried out, 'Where the hell is Milford Junction anyway?' When the lovers were shamed out of consummation by the man's creepy smarmy friend (Valentine Dyall) – 'I'm not angry with you – just disappointed', it seemed, suddenly, that these two had never been lovers at all; they were both too sick to be. Indeed, *Brief Encounter* is the locus classicus of, is, surely, *the* renunciation drama which in *Look Back in Anger* Claire Bloom tries to play so soulfully but which Jimmy Porter so scathingly disrupts. And that's what happened to Lean's film – Jimmy Porter came along. Much of Noël Coward's script was spotted as woman's magazine stuff anyway, but its subsequent complete collapse results, essentially, from the combination of proletarian energy and new morality eroding those conventions within which it had most meaning. The film, however, retains enough truth to win through to a new meaning, about utterly humiliated love. Perhaps audience derision is a defence against a tragedy far deeper than that of separation. This encounter reveals the externally decorous, concealed, internal destruction, by all the guilts in the decency code, of instinct and nerve; of which just enough remained for hope and pain. The last, 'happy' scene thus becomes a nadir of abjectness. This isn't to deny that that code is defensible in many of its points of behaviour. If the old morality seems obnoxious to many now it's for the intensity of its guilts and complacencies, for its contempt for the libidinal even when that's perfectly compatible with social obligations, for the uniformity which it presupposes in human nature, for the reach-me-down crudity of its morality. 'Wives and husbands should put loyalty before joy. Never leave the plain old girl, however mean she always was, for a fresh young lady. Good time girls are cold hearted, and end strangled, or in the condemned cell, or racked by flames and typhus. Promiscuous people are stupid, vulgar and/or nasty. Men should quietly let women nag them. True affection is restrained and asexual: "Make tea not love".'

One other movie gives this code life – J. Lee Thompson's *Woman in a Dressing Gown* (1957). The feckless untidiness of middle-aged housewife Yvonne Mitchell drives her husband (Anthony Quayle) into a brief encounter with his cool, tidy young secretary, Sylvia Syms. If the film is intermittently overwrought, a rhapsody of bad house-keeping, it is so only to catch the furious vitality needed to stop a drab story from being too downbeat for the box-office, and is a probably acceptable convention. Yvonne Mitchell's oven-heat hysteria brings out the frenzy so often a regular part of an apparently mediocre existence, while Sylvia Syms notes the vehement briskness within middle-class blandness. The film has the considerable and un-British merit of being *embarrassingly* moving, as are certain performances of Judy Garland or Giulietta Masina, and of being so more consistently and realistically than most of theirs allowed. A semi-proletarian setting (council house), an American formula, a Jewish actress; as so often, the best British films work from impulses half-in, half-out, of the reigning culture.

'Marriage fatigue' – to adopt a useful phrase from *Escapade* – is rarely a principal theme, as it is in *Woman in a Dressing Gown*. It is fairly frequent as a sub plot or a background situation – the effect of divorce on children, or what to do with one's in-laws (*The End of the Road*). Interesting weirdies, in the Joan Crawford class, include Compton Bennett's *The Years Between* (1946). Hubby (Michael Redgrave) returns from the war to find that wifie (Valerie Hobson) occupies his old seat in Parliament. What mends the marriage? Why, good old homely advice from his staunch old nanny (Flora Robson). Muriel Box's *To Dorothy, a Son* (1954) sets its cap for the distaff side of the box-office, apparently on the assumption that women relish the spectacle of thoroughly hen-pecked males. Struggling composer John Gregson, country-cottaging it, gets it not only from his tyrannical and pregnant wife (Peggy Cummins) but also from glamorous ex-flame Shelley Winters. This battle of the Amazons, a whiningly self-righteous English one versus a sweetly glittering American one, might have been quite Homeric. Alas, a boring plot fobs us off with tittle-tattle about an inheritance. Maybe the pithiest statement of the typical English marriage occurs in Tati's *Les Vacances de M. Hulot*; Darby and Joan promenade a few steps apart, in irritable silence, on their long walks.

In their relatively indulgent attitude to adultery and their cynical reasons for renouncing it, two films in our 'marriage group' look forward to the New Morality and approach the spiritual limits of our period. John Guillermin's *Waltz of the Toreadors* (1962) uses Jean Anouilh's play as trampoline for a realistic look at a traditional subject which might have been sub-titled, Colonel Blimp Loves Again. Here the glamorous, young-in-heart French woman (Davy Robin) is the victim of the sclerotic English colonel (Peter Sellers, in Roger Livesey pastiche). When, after seventeen years' fidelity-in-absence, his old flame returns from Paris to help him quit his tyrannical spouse (Margaret Leighton) and elope with her to happiness, he still can't go, for first one reason, and then another – habit, faint-heartedness, jealousy ... all only too credible, none at all creditable. Sellers floridly makes meanness sympathetic, without losing sight of the fact that it's meanness nonetheless, and Anouilh's suave ferocity is exhilaratingly unleashed when the invalid harpy to whom the Colonel has so long been chained reverses our sympathies in her slashing accusations of his sexual and amorous incompetence. When, at last, the bluff Colonel, cured of his jealousy, cries to his happier young rival, 'To her, my lad', the lusty gusto is only a perversely bluff animalism in the Squire Western tradition (nostalgically emphasized later in *Tom Jones*). His counterpart is another old prevaricator, the village doctor (pallid, black-clad and all too prudent, i.e. the middle-classes). He has long cherished for the Colonel's lady a passion which is pure, platonic, unswerving, silent and quite as gormless as the Colonel's. Margaret Leighton, pallid and distraught, invests some of her scenes with a Brontëian fury of repressed passion. If the film finally capsizes amidst a welter of English romp ingredients involving period uniforms, cars, bicycles, hunts and falling into water-butts, they are to some extent redeemed by Guillermin's dashing style (a French critic described him as 'the Paganini of *mise en scène*'), and don't suffice to destroy the film's misanthropic edge. If the deservingly generous and rebellious ensign gets the Frenchwoman, Anouilh's dry pessimism has sabotaged this too; since she's old enough to be his mother, the future offers possibilities galore of equally tragic yet derisive acrimony.

The defeatism of fidelity inspires Sidney Gilliat's *Only Two Can Play* (1961), adapted by Bryan Forbes from Kingsley Amis's *That Uncertain Feeling*. The opening aubade, a sort of anti-pastoral serenade to the dinginess of furnished lodgings, introduces a trenchant vignette of a mediocre and miserable ménage (Peter Sellers and Virginia Maskell). If the film's sketch of the smooth foreign adulteress (Mai Zetterling) is somewhat stylized, its harsh domestic ironies match, in their earthier, less fantasticated English way, those of Wilder's *Kiss Me, Stupid*. Indeed, it really belongs to the New Morality; for though it ends with morally errant, physically innocent, and abjectly penitent, hubby returning to his punitively-inclined wife, he does so less through decent loyalty (old style) than through his refusal, half through mediocre resentment, half through modest pride, of the advantages of adultery.

Outside the stoic emphasis on marriage as a source of loyal, comforting decency (rather than joy and meaning), the code manifests a certain misogyny. Though this misogyny is far from being self-critical, the self-criticism results in sad acquiescence, rather than improvement. Puritanical guilt can, it seems (under the stress of biological impulse, and wordly common sense, and current optimisms), make concessions to the notion of sex as fun, but only so long as it's all a matter of wild oats irresponsibility, of jovial contempt or imperceptiveness, of the hot foreign piece or the glittering frisky popsy. It's in the good old Squire Western tradition if jovial Kenneth More has a glamour girl aboard the Jag or *Genevieve*, and we're encouraged to presume, if we're so inclined, that she might turn out to be sexually amenable after an evening out (though she's also likely to be a bit of a bitch or teasingly unwilling). Kay Kendall in *Genevieve* is exceptional in being allowed to suggest that a popsy can have character and feelings, is, in fact, a female human being, of whom one could grow fond, for reasons other than one's appreciation of the old girl virtues (i.e. the housewifely equivalent of the old boy qualities).

The depersonalization of the popsy links with the British cinema's extraordinary difficulty, not in finding, but in developing, starlets, female, assorted, innumerable. Given Jean Simmons's haunting blend of delicate technique, Celtic intensity, suburban blandness and uncanny poise, the British cinema finds, between *Great Expectations* (1946) and *Life at the Top* (1965), nothing nearly as interesting as Hollywood's *Angel Face* and *Elmer Gantry*. After years of banal British parts, Janette Scott reveals in, of all films, *Day of the Triffids*, a warm sad tone highly relevant to the sentimental education of semi-detached old morality youngsters. Joan Collins's sullen vehemence inspires *I Believe in You*, but only Hollywood offered her better than popsy roles. Diana Dors became a star as an extra-cinematographic personality, and her only memorable cinematic role has her in condemned cell sackcloth and ashes. Rank makes a brief effort for Diane Cilento, framing her handsomely in George More O'Ferrall's *The Woman for Joe* (1955); but her real complexity is frustrated by her roles' too-simple conceptions of her as *either* bitch, angel or waif. Yvonne Furneaux, disturbing *femme fatale* in *The Beggar's Opera*, and admirable Antonionian heroine in *Le amiche* (1955), had virtually no interesting British roles until Polanski's *Repulsion*. In *Bachelor of Hearts* (1958), Barbara Steele is just a weakly pretty face, and only foreign directors seem aware of the strange, spiky, whiplash strength which renders her so mesmeric in Bava's *Mask of the Demon*, Corman's *The Pit and the Pendulum*, and Fellini's *8½*. Honor Blackman slugs it out with Diana Dors in a saloon brawl in a South African Western, David MacDonald's *Diamond City* (1949) whose gross characterization is altogether different from the potentially Hawksian heroine whom she created for herself in TV's *The Avengers*. Outside *Genevieve*, Kay Kendall's only piquant roles are in Hollywood movies. After Thorold Dickinson's *Secret People* (1951) Audrey Hepburn was put under contract by a British company, who never found a film for her, and simply loaned her out to Paramount, who did. Belinda Lee was lavishly gowned and framed, and Rank's made a promising start as, in Clive Donner's *The Secret Place* (1956) and Brian Desmond Hurst's *Dangerous Exile* (1957), this big, sensual, dreamy-eyed girl is loved by young adolescents, catching erotic overtones which, far from those intended, are all the more fresh and touching. She could be described as a blonde Ava Gardner, or a female Victor Mature, if she weren't also a big, sedate, English Jane Fonda, with intriguing passing tones of emotional sensuality, of what Baudelaire called 'the natural ferocity of blondes', and of tough disgust. Alas, *The Secret Place*, instead of building up from its promising first half to a story about three normal, ill-assorted people, bound by guilt, in a kind of *Huis clos*, fades away into heavy-chases-boy melodrama, and *Dangerous Exile*, after a colourful start, dwindles into Orczy tosh. She nonetheless became a European star, and object of a minor intellectuals' cult.

Virginia McKenna enjoyed some success as a blend of Anna Neagle and Ann Todd. The toughly fascinating Adrienne Corri had some good character parts. After the eclipse of the Gainsborough girls (Margaret Lockwood, Patricia Roc, Jean Kent), who may have lacked subtlety but had a joyous, florid, rude feminine energy, the divorce between respect and provocative sexuality was complete. Romantic roles were allotted to Phyllis Calvert and Ann Todd, whose ladylike restraint conceals whatever it is they have to restrain. Roles abound for such excellent character actresses as Flora Robson, Brenda De Banzie, Margaret Rutherford, Kathleen Harrison, and Thora Hird (in complete contrast to the equal and opposite Hollywood imbalance, all optimism, glamour and little character). While England's young stars languished in their limbos, a constant procession of European girls – Mylène Demongeot, Micheline Presle, Mai Zetterling, Melina Mercouri – and, alas, faded American stars and starlets, streamed to and fro from our shores. They had already been created, they hadn't had to grope for feelings, for their identity, through the fog of British reserve – a fog blackened, it must be said, by the smutty anger of British misogyny, puritanism and shyness. As Orson Welles remarked, British journalists were gratuitously vindictive in assuming the stupidity of any girl who was glamorous or pretty, and John Huston observed, 'The young Englishmen are all women-haters, because they live under a régime of terrifying old ladies, ruled over by a scarcely seductive girl guide. London's no city for men – it's a spinster's capital.'

Ralph Thomas's *Doctor at Sea* (1955) and *Upstairs and Downstairs* (1959) are welcome intimations of thaw in the sex cold war. For their English heroes' feelings for the 'hot foreign bits' (Bardot in the first, Demongeot in the second) include a little tenderness, gratitude and generosity. If the older attitude to sex is as cheap as it thinks sex is, British love stories are consistently moving when dealing with love defeated. The theme is suspiciously rare in Hollywood, and associated with disillusionment by the French. The ambiguities it acquires in the British climate may be exemplified by two films, Guy Hamilton's *Manuela* and Carol Reed's *The Key*.

Guy Hamilton's *Manuela* (1957) centres on a hard-bitten skipper (Trevor Howard). While his men go off to the cafes and brothels of a Mexican port, he remains aboard, sardonically throwing pennies into the sea, for a derisive glimpse of the diving boys' bottoms. He can't quite trust the lovely waif from the devil knows where (Elsa Martinelli), and he feels he lost his ship by yielding to a love which, tragically, he crushes in himself. This effectively atmospheric movie is something of a follow-up to *Passage Home*, with dormitory misogyny (boys' bottoms) replacing the social guilts which run through its more substantial predecessor.

In Carol Reed's *The Key* (1958) William Holden is dismissed by Sophia Loren because, expecting to die, he gave his best friend the key to her flat. Defeatism, the 'old boy net', and misogyny comprise the unholy trinity of respectability. On script level, the film arraigns them. The alternative to Sophia Loren is glum, hairy-faced Oscar Homolka, who invites the hero to come and sing carols with him in the church choir. While they're so doing, German bombers score a direct hit, and the roof falls in. The script couldn't offer a clearer suggestion that fate is blind, that you're no better off at divine worship than in the brothel, that if worship won't save you then it's not love that kills you. The directorial style, however, renders love a cold, gloomy and dubious enterprise, proving that whatever you do is less happiness than gloom. Yet a film with the erotic charge of Buñuel's *Wuthering Heights*, of Borzage's *Man's Castle*, of Vidor's *Ruby Gentry*, could have left us in no doubt that even if Sophia's pleasures do bring doom in their train, a brief encounter with 'La Princesse' is a transcendence. Otherwise, the Briton is resigned to women as to queuing. In *Doctor at Sea* he's gone to escape his landlady's plain but avid daughter, 'a frying pan named Wendy'. But it's out of the frying pan into the fire, for the lady passengers have a gleam in their eye, and even roaring old seadog James Robertson Justice finishes flat on his bed with his leg in plaster, helpless beneath the ministrations of cooing, knowing Brenda De Banzie. In George Pollock's *Rooney* (1958) and in Clive Donner's *Nothing But the Best* (1963) the offending females are again landladies – they represent, in a convenient shorthand, the desperately pretentious 'shabby genteel', girls who have nothing to offer but drab domesticity. Stories of active females and of passive males too shy to back out, are an American as well as an English speciality, and it's a gain in realism, and in sadness, that the aggressive English girl characteristically has nothing going for her but the shyness and weakness of the unappetized male. An associated English speciality is funny sexual bathos, e.g. Ralph Thomas's *Appointment with Venus* (1951), where Venus turns out to be the name of a prize Jersey cow to be rescued from the Germans. Of the many dialogue variations in the same mood perhaps the best occurs in *The League of Gentlemen* (1960), where a frigid gold-digger refuses her fuming husband, with the calm observation, 'You've already had your porridge for this week.' Bathos reaches it's acme in drag humour, a universal archetype rarely more rife or subtle than in its English forms, from Old Mother Riley through Norman Wisdom and the *Carry Ons*. It differs from the transvestite or homosexual variety in that the stress is on grotesquerie, not attractiveness. The impersonation parodies both sexes at once, the failure of women to be desirable and the failure of men to understand them. Yet it has a stoic gusto, a quality of derisive and masochistic affection, which makes it a vulgar, a working-class speciality, tolerated, rather than enjoyed, by respectable taste. They telly-era fad of drag is another matter, eyeing, or perhaps ogling, a feeling that modern smoothness is effeminizing the male, and what he finds in the change of garb is not a switch to a female mode but a switch from the exasperating frustration of active male impulse to a humiliating, but better adjustment. The newer tone tends to follow the American example, where transvestite gags are more closely associated with the humiliation/castration of the male (e.g. *Some Like It Hot*). In France the theme is less emphatic.

Scurrility is, of course, obsessive in English humour, from 'Balloons to you' (Norman Wisdom) to 'These trousers are a bit tight under the circumstances' (Arthur Askey). In *Carry On Spying* skittish acknowledgement of onanism looms when, to Barbara Windsor's patriotic wail 'I only want to do my bit,' colleague Kenneth Williams retorts, 'You'd better do it in your own room, then'. No barrack-room ex-inmate viewing the same film could fail to raise a reminiscent smile on coming across 'The Street of a Thousand Artisans' and in *Invasion Quartet* a unit is called the Special Operations Division so that it can be referred to by its initials. The endemic queer joke may be typified by *The Captain's Table*, with John Gregson looking mildly discomfited as the pansy steward prattles on: 'Oh we know how to look after the tools of our trade.' Joan Littlewood may feign innocence when the Lord Chamberlain complains about the angle at which an actor carries a plank, and Billy Wilder, in Hollywood, ridicules the Legions of Decency for objecting when one man invites another to come and look at his wife's parsley, but audience hilarity leaves little doubt that the first joke is no more geometrical than the second is horticultural. Universal as such humour is, its abundance in British movies suggests that it's doing more than its fair share of work, particularly in combination with the fact that the most moving sex films are the melancholy ones. If such jokes proliferate and, like a baroque ornamentation, seem to take over the spiritual structure of the entertainment, it's because they are a significant indicator of sensibility.

Since the Gainsborough melodramas, with their robust grimness, the romantic key, though not absent from British movies, rarely inspires. One needs only contrast Ralph Thomas's neat, nice *The Wind Cannot Read* with, for example, Albert Lewin's *Pandora and the Flying Dutchman* (a Hollywood-spirited film which happened to be shot over here) or Henry King's *Snows of Kilimanjaro*. The love stories directed by David Lean might be described, on the analogy of 'anti-hero', as anti-love stories. After *Brief Encounter, The Passionate Friends* (1948) and *Madeleine* (1950) wrung from Lindsay Anderson the unkind comment that Lean had changed from the white hope of the English cinema to its white elephant. White is the colour of Lean's muse, for *The Passionate Friends* lyricizes, with crystal-clear photography, the Alpine snows amongst which the platonic, but still guilty, lovers, mooch rather than smooch; and even the darkly Victorian *Madeleine* dwells on its close-ups of Ann Todd of the far-sad face and silky blonde hair. *The Sound Barrier* (1952) is even more oxygenated, with test pilots diving through white cloud-mountains. And this white isn't merely a photographic colour. It is the whiteness of sun on snow, of love lying lightly, beautifully, over a long loneliness, through which a timid, tender crocus briefly thrusts. An unfinished project of Lean's was called: The Snow Goose. *The Passionate Friends* might be called 'The Lovers Who Couldn't Quite', and though cut with an exquisite razor it comes to life only in its climax, when the quiet calm guilts which seem to have all but frozen the heroine's life-force nearly hurl her under an underground train amidst gleaming white tile. *Madeleine* was possibly a defence of women (and even French women) against the xenophobic misogyny of puritanical Scotland. Yet its most convinced moment occurs when the bewhiskered patriarch looks round his new mansion and remarks complacently, 'It has – solidity!' Ann Todd elegantly glided through these films, like another worldly icon for Garbo, or Michèle Morgan, or Veronica Lake. Wistful, fastidious, passive, this moon actress seemed to reflect the fire and warmth, if any, of her leading men, and the energy, if any, of her situation. She acquired her reputation as a romantic lady fortuitously, perhaps, as James Mason's victim in Compton Bennett's *The Seventh Veil* (1945), which really hinges on her softly obstinate refusal, first, of her guardian, then of her other lovers. In Joseph Losey's *Time without Pity* (1957) she makes a desperately poignant foil for the brutal energies of Leo McKern.

One might attribute the emptinesses of Lean's Ann Todd period to an unfortunate conjugation of restraints in director and star. Yet Katharine Hepburn, an undoubtedly active actress, cannot quite fill the interior spaces of *Summer Madness*. The story of an elderly spinster's brief encounter with love, and acceptance of her lover's cynicism, in Venice, starred, on the stage, Shirley

Booth. The film's star is undoubtedly stronger and more glamorous, and it is this which weakens the film. She suggests, rather, a smart, efficient, handsome American secretary who, far from being too plain, shy, and ordinary for love, has missed out by being, quite unconsciously, too brisk, self-sufficient, intelligent, proud and idealistic. Lean dwells on lyrical Venice visuals, thus widening a gap, rather than strengthening the links, between the filmic and the dramatic. Possible links spring to mind. The tourist cine-camera for example is not just a prop, but more a way of life, with all the eager pathos of its devices for automatically 'correcting' reality, turning it into a flat remembered reproduction of a reality that was seen only in terms of cultural cliché and future memory to begin with, bringing it back more dead than alive, turning the holiday into a preview of a souvenir. How hard those tourists gawp, trying to feel ecstasy, trying, oh, so nobly hard.

One can imagine also how much more dry, sharp and hard a tone a De Sica might have conferred on the woman's disillusionment with the bambino. A white gardenia drifts down the dirty canal water as Lean, too gently, opposes, to all that's pure ascetic and cerebral in his heroine, the gentle perfidy of corrupt old Venice – the bambino, her lover's antique shop, her lover's cynicism. The passionate appears as a sunset like a body softly on fire, a red goblet in a shop window, and a fireworks display synchronized with the spinster's one night of love. Yet the feeling for emotion seems transposed from Lean's understanding of stiff, complex, forlorn men. To *Doctor Zhivago*, an intelligent, rough hewn, Hollywood concoction, Julie Christie brings the rough, bitter, vigorous wind, from the steppes of endured suffering, and a complexity which Lean seems to track, rather than initiate. His perfect technique, delicate and strong, resembled a white statue awaiting a collaborator to breathe into it, ardour and madness. It's interesting to think of *Summer Madness* as it might have been treated by the Hal Wallis-Shirley Booth-Delbert Mann team with Anthony Quinn as the lover. For all the lack of visual style, we might well have felt more strongly the swell and cut of desire and pain, before the lonely heroine accepts beauty and pleasure as spiritual forces in themselves (an acceptance very beautifully implied, in Lean's film, by the lunging wave of her arm from the train). For Lean's reticence is both negative and positive; it has a barbed quality, a diffused bewilderment that softens pain but becomes all the more baffled and haunting for being so ethereal. Lean's stylistic finesse has a spark from the Symbolist flame, and his whiteness isn't without that Mallarmean overtone, which rings most clearly through the glittering, crystalline, frozen house in which Lara and Zhivago part for ever. One might view Lean's art as the holding of a refined balance – or equivocation – between his heroes' lyrical, private, strange worlds, and a consensus wisdom: both are admitted, neither denied.

The painful pusillanimity of *Brief Encounter* is reiterated, from another angle, in Carol Reed's version of *The Fallen Idol*, with Michèle Morgan for Ann Todd, a Belgravia tea-shop for a station buffet, a horrid wife for a horrid friend, and an uncomprehending boy for uncomprehending buffet attendants and neighbours. Between Lean's sauve, white aestheticism and the more gritty, ashen, 'commercial class' mood of the Greene-Reed tandem comes the curious tenderness of Anthony Asquith, with or without Rattigan. A gently sad tenderness envelops all human relationships, of which love is the purest, the finest, the, so to speak, vanishing point. Yet his colour too is white. Indeed, woman in white recur – the ballerinas are dancing *Swan Lake* whenever his lovers go to the ballet, and fickle or perfidious women wear white in *French without Tears* (1939), *The Woman in Question* (1950) and *The Browning Version* (1951). Asquith's central feminine figure is a gentle, stoic, ever-young mother, whom the son honours and courts with a thousand tender attentions. (Fay Compton in *Tell England*, 1931, Lillian Gish in *Orders to Kill*, 1957.) Often the Asquith lover is more cosseted, more innocent of the world, than his beloved. In *A Cottage on Dartmoor* (1930) – where Asquith out-Hitchcocks Hitchcock, before Hitchcock became Hitchcock – a married woman finds her ex-lover, on the run, hiding behind the bars of her child's cot. In *Dance Pretty Lady* (1931) the young aristocrat jilts his chorus-girl mistress with the gentle callousness of unawareness. In the thirties Asquith's essentially Edwardian lyricism irradiates some merely competent screenplays and his best films aren't vaporized by the sternest comparison – with Ophüls. But where Ophüls, after years of frustration and inactivity, went on to his great period in the early fifties, Asquith's style, after too many uninspiring assignments, became shyer, tighter, dryer. Something of the old lyricism trickles forth one last time, after years, in *The Young Lovers* (1954). But the emphasis is misogynistic in *The Woman in Question* and *The Browning Version*. The first is a murder mystery, evoking

Pirandello and *Rashomon*, where each of five people suspected of murdering the blousy Madame Astra (Jean Kent) sees, in his flashback, a different girl. Eventually the murderer turns out to be the meek and gentle keeper of a pet shop, who strangled her when she laughed raucously at his offer of marriage. 'It's the gentlest men whom women destroy ...' This resolution is too simple; the conclusion might have left all our options open, challenging our certainties and creating a kind of vertical *La Ronde*. No less bitter is *The Browning Version*, from Rattigan's play. What has broken the spirit of Mr. Coker-Harris (Michael Redgrave), the public school classics master, and made of him a sour tyrant? A despotic headmaster must bear subsidiary blame, but mainly it's Millie, his bitchy young wife from the common classes (Jean Kent). At last, he rallies, faintly, encouraged by the sympathy of one of his young pupils. Asquith does suggest that the incompatibility of Coker-Harris and his wife is reciprocally tragic; but the film so stresses the former's cold suffering and the latter's active infidelities that most of the time we pity the male bitch and condemn the female one. (His rebellion is admirable, but hers is treachery! We even feel it serves her right when the science master [Nigel Patrick] betrays her.) The film's powerful core is Michael Redgrave's Coker-Harris, a *tour de force* reconciling a sour cold mask with every flick and quiver of furious inner tension, derived surely, from the most meticulous observation of the mannerisms of an almost vanished pedagogic type – the classical pedant whose very mouth closes like a cane. This acid-etched portrait is perfectly framed by Asquith's gentleness and here is one of the rare British films with a Renoirian sense of all the nuances of tic, grimace, gesture, posture and silence. *The Passionate Friends* reads as a negative presentation of positive feelings, *The Browning Version* is a positive presentation of negative feelings. Rattigan and Asquith have worked so closely together that on the analogy of the Chesterbelloc it's fair to invent the Rattigasquith. It's all the more regrettable that with *The V.I.P.s* (1963) and *The Yellow Rolls-Royce* (1964) Rattigan achieved his unconscious ambition and actually became Aunt Edna. Before achieving this transfiguration however, he contributed some potentially interesting studies of British love for other directors; *The Deep Blue Sea* for Anatole Litvak (1955), *The Prince and the Showgirl* for Laurence Olivier (1957), *The Man Who Loved Redheads* (ex- *Who Is Sylvia?*) for Harold French (1954), and *Separate Tables* for Delbert Mann

(1958). The last is the best, perhaps because it's American. Against the back-ground of a dreary residential hotel, two stories are rather awkwardly grafted onto one another. The fundamentally decent sex offender (David Niven) dares assert himself against public opinion. The shy spinster (Deborah Kerr) defies her dominating mother. Film stars Burt Lancaster and Rita Hayworth resolve their love-hate jibes and grudges. The film is visually ragged, but, a Chayefskian asperity having crept into it, is powerful enough. *The Prince and the Showgirl* has nothing to do with the English character, since it opposes an American chorus girl (Marilyn Monroe) to a Hohenzollern Prince (Laurence Olivier). A more thoughtful playwright might have developed it into a clash between, on the one hand, America, democracy, idealism, and Momism, with attendant cynicisms (she's a gold-digger) and, on the other, a chivalrous, brutal, Teutonic patriarchy. Rattigan simply extrapolates from the old chorus-girl-cum-Milord theme. A dynamic American girl redeems a poker-faced faint heart from his amorous defeatism, and, thematically, Olivier's adroit pastiche of a galumphing Teuton hangs in space. Since the style is British anyway, one wishes Rattigan had gone the whole hog and told us all about Lilly Langtry and the Prince of Wales. *The Man Who Loved Redheads* is a Viscount whose foible for redheads (all played by Moira Shearer) is his sweet torment from puberty to senility. All the women prove shallow or bitchy and the moral is that man should stay in the club with the other bachelors, drinking. It's a bit sad but less painful and you'll end there anyway. Wolfenstein and Leites contrast the American attitude of their period ('the missed opportunity is comic') with the French ('the missed opportunity is tragic'). In middle-class English films, the missed opportunity is melancholy but inevitable. In this colour-conscious age, it would be interesting to transpose the theme into *The Man Who Loved Negresses*, and give the moral a different flick.

If these films view childhood idyllically, they come down on adolescence like a ton of kindly platitudes. The traditional French cinema shows a tender and permissive sympathy towards this period of unsureness, vulnerability, and questioning, whence *Le Diable au corps* and *Les 400 coups*. Hollywood progressed from the complacent-cosy Andy Hardy view of teenage romance to films like *Rebel without a Cause* and *Take a Giant Step*. In the old fashioned British cinema, adolescent sex remains innocent or delinquent. Drama occurs when teenage immaturity runs ahead of itself or gets reckless or defiant. If there are any bearable films on either theme, I either didn't see them or have completely forgotten them. Ted Willis's screenplay for Peter Cotes's *The Young and the Guilty* (1957) has it that the two amorous teenagers (Andrew Ray, Janet Munro) are really and innocently in love and unjustly suspected by their heavy elders of precocious activities like heavy necking. Shame on you, you older generation, you.

Although a new realism about sex, and the New Morality, which aren't identical, make their first impact in Jack Clayton's *Room at the Top* (1958), they had already appeared, albeit cautiously and gradually, in more traditional terms. With the institution of the X certificate in 1952, a few British films ventured to break down the categories of melancholy resignation, naughty friskiness, and moralized sin, and study sexuality from more or less the same stand-point which D. H. Lawrence had brought to *Sons and Lovers* in 1913, or which, for that matter, Henry Fielding had brought to *Tom Jones* in 1749: the view that sexuality can be as spiritual (or as mean) as anything else.

Something of a pioneering role is played by an Anglo-French co-production, René Clément's *Knave of Hearts* (*Monsieur Ripois*), 1954. An ill-paid clerk alone in London, Gérard Philipe, charms his way around a cross-section of London girls. They include his boss's strong-minded secretary (Margaret Johnston), a sentimental little middle-class girl (Joan Greenwood), a French prostitute (Germaine Montero), a cool and commanding lady (Valerie Hobson) and – almost – her best friend (Natasha Parry). Fate – or an unconscious touchiness – turns an impulsive gesture of his into a crippling accident. But as the two women walk their now helpless captive in his bath chair, he seems to possess both their favours, and eyes a third. Endowed with Clément's characteristic pessimism, and, equally characteristically, a plot in which accumulative repetition prevails over increasing depth or maximum variation, the film anticipates many of the techniques, moods and themes of the rising generation. Here, seen through an often hand-held camera, are London's pluvial skies and drab dragging Sundays, the serried ranks of sash windows in seedy buildings like the stern lorgnettes of decaying dowagers, the amoralism of a youthful outsider struggling for success, the near-castration of male *joie de vivre* by English girls more worldly than they seem.

Its English follow-up also adopts the mode of worldly cynicism. When Sally Bowles (Julie Harris) in Henry Cornelius's *I Am a Camera* (1955) becomes pregnant (father unknown), the hero is eager to marry her, his love helped along by old-fashioned gallantry about damsels in distress. But she's simply miscounted her monthlies, so that her immorality goes unpunished, and his gallantry unrewarded. Cornelius's rather circumspect treatment of Berlin-in-the-thirties disappoints the kinky sixties (though fidelity to Isherwood would have been censored in the fifties). One rather wishes that Cornelius had sacrificed Isherwood's admittedly sharp and agreeable little novel for a similar subject in a contemporary English setting. As it is, it's with a start of surprise that one realizes only eight years separate this heroine from Julie Christie in Schlesinger's *Billy Liar*.

Otherwise, fifties X certificate sexology can almost be divided into two kinds; the devious and the glum. One might expect sex films to celebrate straight sexual ecstasies before going on to problems and perversions. The reverse happens. Eroticism, being regarded as something of a disease, is approached in its problem forms before its attractions dare to be de-stylized. 1956 gave us Herbert Wilcox's *My Teenage Daughter* where Sylvia Syms treads the slippery slope from Humphrey Lyttelton's jazz club to the condemned cell. 1957 gave us Don Chaffey's *The Flesh Is Weak*, about prostitution, and 1958 his *Question of Adultery* (artificial insemination). 1959 offered Terence Young's *Serious Charge* (Teddy Boy Andrew Ray accuses the vicar) and Robert Siodmak's *The Rough and the Smooth*, where Nadia Tiller teases Tony Britton because she only gets her kicks when men rough her up. This last film, both devious *and* glum, was an unexpected box-office success, linking, albeit tenuously, with the Gainsborough vein of sadomasochism. 1960 brought Guy Green's *The Mark* (about a man who interferes with little girls), Ken Hughes's *The Trials of Oscar Wilde* with Peter Finch, and, if it's a British film, Gregory Ratoff's *Oscar Wilde*, with Robert Morley. The former is perhaps a little too elaborate in establishing Wilde as a kind manly family man who deserves our sympathy, the latter more unfeeling, derisory and tonic. Both are interesting, neither altogether adequate to a tempting and difficult subject.

The Flesh Is Weak and *The Mark* merit a closer look. The first film caused consternation in the film industry by proving, not that there was a West End

Old Mother Riley Headmistress: Arthur Lucan

Masculination: By hardship and by gentility

The Belles of St. Trinian's: Alastair Sim

Guns at Batasi: John Leyton, Mia Farrow, Richard Attenborough

Moralities, Old and New

Sailor Beware: Gordon Jackson, Peggy Mount

Woman in a Dressing Gown: Yvonne Mitchell, Anthony Quayle, Sylvia Sims

An everyday loneliness

Knave of Hearts: Gérard Philippe, Joan Greenwood

Secret People: Valentina Cortese, Serge Reggiani

Atrocities: For and Against

Yesterday's Enemy: Stanley Baker

Idol of Paris: Beryl Baxter, Christine Norden
Amusements of the Olden Time

The Tales of Hoffmann: Moira Shearer

Our Mother's House: Yootha Joyce, Dirk Bogarde

Not in front of the children, or the lower orders

The Hellfire Club

Dracula: Christopher Lee, Valerie Gaunt

Blood, milk and water

The Stranglers of Bombay: Paul Stassino, Roger Delgado, Guy Rolfe, Marie Devereux

Dead of Night: Ralph Michael, Googie Withers

The past is a lure, and the future is now

The Damned: Shirley Anne Field

audience for sex, which everyone knew, but that even suburban housewifes would flock to a sordid vice movie, that is to say, that the woman's angle on prostitution needn't be as romanticized as it had been in, say, *Waterloo Bridge*. An au pair girl (Milly Vitale) is lured into vice by loving a seductive ponce (John Derek) not wisely but too well. The film's best quality is exemplified by the girl's encounter with her first client, a sensitive young clerk who only came because his office-mates kept teasing him about his inexperience. He leaves her untouched. The scene's obvious sentimentality is less important than certain positives. It gratifies audience curiosity about the prostitution situation. It begins to bring together the over-moralist and the over-romantic views of vice. It gently urges spectators towards an identification with sinners and scapegoats, and it points out that the respectable middle-classes are guilty of spiritual collusion, not merely by providing most of the clientele but in their everyday sociabilities. The film is directed with a sharply sensual eye, and even if one is disappointed at its eventual subsidence into razor-slashing, and its evocation of the Messina brothers to perpetuate the anachronistic view that even if prostitutes aren't evil, ponces usually are, it's not at all an insensitive film. *The Mark* is another assault on philistinism. Stuart Whitman comes out of prison, to which he has been consigned for interfering with a little girl. Now he faces the task of remaining cured, despite all the pressures to collapsing morale, and therefore relapsing morals, exerted on him by the suspicious local police, by the machinations of a business colleague, by a ruthlessly prying reporter, and by a brief, fearful reflex on the part of the widow (Maria Schell) who has come to love him. Eschewing all melodrama, the script concentrates on everyday tensions. The hero, weakly, clings to his guilt, to his fear of all women who aren't either reassuringly motherly or too young to be dangerous; even the untidiness of his hair and collar and tie is subtly dejected and masochistic. Rod Steiger's strong, helpful psychologist is a tonic assertion of new understandings as neither sinister nor weak. 1961 brought *Victim* which, coming from Relph and Dearden, set the seal of respectability on the devious sex movie, even more than the Oscar earned for the screenplay of *The Mark*. While refusing to lyricize homosexual feeling, Relph and Dearden deftly use the detective story formula to lure us on a Cook's tour round homosexual London. They admirably integrate a convincingly 'tough' plea for tolerance with counters to many a popular misconception about homosexuality. 'Queers are effeminate'; so one is a muscleman. 'You can tell queers by their creepy ways', so one of the queerest looking characters turns out to be a normal 'tec posing. 'Queers are parasites sapping the nation's moral fibre'; so the dignified Establishment deviant in his Rolls-Royce really cares about the welfare of the working man. A cop yielding to a puritanical rage against queers is reprimanded by his superior. The defence of a persecuted minority is all the more cogent in its unsentimentality (queers prey on queers). In the last reel, the film breaks carefully through all its distancing. The apparently normal hero (Dirk Bogarde) with the normally sweet wife (Sylvia Syms) is revealed as having, in his heart, at least, a weakness with which they will both, tragically, have to live.

If *Room at the Top* presents sex earthily and normally, with no emphasis on exotic naughtiness, nor on its tactfully joyless problems, it's not exactly lyrical about it either. The well-to-do young girl's verbal rhapsodizing about the act is a testimony, of sorts, to pleasure, and to her impressionability, yet her superlatives are oddly impersonal, and the final effect, in the context of deception, sad. Even the hero's satisfactions with his mistress (Simone Signoret) take on a tragic futility and guilt. Thus Jack Cardiff's *Sons and Lovers* is probably the first British film whose primary theme is that of self-discovery and self-liberation through love and sexuality. Yet Dean Stockwell's Paul Morel seems a little too tame and equable, and Heather Sears miscast as Miriam. The quarrels between Paul's parents (Wendy Hiller, Trevor Howard) are softened, and even before they have begun we know they'll end in grudging reconciliation. Mrs. Morel's smile is a little too assured and friendly, father too happily hangdog. The film's glum black and whites are far less Lawrentian than the colours needed for the novel's hot close fire-lit interiors as for Lawrence's eye for nature. One may well suspect that the film's producer, Jerry Wald, had spotted that the novel's story-line fits that theme which one finds also in his production of *Hemingway's Adventures of a Young Man* and which no doubt interested him in his projected version of *Ulysses*. In all three stories a young man regretfully breaks free from an idealistic but possessive mother, and he may well have sensed that this theme could be very relevant to American Momism. Both the Lawrence and the Hemingway show Wald astutely compromising between (rather than reconciling) the rising sophistication of mass taste and the harsher, less reassuring aspects of his literary properties. But even if the film takes only its story and dialogue from Lawrence, if it hasn't his electric blend of anxiety and lyricism, and if the older generation oddly eclipse the youngsters, it achieves a tart mellowness, a friendly sourness, and rasping drabness, which are authentic enough.

Lewis Gilbert's *The Greengage Summer* (1961) seems something of a 'rear-guard' film, interested by the New Morality and its appearance among the upper-middle-class young, but not quite able to bear the shock of shifting its own perspectives. One might oppose it to *Knave of Hearts* and *Waltz of the Toreadors* in its confrontation of French naughtiness with English innocence. An English Rose (Susannah York), holidaying in France with her younger sister (Jane Asher), falls in love with another guest at the hotel (Kenneth More), despite his involvement with the manageress (Danielle Darrieux). When he gently and considerately rebuffs her, she toys with the idea of acquiring experience via the boot-boy. All this is in beautiful, glowing tints which evoke a spring time innocence – until the actual seduction scene, when she screws herself to the sticking point with the frantic absorption of whisky and nicotine. It's all very suspenseful because he's a pretty unpleasant boot-boy, slimy and embittered, and she's so sweet. She survives temptation, as so nice a girl was bound to do, but the film runs true to traditional form when the boot-boy charges into her room at midnight to rape her, and falls from a window to his accidental death, while knight-errant Kenneth More, who had meanwhile turned out to be a dashing jewel-thief, sacrifices his chance of escape so as to dispose of the corpse in a nearby river for her, and ends up under arrest, which proves that he loved her after all, and in the right British way, an avuncular and sexless one.

To the producers' great surprise, the film was bitterly attacked at Cannes, as anti-French. Indeed, on the screen, the xenophobic asides heavily prevail over what might, on paper, have looked like a piece of British self-examination. All the English characters have friendly, open, generous personalities. Even their faults are romantic ones, or the understandable tizzies of immature beauty. But the French are represented by the contemptibly pitiable boot-boy, by the Danielle Darrieux character, who is sour, jealous, and grasping, and by her partner, who is an even sourer lesbian.

This xenophobia is regrettable because the film needed only a little less melodrama, and a more even distribution of virtues and failings, to be a very fine one. If we scrub all the melodramatic nonsense about the boot-boy's death; if the Danielle Darrieux character has a great deal to offer her English lover (so that we can see the girl misjudging her, with the cruelty of youth); if the boot-boy's cynicism has a witty apropos that helps our heroine's discovery of the world; if the Englishman isn't a dashing jewel thief but, perhaps, a friendly 'R.A.F.-type' only really at home in clubs and bars; if the French lesbian is replaced by what the heroine fears she herself will become, an English spinster; the film would not only not have offended the French, it might have begun to explore English attitudes in an interesting way. The film has its beautiful photography and a warm and beautiful portrayal of a warm and lively brother and sister brood, especially via Jane Asher.

As it is, both the affirmation and criticism of love in Britain are the prerogative of films subscribing to the New Morality, or repudiating it as circumspectly as Lewis Gilbert's *Alfie*.

30. The Lukewarm Life

Every culture seeks to repress the social and unpleasant aspects of human nature. But since human nature doesn't fall into easily distinct compartments, culture too invariably runs the risk of over-controlling, of denaturizing, human beings, in the hope of protecting man from his all-too-human inhumanity.

It's fairly easy to see how checks on aggression can become checks on self-assertion, and on the life-force itself, producing a guilty, docile, shy and apathetic people. Similarly checks on erotic irresponsibility can produce a depressed, suspicious attitude, not only towards love-relationships, but to all forms of human friendship. If we add to this combination the discouragement of ambition necessary in a relatively stagnant economy, we find all the components of the melancholy tone, or overtones, of many British films; most clearly perhaps in those connected with the public school culture (such as *Passage Home* and *Manuela*).

The other face of this melancholy is complacency, more marked in middle-middle-class films, where the importance attached to the cosy semi-detached little family (aside from loyalties to the system) replaces the austere loyalties of the masculine dormitory. Yet the very modesty of this cosiness implies a stoic repudiation of other possibilities. Further, the stress on privacy is defensive (since privacy is to be used only in conformist ways anyway). Fear of the neighbours, and distaste for crowds, suggest a completely, rather than a semi-detached state, as against a tribal togetherness which often exists more richly in the upper-middle-class level. The well developed middle-class sense of civic responsibility can result from a determination to be irreproachable, rather than an emotionally satisfying concern for others (that is, it can result from inner conscience and outer fears). Complacency characteristically results in hiding real tensions from one's notice (and, of course, the middle-middle-classes are traditionally more idealistic, and squeamish, about everything from blood sports to class tension than the public school classes).

In a psychoanalytic *schema*, a third face of this melancholy would be paranoia. One's own repressed life-force is attributed to others, and its threat to oneself morbidly exaggerated. Hence the middle-class fear of the working-class as an uncontrollable mob (countered by working-class insistence on 'respectability'), and the more general obsession with violent crime, juvenile delinquents, the censoriousness of one's neighbours, and so on. However, it seems that British puritanism instills, against complacency, a high degree of self-criticism, at least in certain areas, whence the cultural strength of the 'nonconformist conscience' and constant twinges of consciousness about taking minorities as scapegoats.

The working-out of the pattern would be far too complicated for our purpose, especially as these tensions aren't unique to Britain; they're built into human nature, and every culture, by definition, finds a different solution to them. When we speak of 'the British character' (by which people too often mean only the upper-middle-class English character) we are, in effect, saying that there area specific British patterns, or tendencies, distinct from, say, the American and the French. By British standards, American culture produces a somewhat hysteric blend of idealism and cynicism, far more aggressive, but, in other ways far more hopeful, dynamic and delusional. The French pattern is at once more mellow and more cynical, more tolerant and more violent.

The characteristic British shyness can be seen as a blend of depression and slightly masochistic paranoia. It appears in such national traits as taking pleasures sadly ('one daren't trust them, even while they're happening'), an exaggerated fear of Teddy Boys and the like, a coldly destructive attitude to others' pleasure (Sabbatarianism), and a tendency to timid, prickly loneliness. It forms, in other words, the whole *Separate Tables* syndrome, which isn't exclusively British, of course, but is generally allowed as a key-signature of British life.[40]

The British like to believe that in the Swedes there exists a race sadder than they, and, usually, attempt to explain this, either in terms of climate, or in terms of Sweden being a progressive country. Some of Ingmar Bergman's films may be more aggressively gloomy than anything our middle-class cinema produced, but it's worth pointing out that, just as *Brief Encounter* is the British equivalent of *Summer with Monika*, so *Separate Tables* is the British equivalent of *Smiles of a Summer Night*. In other words, the more honest and dynamic Swedes remove British complacency and apathy from gloom, being, finally, both gloomier and happier than the restrained and monotonous British.

Because so much upper-middle-class life is a matter of *Separate Tables*, then of course, barrack-room fun looms so large in British war films, giving the barrack-room the cheery togetherness of a school dormitory. In other words, it takes on a meaning often missed by commentators who, with puritan hypochondria, see in it only an outlet for the homosexuality supposedly inculcated by the mono-sexual conditions of public school life. It's tempting to retort that this 'tribalism' is a very healthy and natural thing, that British life at many levels would benefit from more of it, and that it might with advantage be extended to include both sexes.

During the war and post-war years, British movies were well aware that services life, for all its exasperations, had a unity of purpose, and a meaningful togetherness, sadly lacking in peacetime Civvy Street (*vide They Made Me a Fugitive*, and one of the more likeable overtones in *The Intruder*). A formula worked with sympathetic, if, eventually, ill-directed, earnestness, was the 'omnibus' genre.

Its first stage is exemplified by Noël Coward's and David Lean's *In Which We Serve* (1942), Leslie Howard's *The Gentle Sex* (1943), Dearden's *The*

Bells Go Down (1943) and Carol Reed's *The Way Ahead* (1944). Since service life unites people from different backgrounds, their separate stories find, not only a common purpose, but a common interest. Films like Dearden's *The Captive Heart* (1946) and *Dead of Night* (with its omnibus of directors, 1945) exemplify a transition stage; civilians meet and tell ghost stories, P.O.W.s face the problems of readapting to civilian life. A Czech pilot (Michael Redgrave) who escaped the Gestapo by taking on a dead British officer's identity, must now return to his widow. If too tightly tied to soap-opera apron-strings, the element of counterfeit in this plot is significant. If togetherness isn't a dream, it's a lie ... yet that we must accept ... The next stage is to try and show some sort of interdependence, of *virtual* togetherness, in the structures of civilian life. Hence such films as *It Always Rains on Sunday* (a kind of post-Mass Observation study of one day in one district), *Holiday Camp* (a nicer kind of barrack-room, as usual over-condemned by the middle-class ethos), and *Train of Events* (with its communal disaster). Institutional structures include a dance hall (*Dance Hall*), a department store (*The Crowded Day*), Derby Day (*Derby Day*), and so on. Sometimes there is no actual framework at all other than that of an author's particular tone, range or outlook (*Trio, Quartet* and *Encore*, after W. Somerset Maugham, *Meet Me Tonight* after Noël Coward). All of which is quite as defensible as, say, Griffith's *Intolerance*, Dreyer's *Leaves from Satan's Book*, Duvivier's *Un carnet de bal*, or Ophüls's *La Ronde* and *Le Plaisir*.

Indeed, one advantage of the formula is that, since the audience get a varied bill of fare, identification need be less consistent. This might well facilitate characterizations and stories which are just a little odder, sadder, truer, and more, in a semi-Brechtian sense, alienating, yet recognizable, than the principal characters in a one-story feature. Alas, these films usually work things the other way. They simply connect, often arbitrarily, stories which are merely digests of longer stories or collections of secondary, plot supporting cameos. The formula began as a celebration of ordinary, everyday, minor people, individuals freely assenting to the moral order of the group. Gradually purpose and group disappeared, until Don Chaffey's *The Man Upstairs* (1958): a lodging-house's 'separate tables' realize they owe a near-suicide help, not blame.

A handful of interesting films used the formula's special possibilities. 'The Fumed Oak' and 'Red Peppers' episodes of the Noël Coward film *Meet*

Me Tonight (Anthony Pélissier, 1952) are caustic cameos of the mediocre and seedy sides of *This Happy Breed*. They complement, and, arguably, improve on, Greenian melancholy, being less stylized, with their sense of the vicious, stifled energy packed in each little box of life. In the (dimly filmed) Maugham films a little of the author's sharp-eyed disillusionment lingers. *Trio* peeks into the social aspirations and placings of a shabby genteel verger; notes, ambivalently, the outwitting of a flashy Oriental businessman by the equally devious English; and sketches the apathetic, interfering or autodestructive denizens of a sanatorium, living out their lives in petty loathings and hating the consumptive couple who choose a short sweet life together rather than a lingering and lonely postponement of death. Not until the angry young men is that quiet spitefulness, muffled, seething, restrained, but polluting every relationship, again marked as a characteristic British tone.

Characteristic too, and nicer, is the sense of living in an aimless, nonsense world – nonsense because, while life is bearable, it seems to offer no profound emotional satisfaction. From the early fifties on, the harder spitefulness weakens, while this sense of the absurd strengthens. This is, no doubt, because affluence, relieving social tensions, allows a fearful, and meaningful, clinging to status, to relax, leaving a void. Absurdity is the theme of two comedies of middle-class frustration, James Hill's *The Dock Brief* (1962), from a play by John Mortimer, and Peter Yates's *One Way Pendulum* (1964), from a play by N. F. Simpson. Both subjects straddle the frontier between the old and the new British cinema. But they have their roots in traditional idioms and conditions, and, given the fashion-ability of the theatre of the absurd, it's more interesting to make the connection with an older treatment of the theme.

The Dock Brief concerns a sad-faced husband (Richard Attenborough) who, finding his jolly wife's hearty laugh very wearing to his nerves, murders her. He is defended in court by a barrister (Peter Sellers) who, after weaving innumerable fantasies anticipates an outstandingly brilliant performance, does indeed eventually secure his client's acquittal, since through sheer incompetence he never actually manages to say a word in his defence. It occurs to them that they might make a good team ... the plot touches on the resentment of happiness, the substitution of fantasy for reality, and the systemization of malice masquerading as inefficiency (cf. *Nearly a Nasty Accident*). If the film is weakened by its rather slow, obvious quality as a film script, the interplay of the barrister's pompous, self-righteous enthusiasm with his client's placid masochism make an apt enough parable for a strain in the middle-class psyche. 'Inefficiency's the ticket.'

In his novel *The Great Divorce* C. S. Lewis suggested that Hell, far from being a spectacular lake of fire, was an interminable, grey, seedy, rainy suburb. If he's right, then the Victorian semi-detached of *One Way Pendulum* is the staider British equivalent of *Hellʒapoppin'*. What a crazy world: grandma's in her bathchair playing at puff-puffs, father (Eric Sykes) has rigged up a do-it-yourself Old Bailey kit in the sitting-room and has put himself on trial for masochism, which he took up to pass the time (boredom as auto-punitive). Meanwhile, up in the attic, son (Jonathan Miller) bridges the gap between the two cultures, teaching a squad of Speak-Your-Weight machines to sing the *Hallelujah Chorus*. He also stops and starts at the resounding tinkle of a cash-register, a Pavlovian reflex of thrift and affluence. Anchorman of the system is Mum, ironing away in a placid, practical acceptance of everybody's foibles which comes to seem much of a foible itself. In a mad-house of harmless, pointless hobbies – gently obsessional surrogates for real experience – only the teenage daughter retains a little biological fire.

If N. F. Simpson's play falls short of Ionesco's *The Bald Prima Donna* and *Rhinoceros*, it is perhaps because its ideas, however striking, are one-shots that can be integrated or developed in detail only, and are hardly extensible into an exploration of moods and their spiritual links. Yet its mixture of traditional farce types and the tragic-satire of the absurd remind us that Ionesco's plays were inspired in the first place by the characteristic idioms of English middle-class life.

Hitchcock had made just such a point thirty years earlier, in a film whose moral seems not to have been grasped at the time. *Rich and Strange* (1931) centres on a suburban couple (Henry Kendall, Joan Barry), who are bored with their life routine and with each other. They come into a small inheritance and go on a world cruise, to taste a little high life and adventure. She is courted by an English gentleman (Percy Marmont) whom she doesn't treat too kindly. He has a romance with an exotic Princess (Betty Amann) who turns out to be an adventuress and runs off with all his money. His wife, offended rather than hurt, is easily able to forgive him. They're shipwrecked, menaced by Chinese pirates, confront death, and, while confronting it, find something more than companionship: comradeship. They return at last to their familiar sitting-room in their cosy semi-detached. They sit down by the fire once more, and switch on the radio. The gale-warning reminds them of the shipwreck, and they shiver a little, reminiscently. Pussy miaows, and, remembering a cat slaughtered by pirates, they shudder briefly. But that's all. They have settled again into their old rut, a little more disillusioned with each other, but just as bored, and certainly no wiser about life, love, death, existence. They've gone round the world in a grey flannel bathysphere.

The same story, but with the characters suffering from, rather than expecting nothing other than, this meaninglessness, would bring one right into the Antonioni world: Ship Wreck, instead of *Blow-Up*. If the British cinema is generally unconvincing in its attempts to shift from its traditional terms of semi-detacheds and Alec Guinness little men, to the more fashionable European terms of concrete office-blocks and sensual affluence, it is probably because Britain is so little modernized that the new terms are being imitated before being fully experienced. An interesting attempt is Wolf Rilla's *The World Ten Times Over* (1963), a sad saga of two night club hostesses (Sylvia Syms, June Ritchie), who get disillusioned with men (Edward Judd) and after a suicide attempt end up in a — lesbian? — cuddle. This sincere attempt links some small sad worlds à la Sammy Lee with visual essays on the hostile blandness of egg-box office-blocks, conversations in which no-one communicates, and embraces where the lovers' hands lie limply in leather gloves on leather coats, until people and statues in the parks, seem made of the same clammy substance. Rilla can't maintain Antonioni's maniacal visual precision, nor is such a style central to the milieu. But it's more than fashion-mongering, it's an honest try, and what is astonishing is how, even in ersatz, Antonioni's cold, muggy style explores English reserve, loneliness, irresolution (through Edward Judd); the brisk, prim, female's contempt for the male (through Sylvia Syms) and, through the working-class character (June Ritchie), feeling's last desperate attempt to smash the thickening ice, a bitchy-tragic fling at a drunken copulation. If sex is a current obsession it's not because we're all becoming uncontrollable erotomaniacs but because sex seems the last hope of finding anything normally warm in ourselves at all ....

6: Romantics and Moralists

31. Between Two Worlds

While many film-makers have criticized the system and the consensus, they have usually advocated its modification, as it were from within, and on its own terms. A consequent lack of perspective and purchase explains why many of the best English films are connected with French or American producers, directors or literary origins.

However, other film-makers have criticized aspects of the consensus in terms derived from outside the generally shared atmosphere. Even their assent to it has been arrived at through a noticeably different type and texture of thoughts, a more personal temperament or style. If we divide these artists into moralists and romantics, then the moralists include Thorold Dickinson, the Boulting Brothers, Roy Baker, the producer Raymond Stross, Peter Glenville, Joseph Losey and cartoonist Richard Williams. The romantics include Michael Powell, David Lean and Terence Fisher, and, of course, the horror film genre.

Up to a point, of course, the consensus accepts the Romantic urge. Wordsworth's early Romanticism evolved into a kind of puritan authoritarianism – which can, of course, be felt romantically, though lacking the element of revolt and impatience with restraint which Romanticism usually implies. Matthew Arnold (son of Arnold of Rugby, inventor of the public school system, and patron saint of evangelical gentlemen and muscular Christians, also forms of romantic conformism), sets, in his literary criticism, a precedent for that schoolmarm misinterpretation of Romanticism as uplift. Kipling perfected that romantic compound of evangelical-imperialist-militarist sentiment

The Next of Kin: Mervyn Johns, Reginald Tate – 'Are you a wolf in Welsh clothing?'

which haunted the British imagination from W. E. Henley to *The Drum* (1938) and *Zulu*. Outside the schoolroom, a parallel edulcoration leads from the libidinal harshness of *Wuthering Heights* to the love 'romance'.

The films of David Lean crystallize the forlornness implicit in British Romanticism, so much so that his art has special problems. It's often said that nothing is more difficult to establish, in screen terms, than a negative, whether physical or spiritual: the absence of all those feelings which no-one even dreamed of feeling, though they might have. Lean's art is ultimately in this key. The love stories, slow as glaciers, look towards Antonioni's, yet never quite discover what seems to me to be their own theme. Even *The Sound Barrier* remains earthbound. Its plot asks test pilot's wife (Ann Todd) to accept her aircraft manufacturer father's determination to sacrifice her husband in the service of aviation and she answers, predictably, yes. It loses, in gloomy interiors, the other half of its subject: a sense of duty and the intoxications of flying, above cloud-mountains, on pure oxygen. What might have been a technological romanticism, worthy of Wordsworth, and de Quincey too, becomes sub-Balchin. *Great Expectations* asserts the coarse (Magwitch) against the romantic (Estella), whence its force. Almost as energetic is *Hobson's Choice*, from a doughty Lancashire comedy. Yet another ruthless paterfamilias (Charles Laughton) drunkenly tries to pluck the moon from a puddle, and falls to oblivion down a cellar hatchway. No doubt he took the moon for a golden sovereign; thus a poetic universe takes its revenge. The film's flaw is, perhaps, that Laughton, trying to humanize the old tyrant, overdoes it, and makes him merely a petulant big baby. The formidable face of Manchester is lost. Lean's jollification and justification of the patriarchal has a curious complement, in Nicholson and Lawrence, individualistic, self-destructive idealists. *Lawrence of Arabia* recalls Kipling's more complex tales. Lean's muse seems, like Nicholson, Lawrence and Zhivago, poised between authority and independence, official and personal causes, puddle and cirrocumulus.

Lean's white contrasts with Michael Powell's colour by Pyrotechnicolor. Powell has been dismissed as a 'mere' technician, but if so, he's an eccentric one, in the sense of that proverbially English phenomenon, an eccentric Colonel. When stiff upper lip Colonels retire from matter-of-fact activities like strategy and gunnery, they notoriously embrace soft-centred systems of mystical belief. Similarly, where Powell the brilliant technician leaves off, there appears a man with a disciplined foible for romantic mysticisms of every kind: for militarism (his Prussian officers and his Queen's Guards), for the English countryside (*A Canterbury Tale*), for the fate-time warp (*A Matter of Life and Death*), for sex-maniacs (*Peeping Tom*), for a sex-maddened nun on Himalayan peaks (*Black Narcissus*), for the wild Celtic fringe (*The Edge of the World, I Know Where I'm Going!, Gone to Earth*), for the spiritual hothouse of opera-ballet (*The Red Shoes, The Tales of Hoffmann*). He opens up the romantic veins of his sober subjects: even *The Small Back Room,* most of which is the best filmization of Nigel Balchin, blossoms into expressionist D.T.s with David Farrar vainly striving to scramble up the sheer smooth sides of a gigantic Scotch-bottle. The most powerful passage in *The Battle of the River Plate* is the camera's chilling inspection of the *Graf Spee's* grey, silent structure. This vast, complex killing-city becomes a technological Moby Dick, invested with Satanic nobility. Its battles catch the gaudy, moving fervour of battle paintings in regimental messes. Powell is always interested in mechanism as romantic. The veteran officer of *The Queen's Guards* levers his crippled body on a complex rig-cum-cradle. And Peeping Tom's movie camera has two very optional extras. The tripod's front leg conceals a blade with which he bayonets sufficiently beautiful subjects. As he photographs their dying agonies a distorting mirror in lieu of reflector enables them to enjoy the show too, live, and re-infects them with their own fear, squared.

Had Powell and the cinema, and Technicolor, flourished in the first half of the nineteenth century instead of the twentieth, the period, in fact, of Romanticism encountering Victorian realism, Powell might have been working with the cultural grain instead of against it. His cravings are audacious, constant, uncertain, he turns this way and that, restlessly seeking out different genres, styles, symbols.[41] In a sense, he's Britain's Abel Gance. Both directors have a weakness for patriotic rhetoric (Powell's more veiled), both have a weakness for optical shocks (for Gance, 'the camera becomes a snowball', for Powell, 'the camera becomes an eyeball', when the pink-and-mauve eyelid-lining closes over the screen in *A Matter of Life and Death*), and both seek to ornament melodrama by visual style rather than by rethinking into drama.

The heroine of *I Know Where I'm Going!*, trying to say her prayers, discovers herself making a wish while counting the roof beams of the eerie cottage. Altogether the film neatly dovetails the magic world with that of ration-books and faulty telephones, matter-of-factness and the wish to believe that, somehow, somewhere, romantic and occult values obtain. The danger is the debasement of myth to cosy whimsy, but Powell and Pressburger's film reveals a serious belief in the wayward natural forces. Their fierce power is asserted in constant hints and jabs (a close-up of the eagle's beak ripping off a rabbit's ear) which see nature as a Nietzschean whirl of blood and death. The heroine's money power bribes a foolish young boatman to defy the storm. But the hero, sailing her boat through the treacherous whirlpool, overcomes these forces with that protective manliness which, like those of the Hebridean islanders dwelling on the edge of the world, is itself a force of nature. And the gently comic relief about Celtic eccentricity reasserts a certain sharpness. The

Black Narcissus: Nancy Roberts , Deborah Kerr – Truer and tougher than many an exotic romance poem

women kiss kinfolk on their mouth, in a family greeting like passion. The peppery old eagle-tamer potters about with feather-duster and hair-net, mildly evocative of Ollie in drag and calling the hero 'potty' for considering marriage. In this fey land, hearts may be either closer or freer, as they choose, than in the semi-detached family system.

Another form of paganism inspires *Black Narcissus*. A white Anglican order of nuns (Mother Superiored by Deborah Kerr) take over an old Himalayan 'house of women'. But they have to retire defeated, for their faith fails to prevail against the eerie wind, local superstitions (which turn out to be well-founded), secular paternalism (Esmond Knight's amiable despot), the silent challenge of a nakedness-transcending Tibetan holy man, and the impact of the flesh, incarnated in its aspect of vigorous, earthy common sense, by David Farrar, his hairy legs dangling astraddle a humble donkey, and, in its exotic aspects, by Jean Simmons as a jewel-in-nose dancing girl. It's refreshing,

Old Bones of the River: Will Hay – Not Sanders but still a master – of sorts

too, that one of the nuns' errors is wilfully planting English flowers instead of cabbages, and that Sabu should have bought the scent called Black Narcissus from the Army and Navy Stores. Powell isn't the man to resist some abrupt chopping between niceness and melodrama, but the film is truer and tougher than many of the exotic romantic poems that have an honoured place in anthologies of English literature.

In each film, this romantic urge sports a different livery, co-existing with the everyday and with an only mildly pusillanimous humour (the Heavenly Messenger is always heralded by the smell of fried onions). Its recurrent forms are these which best survive the hard-headed tests which Powell does after all apply. His central problem, as an artist, is another permutation of Lean's, his tendency to escape from realism, yet only play with romanticism. The dichotomy remains in his often dry way with strong emotion. Romantic in potentiality is his daring way with technical effects – the behind-the-eyelid effect, or the camera zip-panning to and fro with a ping-pong ball until time stops and players and ball stand transfixed. Too often, invigorating details are frittered on merely decorative details. In *The Elusive Pimpernel* abstract cinema makes its bow, but only to give us visual equivalents of a sneeze. Powell never gives such patterns a more emotional pretext nor adds 'abstract expressionism' to his repertoire.

His four ventures into opera-ballet are both fascinating and dissatisfying. *The Red Shoes* easily out-Mamoulians Mamoulian. It's schematic in its view of ballet life, and in its romantic view of art as diabolical (a view Bergman entertains in *Summer Interlude* and *The Face*). It has suffered the fate often endured by works of art which, without reaching a new level of inspiration, show a new stylistic flexibility of approach (in colour palette). Instantly praised, they appear infuriatingly pretentious for some years afterwards, before finding their own level, which is an honourable one. This survives for its succession of lyrically coloured scenes, and for a climactic ballet which, despite some ugh touches, compromises effectively between late forties simplicity (in Kelly-Donen style) and an expressionism which was Powell's and Heckroth's own – drifting pieces of sad, sickly cellophane suggesting gaiety's futility, some sharp discords.

With characteristic audacity, Powell and Pressburger's altogether renounced this simplicity, and banked everything on an all-stops-out expressionistic clutter for *The Tales of Hoffmann*. This gallimaufry of Gothicisms, this pantechnicon of palettical paroxysms, this meddle-muddle of media, this olla podrida of oddsbodikins, this massive accumulation of immemorial Mighty Wurlitzerisms, follows Offenbach's operetta relatively faithfully and fills in filmically by ballet, decor and by-play, seeking, moreover, an operatic visual style with a splendid disdain of plausibility. It seeks nothing less than to recapture the full blown romantic urge. If that is weakened for us by time, then eclecticism will overwhelm us. The film cocktails up innumerable idioms of nineteenth century Romanticism: the Greek, the Gothic, Balzacian courtesans, doppelgangers, the devil, sexual oddities (Pamela Brown playing a man), and, over and over again, art as the devil's grip. It's not courage this film lacks, it's taste, in the sense of economy and proportion. Sometimes it's ugly, inexpressively, or even when the theme requires beauty. One need only compare the awkward way in which humans and puppets mingle in a symbolic quadrille with the similar mixture in the night club scene in L'Herbier's *La Nuit fantastique*. L'Herbier, however academic, had grown up within a climate infected by Surrealism, by the sombre, toughly Marxist poetry of Prévert-Carné, by Delluc, by Vigo. Powell-Heckroth have as inspirational trampoline the visual culture of Ye Olde Junke Shoppe.

Unreservedly successful are those sequences whose embellishments are photographic rather than architectural – Moira Shearer in dragonfly tights, photographed through a smudged green filter; or a split screen showing four elevations of Moira Shearer in white with a black-cloaked porteur merging into a black background. If often overblown, the film is intermittently breathtaking, an effect which survives repeated viewings. And if we extend, as we should, the revolt against good taste from juke-box baroque and pop art to Odeon Romanticism, it's quite impossible not to see the film as a minor classic, substituting for the elegant all the fascinations and discords of excess.

The next film in the series, *Oh ... Rosalinda!!*, is a four-power *Die Fledermaus*, an underbudgeted blend of opera-ballet-bouffe and topical satire. The Bat is metamorphosed, inventively, into a sort of Harry Lime of love. Powell lovingly adds absurdities of his own to operatic convention, e.g. a duet sung over the telephone is interspersed with each interlocutor's bursts of lyrical dance. The sets are painted rather than built, which weakens it, and it oddly misuses its battery of high-tension talents – Michael Redgrave has more dancing to do than Ludmilla Tcherina. After *Honeymoon*, which floated into only a few cinemas here, despite its inclusion of La Tcherina's stunning total-theatre ballet version of *Les Amants de Teruel*, Powell has abandoned the genre. One can't help wishing he had responded rather to the contemporary ballets flourishing in France and America, ballets whose romanticism is rooted in current idioms and emotions, for Powell's translations of ballet are a good deal more cinematic, as well as 'transparent', than, say, *Black Tights*.

The Elusive Pimpernel is at once dated and facetious, a perilous combination, remediable only by animal verve, as in the Hollywood remake of *Scaramouche*. P & P do achieve a few minor prodigies of visual virtuosity. Quite 'hand-held' in its effect is a dazzling game of Blind Man's Buff, where the aristocratic ladies blindfold George III with a black scarf from under one corner of which he and we can see a whirling circle of lovely, creamy bosoms. Attempts are made to variegate the inevitable but static scene where a dignified lady alone at her dressing table receives and has to read an important note. P&P have her find it on the floor and stretch herself out at full length in order to peruse it. Powell has certainly escaped the visual stuffiness of so many spectaculars. But the human energy is lacking, as it is in another product of Korda's hook-up with Selznick, *Gone to Earth* (*The Wild Heart* in the U.S.A.), with Jennifer Jones as Shropshire's answer to Pearl Chavez. *Duel in the Sun* is a bad taste masterpiece which is also a good taste masterpiece because its sultry vulgarity is merely the idiom of a robust intelligence. Throughout the British film the American star visibly yearns for someone to make a passionate film around her, to whirl her into its demonic dance. From King Vidor's film she recreates postures and gestures of fiery beauty. But P & P, shy, like so many of their generation, in the presence of erotic intensity, fear embarrassment and ridicule, and cut away instead to local colour (harpists, landscapes), and *faux-naif* cliché (the bad squire's black boot stamps on the girl's rosy posey). Powell's respect for unfashionable genres is in itself admirable but here he accepts their worst rather than their best. A schematic colour symbolism offers transient compensations for dramatic hollowness. The red of the huntsmen contrasts with the black of the church-going middle-classes, both groups being determined, in their different ways, to hunt down the free, fey, fox heroine. The result is neither Selznick, Mary Webb, nor P & P – for Romanticism is passion creating its own universe, or it is nothing.

The recent deluge of Technicolor horrors might have offered Powell a congenial climate for his lyrical propensities. It's characteristic of his ever-astonishing mixture of gifts that his near-miss to a masterpiece, *Peeping Tom*, is a very different kettle of fishiness. The story-line is excessive enough to carry almost any amount of dramatic soft-pedalling. In a sense, it craves cool style, for its cameraman (Carl Boehm) is secretive, passionless, lonely. Appropriately for a tale of repressions and inhibitions, the film is built on a network of symbols, admirably summarized by Ian Johnson. The eye-mirror-camera-bayonet cluster recalls the brain surgeon with the *camera obscura* – another 'cutting voyeur' – and P & P's trade mark as *The Archers* – a close-up of an *arrow* smacking into a bull's-eye. Little need to dwell on the erectility of bayonet-tripod, while Mark Lewis's job as a *focus-puller* underlines the voyeur's association of seeing with sexual protuberance. The old woman who 'sees through' the quiet young man to his real nastiness is blind (is she not related to the Celtic women with their 'second sight'? Indeed, Anna Massey, playing her daughter, looks like Pamela Brown in *I Know Where I'm Going!*). Mark has his tripod, the old woman has her stick; he his mirrors, she her insight. The Oedipal situation is lovingly elaborated. Mark paraphrases on his models the experiments his father, a world-famous psychologist, inflicted on him. These experiments, in the effects of fear, include throwing a lizard (cold-eyed phallic 'snake') on to his bed, shining a bright light into his eyes, showing him his own films. Mark has kept his father's films of his experiments – as also shots taken by his father of his second wife. A bosomy young thing whom he married six weeks after Mark's mother's death, she looks like the nude models whom Mark now photographs to earn pocket-money (among them we may recognise Pamela Green and Susan Travers, garnished with a disfigured lip). Thus the film abounds in films-within-films. Opening with Mark's own film of a murder, it takes in its stride both the film on which Mark is working at the studio and Mark's father's films of young Mark. The film's plethora of in-jokes out-*Cahiers Cahiers*. Mark's father is played by Michael Powell. The director of the feature film is played by Esmond Knight. The hero is called Mark Lewis, presumably after the film's script writer, whose name is Leo Marks. Pamela Green was made famous by a photographer called Harrison Marks. The Esmond Knight character is called Arthur Baden. Baden-*Powell* also looked after little boys and trained their characters. Mark gets involved with red-haired women only (like most Powell heroines). He describes himself as a correspondent from the *Observer* and his father tells him to 'Look at the sea', 'Look at the see' being what his victims do in the *mirror* which replaces the *reflector*. The black-and-white flashbacks to clinical child-torture relate to the coloured present in a way reminiscent of Resnais's *Nuit et brouillard*. This film is built on refusing to allow the audience to hate the torturer, on a cold hysteria of frustrated indignation, stoked up by the sacreligious idea of casting Moira Shearer as a bit of a bitch, fit fodder for a sensitive sex murderer. Suicidally impaled on his own machine Mark, in dying hallucination, is reconciled with his long-dead father. Here art reveals, again, its diabolical root.

Reconciliation with the diabolical is, indeed, an underlying lietmotif in Powell's films. It underlies the close association between the gallant Prussian officer and the Nazi cause, as it underlies the cruel paganism of *I Know Where I'm Going!*, where the hero subdues nature, or rather survives it, because he has its own sharp intensity. Indeed, Powell has a fondness for leading men with a certain sharp fierce glance or voice – Roger Livesey, Marius Goring, Anton Walbrook (and, in a different modality, David Farrar), just as his heroines are often half-witches. Ironically, the one film in which he needed to explore emotional intensity in depth (*Peeping Tom*) depends on what is, in effect, the 'deadpan' pleasantness of Carl Boehm, and the dimension lacking in *Peeping Tom* is more vividly asserted in Polanski's *Repulsion*, via the confluence of Catherine Deneuve's nervous tension and Polanski's eye for the eerie everyday.

Yet it is in this unending game of hide-and-seek between the uninhibited and the diabolic, the patriotic and erotic, the traditional and the technological, the Tory and the pagan, that Powell's work finds much of its fascination. One can endlessly establish spiritual concavities, the fact remains that the convexities are intricate and fascinating. Perhaps his most 'perfect' film is a child's Arabian Nights fantasy, *The Thief of Bagdad* (1940), for which he shares directorial credits with Ludwig Berger (German specialist in trick-and costume-films) and Tim Whelan (an efficient Hollywood craftsman). This too carries many distinctly Powellian notations. Almost its first shot is of a painted eye on a ship's brow, surging into close-up. Its story (by Miles Malleson) includes the theft of the all-seeing eye (*Peeping Tom* indeed!) from a Tibetan temple (*Black Narcissus*). The giant genie from the bottle (beautifully played by Rex Ingram) prefigures the gigantic bottle in *The Small Back Room*. Its tricks with time prefigure *A Matter of Life and Death*. If it never quite transcends the sphere of children's film, it remains one of the classic screen fantasies, along with Roy Rowland's *The 5,000 Fingers of Dr. T.*, Joseph Von Baky's *Münchhausen*, and Albert Zugsmith's *Evils of Chinatown*. Its scope and audacity, its morning freshness, reduce even Cottafavi's *Hercules Conquers Atlantis* to pretty small beer.

One craves, perhaps, a venture into those dark interiors where the fantasies of *The Thief of Bagdad* interpenetrate with those of *Peeping Tom*. Whence their centrifugality? The comparison with the director of *The Citadel* is pertinent. Vidor, intellectually, perhaps, less cagey and sophisticated than Powell, has retained an authenticity of emotional excess which endows his films with their genuine mysticism, founded on human energy. But Powell lived in a class, and a country, and a generation which suspects, fears and undermines emotion. Thus his diversity of qualities rarely find their holding centre. Between himself and Hoffmann he interposes the opera-ballet convention (whereas the – American – Corman-Crosby team, in their horror films, create a coherent universe blending aspects of Poe, Wilde, Freud and colour expressionism). It would not be unreasonable to see Powell's indirectness as the Pirandellism of scepticism, to see his ballet films as preludes to an *8½* which he hadn't the egoism to make. One would dearly like to see him tackle those science-fiction subjects which have a built-in excess – C. L. Moore's *Shambleau*, Richard Matheson's *I Am Legend*. And he is the only British director who could have brought to the screen Ian Fleming's James Bond, rather than his boring technological surrogate.

He remains an upholder, through its lean years, of the Méliès tradition. Several of his films generously reward innumerable viewings (notably *A Matter of Life and Death*, *The Red Shoes*, *The Tales of Hoffmann*, and *Black Narcissus*). *The Edge of the World*, *The Small Back Room*, and *The Thief of Bagdad* attain some sort of perfection in very different genres, and most of his failures remain more interesting than the successes of now fashionable Hollywood auteurs.

The popular cinema is, of course, perenially suffused with a pale pink romanticism which nonetheless isn't always only pop. With Batman and Shirley Temple now in intellectual vogue, who will begrudge this writer his foible for *The Wicked Lady* (Leslie Arliss, 1945)? This, the most rumbustious of Gainsborough's costume melodramas of the forties, is a tomboy-bitch saga whose commercial expertise, notably in the cunning balancing of our sympathies, is quite as fascinating as *Gone with the Wind's*, while its sexual innuendoes are rather more knowing. Intriguing, too, is Terence Young's *Corridor of Mirrors* (1947). Its decadent hero (Eric Portman) reconstructs Renaissance Venice in his grounds and dreams himself into living in those spacious days instead of in this age of austerity and democracy. The theme is less eccentric than might appear, even to its enervating pallidity, when one remembers how much English poetry testifies to a penchant for a sugary, yet subtly misanthropic, romanticism. The subject might have been rather more pointed had its hero been nostalgic for the Elizabethan age.

The period romances which offer escape from wartime and postwar austerity may be divided into two strains. The first exhibits both vulgarity and vitality, the other, neither. The first group is constituted by the Gainsborough films, conceived on the novelette level, but distinguished from their American counterparts by a certain grimness. They include Leslie Arliss's *The Man in Grey* (1943) and *The Wicked Lady* (1945), and Arthur Crabtree's *Madonna of the Seven Moons* (1944) and *Caravan* (1946). Offshoots of the genre include Compton Bennett's *The Seventh Veil* (1945) and David MacDonald's *The Brothers* (1947), the latter easily superior to most of the Hawks and Walsh films touted by auteur-theory connoisseurs. The genre was driven headlong to disaster when Rank's new régime at Gainsborough edulcorated it with middle-class 'class' (e.g. *The Bad Lord Byron*, *Christopher Columbus*). Probably the best of the refined films are *Saraband for Dead Lovers*, Alexander Korda's *An Ideal Husband* (1947) and Thorold Dickinson's *The Queen of Spades* (1949), which merits further exegesis later. Gabriel Pascal's *Caesar and Cleopatra* (1945) and Duvivier's *Anna Karenina* (for Korda, 1948) are the titanics of the genre. The former combines Shaw's boring passionlessness with empty expanse. The latter is framed to accommodate passion of which the actors show little sign.

The tendency to deficient vitality probably relates to the conspicuous absence of romantic feeling in contemporary terms (except for *Pandora and the Flying Dutchman* (1950), which, like its producer-writer-director, is essentially American. With the *musée imaginaire* of myths promised by its title it combines its Delvaux-like sequence of a jazz band playing, by mutilated Greek statuary, on a nocturnal beach, and the moonlit sacrifice of a sports car to love Goddess Ava Gardner. If we define Romanticism as beauty taken to a pitch of promise that hurts, it has its modern terms, as Vadim, Fellini, Tennessee Williams, Antonioni and everyone but the British know. Most of Swinging London is its small change – or counterfeit.

The weakness of the romantic urge arguably underlies both the rarity of personal vision among directors and writers, and the apparent absence of auteurs in British films, few of which bear the obvious imprint of a particular directorial personality. Most critics would concede a personal style or thematic to, probably, Asquith, the Boultings, Dickinson, Endfield, Fisher, Leacock, Lean, Lee Thompson, Losey, Powell and Reed. A few might claim an ability to distinguish, blindfold, between a Gilbert and a Leacock, a Dearden and a Frend, a Mackendrick and a Crichton. Indeed, once one begins to consider the British cinema, in terms of the auteur theory as applied to Hollywood, it becomes evident that the two industries are in much the same position. Possibly the real objection to British cinema is, not its endorsement of the consensus, but the content of that consensus, in contrast to the content of the Hollywood consensus. The position is further complicated by the fact that many artists endeavour to fit their style to their subject, so that one has really to ascribe auteur *status* to chameleons like René Clément in France, Alberto Lattuada in Italy, or John Huston in the U.S.A. The British cinema offers two such directors: Alberto Cavalcanti and John Guillermin.

Cavalcanti's career spans many years and many phases, from the French avant-garde of the twenties, through English documentary of the thirties, to Ealing in the forties, and Brazil and Europe again in the fifties. His assimilation is almost too complete. But perhaps only a European's objectivity preserved Greene's critical detachment in *Went The Day Well?*. It may be that his most personal British film is *They Made Me a Fugitive* which, as Arthur Vesselo noted at the time, recalls the German cinema of the twenties. Vesselo presumably meant to stigmatize its brutality as decadent, but the *rapprochement* fits the strange poetry distilled by its strange blend of humour, brutality and seedy studio realism. If Guillermin's topics meant anything, he would appear as a right-wing apologist. Auteur theory procedures would work from the *Daily Express*-spirited combination of *Never Let Go* and *Guns at Batasi* to suggest that the *real* meaning of *Town on Trial* was the detective's losing the chip off his shoulder about class, and that *Waltz of the Toreadors* related to Vichy defeatism via the play's author, Jean Anouilh. But there's no definite reason to suppose that any of these subjects were anything for their director other than personal stories to be enhanced by the swing and energy of his style. This indeed is remarkable among British directors for its long, sharp, swinging and scything camera movements, often in neatly complex geometrical intersection with the action. Stylists who have never found their subject aren't rare in British films, and include Seth Holt (whose strong spare boldness is reminiscent of Losey and Endfield) and John Moxey (whose *The City of the Dead* is a little spatial *tour de force* like Gregg Tallas's *Siren of Atlantis*).

32. A Gothic Revival

Yet the British cinema evolved its own Romantic genre: the horror film. A minor cycle of gruesome crime films with Victorian backgrounds indicate the 'zone' between Gainsborough grimness and horror proper. They are almost invariably shorn of their purple passages by the British censor, so that British spectators of *Jack the Ripper* (1958), *The Flesh and the Fiends* (1959), *The Siege of Sidney Street* (1960), and *The Hellfire Club* (1960) have had to content themselves with that atmosphere of gloomy criminality which murder fans so often find satisfying in itself. A French critic, Jean-Paul Török, has spoken of their 'black romanticism, whose beauty springs from an accumulation of sordid cruelties'. The same phrase applies also to the very physicality of three films all dating from 1958, Robert Day's *Corridors of Blood* (surgery before anaesthetics) and *Grip of the Strangler* (which opens on spectators having orgasms at a public hanging) and Henry Cass's *Blood of the Vampire* (a grim colour piece about a prison governor (Donald Wolfit) using convicts as his blood bank behind prison walls of blood-orange brick). The traditional cinema mainstream discovers the romanticism of cruelty and tyranny at about the same time as the angry young men burst through. A belated but heavy blossom of the stock is James Hill's *A Study in Terror*, an apocryphal encounter between two eminent Victorians: Sherlock Holmes and Jack the Ripper.

A related group, less dour, nearer the convulsive emphases of grand guignol, are Anglo-Amalgamated's little trio of 'piercing' films, Arthur Crabtree's *Horrors of the Black Museum* (1959), Sidney Hayers's *Circus of Horrors* and Michael Powell's *Peeping Tom* (both 1960). The first begins with a succulent blonde eagerly unwrapping a Post Office parcel, which turns out to contain a pair of binoculars, a gift from an admirer. Their focusing knob thrusts a concealed spike into each of her eyes. Michael Gough plays an unhinged criminologist whose subsequent crimes include screwing ice-pincers into an evil old lady's neck, clipping a portable guillotine on to a tart's bed-head, dipping an inquisitive guest into a vat of acid from which he emerges a skeleton, and so on. A little more style informs Sidney Hayers's film; a megalomaniac plastic surgeon (Anton Diffring) takes over a circus, and staffs it mainly with sumptuous-bodied young ladies whose disfigurements he has repaired. He prefers the degraded women (prostitutes, pickpockets) as more loyal and when they try to leave him little accidents occur. That is to say everything that thrills the audience of real circuses by not quite happening, happens. The knife slices the living target's pretty throat in two, the trapezist falls, the lions get their tamer, the gorilla grabs a passer-by, and so on. All of which proving how narrow is the dividing line between a morbid X film like *Circus of Horrors* and the sawdust and tinsel of family fun.

Puritanism about violence apart, the horror film tends to be aesthetically infra dig. The assumption is that strong ideas are crude artistic effects as compared to sensitivities of style. Yet it's dubious whether they're any less difficult to think of, and handle, than various routine effects which get acknowledged as 'quality' style. Even when handled unrealistically, they may, in an obscurantist culture, rewardingly stimulate the spectator's thinking, and his awareness of his own, and others', latent possibilities, both useful artistic functions. The genre can, after all, trace a direct ancestry from the eighteenth century Gothic novel, and similarly merits attention. Hammer films, since going soft, have won tolerant critical smiles but our defence of the genre applies only to those scenes which aroused disgusted protest when they appeared. As Török remarked, 'horror has become in Great Britain a new genre of cinema, clearly defined, with its own rules and its own style. One hears, and rightly so, a great deal about Free Cinema. But, by its power of suggestion, its frenzy, its invitation to voyage towards the land of dark marvels and erotic fantasy, is not the horror film the real British "free cinema"?' In other words, English pulp movies reactivated the Theatre of Cruelty some years before the English rediscovery of Artaud.

A more realistic brand of guignol has inspired Hammer movies as drearily formularized as their titles: *Maniac, Paranoiac,* and, least bad of the cycle, Silvio Narizzano's *Fanatic.* No door is left uncreaked, nor door knob unturned, and since Hammer are notoriously stronger on persistence than on originality, only inability to spell can have prevented them from working their way through Auto-, Dipso-, Klepto-, Mono-, Megalo-, and Pyro-, not forgetting all the -phrenes, -philes, -phebes, -ists and -ites. Seth Holt's *Taste of Fear* (1961) has his force, but the genre acquires some sort of artistic justification when younger directors adapt it. Reisz's *Night Must Fall* (1964) craves indulgence and points the way to Polanski's *Repulsion* (1965).

The traditional apparition has accompanied into eclipse his underlying combination of folk-lore and Christianity. Ealing's supernatural omnibus, *Dead of Night* (1945) has only one such ghost, and that in a comic story with Basil Radford and Naunton Wayne as ghost golfers. Otherwise, its tales are of dreams, premonitions, hallucinations and paranoias. The dream hearse driver preludes the real bus conductor, the doll controls the ventriloquist, the mirror projects its past into the present room. Finally the whole film is revealed as a dream – but as the dreamer's day begins it reiterates the beginning of the dream. The intertwining of what used to be thought of as semi-documentary realism, and a universe like a parallel-tracked Moebius loop, is quiet and oppressive. A pity that *The Night My Number Came Up* (Leslie Norman, 1955), Ealing's subsequent venture into dream predestination, restricted itself to regulation characters and emotions, betraying its stoic, agnostic, view of the supernatural as another system, no harder, after all, than this. Neither *The Queen of Spades,* of which more later, nor *The Innocents,* the only serious attempts to revive traditional phantoms, were conspicuous for their box-office success. The latter might have been rather more interesting had it ceased to be a ghost story at all, and been a straightforward soul-fight between, on the one hand, the well-meaning sweetness and light of governess Deborah Kerr, and, on the other hand, the erotic and sadomasochistic egoisms of a gamekeeper (à la James Mason-Laurence Olivier) and a housekeeper (à la Barbara Steele).

The occult retains much of its fascination, and may well intensify it, as providing not only a pretext, but also an additional dimension, for orgiastic ambivalence. Jacques Tourneur's *Night of the Demon* (1957) has lately attracted a little appreciation, though one may prefer Sidney Hayers's more adventurous *Night of the Eagle* (1962), with dons and their wives casting spells on their rivals in their race to the top. This C. P. Snow's nightmare is decked out with needle-sharp zooms and edgy close-ups, which magnify the astutely observed tics and gestures of modern professional people and make of the emotional tensions behind them a trampoline into demential realms. The camera moves from the occult samples, laid out on the kitchen table, accusatory of insanity, over to the groceries, calm reminders of sanity, with which, alas, they obdurately co-exist. Tape recorders, telephones, door-bells, all the semi-impersonal contacts of modern life, become part of a paranoid network, and the film's horror is the interpenetration of our too-sane rationalism by a mercilessly 'Hobbesian' meta-universe where only logic is that of arbitrary trickery. The first part of this minor film fascinatingly links the vacuous eeriness of the tape recorder in *La Notte* with hallucinatory realms.

Whereas American SF emphasizes monsters threatening hero, home town and the world, and having to be blasted by the U.S. Army into kingdom come, British films about libido-on-the-rampage emphasize the living dead and nineteenth century settings (thus vampire, werewolf, mummy and Frankenstein Monster). Their principal contemporary theme is a quiet, sinister, de-personalization, in, notably, Val Guest's *The Quatermass Experiment* (1955) and *Quatermass 2* (1957), Wolf Rilla's *Village of the Damned* (1960), Anton M. Leader's *Children of the Damned* (1963) and John Krish's *Unearthly Stranger* (1963).

A recurrent problem in screen SF is how to relate the alien entities and situations to the familiar. If this intriguing quintet lack the virulence of their Hollywood counterpart, Don Siegel's *Invasion of the Body Snatchers* (1955), it's not because their basic ideas are any less inventive – if anything they are more so – but because modest British calm and timidity soft pedals, not the facts, but the experience. If the first Quatermass survives two viewings, it is largely on the strength of Richard Wordsworth's slow, agonized deterioration into the thing that transforms, first, his limbs into cactusoid lumps, and eventually, his body to fungus. Physical, spiritual and moral atrocity counterpoint the metaphysical and collective threat. Its successor has a fine pattern of ideas, with 1984-guards-in-1958-Britain, and Shell's Milford Haven refinery seeming, in 1957, uncannily technological. Huge towers, allegedly containing synthetic food for easing the world food problem contain, in fact, a black acid slime, serving a malevolent and superior intelligence. A pity that the 'puppetization' of cabinet ministers, police-chiefs, etc., results in human interest almost as uninteresting as the crushingly banal gun-play climax.

The Quatermass films express a very British hostility to progress, technology and the future – a hostility too undiscriminating to be considered a melodramatic harbinger of *The Red Desert*. The two 'damned' films, both developed from John Wyndham's *The Midwich Cuckoos*, express the nightmare obverse of the theme of pre-pubertal innocence (and relate to a childbirth theme indicated elsewhere). In the first place, these children are innocents with a vengeance – parthenogenized changelings fathered by some Process X from Out There. The children exhibit a coldly precocious contempt for their elders, and their unified intelligence and mental energy pose a terrifying challenge to the human race. More particularly in view of a tussle between the military hawks, who want to blast the entire village out of existence, and the scientific dove (George Sanders) who prefers to study them first and then deploy minimal, selective and self-sacrificial mental pressures. Since the equation 'science = atom bomb = World War III' was never far from audiences' minds during the fifties, the film repudiated a political overemphasis. Yet this is a disappointing substitute for a (commercially more dubious?) theme, tracing out the conflicts of love and hatred between parents and children who are only *part* changelings. Losey's *The Damned*, of which more later, works the theme back towards social possibilities, i.e. realities.

The equally 'cold' children of the damned are envoys sent through time by our posterity, to help us avert a hideous disaster (by implication, World War III) which has ravaged them and lies in wait for us. Two commonsensical detectives gradually realize what's afoot and hunt the children down through various realistic locations and encounters to their hideout, a blitzed church. They are ringed by tanks and rockets, and an inadvertently dropped screwdriver unleashes the barrage which simultaneously destroys the children and humanity's chance of peace. The two films have some interest as dream-paraphrases of the battle of the generations, in perplexingly rapid cultural change. The latter film aligns itself with the Aldermaston marchers.

A little too pedestrian in maintaining its realistic frame of reference, a little rudimentary in its tracing of spiritual possibilities, this boldly pessimistic movie may be twinned with *Unearthly Stranger*. This concludes with the revelation that inhuman aliens are camouflaged among us by intense telepathic power. When concentration slackens, their human metabolism falters (so that salt tears leave burn marks on a housewife's face). All these creatures are women (women, like children, tend to be outside the safe system ...). Yet, despite one or two fine shocks, man-and-wife relationships are ultra-conventional, and a high-voltage hysteria is restricted to scenes between two civil servants (John Neville's hypersensibility, burning like dry ice). Appropriate as such comradeship may be to the film's misogyny, the renunciation of deeper themes restricts it to a minor, yet interesting, atmosphere piece.

33. Terence Coloured

After the success of the Quatermass films, Hammer decided to venture a quick, not-too-serious remake of the well-tried Frankenstein theme. The directorial chore was assigned to Terence Fisher. Many of his previous assignments featured scenarios of almost memorable mediocrity, gummed together around superannuated Hollywood stars. But from the first day of shooting *The Curse of Frankenstein* (1957), Fisher and actor Peter Cushing discovered their common admiration for the icy idealism of the bad Baron. Soon realizing, after the first day's shooting, that their film was outraging its brief, Fisher and Cushing allowed its ambivalence a freer vein.

Hammer's Frankenstein series reproduces, on a popular level, the intellectual rediscovery of Sade, in three ways. First, script (by Jimmy Sangster) relishes poetic injustice (anyone foolish enough to believe in human goodness gets it). Second, the Baron (Peter Cushing), in contrast with Mary

Shelley's febrile idealist, represents both the cold cruelty, and the courage, of science, thus paraphrasing that unmoved detachment from one's atrocities which, *pace* the *Marat-Sade*, is one of the aspirations of Sade's debauchees. And just as the Sade libertine becomes the unmoved mover, matching God, so this Frankenstein reproduces not only the hubris, but the coldness, of materialism. In contrast to the Gothic setting of the novel and of the American film, Fisher's movies are in the visual key of Oscar Wilde. Cushing and Lee are perfect dandies – but aloof, cold, proud, celibate, deadlier by far than Wilde's, very near the surgeon-torturers of Baudelaire. These days Wilde's idea of evil wouldn't raise a long-haired teenager's eyebrow; but the blend of Technicolor elegance and cold savagery gives something at once frozen and libidinous.

The first film's immorality is cautious. Frankenstein murders his trusting old Professor and transplants his brain into the Monster, where it endures a grisly mental deterioration. Eventually Frankenstein in his turn is tricked by his assistant, and left incarcerated in a brutal nineteenth century asylum, where he'll be whipped into mental deterioration himself. On paper, therefore, the film is even more sternly anti-scientific than the original novel or the film. But Cushing's dignity, and the very *Schadenfreude* of the final twist, demoralize it.

Its successor, *The Revenge of Frankenstein* (1958) achieves the Sadeian reversal of moral orthodoxy. By a trick the Baron and his accomplice get the guillotine blade to decapitate the priest sent to perform the last rites. Later, in Germany, a certain 'Dr. Stein' selects from his charity patients the choicest chops as components of his Creature. This rascalry is so nonchalant that the audience reverses its usual moral preferences sufficiently to be pleasantly rather than unpleasantly shocked by the happy end. For the last scene shows 'Dr. Frank' setting up practice in Harley Street. His first patient is a beautiful girl who clearly finds her butcher-to-be most stimulating.

Christopher Lee as *Dracula* (1958) has such strength and grace in his movements, and the torments of his pale victims in pastel-shaded negligées, are so palpably erotic that, J. P. Török argued, the film suggests, if it only ambiguously asserts, a Sadeian polarity. For, after all, the women who choose the vampire's caresses to life, are *martyrs* to pleasure. Count Dracula becomes then the 'soul' of erotic egoism, at bay in a Victorian era which, far from being characterized as, in contrast to ours, puritan and repressive, is opulent, materialist and rationalist (very like ours). Even the cross which destroys the vampire is despiritualized. It's used like a special kind of hypodermic needle, a ritual prophylactic. Essentially, the vampire hunter is as materialistic as Sherlock Holmes; and it's real dream-stuff that his demure wife (Melissa Stribling) should be concealing vampire and coffin in the cellar of his own home.

Morally, the films are rather more ambivalent than critics realized, being at once Sadistic and tragic. The interweaving of moral and physical detail may be exemplified by *The Mummy* (1959). An Egyptian high priest, guilty of craving the Queen, has his tongue torn out by the roots before being wound in a white shroud and buried in her tomb. These Oedipal and castratory references are developed even further into perversity by his subsequent mutilations. Revived by Egyptologist Peter Cushing, he sees in an English girl the reincarnation of his beloved. He returns, to destroy them, no doubt, but to protect, and love, her. As reward he has two great holes shotgun-blasted in his chest, like craters for breasts, and dies in a swamp, his white bandages smeared green and gold by mud and slime. (Psychoanalytically, the mutilated phallus is turned into dead femininity and excrement.) Yet, like Heathcliff, the strength of his love has reversed the natural course of life and death.

A similar ambivalence typifies the moral ironies of *The Curse of the Werewolf* (1961). A beggar (Richard Wordsworth), with an incautious confidence in human charity, is made to crawl, ignominiously, and then, as appropriate reward, thrown into prison. As the years drag by, he becomes demented, and, when the jailer's daughter takes pity on him, rapes her. But his moral deterioration goes one stage further. The dying girl gives birth to a son, who, in late adolescence, begins turning into a werewolf, at each full moon. He has, in the end, to be shot by his loving adoptive father. In *The Brides of Dracula* (1960) a proud Countess (Martita Hunt) is reluctant to kill her vampire son (David Peel) as duty enjoins and instead attaches him to a long silver chain. He rewards her maternal kindness by making her his victim, and vampire in her turn. As if in acknowledgement of her kindness, however, the script postulates that even after death, she is able to repent. Thus death-moral death becomes a country into which one advances gradually, as in Cocteau's *Orphée*.

Innumerable scenes derive their strength from the interweaving of moral and psychological overtones with Fisher's physical approach to visual style. In *The Brides of Dracula,* an old sorceress lies over a grave, urging the corpse below to struggle up through the earth to her new vampire's life. 'I know it's very dark, my dear, but you must try, try ...' she urges, clutching the earth convulsively as if to help the corpse below to rise out in necromantic counterpart of childbirth.

This dreamlike physicality depends on Fisher's idiosyncratic readiness to sacrifice strong dramatic emphases for the continuity of a scene as a dramatic whole. Another consequence is the prominence, in nuancing the dramatic, of sensuous and tactile elements. Technicolor becomes cruel. Frankenstein, cutting out organs, wears yellow and leather oilskin aprons which stimulate our epidermal sense. Eyeballs, placed, with their tangle of nerves, in a glass tank,

Beat Girl: Christopher Lee, Gillian Hills, Delphi Lawrence – Dracula spots another victim

follow a Bunsen flame as it is waved to and fro close to them. Its reflection in the glass tank 'touches' them, underlying their hideous exposure. Always there is blood – as Melissa Stribling lies panting and ecstatic after Dracula's visit, her vaporous negligée is drenched in her blood, sucked and spilled. We are given two views (neither in close-up) of a pickpocket's (wantonly) amputated arm. The first shows its tattoo (stressing its owner's life experiences). The second reduces it to a cross-section of red meat round bone (is that all our life-stories come down to?).

At other moments, the colour sings. The vampire's avid victim (Carol Marsh) walks in her grave-clothes through a wood whose autumnal tints are enswathed in a bluish mist which is cinematically beautiful precisely because it resembles the real thing less than an ectoplasmic emanation, a voluptualization of nature, a Symbolist world.

The Brides of Dracula: Andree Melly, Yvonne Monlaur – 'Technicolor becomes cruel'

The Stranglers of Bombay (1959) becomes, in effect, a grisly succession of thuggee atrocities. It was originally intended to break with the tuppence-coloured style and return, in black and white, to the 'documentary' sobriety of Guest's *The Camp on Blood Island*. It is unintentionally, therefore, that it becomes, in Michel Caen's words 'a very beautiful catalogue of tortures ... a young Hindu girl (Marie Devereux) whose stunningly exposed bosom is of quite demential sumptuousness, contemplates the atrocities with a pleasure so intense (and so evidently erotic) that she glistens with sweat ... I am astonished by the presence of this proud figurehead of female sado-scoptophilia, who can have escaped the scissors of Auntie Censorship only by some miracle ...'

Hammer's 'grand series' owed their success to a chemistry of moods: physical atrocity interacting with moral irony + dandy coldness + sensuousness + Victorian nostalgias + Victorian materialism. The scripts have few virtues other than their nicely calculated acquiescence in injustice, while Fisher refuses to emphasize the horrific at the expense of the dramatic scene as a whole – that is, of a more generalized human interest. The Sadistic tone comes, ironically, from a reserve which, accidentally or intuitively, finds a cruel synthesis between atrocities and *temps-morts* and turns everything into moral apathy. Their spell may prove ephemeral; yet spell they cast.

34. Shammerteurism

Hammer's subsequent movies suggested that the studio thought in terms only of general theme and production values. The image lingers, but the spirit is weak. Fisher and other directors acquiesce in scripts which, having thought of one good twist on a theme, allow everything else to relapse into cliché and *déjà vu* (the same sets, actors and characters, thinly revamped). *The Two Faces of Dr. Jekyll* (1960) has three good ideas, (1) ugly Jekyll becomes handsome Hyde, (2) ladies' man Hyde seduces Jekyll's bitchy wife, so (3) what does Jekyll do about it? Thereupon it abandons its many fascinating possibilities for ideas like murder by serpent plumbing.

The weaknesses of *The Gorgon* (1964) deserve closer attention. It gives the Gorgon the syren's voice, and locates her in Bismarck's Prussia, within singing-at-dusk distance of a mental home. The black-and-orange duskscapes make a fascinating 'zone' between authoritarian chains and the syren's song. We're beautifully poised for a Marat-Sade meditation on order and liberty, authority and eroticism, the system and the dream, benevolent despotism and suicide, rationalism and the romantic agony, reality and hallucination.

In the event, alas, the Greek Gorgon lives in a Gothic castle (the same old set again). The script minimizes the erotic and the hallucinatory, and wastes all its time discussing whether a Gorgon exists, when she must do for the film to be named after her. Behind such tactics there stands, presumably, the British censor refusing the 'sensational' use of mental illness.

After, or rather while, sampling *The Gorgon*, *The Evil of Frankenstein* and *The Curse of the Mummy's Tomb*, all 1964, I dreamed that I was touring the script crypt at Bray. There Major Carreras cracked his bull whip over the sweating backs of the toiling writers, who moaned at their task while an assistant producer beat out the typing speed on his kettle drums. The light of the full moon poured in through the Gothic windows, and producer Anthony Hinds stared in horror at his hands, as they grew hairy and twitched – another script idea was taking them over, and he was turning into one or another of his dreaded alter egos, John Elder and Henry Younger. Young Baron Sangsterstein was there, cackling hideously and with fiendish cunning sewing together bits of scenarios from the old Universal book. The dialogue was inserted by a very old librarian entirely wrapped in off-white bible-paper; he was consulting a stack of stone tablets whose hieroglyphics were cliché when the riddle of the sphinx was only a gleam in the High Priest's eye.

The Kiss of the Vampire (Don Sharp, 1962) was the last film to offer any hope of Hammer's muse receiving the love-bite of life. The lordly vampire assembles his disciples for orgies in his stately castle, terrorizes the simple peasantry, and is vanquished, at last, by a dour doctor whose black clothes, Calvinist ferocity, and middle-class status adumbrate a fascinating antithesis: vampirism versus puritanism. The *raison d'être*, indeed, the beauty, of Calvinist severity is affirmed when the doctor purifies the bite made by a lovely vampire in his wrist by pouring whisky over it and then setting fire to it. Art, too, is dangerous: two vampires, brother and sister, 'mesmerize' a young bride during the playing of a passionately romantic piano piece. And just as *The Brides of Dracula* nuanced the traditionally Manichean distinction between the living and the undead, so, here, the newly vampired of this sub-species can brace daylight for short periods, if it's an overcast sky. For all that, the film doesn't escape the pitfall of its theme. Far from raising immorality to the level of vampire horror, it reduces vampirism to immorality, which, for censorship reasons is, in its turn, reduced to rather sedate orgies. Sharp, no mean stylist, doesn't really believe in the supernatural. The cold wind tearing autumn leaves remains simply a cold wind tearing autumn leaves.

35. Flesh and Fantasy

One might not expect too much from an English foray into the peplum (classical epic done into visually elegant pulp fantasy). Yet Don Chaffey's *Jason and the Argonauts* (1963) isn't to be omitted from any account of this minor, but interesting genre. American ventures in the genre stress either a Biblical-puritan morality (*Ben-Hur*) or a Darwinian ferocity of will (as does the Kirk Douglas Ulysses). The Italians incline to a leisurely, sensual, sometimes poetic clarté. The one British film imbues the genre with a bold, solid sobriety which evokes *Western Approaches* and which counterpoints fascinatingly with the hazards of myth (a disastrous finale, involving a skeleton army, I consider a producer interpolation). The film is British also in its misogyny (the ship's protective figurehead, the goddess Hera, rising like a cobra from the sea to hiss her secrets into Jason's ear), in its fascination with father-figures (the taciturn and selfish benevolence of the Triton), and its stoic sense of duty, of system and of fantasy as anti-fantasy. The scriptwriters have placed the human peripetia in the framework of a domestic spat among the Gods. Smoothly Hera (Honor Blackman) teases Zeus:

'You will cease to exist when men cease to believe in you,' to which her spouse replies,
'You know that? Yet you remain with me?'
'You despise my weakness?'
'No, I find it – almost human.'

Inspired less by Pirandello than by Richard Garnett's *The Twilight of the Gods and Other Tales,* these terse lines juggle brilliantly with a variety of

Guns of Darkness: David Niven, David Opatoshu, Leslie Caron – Pacifist principles on trial in the face of violent reality

themes, all but yoking the stoicism of Homer with the protesting scepticism of Euripides and the nostalgia of public school classicism.

36. The English Moralists

The boundary between those moralists who subscribe, albeit critically, to the middle-class consensus, and those who, insofar as they assent to it, do so with some degree of spiritual independence, cannot be hard and fast. But a difference of emphasis may be illustrated by comparing *Guns of Darkness* (1962) with Thorold Dickinson's *Secret People*. Asquith's film involves a British businessman in a foreign revolution, and suggests a new focus for a standard code of moral decency and obligation. The second asks us to identify with a foreign girl's involvement, in Britain, in her own country's revolution, and maintains a humanist stance in terms of more searching queries about

morality and identity. If Asquith typifies English liberalism at its most open, Dickinson's liberalism impels itself towards the radical pole. Whereas Asquith remains within the ambit of home counties gentlemanliness, Dickinson, of not dissimilar generation and background, arrives at an internationalist perspective. He makes a documentary about the Spanish Civil War (*Spanish A.B.C.*, released 1940). *Men of Two Worlds* (1946) looks at Africa in transition through the eyes, not of a Sanders or even a Windom, but of an African. *Hill 24 Doesn't Answer* (Israel, 1955) shares Israel's military struggle in a spirit, and a style, not dissimilar from Renoir's *La Marseillaise*. This spiritual breadth is matched by a stylistic range which, in a small oeuvre, nevertheless runs the gamut from documentary, through reconstructed documentary like *The Next of Kin* (1942) and through the claustrophobic period melodrama of *Gaslight* (1940) to the supernatural fantasy of *The Queen of Spades* (1949).

Indeed, the complementarity with Clément might be taken further, Clément's tragic cynicism contrasts with the – no less tough – moral affirmations of his English counterpart, the key to whose inspiration is, perhaps, this blend of sensitivity and dynamism, of human warmth and of a melodramatic force which expresses also a certain spiritual ruthlessness. While Asquith, whose *Tell England* (1931) and *A Cottage on Dartmoor* (1930) were worthy of the Russian silents in their visual flow, dried up stylistically as he effaced himself spiritually, Thorold Dickinson's *The Queen of Spades* and *Secret People* (1952) retain this early fluidity, taking it, at moments, to the point of the handheld rapidity associated with Godard and the New Wave. The interplay in *Secret People* between the dancing of Audrey Hepburn and the camera yields an aesthetic pleasure of its own, in its lively conjugation of two mercurial, dynamic sensibilities. Dickinson, like an English Visconti, blends the chameleonic and the leonine.

It's all the more regrettable that most of his films lie outside our time, place and theme. And it's not altogether accidental, for it is precisely this sensitive dynamism that fades from the British cinema generally between 1945 and 1958. *Secret People*, significantly Dickinson's last British feature, before his United Nations period, matches Losey's ruthlessness of thought and feeling. Losey, an American expatriate, adumbrates the cosmopolitan sixties.

A terrorist organization, operating from London, asks a foreign refugee (Valentina Cortese) to help them assassinate the dictatorial General at whose orders her father, a peace-loving writer, was murdered. She overrides her scruples only under the simultaneous pressure of a passionate love for, and moral and actual blackmail by, one of its members (Serge Reggiani). The attempt fails, and an innocent nurse is killed. Inadvertently, through nervous guilt, the foreign girl then betrays the organization to Scotland Yard. For fear of reprisals, she has to be announced as dead, and given a new face and identity. Lonely years later, she discovers that her hardened, pitiless lover is now inveigling her younger sister (Audrey Hepburn) into his organization. She saves her, at the cost of her own life.

Its restatement of human values and conscience was, in 1952, at the meanest epoch of the Cold War, rather more radical than may now appear. The post-war generations are, of course, so used to notions of mass destruction as the normal business of nations in wartime, and given a political context, that scruples about individual assassination are liable to seem rather exquisite. What else is James Bond about? And, at least as so far as the wider public was concerned, it was perhaps unfortunate that the film was set in the thirties. Had the fascist General suggested pre-war Spain, and the assassins Stalinists, the story's ethical balance might well have been very sharp. But the thirties suggested, to most people, Hitler and Mussolini. By that association, the film, in postulating the bomb and the pen as alternatives, seemed to be reducing the liberal conscience to a scrupulous, pacifistic ineffectiveness. Confronted with a Hitler, a Mussolini or a Franco, there's little doubt that, if the pen is mightier than the sword, it's only because it can lead to the unsheathing of so many swords that the potential aggressor prefers to replace his own in its scabbard. Yet another area of reference might have offered an Eastern European régime as the dictatorship and a band of aristocratic émigrés as the terrorists, and indicted these Jack D. Rippers who try to fight Communism without understanding its appeal and so perpetrate fiascos like the Bay of Pigs, or put back the possibilities of internal evolution by the pressure and power of ideas. Perhaps this was as contrary to public understanding of politics as Ken Russell's *Billion Dollar Brain* one-sixth of a century later. Sensitive though the film is, one may feel oneself, quietly, fighting its argument, even, withdrawing from it, as it goes – much as one may feel oneself diverging from the logic of Camus, when his moral scrupulousness leads him to an analogous cult of pious inaction, of negative scruple, of what Catholic orthodoxy terms 'angelism'. *Secret People* might in fact have gained in depth if its terrorist villain had also been something of a hero, a Sartrian Machiavellian whose hard lucidity, whose acceptance of *les mains sales,* attracts as it terrifies us.

It's worth relating one's reserves in this basic issue, for the film's quality then emerges more clearly. Its heroine – so sensitively played – is a classic screen incarnation of the liberal conscience in the modern world, torn as she is in so many ways – between her idealism and her hatred of Fascism, between her love of her father and her love for his ideals, between her fear of her lover and her responsibility for her sister, between her loyalty to her country of origin and her loyalty to the country to which she fled, between her own guilt and her trust in the law – which half-betrays her. The scene in which she hysterically breaks down under kindly and unsuspecting questioning at Scotland Yard resolves two sets of tensions and renders, in a way matched only by Losey, the inseperability of one's moral principles and one's deepest, most spontaneous emotions.

Indeed, the film takes its cruellest turn just when most films finish. The police have scattered the terrorist gang. The heroine, already uprooted from her homeland, is uprooted again, from not only her English friends, and all that remains of her family, but even her own identity, her own body. Her name and her face are erased. In a free country, she has become an un-person – the ultimate refugee, a punishment crueller than death, not for her own guilt, merely human though it was, but for her remorse. Her complicity takes up the film's third theme, that of the secret people within us, emerging only as pressures liberate them (a view of character not so far from Sartre). She is uprooted, also, from her moral integrity: finally, her heart is so exhausted that her death, at her lover's hand, protecting her sister from him, has a tragic quality of, as in *Lear,* death restoring happiness. This sacrificial altruism returns her to her own identity, and her motherliness, as it wipes her from the face of the earth. As a result of Reggiani's charm, specious though it is meant to be, there hovers within this complex and spiritually volatile film its own anti-thesis: the story of a sensitive terrorist who realizes what he is doing to himself and to others, and must go on doing it.

The Queen of Spades: Anton Walbrook – Existential paradox of life's discontinuities; freedom, anguish and a sense of fate

Films of this period are currently at their awkward age, and by current tastes the picture of working-class-immigrant life may seem too sweet. But with a little distance the film now reveals itself as the English, liberal, middle term between Wajda's *Ashes and Diamonds* (less gruelling, as the English experience is, but no less authentic, is its subtlety), and *La Guerre est finie*, Resnais's study of subversives in stoic exile.

The romanticism of *The Queen of Spades* enfolds a violently cold irony about ends and means, hallucinations and deceptions, disrupting identity and spinning man into an exiled nothingness like absurdity. It's curious that if one takes certain romantic stories which involve the supernatural, say Balzac's *La Peau de chagrin* (*The Wild Ass's Skin*) and diverts them of their romantic grandeur one rapidly arrives at an existentialist parable, concerning, in this case, commitment,

solidarity, and the destruction of being by ambition. The interpretation of Pushkin by the director of *Secret People* achieves just such a duality. What may at first seem sheer brio, turns certain apparent flaws into radical extensions of meaning.

The director joined the project after it had been shooting some weeks, and it's hard to see how, otherwise, the film could have been anything but a lost middlebrow cause, artistically as well as commercially. The story might have seemed an original blend of *Dead of Night* (with its ghost), Gainsborough melodrama (with its bullied and bullying hero-villain), and of *Great Expectations* (with its frightening, secretive old lady). In the event it dissatisfies, since only a ghost unites a middle-aged officer and an old lady whose human contacts are conspicuous for their tenuousness and negativity. Moreover, topic and mood are fairly remote from British preoccupations or style. As in the case of *The Innocents*, one's impulse is to interpret the supernatural in human terms. And this might have been an interesting way of handling the story of social ostracism, gambling fever, and the exploitation and degradation of others as the wheel of fortune spins.

For the aesthetically more finely attuned, sheer style provides a substitute for the relevance, in its time, of its romantic terms. These swift, thrusting tracks and pans, counterpoint the romantic atmospherics, with little crescendoes, explosions of feeling. The perilously disparate casting (Ronald Howard's Asquithian Englishman, Anton Walbrook seething with Teutonic near-expressionism, Edith Evans' wrinkled rubber mask stifling her into passive nonentity, Yvonne Mitchell's beautiful blend of Jewish warmth and English idealism), whirled into this dervish dance, suggests that each of us lives in a world which can never interfuse with others. Visual style pulls the film together; story and casting pull it apart; in its sense of human contact it is 'anti-Renoir'; society is the collision of solitudes. *Secret People* ... Avarice, formality, innocence, dream, the nature of life itself, encase us in little paths, boxes and convulsions of our own. Dickinson's films, baroque in their diversity, in their volatile mixture of strength and adaptability, are baroque also in a deeper sense. Superficially, the rationale of the style would seem to be its conjuncture of sensitivity and showmanship. One deploys one's effects to render nuances of feeling and to move the spectator. But their mercuriality is such that, sensed as one would a painter's or a poet's style, the cinematographic quality becomes that of an imperious form overlying assertions and contradictions whose synthesis must be radical uncertainty. We are led straight towards the existentialist paradox, of being and not-being, of life's discontinuities as freedom fraught with anguish and, curiously, a sense of fate. Given such sensitivity, the melodramatic elements transcend themselves and are experienced, not only with suspense, but with pain. A happy end becomes impossible, since merely to have suffered as much as this is a denial of a benevolent universe. The intricacy of the patterns all but undermines, or, at least, indefinitely postpones, any possible end. Not until Losey does so philosophical a stylist appear in British movies. The two exiles, liberal emigrant and Democratic immigrant, are fascinatingly complementary figures.

Though the Boulting Brothers operate from within the consensus, they, too, are outsiders, by reason of the narrowness of their base. Their early films (*Pastor Hall*, *Thunder Rock*) mark them as earnest evangelicals. Their satires, coming near the end of their rightward move from Labour to the Liberal party, are the flip side of a painfully disappointed earnestness.

Their first two films, *Pastor Hall* (1940) and *Thunder Rock* (1942) establish their baseline in moralistic drama. After three documentary features (*Desert Victory*, 1943, *Tunisian Victory*, 1944, *Burma Victory*, 1945) a fictional semi-documentary symbolizing Anglo-American friendship, *Journey Together* (1945), inaugurates a trio of films connecting moral fibre with political problems (*The Fame Is the Spur*, 1947, *The Guinea Pig*, 1948).

In the last two films, problems of the left are considered sombrely. Taken as a pair, they distinguish loss of purpose from the need for a long, devious reformist haul. An interwoven theme is that of disenchantment with human nature. Politicians let the sword of purpose rust into its scabbard. Privileged 'gentlemen' send the friendly eager beaver to Coventry.

In the light of this disillusionment, an apparently non-moralistic subject takes on ulterior meaning. Their version of *Brighton Rock* is, like Greene's novel, a meditation, not only on a small-time gangster, but on human nature, and its lost ideals. The razor murderer Pinkie (Richard Attenborough) has had a Catholic education, the nice girl (Carol Marsh) who loves him remains, in the film, ironically unaware of the bitter truth, which, in the novel, is 'the worst horror of all'. Invincible ignorance is our bliss. But the real antithesis to Pinkie is incarnated by Hermione Baddeley as Ida, the blowzy, raucous, rude, promiscuous 'angel' of a human decency which may be mediocre to the point of seediness but which is prickly and real. *Brighton Rock* is the first of three films expressing a worried awareness of moral mediocrity. *Seven Days to Noon* and *High Treason* re-connect it with political problems. Both deal with fanatical idealists who set themselves above authority, representing the common man. The first anticipates and exaggerates the link between C.N.D. and direct action. An idealist scientist (Barry Jones) purloins an atomic device and threatens to destroy himself and London unless the British Government promises to renounce atomic weapons. The metropolis is evacuated while he holes up with his unwilling companion, a tired middle-aged prostitute (Olive Sloane) who rather reminds us of Ida, the enthusiastic amateur in *Brighton Rock*.

Though her pleas fall on deaf ears, she is saved from the scientist – whom we can, almost, respect – by the efficient organization of the authorities. In *High Treason* respect for the dissidents has gone. A network of conspirators mislead and manipulate a great many common people, and the countervailing force is the moral ascendancy of the police. In other words, the three films show a decreasing faith in the common man, and an increasing reliance on authority.

As if sensing that with *High Treason* they had gone too far, and involuntarily reached a McCarthyite position, the Boultings retired from political topics for a while. Any anti-nonconformist moral 'Don't dare to be a Daniel, don't dare to stand alone, which, in the absence of reasonable dissent, could seem implicit in the two films, and of course *Suspect* later, finds some sort of counterpoint in the (admittedly morally uncontroversial) *Single-Handed* (1951), where an ordinary seaman (Jeffrey Hunter) with a high-powered rifle holds off a German battleship.

In this area the Boultings compare interestingly with Val Guest. *High Treason* is a combination of *They Can't Hang Me*, *80,000 Suspects* and *Quatermass 2*. Ida incarnates a Rabelaisian streak lacking in the tenser Guest. In a general way the Boultings seem more indulgent to an idealism, however warped, as the motive of dissident behaviour, although Guest allows the most overt justification of traditionally nonconformist attitudes in the (not altogether typical) *Yesterday's Enemy*.

After a miscellany of more relaxed, less interesting, movies, the Boultings discover a new tone with *Private's Progress* (1956). It's ostensibly a wartime subject, but its pictures of *servitudes et grandeurs militaires* makes it easily the most evocative film on national service drudgeries and idiocies. Officers, gentlemen and aesthetes aren't spared. Dennis Price leads a daring commando raid whose objective is to save some art treasures (!), and then steals them, leaving Ian Carmichael, as the innocent petty bourgeois, to carry the can. Then follows a series of satires whose butt is the depressing selfishness of absolutely everybody, from the highest to the lowest in the land.

In other words, both the high expectations of their earlier films, and the mild paranoia of *High Treason*, have been surmounted, and replaced by a still pained, but a humorous, acceptance that idealism is neither here nor there, but a kind of lonely warbling in orbit. On the other hand, the 'Daniel' of earnestness never quite lets the bastards grind him down; a decent disgust and a prophetic sense of moral decay, stay with us, and him.

Critics roundly deprecated the vulgarity of *I'm All Right Jack*, particularly of the worker who always stammers on the letter 'f'. But behind the Boultings' vulgar humour is a kind of pain, overcome by humour, and switched back to a scathing tolerance, and it's this that gives these jokes their weird absence of indignity (oddly, their one essay in straightforward low farce, *A French Mistress*, 1960, fell quite flat).

Conversely, it's arguable that it's because of their exacting idealism that in *Seven Days to Noon* the representative of mediocre decency tends to be a bit of a tart whose chances of happiness are somewhat foredoomed. To the honest puritan the common and the seedy are one. This argument needs care, because it's often by making the spokesman for one's case as unpromising as possible, that one generates intense moral suspense, a greater complexity of sympathies, a two-way involvement and a subtle yet emphatic affirmation. *Seven Days to Noon* would be much less interesting if Olive Sloane were replaced by, say, Kathleen Harrison, or Huggetts-era Petula Clark. Its moral norm lies between its extremes, though nearer one than the other.[42] Ida, a little patronizingly, and the prostitute, somewhat sardonically, express the Rabelaisian streak which imbues the satires and enlivens the Boultings' inspiration. Yet, given the general line of the earlier films one can't altogether dismiss the feeling that in their concern with denouncing fanatical moral idealists, the Boultings are expressing the pressure of a very similar idealism in themselves – which is subsequently kicked upstairs, into orbit, in fact ....

For, after all, it's hard to see from what moral basis, other than a purely categorical imperative, the Boultings criticize us. Why should we work as hard as we can? What's so uplifting about humping crates about? If the boss pays as little as he can why shouldn't we work as little as we can? Isn't this middle-class eager-beaver showing us all up with his shot-hot efficiency, a bit of a pest? What priority does his enthusiasm for promotion deserve over our traditionally leisurely English style? If the middle-class clerk of *The Battle of the Sexes* earns our applause for fighting off the American efficiency expert, why shouldn't the shop-stewards put a ring through the nose of this Stakhanovite bull in a traditional china-shop? A fair day's work for a fair day's pay is a fine slogan, but what's fair? In what way does this one-man mission to improve the world by speeding up the wheels of industry differ from the one-man missions of scientific and political masterminds? Is it really common sense that the main obstacle between England and prosperity is the bloody-mindedness of the English worker? If so, what uncommon sense is it that so many other nations, from the ultra-individualistic Americans at one extreme, the well-disciplined Germans at the other, and the stolidly Socialistic Swedes in between, possess? Could the malaise of labour relations not be due to a situation to which all sides unconsciously contribute, rather than to the innate moral inferiority of the average Englishman?

Thus one may sense a certain affinity between Boulting satire and a moralism which is negative in effect and which reinforces the use of working-class as social scapegoat. This is surely not deliberate, since the butt of the Boultings' satire is not uniquely, and not even primarily, the working-class, and it would be absurd to align them with those who begin by impartially lamenting British slackness at all levels and then go on to urge more incentive for employers and a firmer line with employees. (The cure for Britain's troubles is, as usual, more stick for you and more carrot for me). And, of course, we can all identify with Ian Carmichael's enthusiasm, even if in real life we're as bloody-minded as the rest of the platoon, or union chapel, or chief clerks. The Boultings also insist that work-frustration comes as much from above as from below.

It's after the satires, and almost into the seventies, that the Boultings seem to have got moral exigence and disillusionment out of their system and produced a straight working-class drama, which is at once tolerant, appreciative and rather beautiful (*The Family Way*). Curiously, *The Twisted Nerve*, whose study of a psychopathic sex maniac sets out to out-Psycho *Psycho*, by intensifying its everyday realism, disturbed and disgusted many critics, maybe because ex-puritans can bring a similar ruthlessness to their tolerance, and remain subtly at odds with those whose tolerance has had no reason to fight through its (broader) limits. Yet 'intellectual' reaction to the film, as to the satires, was rather depressing, since the satires' success was amply merited by their relatively authentic and lively expression of social realities. They're key movies of the period, and even *High Treason* is not without pertinence in indicating the discontents and cruelties which political idealism may dissimulate.

If the Boultings are nonconformist at heart, Michael Relph and Basil Dearden incarnate a kind of stern Anglican officerdom. It's been said that every director appears in his own films, either in a fairly straightforward disguise, or as his *alter ego*, quite often of the opposite sex. It's a fine parlour game for the more refined exponents of auteur theory. At one extreme, Hitchcock himself walks briefly through a scene; at the other, it's arguable that both male rivals in *The Devil Is a Woman* resemble its director, Josef Von Sternberg, and the leading lady, Marlene Dietrich incarnates his *anima*. In the British cinema, Michael Powell's doppelgänger would be Roger Livesey; the Boulting Brothers would be Ian Carmichael; and in my mind's eye Relph-Dearden would be Cecil Parker in *I Believe in You*. *The Mind Benders, Sapphire, Victim*, with perhaps the two Bryan Forbes subjects, are their contribution to our canon of key movies, for here, curiously, they come nearest a full-length and first-hand police attitude towards their subjects. Just as a good detective is, as a priori, ready to suspect everyone involved, so, here, R-D are ready to think cynically about everyone from immigrants to civil servants.

Their nearest American counterpart is Stanley Kramer, whose preoccupation with morality as social morale resulted in such movies as *Judgment at Nuremberg* (with its handy-dandy interchange between American justice and Nazi war criminals), *The Caine Mutiny* (ironies of discipline), *The*

Defiant Ones (with criminals as heroes), *High Noon* (for Americans, a stinging indictment of American civic irresponsibility) and *Ship of Fools*. A welfare worker's view of crime underlines *My Six Convicts* as *I Believe in You*. Kramer, working in the context of irrepressible American individualism, has to think relatively hard and clear to justify authority. Relph-Dearden have as good a case, but too easy a pitch on which to play.

Kramer, as apologist for order, is their master, even though he too is critically unfashionable. A parallel comparison is worth making against Howard Hawks, and they don't come out at all badly against this trendy veteran whose work homes in as easily on the American creed of tough individualism as theirs on English establishmentarianism. Hawks celebrates self-assertiveness and disdain of authority, Relph-Dearden a modest submission to reasonable authority. Hawks is sardonically, but not aggressively, agnostic, R-D believe in (or believe in acquiescing in) either a decent Christianity, or Christianity as decent. Hawks celebrates self-reliance, R-D a sense of responsibility. For Hawks the major manly motive is bold pride, for R-D a fear of shame. Hawks's lucid admiration for a nihilistic loyalty to the manly job compares with R-D's celebration of stoic faith in what one's leaders demand. For Hawks's men, women are desirable but dangerous, while for R-D's men they are less desirable than estimable. Hawks women match his men, in being aggressive and masculine, but are more hedonistic and therefore more human. R-D's women match their men in being loyal and conscientious, though they have impulses to be more emotional and less principled. Hawks and R-D share a concern with the team and the job (*Rio Bravo*, like *The Blue Lamp*, is a cops' saga). Both use a simple, efficient style, R-D angling more heavily, but also tending to track-in to close-up for climax. Both emotionally underplay. Both accept cliché by the bushel, yet retain a certain sincerity. The current intellectual admiration of Hawks as a moralist overlooks the fact that he never makes the slightest attempt to square his simple-minded and repetitious scheme with reality. R-D make some effort at doing so, thus being more irritating, and more interesting. If Hawks is currently 'in' it's because his attitudes are American, and spreading, while if R-D remains unexamined it's because theirs are English establishmentarian, and contracting. But since there's a Hawks cult only moral and aesthetic good can come from propagating an R-D one too, as a counterbalance to it. Their lesser films, like his, express an honest conformity and enshrine often poignant and beautiful touches in that key.

The elements of doubt, disgust and despair which R-D so rigorously exclude quietly but insistently infiltrate the films of Roy Baker, an auteur whose spiritual attitude, a kind of fair-minded pessimism, precludes open revolt as it precludes acceptance. That stoic British acquiescence in arbitrary order reveals its secret roots in an existentialist scepticism which, settling for pragmatism, never, quite, discovers its full potential. His best films are in the class of Dickinson and Losey.

Before going to Hollywood in 1950 he had established himself as a thoughtful director in diverse genres, from the amnesia thriller (*The October Man*, 1947) to the stiff upper lip naval film (*Morning Departure*, 1950). But the limiting niceness of the quality British film abruptly disappeared when at Fox he made two 'psychopathic' thrillers. *Don't Bother to Knock* (1952), starred Marilyn Monroe as a psychopathic babysitter, and was followed by *Night without Sleep* (1953) and a gruelling desert Western (*Inferno*, in 3-D, 1953).

Tiger in the Smoke (1956) joins *Sapphire* and *Blind Date* in the series of 'detective stories with a difference' which was a Rank formula of the time. Margery Allingham's novel recalls the work of Charles Williams in relating the surface of upper-middle-class English life to spiritual struggles between good and evil, considered as metaphysical forces. Less specific, and therefore more interesting in tracing out this near-banal opposition, Margery Allingham's novel centres on a homicidal maniac (Tony Wright). Once called Johnny *Cash* and now called Jack *Havoc*, he terrorizes a rural canon (Laurence Naismith) and his daughter (Muriel Pavlow) in the course of his search for a treasure which he believes to be 'priceless'. But when he finds it it turns out to be worthless for it is *beyond* price, a symbol of the spiritual values which he can never understand.

Baker's film transcends the intrinsic limitations of allegory by its skilful dialogue and atmospheric toughness. For all its melodrama, it comes, at moments, nearer the fuliginous lyricism of Bernanos than the Greene films. The opening sequence particularly, with its street-band of wretched and embittered ex-servicemen tramping through London fogs, dogging the city-gent with scrannel music, is a superb image for a world 'possessed' by the equal and complementary evils of unaware complacency and craven spite.

The contrast carries class overtones, like the skipper/crew conflict in *Passage Home* and the first-class/steerage conflict in *A Night to Remember*. But class conflict is only one aspect, albeit a major one, of a deeper, more pervasive evil. Certainly class breeds spite. The buskers, like the steerage passengers, are forgotten by society, which, unaware of being unjust, is no less culpable. Similarly, skippers Peter Finch and John Mills find some sort of redemption by their role in combating the greater evil (the storm, the Axis), but they must accept blame for the lesser evil (oppressing or torturing men under their authority). The merchant crew prove loyal – or supine; the Italians are humane or weak. But the buskers, like the steerage, cut loose. It's not that they become demoniacal; something demoniacal uses injustice to emerge. The barbed force of Baker's films lies in his feeling for evil as being *both* result of injustice, *and* an impersonal force which, lurking in the nature of man, takes him over.

These are precisely the opening terms of *The Singer Not the Song* (1960), an English Western set in Mexico. Its theme is the hidden complicity, and love, between good and evil. Father Keogh (John Mills) arrives at the hamlet of Quantana to replace Father Gomez (Leslie French). He finds him hounded and degraded by the bandit Anacleto (Dirk Bogarde) and his gang of killers. The new priest's energy and courage compel Anacleto's hostile admiration, and Anacleto's beloved, Locha (Mylène Demongeot), falls in love with him. After a spiritual – and Machiavellian – battle of wits and wills, Anacleto is shot in a street battle. In striving to save the dying man's soul, the priest dies too.

Behind the obvious antithesis the inner complicity of the two adversaries clearly emerges. Anacleto, too, is champion of a creed – a cruelty, a love of evil, which is more than functional, more than egoist, just as Ahab's thirst for vengeance transcends egoism. He is devoted to his vision of the world as a place where the weaker are the prey of the stronger. It is important to him that good be challenged on its own terms – corrupted, converted – as he would be ready to be, could good prove its credentials in terms of spiritual realism. He refuses to allow his men to kill the new priest, for death would spare the good man the spiritual defeat which is at stake. Indeed, Anacleto kills another bandit, his closest friend, 'Old Uncle' (Laurence Naismith), for trying to kill the priest (just as Henry slays Becket). Behind Anacleto's creed is a sincerity analogous to Sade's challenge to Christianity. In his response

Keogh, too, abandons the 'worldly' and British scale of values in which 'order' is the highest good. Anacleto embarks on a series of totally gratuitous, alphabet murders, to break Keogh's nerve, by turning his altruism against itself. But Keogh stays – so becoming, in a sense, co-responsible for the murders, certainly in being as indifferent to the lives of others as Anacleto. When, finally, Keogh betrays Anacleto to the law, so breaking his given word, Anacleto is doomed. But he has won, Good has revealed its helplessness, its dependence on lies, on evil.

Intermingled with the moral struggle is a love story. The priest's concern for Anacleto's soul is a passionate one. So is the killer's concern for the priest. As they lie dying intertwined in the dust (one recalls *Duel in the Sun*), the killer makes an act of contrition, to please the priest, who dies fulfilled. Anacleto, surviving him by a few moments, smiles that he loved the singer, not the song. A certain sexuality is hinted by the men's aberrant dress (leather trousers, cassock), and in this context the priest's kindly indifference towards Locha's love for him assumes strong overtones of an inadequacy like perversity. He doesn't *know* heterosexual temptation. He loves only God, is ice-cold to human love. Anacleto, killer that he is, loves both the girl (although she rejects him) and the priest (although he rejects him). Of the two men, he is incomparably the most generous and vulnerable lover, and, as a man, the priest's superior.

Artistically, the film's flaw is, perhaps, the Englishness creeping into the playing of the three principals. Dirk Bogarde's feline ways are only just steely enough to enable belief in his atrocities, while Mylène Demongeot seems vainly waiting for a chance to unleash her sadness. The film's defect is not a matter of merely superficial verisimilitude, for this Mexican village is clearly 'everywhere'. Through English restraint, the metaphysical conflict lacks, at times, during this engrossing and admirable film, the continuous intensity which Baker might well have reached more easily with an American cast. As it is, his sense of evil endows the calm, decent gestures of moral affirmation with the fragility of hope in a nightmare. Similarly, horror movies apart, the most dreamlike English film since *Odd Man Out* is *Tiger in the Smoke,* another study in lonely, passive delirium, with its fog, the separation of husband and wife, and the former's abject helplessness (bound and gagged in a wheel-chair) through most of the picture.

As Roy Baker's vision completes R-D's, so Val Guest's finds its complement (rather than contradiction) in the wily irreverence of Frank Launder and Sidney Gilliat. Their partial autonomy from the consensus may well be linked with the cultural patrimony betrayed by their specialities (farce; life on or below the lower-middle-class level; and Celtic topics). Both wrote for Will Hay during the thirties, and widened the breach in class barriers with *Millions Like Us* (1943) and above all *Waterloo Road* (1945). As Labour's popularity waned, however, they turned to other fields. Launder specializes in the Celtic subjects (*I See a Dark Stranger, Captain Boycott, Geordie, The Bridal Path*) and the St. Trinian's farces. Gilliat faintly recalls Hitchcock's feeling for the shabby genteel (*London Belongs to Me*) and thrillers (*Green for Danger, State Secret, Fortune Is a Woman*), though without Hitch's sado-pessimistic depth. Launder's *The Happiest Days of Your Life* is one of the brightest post-war comedies. Their marital comedy, *The Constant Husband,* is more sophisticated, because more amoral, than the Boultings' *Josephine and Men*; conversely, their direct satire (*Left Right and Centre*), is too insouciant to hit memorably home. Yet, as one prefers Zampi to post-*Titfield* Ealing, so one may relish the sad-warm-dour comedies L-G produce: Basil Dearden's *The Smallest Show on Earth,* for its marvellous gel of Sellers, La Rutherford, Bernard Miles and Virginia McKenna, and Robert Day's saturnine *The Green Man. The Blue Lagoon* (1948) might be regarded as a sort of ultra-Celtic fringe film, but its romanticism is insipid, and Launder-Gilliat are a soft touch for the pseudo-subversive milk-and-water-old-high-Tory-turned-consensus humour jinks and japes of *The Story of Gilbert and Sullivan.* Yet their consistent freshness and mischief, their cheerful lightly-and-slightly anarchism, their relaxed romping in and out of the system's little loopholes and bye-ways, is always a welcome break from the rigid ideological routines and closures which characterize so many films. And they give great scope to the weariness, the cynical drollery, the dour eccentricity, of Alastair Sim. Robert Tronson's *Ring of Spies* (1963), which they produced, achieves, at last, a sensible matter-of-fact approach to the espionage theme of *High Treason, Suspect, The Mind Benders* and so on. An adaptation of the Gee-Houghton-Lonsdale case, it shows Houghton (Bernard Lee) as an amiable, weak, disheartened man who'll never make it into the upper crust, knows he's not much good, would like a new car and a nice house, and when he's with his hard, prying Polish mistress just mutters wearily, 'Oh what's it all matter anyway?' The film isn't inspired and can't quite bring itself to give even these mediocre little devils their due. For one can no more explain spying entirely by weakness than one can explain gangsterism by cowardice. Both need a certain nerve. But at least it overlaps with a prosaic commonsense.

Whereas Roy Baker's films emphasize the ethical conflicts in relation to philosophical and social structures, J. Lee Thompson and Peter Glenville emphasize the psychological and emotional hinterland of moral decisions. Lee Thompson uses melodrama, not gratuitously, but in determination to ram right into the complacent spectator the full pain and terror of the emotional extremes against which moral principles must assert themselves. *The Weak and the Wicked* (1953) and *Yield to the Night* (1956) attack the common English assumption that the criminal has forfeited, as well as his liberty, any real right to comfort or respect, and that the prime means of penology is the infliction of humiliation, exasperation and pain. His attack on complacency often takes the form of a seemingly perverse attack on the consensus. *I Aim at the Stars* (1960) fails to make some sort of sense out of the ethical paradoxes involved in the career of Wernher von Braun, mastermind of both Hitler's vengeance weapons and America's space programme. Understandably British audiences let it die, but it's surprising that the critics too resented rather than appreciated the brutal moral paradoxes which counter the implications of *Suspect* and which, it can't be denied, anticipate those of Rolf Hochhuth's plays. If Lee Thompson, rigorously scrutinizing liberal tendencies to sentimentality (like overlooking the Hindu-Moslem massacres when discussing imperialism), and sometimes concedes too much to an illiberal consensus, this seems to me, like the ferocity of his films, the flaw of a resolutely self-critical moralist. He is a liberal who, rather than denounce others, challenges himself. He deals, and validly, with massive blocks of brute emotion, rather than nuances of thought, thus relating to the common British practice of responding to moral issues in a fundamental way, rather than with a more intricate and rationalist type of moral analysis. He is a melodramatist because he is a fundamentalist. If one puts *No Trees in the Street* alongside *North West Frontier*, one may see him as a 'Labour imperialist', a position which is as common among Labour veterans as it is rare among the

Socialist intelligentsia. If he is the ideal director for Ted Willis, it is precisely because his vehement style explodes the complacency which has virtually destroyed the creative artist Willis used to be. His British films suggest a moral upheaval, which, ahead of its time, could find only feelings, devoid of concepts, and, being isolated, easily capitulated to the lashback of self-criticism. The mood is not so far, after all, from certain traits in the work of Lindsay Anderson and the younger generation, of which Lee Thompson is a kind of strayed uncle.

More conspicuously serious, less passionate, less, in the end, involving, are Peter Glenville's three essays in moral failure (*The Prisoner,* 1955, *Term of Trial,* 1962, *Becket,* 1964).

Few producers have followed as discernible a moral line as Raymond Stross, who once described himself as a Continental-type producer who made British films, and that isn't a bad description. He's made his share of purely commercial movies, and many of the others suffer from an overdose of melodrama. This is, of course, often a way of avoiding moral and psychological points which a bold theme demands but which, at this time, wouldn't have been countenanced by distributors, and possibly not, though this is far more dubious, by the unprepared public of the time. Nonetheless, during the early fifties, certain of his films, even if in the end they succumbed to the conformist straitjacket, were visibly squirming and struggling and heaving convulsively around inside it. It is for precisely that originality that serious criticism considered them infra dig. The subversive beauty of vice (Marta Toren, Anouk ...) informs *The Man Who Watched Trains Go By* (Harold French, 1952) and its sullen glamour was a bold and precious affirmation at a time when prostitutes in British movies had to be invariably whining, petulant and unattractive. Terence Young's *Tall Headlines* (in whose shadows dwell the condemned man's family) indicted that paralysing middle-class shame which serious Ealing movies unquestioningly affirmed. A highly sympathetic defiance of good taste underlies both *The Flesh Is Weak* and *A Question of Adultery* (1958) (A.I.D., alas, is a pretty unappetizing form of sexual scandal). Two films destined for the world market, with Robert Mitchum, Robert Aldrich's *The Angry Hills* (1959), about Greek partisans, and Tay Garnett's *A Terrible Beauty* (1959, expecting us to identify with almost pro-Nazi I.R.A.), are flatly executed, but the problems they pose, about violence, vengeance and

Machiavellianism, aren't at all unworthy of two other intriguing misfires, Dassin's *Celui qui doit mourir* (*He Who Must Die*) and *La Loi* (*Where the Hot Wind Blows*).

The first two-thirds of Cyril Frankel's *The Very Edge* (1963) achieve a rare desensationalization of rape and its everyday aftermath. It's cliff-hanging climax disappoints after the successfully thoughtful development achieved in Guy Green's *The Mark* (1961) and Sidney Furie's *The Leather Boys* (1963).

37. Have Scalpels – Will Travel

Where American ideology tends to glorify the processes of ambition, competition and conflict, British culture is based on a feeling, at once less sentimental and less cynical, that all these things must be kept in check by responsibility, co-operation and compromise. If the American vice is ferocity, the British is stalemate and stagnation. Both creeds have their own kinds of complacency (the American: 'conflict never hurts anyone unless they deserve it', the British: 'conflict doesn't really exist, you know, and if it does we shouldn't make it worse by admitting it'). Much harder-edged about this than the native product are the films made here by American émigrés, whether under co-production arrangements, or as refugees from McCarthyism, or working for British companies, or as 'runaways' from Hollywood's high production costs. Jules Dassin's *Night and the City* (1950), explored London's underworld with, not the neo-realism for which critics looked in vain, but something of the visionary sadism of Gerald Kersh, an author whose brutal best-sellers have understandably frightened British producers. Edward Dmytryk's *Give Us This Day* (1949) and *Obsession* (1949) are no less convulsively pessimistic, and even if Cy Endfield's *Hell Drivers* (1957) and *Sea Fury* (1958) lack the social analysis of his Hollywood *The Sound of Fury*, their harsh energy is exhilarating and disturbing.

But the richest application of American patterns to British themes is made by Joseph Losey. His American energy, with a bedrock puritanism re-energized, rather than diluted, by a sophisticated acuity, takes in psychoanalytical factors, social pressures, and a psychology as aware as Sartre's of voluntary self deception. His earlier British features begin an awkward, yet explosive, and sometimes Marcusian, interrogation of man in society.

From the distributor's angle, *The Sleeping Tiger* (1954) is a low budget amalgam of two genres: the 'young thug' story for thick-ear fans, and the 'bitch wife' story for the distaff side. One can imagine it as a late thirties Warner Brothers heavy, with Humphrey Bogart, Bette Davis and either Claude Rains or Leslie Howard. Here Dirk Bogarde plays the young Teddy Boy whom liberal psychologist Alexander Knox picks as his guinea-pig, to live-in for six months, as one of the family. The psychologist's ambitious, snobbish, corporal punishment-favouring wife (Alexis Smith) moves from utter contempt for him to devouring love. Her too coldly reasonable husband seems more interested in his soul-fight with the boy than in her. In different ways, their attitude to the boy begins in superiority and goes on to selfishness. But, after the husband has shielded him from the law, the boy throws off his father-fixation, and can't continue the affair. The wife tries to goad her husband into destroying him, but only destroys herself – driving to her death through a poster of the Esso tiger – the original unamiable one.

Losey has to contend with the limitations of the genre, and his approach is altogether at odds with British critical fashion of the mid-fifties. Whereas they demanded a toning down of emotional excess, the ballasting of the story-line with realistic detail, and a location atmosphere, he concentrates on a morality about passion in society, that is, on a structure of passionate actions and reactions. The spectator must feel maladjusted passion in its excess as in its inadequacy, yet it must not be so persuasive as to silence criticism. Thus a certain unreasonableness, integrated with the variety of incompatible viewpoints, does the work of Brechtian comment. Exaggeration becomes deflation. One identifies with, and criticizes, the character's attitude simultaneously. Nor must any one character in its turn, become a scapegoat for the others, for all are part of, all make, the situation. The situation in turn must not be accepted un-critically: that is to say, the criticism of the characters involves criticisms of the values which they acquire from society, and criticism of the situation involves criticism of the social factors which bring it about. A snag is, of course, that the more general the values, the less the spectators can criticize them, the more general the factors, the less we can see 'beyond' them. Against this one can to some extent oppose the powerful contradictions within the character.

Hence a tendency for Losey's early films to become, in one sense, a series of *temps-forts* (as the nihilist Godard styles even climaxes into *temps-morts*, so the moralist Losey affirms even *temps-morts* as revelations of underlying passions, as unconscious decision). The characters, like the society of which they are part, must be both justified and unjustified. A structure of complex and rapid moral switches produces a hot-cold effect which, superficially, may seem, not so much to the 'unthinking' intuitive spectator, as to the 'superior' spectator, clumsy and naive.

In the context of a later publicity campaign the film's expose of latent violence among suburbanites may evoke the reflection, 'I've got a tiger in my Tudor villa', but its moral pattern is more complex and less sentimental than traditional appeals to the moral masochism of the more sensitively evangelical bourgeoisie. For the ultra-liberal (but not yet radical) argument that the latent violence of the respectable is of the same order as the actual violence of the delinquent is not very useful against the rejoinder that society has nonetheless good reasons to distinguish between the two. The film hinges on a conversion. Treatment frees the thug from his unconscious compulsions, i.e. the argument is not to squeamishness about punishment, but to the efficacy of a certain combination of minimum force and remedial action, as against a mindlessly punitive reflex. The latter attitude to the delinquent is seen as a fascinated ambivalence (the rigidly respectable wife goes from hatred to passion). Yet the film also repudiates the unconsciously conformist, liberal proposition that if psychiatry justifies itself it is as the trick-cyclist squad of the thought police. The transference here is possible only because the psychiatrist breathes a very deep breath and takes his patient's side on a minor matter against the police, although he knows he's guilty. Here, the psychiatrist outgrows his 'detachment', takes on his shoulders the risks and burden of commitment. This decision of his involves no 'blanket' condemnation of the police; the Inspector (Hugh Griffith) proves, in the end, an understanding soul. Nor does this, in its turn, involve a blanket idealization of the authorities. The Inspector's action is not automatic. He is a very emotional man, and markedly Welsh, i.e. 'regional' rather than Establishmentarian. The distinction between man and uniform is clarified in *Blind Date*, where the justice and humanity of the Welsh detective (Stanley Baker) contrasts with the smoothly cold heart of his Establishment colleagues who uses 'the book' as a cover for corruption.

Although some of Losey's scenes are directed against assumptions about class ('the middle-classes are intrinsically peace-loving') they're not directed against a specific class as such. His films abound in lower-, middle- and upper-class villains. The psychiatrist's wife, in many ways a 'typical' hang-em-and-flog-em Tory, is, it is stressed, actually American, and from the wrong side of the tracks (none so fiercely respectable as those who've had to struggle for it ...). Indeed, to see only a right-wing moral would be quite easy: 'class will out, for the thug from the good military family turns out to be decent, after a little adjustment, but, just you put her under stress, and your supposed lady with the wrong background will revert to type all right'. This interpretation is theoretical rather than actual, since the whole pattern hinges on the psychiatrist's liberalism, and, most of the time, the wife is the person she has come to be, as well as the person she was. Further, the delinquent conflates Teddy Boy and gentry, thus undermining class differences. The film has its right-wing affinity, via the moral individualism of puritanism ('class is no excuse, no determinant'). But this is cancelled, in its turn, by the emphasis on situation as a determinant of the individual's reactions. In other words, class is a special type of situation. The film's attitude to class and character is nearer Sartre's than that of what Marxists often call 'vulgar', i.e., simple-minded, 'Marxism'.

The doubleness of delinquent and wife is compounded by the curious physical resemblance established between wife and maid (Patricia McCarron). The resemblance is all the more striking in that they are opposite characters. Milady wants to bully Bogarde (because he's rude, i.e. challenges her politeness with truth), while Bogarde bullies the maid (who obeys his accent as much as his threats). The two women are alternative outcomes for the same temperament, one shaped by her achieved class into a quiet arrogance, the other into deference. In another sense, they establish a national contrast. The American girl is ambitious, the English girl pusillanimously resigned. Like many of Losey's, the film is strengthened by the mutual reinforcements possible between left-wing egalitarianism and American individualism. Indeed, his criticisms of attitudes may relate to that persistent *vigilance* vis-à-vis the establishment, that suspicious scorn of those who claim to be 'responsible for us', which appears also in films by such right-wingers as Tay Garnett and King Vidor.

A marked feature of Vidor's *Beyond the Forest* is the resemblance of mistress (Bette Davis) and her Indian maid. Here, perhaps, the implication is that the discontented are tormented by themselves; thus the Indian girl is free, her mistress is not. For Vidor, a corollary of the denial of the significance of class is the insistence that ascendencies arise purely on the basis of life-force. The whip and the slap which recur in his films, often going from the weaker sex to the stronger, express this force as something other than physical strength, as something as magic as life itself. Losey's films share these motifs, but tend to use them, instead, as a symbol for 'unjust ascendancy', whether of life-force, class, authority, or anything else. Class privilege is a salient form of 'unjust ascendancy', a pervasive one, and worth stressing because less easily recognizable than thuggery, But it remains only one form. From another angle it might be said that Losey had embarked, earlier than most, on the integration of Freud and Marx, on the double insistence on individual responsibility and social matrices, a process which though fraught with difficulty may possibly prove the basis of a new 'holding centre' for the decencies within Western democratic humanism.

The psychiatrist too undergoes a 'conversion'. His marriage, apparently so contented, is revealed as hollow. It's a collusion between his wife's satisfied social climbing and the complacency hinted at by his Antarctic smile. Complacent too is his attempt to impose on his patient-prisoner a kid glove tyranny about 'keeping proper hours', and later his attempt to cover the cynical facts of life by a pseudo-rationalist sentimentality. He pretends to the thug that he used 'sweet reason' to persuade the maid's fiancé not to make a complaint against the police, when he in fact bribed him with cash. The pretence that reasonableness does the work of self-interest is sentimentality, not quite sterile but invariably confusionist. Nonetheless, when the psychiatrist has to change sides, and shield his patient, against the law, and at personal risk, he makes the right decision. Later, in an awkwardly contrived situation, he 'tests' his wife. He sees that her passion for the boy is so shallow as to have been quickly smashed by the vindictive upthrust of outraged pride, while her feelings towards him are of indifference. There is a tragic irony in her case, too. How far is her indifference a result of her husband's cold impartiality? Tragic, rather than vindictive, is the film's attitude to the irruption of a real sexual passion into her too-well-ordered life. A visit to a Soho drinking club, a kind of haven for the maladjusted and the classless, to which, without knowing it, she belongs, and which, for that very reason, she despises, rounds out the theme. Not only is the thug a social misfit; so is she, even in the fraternity of misfits. The question: 'What shall we do with the delinquent?' becomes 'what shall we do with the respectable?' Unless both questions are answered, neither can be answered.

A thirty-minute short for Hammer, *A Man on the Beach*, centres on the antediluvian cliché of the wounded criminal (Michael Medwin) holing up in a cottage owned by recluse Donald Wolfit, who turns out to be blind. Losey lets us in on the secret of the old man's blindness from the beginning. Thus the film intermittently becomes a grotesque choreography for harsh, hostile, suspicious loneliness. More substantial is *The Intimate Stranger*. The marriage and career of a young American film director working in England (Richard Basehart) are all but ruined by a jealous assistant director (Mervyn Johns). He provides a young actress (Mary Murphy) with the personal information needed to support her blackmail story of a previous love affair. If, as some critics have suggested, the film land setting, and the atmosphere of persecution and bewilderment, recall the McCarthyite witch hunts, then the suggestion must be that a kind of envious negativity can have as paralytic an effect on English life and thought. For the film emphasizes that the director had to leave Hollywood on account of his own arrogance, and that this is a kind of complementary sin to the assistant's. Its deeper resonance is its crystallization of the vulnerability, the superficiality, of our knowledge of one another. The director, briefly, falls in love with his blackmailer, suggesting that the 'fake' life is, in fact, his own unlived life, and so making a cogent criticism of his own emptiness, of his own unconscious duplicity. The persuasiveness of the blackmailer's case shows how extensively 'real' life is based on fictions, how, by lazy acceptance of plausibilities, we reduce reality to a B movie ....

Time without Pity is the first British film to offer Losey a plot, and a production set-up, congenial to his own interests, and in which he can work with, rather than across, the grain of his story-line. When his son is found guilty of murder, a distinguished writer, David Graham (Michael Redgrave), pulls himself out of his self-pitying alcoholism just long enough to track down the real murderer, racing car manufacturer Robert Stanford (Leo McKern). When he can't touch his conscience, he makes his own suicide look like murder, for which Stanford will hang. The film, is, in essence, a soul-fight of the kind which American regional puritanism bequeathed to Ince Westerns and which never altogether disappeared from the American cinema. But Losey's sense of society transforms the film into a network of soul fights, between the writer and every individual who refuses to make justice his concern, from the newspaper editor paying off old scores to the vague old woman living alone amidst her slashing-and-clacking clocks. Not that the writer can allow himself a crusader's complacency. The unconcern of others only mirrors his irresponsibility, which ceased but a few hours previously; and his son, understandably, cruelly, repudiates him, from the condemned cell. The brutally energetic industrialist and his frigidly refined wife (Ann Todd) form a mutually torturing couple not unworthy of Strindberg, and crystallize the cruel hollowness formed by the complicity of British philistinism with British puritanism (this aspect of the film anticipates a possible permutation out of *Look Back in Anger*, *This Sporting Life*, and *Life at the Top*. What would have happened if Alison Porter had married Machin and he'd been jumped up to trainer-manager of the rugby club?). His wife represents the refined, negative society that rejects all that he stands for, denies him acceptance and meaning; he tortures her, as Soames does Irene in *The Forsyte Saga*. Stanford's brutality is the expression of a superabundant energy which can find no satisfaction, only palliatives, in power and speed, which he uses as drugs, to leave his emptiness and his guilt behind. But the writer waits at the finishing-post, which is also the starting-post, of the high-speed circuit. The vicious circle of the race against guilt in the stony arena is a superb example of moral tension, *physicalized*. Michael Redgrave's trenchant volatility, chiselling against McKern's granite violence, has never found a more resonant director than Losey.

From a box-office point of view, *The Gypsy and the Gentleman* is a baffling project. Its simultaneity with Brian Desmond Hurst's *Dangerous Exile* suggests that the Rank Organization was trying to revive the Gainsborough melodrama, a sympathetic purpose, though both films missed where *Tom Jones* was later to hit. Losey said, 'One of the reasons why I undertook *Gypsy* ... was that I thought I'd found an opportunity for a piece of pure style,' and certain compositions and colour schemes were inspired by Thomas Rowlandson. Though the mood is one of turbulence rather than of nostalgia for 'Merrie England', one may regret certain restraints: the bloodlessness of the bare knuckle boxing match, the no-more-than-one-scream from Dr. Forrester's

private Bedlam, with its grim possibilities in the way of utilitarian money-making. In retrospect it appears less an *exercise de style* (though it has the visual impact of a good Western) than a fancy dress draft for *The Servant*.

Deverill the gentleman (Keith Michell) gets himself ruined by the Gypsy Belle (Melina Mercouri), but his real enemy is within him, the spiritual fecklessness bred by privilege. And she, too, is her own executioner.

The whip motif interweaves with the theme of class smashing natural emotional ties. Belle herself is a half-breed – her gentleman father abandoned her mother, who also abandoned her, for 'the gyppos leave the mixed ones to die'. Race is a form of class. Deverill protects a skivvy from her slaps, and our first response is to admire his gentlemanly concern for social inferiors, as compared to her upstart's brutality. But Belle makes him admit the truth; the skivvy is his love-child, so, as a father, he's derisory. A whole parable about

The Gypsy and the Gentleman: Keith Michell, Melina Mercouri – The spiritual fecklessness bred by privilege

social responsibility underlies that twist. Equally, he wants to prevent his sister marrying a doctor; for him, the profession isn't noble enough; in fact, no profession could be noble enough, compared with the privilege of abusing one's privileges. The crowning wickedness to which Belle goads him (certifying his own sister) is hardly more than a tautology of what he has done already (he simply shifts his sister from one doctor to another ...). One can't help reflecting that what hurts Deverill is not simply his sister's suffering, but the awful realization that Belle has shamed him, has deprived him of his aristocratic superiority. He has become a dependent money-grubber, like the rest of us.

So far as status is concerned the 'freest' characters are the young doctor, the actress (Flora Robson) and the blacksmith-boxer (Nigel Green). The sawbones wants to forget all about his fiancée's inheritance (though this ingenuous idealism goes with the weakness of inexperience). Rather stronger is the 'great lady' of the stage. She too has a servant, Coco, a young coloured boy whom she treats with absurd indulgence, even when he steals a gold coin. This comic little theft is like a quid pro quo for his status as pet (all servility degrades). But her human concern for him is real, and she shows her mettle in extricating Deverill's sister from the madhouse. Her attempted impersonation of aristocratic authority is foiled, by her fame (Forrester recognizes her), but as she reminds him, she has influence in high places, and he yields. Fictions are self-defeating, social facts are efficacious. She is classless – by professional success – and free – to be concerned.

Belle is classless too – as a semi-gyppo, and a thief. She's magnificent, and sympathetic, in her gold-digging, because (a) sexual privileges are no less sympathetic than hereditary ones, (b) she's the underdog, (c) she's trying to get money for horse-trader Patrick McGoohan, whom she loves rather more generously than Deverill loves her. Love is all her existence; marriage she scarcely understands. But when her lover uses the money she gives him to start bargaining for a pretty young gypsy-girl as concubine (on all levels, money speaks ...) she turns them away, crying 'Get off my land!', like a Deverill herself. In their turn, the Gypsies are quite ready to sell their daughter, as she to be sold – a mirror of the heiress theme. And Belle, who sells her body to Deverill, twins with another man who sells his body to Deverill – the blacksmith-prize-fighter whose purse Belle steals and who refuses Deverill's paternalist compensation, as implying the loss of his good name. He understands *order,* and he has *self-respect,* perhaps because, fighting apart, he has a modest status and trade. The Gypsies are rootless – nomads and thieves – because beneath any social standing. When Belle orders them off her land, they retaliate by sacking the Deverill mansion. By so doing, they bring to light the faked will. Disorder remedies disorder (but haphazardly). For in a disorderly order, the forcefulness of Deverill and Belle, in itself a glorious explosion of life-force *against* class barriers, becomes irresponsible and predatory, and concludes in masochism (for as Deverill is exploited by Belle, so is she by the man she loves). Though the Gypsies are barbaric in ransacking the mansion, they are no more so than Deverill himself, since he has been selling its treasures to pay for his debauch.

In a sense, this is a film noir in Technicolor, but in another sense it negates the genre's negation, to the effect that fate or the system will cross us whatever we do. Here, we see, or we feel, the characters' mistaken choices. Deverill might have taken his uncle's advice, and learned to be something as egalitarian as the system allowed, that is, a 'good master'. Even so, the phrase jars on our modern minds, and sets us in a mood to think in social terms when Belle is insulted for her race, or when we compare, in our minds, the Deverill mansion with Belle's tent in the forest (a subsequent cut from stately home to forest downpour hints at the demoralizing squalor of her existence). Deverill finds in his cellar a bottle of wine, brought from France 'when they still had a king'. Irresponsibility lost that king his throne, and his head. Someone, somewhere, had the idea of a revolution, involving principles and social progress, instead of the horse-trader's blind opportunism and revenges.

But though Losey ties in social and personal relationship – more concretely than *bien-pensants* find comfortable – he isn't saying that meaningful decent personal relationships are possible only in an egalitarian democracy. Deverill is matched by his uncle, Belle by the actress, her lover by the blacksmith, one doctor by another. Nonetheless, the Gypsy and the gentleman have in common their social irresponsibility. Unearned privilege oppresses the character, as much as underprivilege; people being what they are, privilege implies its abuse.

Melina Mercouri's performance is almost embarrassing to the English spectator, for the best of reasons: its uncouthness, shot through, particularly in the film's second half, with the deepening sadness of a lucidity never quite attained, and, in extremis, denied.

In one of his finer moments, Deverill lucidly and honestly admits to his fiancée that he doesn't love her, and her quiet affirmation of friendship establishes what his life could have been, had his social background been such as to engage his sense of responsibility on a broader front. In a similar way, dream-girl Margit Saad's sexual gift of herself to Johnny in *The Criminal* has a cool, sharp, reserved incisiveness, implying a classical, rather than a romantic attitude to love, as passion indeed, but as infatuation, i.e. a subtle but no less pernicious form of egoism, which is what it becomes for Deverill, for Tyvian in *Eva* and for Tony in *The Servant*. For Losey, as for Freud, overt sexual passion is only one passion among many – Graham in *Time without Pity* is, almost, kept alive, by the sheer frenzy of his love for his son and his guilt. If Losey is an admirable portraitist of passion (with its battle for ascendancies, its devious egoisms) it is because it has, for him, no moral privileges. On the contrary, for him as for Freud, it takes its character from the morality which nourishes it. Paradoxically (given its Nietzschean sense of energy) there is no indulgence of amorality in Losey's work, less than in that of John Huston (another director who owes much to American regional puritanism), less even than Buñuel (with his, moral, weakness for Sade). There is a streak in Losey's work of a (highly sublimated) moral pessimism, just as his sense of interpersonal ascendancies is healthily disquieting: both are American traits. In more ways than one, he is, as an American, a Freudian and a Democrat, an 'anti-Dostoevsky'. It's a position almost too easy for an artist in a popular medium to adopt (vide Richard Brooks's version of *The Brothers Karamazov*), and it's all the more difficult to adopt validly, whence Losey's stress on conflict and paradox. Losey's films accept liberal principles, but accept them in a basic, that is, a radical way, so forcing liberalism to that internal crisis, that attack on traditional complacencies, which has made, for some of the liveliest minds of the rising generation, liberalism seem a dirty word. Analogies with Camus and Sartre impose themselves. But where the existentialists suppose in human nature a somewhat curious instinctlessness, Losey maintains the severity implicit in Freud at a point which, like Sartre's moralizing, balances on a knife-edge between pessimism and a liberating intransigence. His work adumbrates a new kind of moral tone, both puritan and Nietzschean, rationalist, yet bursting with libidinal vigour. His subsequent collaboration with Pinter is as inevitable as it is surprising. Pinter's absurdities of the interpersonal are precisely what Losey's ferocity cannot but, intuitively, explain, and, in a valid, challenging, sense, moralize. The director fits the scripts as a hand fits a glove.

Blind Date (in the U.S.A., *Chance Meeting*), a detective story, reverts to the scale and style of *Time without Pity*. A struggling young Dutch painter (Hardy Kruger) in London gives a few art lessons to a proud rich woman (Micheline Presle). They fall in love. After several meetings in his white, bare studio, he, for the first time, goes to her home, when she is found murdered. The police describe her as the mistress of an important Foreign Office personage. It is suggested to the Inspector in charge of the case (Stanley Baker) that his career would be advanced were charges successfully pressed against the boy. But Inspector Morgan credits his story, and the apparent victim is finally revealed as a murderess. Dropping her guard for a split second, she inculpates herself, and the boy goes free.

Artist and detective are both hunters after truth, each in his own specialized, limited, slightly oblique way. The painter, arrogant and innocent, seems to hover on the edge of life's complexity, sensing, yet denying it. In London, alone, he paints pictures of Dutch miners, honouring his father. Truth, for him, is the truth of form, physical enough, but also something of an abstraction from life. He scolds his none-too-serious pupil for drawing a shoulder lifelessly, and bares his own: 'This is a shoulder, it's flesh and blood, scratch it, it bleeds'. She adds: 'Kiss it, it trembles'. We first see him, before his disillusionment, hop-skip-and-jumping along the pavements, enviably free, but half a child. Outside his art, there are obvious things he can't, won't, see: the heavy opulence of his beloved's apartment, with dolphins and putti-taps, a nouveau riche love-nest if ever there was one, and as the detective spots at first glance. The detective has an eye for life, an eye that's hardly artistic, but just as incisive and just as salutary. 'That woman isn't a giver, she's a taker. My father was a chauffeur, so I know all about that'. There is a minor early exchange, typical, in little, of the drastically self-effacing quality of the best scriptwriting. The painter, under suspicion, states, 'I washed my hands ...' The detective: 'Why, were they dirty?' The painter: 'I was curious to know the scent of her soap.' The conflict between the smooth establishment view of the system, and

Morgan's intuitive belief in the boy's insight, born of the experience which is his equivalent of the artist's vision, gives a special depth to his Racinian choice between justice and career. How unkind fate, and they, will be to him we don't know; but he has made the right choice. Yet his intuition can only be touched because the boy persists, is active, questions, probes. In a way they have exchanged modes: it's the boy who queries, the detective who intuits. The artist stands on his rights, from the beginning. He's not afraid to question the 'fatherly wisdom' of the police, and it's just as well for him that he isn't. He never resigns himself to anyone else's hands. Truth is not the monopoly of any one profession, of any one approach. It springs from a dialectic, the reciprocal challenge-and-respect of the diverse insights of honest men.

The dishonest woman, too, stumbles on her moment of truth – with disastrous consequences for herself. Once she has committed herself to destroying her lover, and to living a lie, then all that is living in herself, lust and pity, fusing, for a moment, into a tenderness like love, can only destroy the rest, and be destroyed by it. Much of Losey's tonic moral harshness comes from the way in which his characters' virtues only help them on the road to destruction. Just as living is generosity, so meanness is suicide. And Losey's films become tragedies without being nihilistic.

Finally, the painter walks away into the sunlight, and catches a bus, only a little less carefree than he was at the beginning. We've already seen that he lives in the present (in terms of flesh and the scent of the soap) and that with his deeper loyalty to his art and his father goes an admirable spiritual freedom and resilience. He's lucid; having escaped from the trap his woman set, he cuts clean with the past. Clearly, his wasn't a great love. But if he leaves the police station without a stain on his character, he also leaves it without a mark on his heart. He's free again, but what has he learnt? Is his the artist's eternal virginity? Or is that, in some ways, a sterile, a Godardian, freedom? The detective, though nearer corruption, is, perhaps, the deepest moralist of the two, with his acceptance of the social role, his application of his father's wisdom, rather than idealization of his image, and it's his career which may suffer. But both functions have their nobility, their complementarity.

The Criminal opens with a game of poker. Hard men peer intently at their cards, on whose fall, perhaps thousands of pounds, even some lives, ride. An intensity of suffering reveals the underlying masochism of the compulsive gambler. The camera tracks back. The men are convicts in a cell, playing for snout. The prison is society, society is a prison, insofar as it's a 'system' of human greed, a system to which the criminals condemn themselves. Bannion (Stanley Baker) may seem an ostentatiously free man, in that he's a very prosperous criminal, one of the (in the noblest sense) Nietzschean elite, like the master-craftsmen of *Du Rififi chez les hommes*. Society hasn't broken him. In his greed he's less neurotic than some, and, apart from his tragic flaw, he's the non-neurotic criminal, the man well adapted to a criminal society. Even within the prison he has almost as much physical freedom as, and more spiritual freedom than, his old antagonist. The Chief Warder (Patrick Magee) clashes his keys against the steel banister in rhythm with the prisoners' angry clattering of their tin mugs on cell doors. The prison governor, with his *New Statesman*, sees Bannion as a not ignoble enemy. But Bannion's luxury flat is a prison too, until he

finds the woman (Margit Saad) who has freedom, who is his freedom. She materializes, in his bed after a party, like a gift from the Gods, like a hedonistic grace. But the gift to her of a too-ostentatious – and unnecessarily ostentatious – ring becomes his downfall – because he can never quite break free from his inner prison – and he dies, squalidly, grubbing in the snow-covered earth beneath which his useless treasure lies; screaming, moreover, in dying terror of Hell.

The system finds another image in *The Damned* – a film which criticizes, in reminiscent terms, the Val Guest view of society. Sheltering from a gang of Teds in a seaside town, American playboy Macdonald Carey and pick-up girl Shirley Anne Field stumble into a secret bunker where civil servant Alexander Knox is rearing a weird breed of ice-cold, radioactivity-proof children in preparation for the day after The Bomb. (And if there's no day of the bomb, what life will theirs have been?)

This coldly convulsive ethos is only the last stage of the dialectic of British sang-froid and British cold-bloodedness. Around a seafront statue of George III cluster the Teddy Boys. Their leader, King (Oliver Reed), sarcastically sports a Guards brolly and accent, asserting, not only the contrast, but the continuity, of militarism and hooliganism. (Losey's approach to phenomenon, like Freud's, is dialectical, rendering him keenly conscious of the way in which opposition leads to resemblance, and inspiring his pairs of antagonists and accomplices: Tony/Barrett in *The Servant*, Tyvian/Eva in *Eva*, the King and King.) The Teds think sex is filthy – and King uses his pretty sister as bait for men whom he can 'indignantly' beat up and rob. Yet his incestuousness has its genuinely protective tinge. King seems to represent puritanism's rear-guard: Shirley Anne Field escapes from him in the American's motor launch, called, pointedly, *Dolce Vita*. There is a passionate nostalgia of opposites between the cold, reasoning bureaucrat and the forcefully passionate artist. Sculptress Viveca Lindfors sports black leather trousers, and, with a facetious *femme fatale* gesture, resembles her own statue of a 'graveyard bird'. Her violence, though, is personal, emotional, protective. It is a revelation of, and therefore a counter to, society's. When a philistine Ted takes a hatchet to her work she closes with him without a second's hesitation. The bureaucrat's violence, constructive in intent, is impersonal, rational, merciless. He shoots the sculptress he once loved to keep his secret. Still

The Criminal: Stanley Baker, Edward Judd, Margit Saad – The world as a prison yet a woman who offers freedom under surveillance by a helicopter, *Dolce Vita* drifts out beyond territorial waters. The lovers, believing themselves free at last, but contaminated by radio-activity, are doomed to a hideous, lingering death (so much for the ivory tower, the *Playboy* penthouse ...). The black leather boys have an almost touchingly old-fashioned warmth, their brutality a certain personal quality, in contrast to the most dangerous 'anti-violence' of all, the calm expectation of the Day of the Megadeaths. Yet the bureaucrat's concern for his wards' mental health is, in its turn, *like* kindness, compared with the military's old-fashioned, no-nonsense demands for even stricter surveillance, for the abolition, in the name of security, of all privacy. As it is, the children's brave but losing battle against their 'Big Brother' TV surveillance, their foredoomed attempts to escape from their sterilized universe, the poetic myths through which they endeavour to explain their own origins and existence, have the chilly tragedy of *L'Année dernière à Marienbad*. Only this is Weymouth, 1961 ...

In some details, the film's view of the English is schematized, The Teddy Boys are a phoney lot, and although Viveca Lindfors triumphantly displays the warmth and attack worthy of Losey at his best, he seems otherwise, more distant from his players than usual. A certain passivity and distance attaches to its central characters. The film was ravaged and re-shot by its producers. Yet, for all its defects, it remains exciting for its structure of ideas, for its use of landscape, and for innumerable images – King clambering over moonlit tombs like a graveyard bird – a guard's rubber-gloved hand sending the children's toy globe spinning while they sleep ....

With his next film, *Eva*, Losey turned to a European producer, and away from the British formulae, within which he had had to work. His subsequent film, *The Servant*, confirms his (relative) freedom; *The Damned* is the last film in which Losey had to work within a form so closely determined by the middle-class traditions which have been our theme.

38. Suspended Animation

Although *Animal Farm*, the only cartoon feature to come within our brief, has been mentioned elsewhere, it would be regrettable to overlook certain short cartoons which display many parallels to feature motifs. They merit critical attention more particularly in that while cartoons are often reviewed, they are rarely criticized, partly because they fit only awkwardly into the cinema's feature-slotting structure, partly because many of the best move at memory-defying speed and are rarely given as many viewings as they need for their intellectual structure to sink in. Commercially speaking, the British cartoon can hardly clamber into the ring, being kept out by American dumping, coupled with the aesthetic conservatism of circuit bookers. TV commercials have subsidized most British cartoons, which are made more for love, or prestige, than money, and often bring a wild purity to their themes.

Most traditional of the cartoon producers are Halas and Batchelor, whose *Animal Farm* was in the Disney tradition. Their graphic progress since then may be exemplified by the *Hoffnung Symphony Orchestra*, a bright, *après-Punch* piece spiritedly solving the problem which gave every Hollywood cartoon unit, from Disney to U.P.A., such difficulty; how to reconcile emphatic laugh gags with smartish-post-Disney graphics. Their *Automania 2000* is a Tati-spirited spoof on technology and piecemeal planning, with cars enjoying a population explosion and covering the globe with a mile-high traffic jam.

A newer school of cartoonists perform upon that Goonish cusp between the old and new, humour and satire. The Canadian George Dunning is responsible for whimsies with a barbed irony. *The Wardrobe*, *The Flying Man* and *The Apple* are as near American wryness as any English tone. The last in particular has a curious sense of futility-in-apparent-freedom, of obsessions acted out against indefinite and limitless space, with a tick-tock timing at once perky and derisive.

The Australian Bob Godfrey's *Polygamous Polonius* spiritedly crystallizes the struggle of the British soul against being smothered by the schoolroom attitude to art. A 'nice' lecturer blithely prattles away about all sorts of sexy paintings, blandly ignoring their outrageous provocations, despite continuous interruptions by an obstinate little man who persistently metamorphoses into hopefully romantic or impressive or ingratiating disguises (toreador, scoutmaster, et al.). All to no avail; she won't be seduced, and crushes him into matrimony.

Do It Yourself Cartoon Kit is a prestidigitous jingle-jumble of iconographics, from Goonish to Gothic, by way of empire-builders' emblems, admen's knickknacks, cultural doodads and assorted oojamaflips. It weaves a pixilated and reciprocally destructive choreography from the diverse and irreconcilable notions that obfuscate our insights, titillate our palates, manipulate our loyalties and masquerade as satisfactions. *The Plain Man's Guide to Advertising* redoubles the attack. *The Rise and Fall of Emily Sprod*, whose theme, if any, remains obscure to me, unless it's a continuation of the Polonius film's, features some irreverent yet ultra-beautiful play with paintings and suggests that Godfrey might develop towards cartoons which are only incidentally humorous, and, primarily, dream-like, satirical or even macabre, along the lines of the Polish school. For the Poles share the British ambivalence towards the past – even if theirs went out with a bang in 1939, rather than with a balance of payments whimper, and even if Poland, always occupied, yet obstinately a traditional entity, contrasts with Britain, never occupied, except by its own myths ...

Pop art imagery kicks off from contemporary American imagery (subsequently reaching back as far as the thirties) and from pre-1914 British imagery. Marilyn Monroe meets Sergeant Pepper. A reigning matriarchy meets a deposed patriarchy. The loss of a simple, proud, direct male energy, that was felt to have reached its climax in Edwardian times, appears in many a cartoon, even before the satire boom. If fractricidal strife, and ironies of cool and rage, are the covert theme of *Tom and Jerry* and the American cartoons, the corresponding English theme is a derisive nostalgia – not always the same thing as satire. Richard Williams's *Love Me, Love Me, Love Me* is a sharp send-up of British mediocrity as being self-protective masochism. Our hero, Squidgy Bod, is shy, accident-prone, and always wrong; people love him. Thermus Fortitude is strong, efficient, and always right, and people hate him, excepting his own true friend, a stuffed alligator named Charlie. He takes a correspondence course in lovableness, and soon everybody loves him, except Charlie, so Thermus throws him out of the window, where he gets trampled on by Squidgy Bod. Charlie, though described as stuffed, seems to be the most living character of the trio – spontaneous (as a loving, wild, pet) and dangerous (being an alligator), he is all the positive emotion repressed and depressed by British phlegm. The parody of the fable form, the medieval MS effects, the spoof Biblical idiom, and gilt-edged olde saws, send up a whole battery of moral traditions, or concoctions, and all in all this cartoon is almost as classic a crystallization of the British character as Tex Avery's *The Cat That Hated People* of the American.

Other cartoons are philosophical fables. Richard Williams's *The Little Island* is a radical and savage allegory about three creatures, monomaniacs devoted to truth, goodness and beauty, respectively. The tension between this unholy trinity of human ideals escalates to apocalyptic proportions, as they metamorphose through various historical forms. Goodness becomes, *inter alia*, choirboys and mailed blue fists smashing down from heaven (harbingers of the glove in *Yellow Submarine*). Beauty becomes Greek dancing and Wildean decadence. Truth, most 'impartial' of the three, simply comes up with the H-bomb, whereupon the other two dwindle reluctantly, into fear and common sense. Williams forcefully invests this nineteenth-rather-than-twentieth-century antithesis with twentieth-century angst, and his sharp, strong, sardonically ornate graphics and logic attain a quite convulsive anxiety. One can see it as a summary of three traditions (the Greek, the Hebrew, the scientific) tearing humanism apart. And it's all the more interesting for inter-relating abstract forces, in the idealistic tradition of Christian Platonism, with the dynamism of dialectical materialism – or of interacting psychic forces. (Indeed, I initially misunderstood the film as sketching the Protean conflicts of ego, super-ego and id.) We are all disturbingly caught in a cultural transition, and far from being a fairly straightforward and sentimental plea for less monomania and more tolerance, the film catches, expressionistically, something of the emotional terrors posed by intellectual perplexities in this era when rival philosophies brandish at one another, not Hellfire in the next life, but the H-bomb in this one.

Apocalyptic, if more fundamentalist, are the cartoons of the Hungarians Joan and Peter Foldes, *Animated Genesis* and *A Short Vision*. The latter film, inspired by the irritatingly righteous, albeit naggingly plausible, spirit of C.N.D. insists, with its strong sculptural visuals, pointedly reminiscent of Henry Moore's wartime sketches of Londoners sleeping safely in tube shelters during the blitz, on making us feel, in skin and sinew, the unleashing of an atomic device that melts the bone under the face and snuffs the last spark of life from a blackened, superfluous, and shameful planet. The cartoon film, too, can be a moral sledgehammer.

Notes

1. Raymond Durgnat, *A Mirror for England: British Movies from Austerity to Affluence* (London: Faber & Faber, 1970).
2. John Hill, *Sex, Class and Realism: British Cinema 1956-1963* (London: BFI, 1986), p. 2.
3. Jeffrey Richards, *Visions of Yesterday* (London: Routlege & Kegan Paul, 1973).
4. Sue Harper, *Picturing the Past: The Rise and Fall of the British Costume Film* (London: BFI, 1994), p. 107.
5. Melanie Williams, '"Twilight Women" of 1950s British Cinema', in *The British Cinema Book*, 3rd ed., ed Robert Murphy, (London: BFI, 2009), p. 287.
6. Raymond Durgnat, *The Crazy Mirror, Hollywood Comedy and the American Image* (London: Faber & Faber, 1969).
7. Raymond Durgnat: Interview (1977), in the UCLA Film Department at University of California where Durgnat was a Visiting Professor. The full interview is published in *Rouge* (2006) and is online at www.rouge.com.au/8/interview.html.
8. *Movie*, edited by Ian Cameron was first published in 1962. V.F. Perkins, Robin Wood, and Paul Mayersberg were regular contributors. Durgnat contributed in 1965, using the pseudonym O.O. Green for articles on Josef von Sternberg and Michael Powell (*Movie* nos. 13 & 14 respectively), and his own name for 'Two Christian Films' (Richard Brooks) and on *Belle de Jour* (nos. 12 &15 respectively). Durgnat wrote more frequently for *Movie*'s contemporary, *Motion*, edited by Ian Johnson.
9. Interview, op. cit.
10. Raymond Durgnat, *A Mirror for England*, op. cit., p. 25.
11. 'Auteurs and Dream Factories', in *Films and Feelings* (London: Faber & Faber, 1967), pp. 61–86.
12. *The Unquiet Grave: A Word Cycle* (1944) was written pseudonymously as Palinurus, by Cyril Connolly,

13. 'Auteurs and Dream Factories', op. cit.

14. Referring to William Empson's *Seven Types of Ambiguity* (1930).

15. Raymond Durgnat: Interview (1977).

16. *Monthy Film Bulletin*, June 1951, pp. 277–8. The review was by GL (Gavin Lambert).

17. Interview, op. cit.

18. *Films and Feelings* (1967). It brings together articles published in *Projektio*, *Films and Filming*, *The Architectural Review*, *The Burlington Magazine*, and parts of his postgraduate research at the Slade School of Fine Art.

19. *The Strange Case of Alfred Hitchcock* (1974), pp. 137–140.

20. *A Mirror for England*, op.cit., p. 22.

21. Ibid., p. 23.

22. Interview, op. cit.

23. *A Mirror for England*, op.cit., ibid., p. 240.

24. The French Roman Catholic author of *Journal d'un curé de campagne* (1936), whose work was adapted to the screen by Robert Bresson (1951).

25. In both *Hungry Hill* and *Great Expectations* the evolution is associated with a loss of masculine toughness, a shift to the feminine. Cecil Parker and sons die, leaving Margaret Lockwood. In the Lean film, the strongest and the nastiest men both disappear. Similarly, Gladstone blows up, but Genevieve soldiers on. The shift from masculine to feminine arguably links with middle- (rather than upper-) class fear of the 'rough', but its complications are beyond our scope here.

26. I wouldn't deny that the working-classes are quicker to threaten physical violence than the middle-classes; but this film also implies that they're wickeder which is another matter.

27. Other celebrations of the special relationship include the (Liberal) Asquith's *The Way to the Stars*, the (then Labour) John Boulting's *Journey Together* (also 1945) and Powell's *A Canterbury Tale* (1944), where a misguided church magistrate (Eric Portman), who possibly personifies the puritanical middle-class, pours glue on the hair of girls who date G.I.s. The notion of Britain and America as buddies locked in complete identity of interest remains unchallenged until two films produced by the American Harry Saltzman: Terence Young's *Thunderball* (1965) and Ken Russell's *Billion Dollar Brain* (1967). Zampi's *Top Secret* (1952) and Asquith's *The Young Lovers* (1954) are irreverent about the cold war.

28. The Norman Wisdom and *Carry On* comedies, proletarian in tone and reference, are touched on in a later chapter, consecrated to the English sense of humour. Films about strikes, which include Bernard Miles's *A Chance of a Lifetime* (1950), Robert Hamer's

His Excellency (1951), the Boultings' *I'm All Right Jack* (1959), and *The Angry Silence* (1959), certainly reflect ideas of the working class, but are dealt with under the general heading of political attitudes. Films about National Service are a disappointing lot, apart from the Boultings' *Private's Progress* (1956) and Gerald Thomas's *Carry On Sergeant* (1958).

29. And what, since writing this, we've got is *Curry 'n' Chips*, an admirable answer (scandalous comedy) to the pitfalls indicated above.

30. Throughout this book the word 'puritan' is used in its modern loose sense, to mean vigorous demands on moral sincerity together with a disapproval of sensual pleasure. It's a cultural inheritance from Puritanism proper (Calvinism) and the renewal of nonconformism by the Evangelical Revival (Methodism). Theologically contrasted, they're alike in the two points mentioned above, and had extensive influence among C of E, rationalists, agnostics, etc.

31. Maybe the Steiger, Van Eyck and Tiller characters were all too cold and unsympathetic for British audiences. But the film's hint of a British decline may have helped to puzzle and hurt the audience in an E.10 hall, who began sighing and jeering about ten minutes after the Briton disappeared and couldn't contain their derision at the 'heroic' end.

32. Though several American films look on the upper-class English as 'perfidious Albion', notably King Vidor's *Northwest Passage*, John Ford's *The Long Voyage Home* and Richard Fleischer's *The Vikings*.

33. At the same time the film stresses the extent to which capitalist enterprise (concrete manufacturers, etc.) are overflowing with plans for rehousing the poor, and rarin' to go. It's a humane film, but by no means a left-wing one, as it's often assumed to be.

It even comprises a built-in caveat about the dangers of bureaucratic regimentation when the new blocks materialise. The camera watches in deadpan fascination as a dreary killjoy caretaker recites the list of prohibitions which it is his sacred trust to enforce. This isn't a bad guess, since this fellow's grandson turns up in *Sparrows Can't Sing*. But this is also a *Matter of Life and Death* attack against the planners' Utopia, and it seems odd to accommodate it in such a film, if not for its anti-Socialism moral.

34. Ealing's response to affluence is uneasy. Contentment resists mass media glitter, whether TV (*Meet Mr. Lucifer*, 1953) or film-fandom (*The Love Lottery*, 1953). With its danced dreams, the latter parallels *The Band Wagon* as *Evergreen* paralleled pre-war Hollywood musicals. Too late for Sinatra, too early for Elvis, its timing is awkward – and its temptations never scarcely tempt.

35. The Rank 'industrial' series take their cue from the Clouzot, and have its boldness without its thoughtfulness. The contrast with Wessex reiterates a familiar English pattern. The right-wing has the rhetoric, the left-wing the conscience; a little too much, perhaps, to accept the insolence and amorality which loom so large, in entertainment. Here no doubt, is one *internal* reason for the British left-wing's difficulty in appealing to its own class. Paralysed by its own idealism, denying itself the energy, the accuracy and the appeal of all those cynical and *sub rosa* attitudes which so consistently motivate human behaviour, it consistently slides into the guilt-inducing, the worrying, the schoolmasterish, and, indeed, the obscurantist.

This isn't to put Wessex further left than Liberal. All their films can be seen as, primarily, tragic, or warning, studies in moral fibre, the old girl net expressing misgivings about the Welfare State, but with class neutrality. *Raising a Riot* praises helpful *private* schoolmarms, condemns 'official busybodies'.

36. This isn't to say that the easy acceptance of authority represented a strong authoritarian presence. The emotional climate was, if anything, less authoritarian, more easygoing, than in other European countries (whether or not the police were detested), and the heavy father represented, if anything, a nostalgia shared between fathers and sons. There was a ready identification with a personal, man-to-man authority, a need, even, for the reassurance, of its ultimate presence, and its principal cause was probably the absence of the constraints improved by pre-war hardships, by the softening of puritanism, by affluence, by the easing of class snobbery, by the soft line in education, and so on. A far from diffuse guilt and anxiety about all this indulgence was relieved by stories of reasonably stern father-figures quietly imposing themselves when necessary. Behind this acquiescence in authority from below there lies the lower-middle-class emphasis on authority as protection from the 'mob', working-class self-policing, entertainment wish-fulfillment upwards, and so on. In general, real authority figures tended to be less heavy than the general public (especially the cinema's middle/working overlap) expected, and would have liked. Our section heading 'System as Stalemate' emphasizes the extent to which such acquiescence helped to perpetuate that locking up of the youthful initiatives and the proletarian talents about which the angry young men and their successors were concerned. In any case this easy acquiescence short-circuited the analysis and exploration of every subject in which it was involved.

37. Other successful exports include (a) some Korda epics, (b) wartime documentaries, (c) 'prestige' pictures like *The Red Shoes* and *Trio*. The first are extremely expensive, the

second a wartime phenomenon, the third catch the 'arthouse' (middle-brow) audience. The most successful of the Korda epics was *The Private Life of Henry VIII*, in theme and tone not at all dissimilar to the Gainsborough pictures.

38. The idea that the war explains an increase in violence (whereas the evidence, on balance, suggests that there was more violence before the war, and even more before World War I) probably registers an increased sensitivity to, and disapproval of, violence.

39. The film was meant to prove to another doddering 'system', the film industry's, what could be done on a B-feature budget, and it's a thousand pities that its very able demonstration is lost on a boring vindication of British bureaucracy, which isn't exactly famous for its piping-hot security.

40. If British films can be as low keyed as they are, it is because the British audience is very emotional in its response to quietly-stated emotions. In much the same way, if the British put dampers on their emotional expression, it is not because they are unemotional but because they are afraid of embarrassing others by forcing them to share or repudiate their emotion. The tendency to emotional stereotypy is reinforced by an emotional intensity which makes it difficult to respond to anything new or complicated. The British quieten their lives as much because their reactions are strong as because they're indifferent. Naturally, once emotions are kept in rigid check a secondary loneliness and fear set in. The precariousness of this balance is the theme of many English films.

41. Emeric Pressburger, a Hungarian scriptwriter, shared joint producer-writer-director credit with Michael Powell on all his films from *One of Our Aircraft Is Missing* until *Ill Met by Moonlight*. Their relative share and influence is difficult to determine, since Powell's solo efforts before and after have much in common with the tandems, and Pressburger's solo British films relatively little. P & P also produced *The End of the River* (1947), based on *Death of a Common Man*, an interesting piece of tropical exoticism, by the American explorer Desmond Holdridge.

42. A possibility which is regularly overlooked by critics in all the narrative arts. They look for symbolism, and overlook the possibility that the author's norm lies between all the characters, is a kind of addition of all the tensions. But drama, almost by definition, is conflict, that is to say, allegorical-symbolical logic is only one of its modes. As often, the protagonists represent 'thesis' and 'anti-thesis', the synthesis being felt but unstated. The example of *Seven Days to Noon* is analogous to that of *Orphée*, argued in *Films and Feelings*.

Lists

The following lists indicate, in telegrammatic form, other perspectives on the British cinema:

Shots in the Dark, covering the release period January 1949–February 1951, claims to omit no major film of the period, and selects the following British films:

Trio, The Blue Lamp, Blue Scar, Dance Hall, The Queen of Spades, Give Us This Day, Kind Hearts and Coronets, The Happiest Days of Your Life, The Passionate Friends, Christopher Columbus, Chance of a Lifetime, The Small Back Room, The Third Man, They Were Not Divided, Scrapbook for 1933.

Bosley Crowther, *The Great Films: Fifty Golden Years of Motion Pictures* (G.P. Putnam's Sons, 1967) includes, among 50 Great Films, and a Supplemental List of 100 Distinguished Films, *In Which We Serve* and *Henry V* as 'great', and, as 'distinguished', *The Bridge on the River Kwai, Brief Encounter, The Fallen Idol, Great Expectations, The Lavender Hill Mob, The Red Shoes, Room at the Top, The Stars Look Down.*

Penelope Houston, *The Contemporary Cinema Dictionary* (Penguin, 1963), lists the following British films: *O Dreamland, Thursday's Children, Every Day Except Christmas, The Winslow Boy, The Browning Version, The Importance of Being Earnest, The V.I.P.s, Room at the Top, The Innocents, Knave of Hearts,*

It Always Rains on Sunday, Kind Hearts and Coronets, Father Brown, Great Expectations, Oliver Twist, The Sound Barrier, Summer Madness, The Bridge on the River Kwai, Lawrence of Arabia, Blind Date, The Criminal, The Man in the White Suit, Mandy, The Ladykillers, Sammy Going South, Hamlet, Richard III, The Prince and the Showgirl, We Are the Lambeth Boys, Odd Man Out, The Fallen Idol, The Third Man, Outcast of the Islands, Our Man in Havana, The Running Man, Terminus.

The following British films were nominated for principal Oscars, 1946-62 (capital letters indicate awards):

Automania 2000, Black Narcissus, Blithe Spirit, Brief Encounter (3), *THE BRIDGE ON THE RIVER KWAI* (5a, 1n), *Caesar and Cleopatra, The Captain's Paradise, The Conquest of Everest, The Cruel Sea, DAYBREAK IN UDI, Dylan Thomas, The Entertainer, The Fallen Idol, Genevieve, GREAT EXPECTATIONS* (1a, 3n), *Giuseppina, The Guns of Navarone* (3n), *HAMLET* (2a, 3n), *The Hasty Heart, HENRY V* (1a, 2n), *The Horse's Mouth, Journey Into Spring, The Ladykillers, THE LAVENDER HILL MOB* (1a, 1n), *LAWRENCE OF ARABIA* (6a, 2n), *The Man in the White Suit, The Mark, Odd Man Out, Passport to Pimlico, The Pickwick Papers, A Queen is Crowned, THE RED SHOES* (2n), *Richard III, ROOM AT THE TOP* (2a, 3n), *THE RUNNING JUMPING & STANDING STILL FILM, SEVEN DAYS TO NOON, Sons and Lovers* (6n), *The Sound Barrier, The Tales of Hoffmann, They Planted a Stone, Tunes of Glory, The Years Between.*

Georges Sadoul, in his *Dictionnaire des films*, has entries for the following relevant films:

Pygmalion, The Way to the Stars, Night Mail, Dead of Night, Hue and Cry, Passport to Pimlico, Knave of Hearts, In Which We Serve, Brief Encounter, The Lavender Hill Mob, Night and the City, Gaslight, Hill 24 Doesn't Answer, Man of Aran, Kind Hearts and Coronets, The Private Life of Henry VIII, The Bridge on the River Kwai, Time without Pity, The Criminal, Whisky Galore!,

The Man in the White Suit, The 'Maggie', The Red Shoes, Odd Man Out, The Fallen Idol, The Third Man, A Taste of Honey, Tom Jones, The Overlanders.

The following films were given longer reviews in *La Revue du cinéma* (May 1946–October 1948) and its offshoot, *Cahiers du cinéma* (from April 1951 to December 1964).

Hamlet, Great Expectations, Dead of Night, Brief Encounter, The Rake's Progress, A Matter of Life and Death, Odd Man Out, They Made Me a Fugitive, Henry V, Give Us This Day, Pandora and the Flying Dutchman, Laughter in Paradise, The Lavender Hill Mob, The Man in the White Suit, The Galloping Major, I Know Where I'm Going!, Outcast of the Islands, Mr. Drake's Duck, Scott of the Antarctic, The Life and Death of Colonel Blimp, Hunted, The Sound Barrier, The Card, The Importance of Being Earnest, Mr. Denning Drives North, The Planter's Wife, Tom Brown's Schooldays, The Hour of 13, The Cruel Sea, Genevieve, Heart of the Matter, The Magic Box, Knave of Hearts, The Personal Affair, Trent's Last Case, Trouble in Store, The Stranger Left No Card, Father Brown, Romeo and Juliet, Hill 24 Doesn't Answer, Richard III, Gideon's Day, Tarzan's Greatest Adventure, Together, Time without Pity, Peeping Tom, Oscar Wilde, Blind Date, The Criminal, Saturday Night and Sunday Morning, The Singer Not the Song, Village of the Damned, Billy Budd, Lawrence of Arabia, A Taste of Honey, The Servant, The Pumpkin Eater, The L-Shaped Room, The Damned, Only Two Can Play.

A review of *The Key* in *Cahiers* No. 89 is symptomatic. 'Carol Reed's direction of this high budget movie, as in his treatment of an originally piquant anecdote, is only the mask of the most total absence of invention. Nonetheless it remains the best British film for a long time.'

Movie No. 1 (1963) ranks British directors in the following hierarchy:

BRILLIANT: Joseph Losey. VERY TALENTED: (None). TALENTED: Hamer, Holt, Reisz. COMPETENT OR AMBITIOUS (a somewhat equivocal heading!): Anderson L., Annakin, Asquith, Baker R., Boulting J. and R., Cardiff,

Carreras, Chaffey, Day, Dearden, Frend, Green, Guest, Guillermin, Hamilton, Hughes, Jackson, Leacock, Lean, Lee, Lee Thompson, McCarthy, Moxey, Neame, Powell, Rakoff, Reed, Richardson, Rilla, Toye. THE REST: Amyes, Asher, Baker R. S., Berman, Bennett, Box, Burge, Carstairs, Cass, Crabtree, Crichton, Czinner, Endfield, Fairchild, Fisher, Guillermin, Allen, Hurst, Kimmins, Launder, Lemont, Lewis, MacDonald, McClory, Norman, Pollock, Sewell, Shaughnessy, Thomas G., Thomas R., Wilcox, Young T., Zampi.

A First Draft Pantheon (drawn from all British films mentioned in the index)

A. MAJOR MOVIES

Billy Liar, Blind Date, Blow-Up, Brief Encounter, The Browning Version, The Citadel, The Criminal, Chance of a Lifetime, The Damned, The Entertainer, Give Us This Day, Great Expectations, The Gypsy and the Gentleman, The Happiest Days of Your Life, Heavens Above!, Housing Problems, How I Won the War, I'm All Right Jack, It Happened Here, Kind Hearts and Coronets, King & Country, Knave of Hearts, The Leather Boys, The Little Island, Live Now Pay Later, The Long and the Short and the Tall, Look Back in Anger, Love Me, Love Me, Love Me, The L-Shaped Room, The Man in the White Suit, Men of Two Worlds, Millions Like Us, The Next of Kin, A Night to Remember, Nothing But the Best, Odd Man Out, Orders to Kill, Passage Home, The Plain Man's Guide to Advertising, Poor Cow, Private's Progress, The Queen of Spades, Reach for Glory, Repulsion, Road Sweepers, Room at the Top, The Running Jumping & Standing Still Film, Saturday Night and Sunday Morning, Secret People, The Servant, The Singer Not the Song, The Skin Game, The Sleeping Tiger, Sparrows Can't Sing, Tell England, Thursday's Children, Time without Pity, Tramps, The War Game, Waterloo Road, Woman in a Dressing Gown, Yellow Submarine, Yesterday's Enemy.

B. IMPORTANT MOVIES

The Angry Silence, The Battle of the Sexes, Billy Budd, Black Narcissus, Blackmail, The Boys, The Brides of Dracula, The Bridge on the River Kwai, Brighton Rock, Coal Face, A Cottage on Dartmoor, Cry, the Beloved Country, Carry On Nurse, Children on Trial, Circle of Deception, Dance Pretty Lady, David, Dead of Night, Do It Yourself Cartoon Kit, Dracula, Dunkirk, The Edge of the World, Everybody's Nobody, The Family Way, Fires Were Started, The Flying Man, Gaslight, Guns at Batasi, Guns of Darkness, The Heart of the Matter, Hobson's Choice, I Know Where I'm Going!, Industrial Britain, The Intimate Stranger, Jason and the Argonauts, The Kidnappers, Listen to Britain, The Loneliness of the Long Distance Runner, The Love Match, Love on the Dole, Man in the Moon, Man of Aran, March to Aldermaston, A Matter of Life and Death, Night and the City, Night Mail, Old Bones of the River, Oh, Mr. Porter!, Once a Jolly Swagman, One Way Pendulum, Our Mother's House, Peeping Tom, Polygamous Polonius, The Pumpkin Eater, The Rake's Progress, The Red Shoes, Refuge England, The Revenge of Frankenstein, Rich and Strange, The Rise and Fall of Emily Sprod, Rotten to the Core, Sailor Beware, Sapphire, The Song of Ceylon, The Stars Look Down, The Stranglers of Bombay, Summer of the Seventeenth Doll, The Tales of Hoffmann, Term of Trial, They Drive by Night, They Made Me a Fugitive, The Thief of Bagdad, This Sporting Life, Tiger in the Smoke, Together, Tom Jones, Tunes of Glory, Up the Junction, The Valiant, Victim, The Way Ahead, The Way to the Stars, Whisky Galore!, Windom's Way, Yield to the Night.

C. The category below this would include delightful, interesting or erratic movies, such as, *Genevieve, Hamlet, Lawrence of Arabia, Passport to Pimlico, The Wicked Lady,* etc.

References

Balcon, Michael, cited in Tynan, Ken, *Ealing's Way of Life* in *Films and Filming*, December 1955.

Berger-Hamerschlag, Margareta, *Journey Into a Fog*, Gollancz, 1955.

Bratby, John, Alas, *The People Are Not With Us* in *Ark* 28, Summer, 1960.

Crowther, Bosley, *The Great Films: Fifty Golden Years of Motion Pictures*, G. P. Putnam's Sons, 1967.

Empson, William, *Some Versions of Pastoral*, Chatto & Windus, 1935.

Forman, C. Dennis, *Films 1945-1950*, British Council, 1952.

Houston, Penelope, *The Contemporary Cinema Dictionary*, Penguin 1963.

Inglis, Brian, *Private Conscience – Public Morality*, André Deutsch, 1964.

Kracauer, Siegfried, *From Caligari to Hitler: A Psychological History of the German Film*, Dennis Dobson, 1947.

Lewis, C. S., *The Great Divorce*, Geoffrey Bles, 1946.

Mitford, Nancy, *U and Non-U* in *Encounter*, 1955.

Oakley, Charles, *Where We Came In: Seventy years of the British film industry*, Allen & Unwin, 1964.

Orwell, George, *Inside the Whale and Other Essays*, Penguin, 1957.

Perkins, V. F., *The Talent Histogram* in *Movie*, No. 1, June 1962.

Raven, Simon, *The English Gentleman*, Anthony Blond, 1961.

Riesman, David, *The Lonely Crowd*, Yale University Press, 1950.

Robson, E. W. and M. M., *The Shame and Disgrace of Colonel Blimp*, The Sidneyan Society, 1943.

Robson, E. W. and M. M., *The World is My Cinema*, The Sidneyan Society, 1947.

Screencomber, in *Kine Weekly*, 1939.

Spottiswoode, Raymond, *The Friese-Greene Controversy: The Evidence Reconsidered* in *The Quarterly of Film Radio and Television*, Spring 1955.

Török, Jean-Paul, *H-Pictures (I)* in *Positif*, May 1961.

Török, Jean-Paul, *H-Pictures (II)* in *Positif*, July 1961.

Trevelyan, G. M., *History of England*, Longmans, 1926.

Valobra, Franco, *Term of Trial* in *Cinema Domani*, No. 6, November/December 1962.

Vesselo, Arthur, *The Quarter in Britain* in *Sight and Sound*, Autumn, 1947.

Williams, Raymond, *Culture and Society, 1780–1950*, Chatto & Windus, 1958.

Winnington, Richard, *Drawn and Quartered*, Saturn Press, 1949.

Wiseman, Thomas, *Cinema*, Cassell, 1964.

Wolfenstein, Martha and Nathan Leites, *Movies: A Psychological Study*, The Free Press, 1950.

Bibliography

These items are selected as interestingly dovetailing with, or counterpointing, the approach in this book. We make no claims to exhaustiveness.

A. General

I. BOOKS, PAMPHLETS

BALCON, Michael, HARDY, Forsyth, LINDGREN, Ernest, MANVELL, Roger, *Twenty Years of British Films 1929-1945*, Falcon Press, 1947.

CARRICK, Edward, *Art and Design in the British Film*, Dobson, 1949.

GIFFORD, Dennis, *British Cinema: An Illustrated Guide and Index to 5000 Films*, Zwemmer-Tantivy, 1968.

GRENFELL, David, *An Outline of British Film History 1896-1962*, British Film Institute duplicated typescript.

GRIERSON, John, *Grierson on Documentary* (3rd edition), Faber, 1967.

LOVELL, Alan, *The British Cinema: The Unknown Cinema* (duplicated typescript for British Film Institute Education Department seminar, unpublished), 1969.

OAKLEY, Charles, *Where We Came In: 70 Years of the British Film Industry*, Allen & Unwin, 1964.

ROBSON, E.W. and M.M., *The World is My Cinema*, Sidneyan Society, 1947.

ROTHA, Paul, *Documentary Film* (3rd edition), Faber, 1952.

II. ECONOMICS, FINANCE, BUSINESS, ORGANIZATION

BALCON, Michael, *Michael Balcon Presents: A Lifetime of Films*, Hutchinson, 1969.

DUNBAR, Bob, *Inside the Straitjacket: Setting it Up* in *Definition*, No. 3, 1961.

FORBES, Bryan, *Breaking the Silence* in *Films and Filming*, July 1961.

KELLY, Terence, *A Competitive Cinema*, Institute of Economic Affairs, 1966.

KNIGHT, Derrick and PORTER, Vincent, *A Long Look at Short Films, An A.C.T.T. Report on the Short Entertainment and Factual Film*, Pergamon Press, 1967.

RIDER, David, *Animation: Cambridge Caper* in *Films and Filming*, January 1966.

SINGER, Andrew, *Inside the Straitjacket* in *Definition*, No. 2, 1960.

SPRAOS, John, *Decline of the Cinema: An Economist's Report*, Allen & Unwin, 1962.

TABORI, Paul, *Alexander Korda*, Oldbourne, 1959.

WINNINGTON, Richard, in *Drawn and Quartered: A Selection of Weekly Film Reviews and Drawings*, Saturn Press, 1948.

WOOD, Alan, *Mr. Rank: A Study of J. Arthur Rank and British Films*, Hodder & Stoughton, 1952.

WOODS, Frederick, *Take That You Swine* in *Films and Filming*, August 1952.

III. ARTISTIC STATE OF THE BRITISH CINEMA (IN CHRONOLOGICAL ORDER)

1947: ANDERSON, Lindsay, *Angle of Approach* in *Sequence*, No. 2.

1949: ANDERSON, Lindsay, *British Cinema – The Descending Spiral* in *Sequence*, No. 7.

1950: CORNELIOUS, Henry, DICKINSON, Thorold, HAVELOCK-ALLEN, Anthony, JOHN, Rosamund, LAUNDER, Frank, LOW, Rachel, MINTER, George, MORGAN, Guy, WRIGHT, Basil, *Round Table on British Films* in *Sight and Sound*, May 1950.

1952: QUEVAL, Jean, *Où va le cinéma anglais?* in *Cahiers du cinéma*, No. 13.

1957: BOLAND, Bridget, EVANS, Jon, MARCORELLES, Louis, RILLA, Wolf, ROTHA, Paul, WRIGHT, Basil, *What's Wrong With British Films?* in *Film*, No. 14.

1958: ANDERSON, Lindsay, ANNAKIN, Ken, ENDFIELD, Cyril, HAMILTON, Guy, *The State of the British Cinema* in *Film*, No. 15.

1962: PERKINS, V. F. (for editorial board), *The British Cinema* in *Movie*, No. 1.

1966: OLMI, Massimo, SILLITOE, Alan, RANIEN, Tino, JEANCOLAS, J. P., *Etapes du cinéma britannique* in *Jeune cinéma*, No. 19.

B. Criticism, Comment, Exegesis

AGEE, James, *Agee On Film: Review and Comments* (1941-8), Beacon Press, 1964.

ANSTEY, Edgar, HARDY, Forsyth, LINDGREN, Ernest, MANVELL, Roger, eds, *Shots in the Dark (A collection of reviewers' opinions)* (January 1949-February 1951), Allan Wingate, 1951.

CALLENBACH, Ernest, *The Understood Antagonist and Other Observations* (on documentary) in *Film Quarterly*, Summer 1959.

CAVANDER, Kenneth, GILLETT, John, GRENFELL, David, HILL, Derek, HOUSTON, Penelope, ROBINSON, David, ROUD, Richard, *British Feature Directors: An Index to Their Work* in *Sight and Sound*, Autumn 1958.

DURGNAT, Raymond, *Bureaucrats and Saboteurs* (on documentary) in *Franju*, Studio-Vista/University of California, 1968.

GIFFORD, Dennis, *Cinema Britanice* in *Cinemateca do Museu de Arte Modernado*, Rio de Janeiro, 1960.

JACOBS, Lewis, *Free Cinema* in *Film Culture*, No. 17, February 1958.

JOHNSON, Ian, *The Decade-Britain: We're All Right, Jack* in *Films and Filming*, September 1962.

JOHNSON, Ian, *Have the British a Sense of Humour?* in *Films and Filming*, March 1963.

ROBSON, E. W. and M. M., *The World is My Cinema*, Sidneyan Society, 1947.

TÖRÖK, Jean-Paul, *H-Pictures (I)* in *Positif*, May 1961.

TÖRÖK, Jean-Paul, *H-Pictures (II)* in *Positif*, July 1961.

WINNINGTON, Richard, *Drawn and Quartered*, Saturn Press, 1948.

WOLFENSTEIN, Martha and LEITES, Nathan, *Movies: A Psychological Study*, Free Press of Glencoe, 1950.

YOUNG, Vernon, *Movies and National Character: The Empirical English* in *Films and Filming*, February 1969.

C. Individual Directors, Auteurs, Films

I. BOOKS, PAMPHLETS

NOBLE, Peter, *Anthony Asquith*, British Film Institute, 1951.

ANDERSON, Lindsay, *Making a Film: The Story of Secret People*, Allen & Unwin, 1952.

TYNAN, Ken, *Alec Guinness*, Rockliff, 1953.

COWIE, Peter, *Korda* in *Cinéma d'aujourd'hui*, No. 6, June 1965.

LEAHY, James, *The Cinema of Joseph Losey*, Zwemmer-Tantivy, 1967.

LEDIEU, Christian, *Joseph Losey*, Pierre Seghers, 1963.

MILNE, Tom, ed., *Losey on Losey*, Secker & Warburg, 1967.

GIBBON, Monk, *The Red Shoes Ballet: A Critical Study*, Saturn Press, 1948.

II. ARTICLES

Anthony Asquith

COWIE, Peter, *This England* in *Films and Filming*, October 1963.

DURGNAT, Raymond, *The V.I.P.s* in *Films and Filming*, October 1963.

MANVELL, Roger, *The Doctor's Dilemma* in *Films and Filming*, April 1959.

MANVELL, Roger, *The Millionairess* in *Films and Filming*, December 1960.

ROBSON (*The Demi-Paradise*), op. cit.

SMITH, John Harrington, *Oscar Wilde's Earnest in Film* in *Quarterly of Film Radio and Television*, Fall 1953.

Winnington, op. cit.

Richard Attenborough

RATCLIFF, Michael, *The Public Eye and the Private Image of Richard Attenborough* in *Films and Filming*, August 1963.

Roy Baker

TÖRÖK, Jean-Paul, *Le Cavalier noir: plus noir que vous ne pensiez* (*The Singer Not the Song*), in *Positif*, No. 45, May 1962.

Dirk Bogarde

WHITEHALL, Richard, *A Great Actor Who Has Never Appeared in a Great Film: Dirk Bogarde* in *Films and Filming*, November 1963.

Boulting Brothers

AGEE, James (*Thunder Rock*), op. cit.

DURGNAT, Raymond, *Heavens Above!* in *Films and Filming*, July 1963.

KOSTOLEFSKY, Joseph, *I'm All Right Jack* in *Hollywood Quarterly*, Fall 1960.

WINNINGTON (*Fame is the Spur* and *Brighton Rock*), op. cit.

Renato Castellani

JORGENSEN, Paul A., Castellani's *Romeo and Juliet: Intention and Response* in *The Quarterly of Film Radio and Television*, Summer 1955.

LANDSBERGIS, A., *Romeo and Juliet* in *Film Culture*, No. 2, March/April 1955.

Alberto Cavalcanti

AGEE (*Went the Day Well*), op. cit.

DESTERNES, Jean, *Variations decoratives sur un thème noir – They Made Me a Fugitive* in *La Revue du cinéma*, No. 9, January 1948

MONEGAL, Emir Rodriguez, *Alberto Cavalcanti* in *The Quarter of Film Radio and Television*, Summer 1955.

Jack Clayton

KAEL, Pauline, *The Innocents and What Passes for Experience* in *I Lost it at the Movies*, Little Brown, 1965.

René Clément

BAZIN, André, *M. Ripois avec ou sans nemèse* in *Qu'est ce que le cinéma?*, Vol. 2, Éditions du cerf, 1959.

Henry Cornelius

WEINBERG, Herman G., *I Am a Camera*, in *Film Culture*, No. 4, Summer 1955.

Jill Craigie

ANSTEY and eds (*Blue Scar*), op. cit.

Charles Crichton

ANSTEY and eds (*Dance Hall*), op. cit.

Jules Dassin

ANON, *Le Fer et le feu* (*The Ashphalt Jungle* and *Night and the City*) in *L'Age du cinéma*, No. 1, March 1951.

JACOB, Guy, *Jules Dassin: Un petit homme à la mer* in *Le Cinéma moderne*, SERDOC 1964.

TYLER, Parker, *The Myth of Technique and the Myth of Reality* in *Sex, Psyche and Etcetera in the Film*, Horizon Press, 1969.

Robert Day

COWIE, Peter, *Corridors of Blood* in *Films and Filming*, November 1962.

Basil Dearden and Michael Relph

ANSTEY and eds (*The Blue Lamp*), op. cit.

Thorold Dickinson

ANSTEY and eds (*The Queen of Spades*), op. cit.

BENAYOUN, Robert, *Les Morts dirent leurs secrets: à propos de Queen of Spades* in *L'Age du cinéma*, No. 1, March 1951.

Edward Dmytryk

ANON, *Un sadisme metaphysique: Obsession, Give Us This Day* in *L'Age du cinéma*, No. 1, March 1951.

ANSTEY and eds (*Give Us This Day*), op. cit.

PAXTON, John, *Coffee in a Teacup: Notes on an English Adventure* (*So Well Remembered*) in *Hollywood Quarterly*, Fall 1947.

ROY, Claude, *Donnez-nous aujourd'hui* in *Cahiers du cinéma*, No. 1, April 1951.

Diana Dors

WHITEHALL, Richard, *D.D.* in *Films and Filming*, January 1963.

Charlie Drake

DURGNAT, Raymond, *The Cracksman* in *Films and Filming*, September 1963.

Julien Duvivier

AGEE (*Anna Karenina*), op. cit.

WINNINGTON (*Anna Karenina*), op. cit.

Terence Fisher

BOULLET, Jean, CAEN, Michel, LEBRIS, Alain, NURIDSANY, Michel, ROMER, Jean-Claude, THIRARD, P. L., *Terence Fisher* in *Midi-Minuit Fantastique*, No. 1, May-June 1962.

BOUYXOU, Jean-Pierre, *The Curse of Frankenstein, Revenge of Frankenstein, Frankenstein Created Woman, Frankenstein Must be Destroyed,* in *Frankenstein, Premier Plan,* No. 51, 1969.

CAEN, Michel, *Entretien Avec Terence Fisher* in *Midi-Minuit Fantastique,* No. 7, September 1963.

CUTTS, John, and DURGNAT, Raymond, *Horror is My Business: Terence Fisher* in *Films and Filming,* July 1964.

DURGNAT, Raymond, *Eros in the Cinema,* Calder & Boyars, 1966.

TAVERNIER, Bertrand, *Entretien avec Terence Fisher* in *Midi-Minuit Fantastique,* No. 10-11, Winter 1964-5.

Bryan Forbes

BAKER, Peter G., *Whistle Down the Wind* in *Films and Filming,* September 1961.

HAALA, Erika, *Zurnige Schweigen: der denkende Mensch und die Masse* in *Filmanalysen,* No. 1, Altenberg, 1961.

KAUFMAN, Stanley, in *A World on Film,* Harper & Row, 1961.

Carl Foreman

BAKER, Peter G., *The Victors* in *Films and Filming,* January 1964.

FOREMAN, Carl, *The Road to the Victors* in *Films and Filming,* September 1963.

Lewis Gilbert

CUTTS, John, *Carve Her Name With Pride* in *Films and Filming,* April 1958.

Sidney Gilliatt

WINNINGTON, Richard (*Millions Like Us, Waterloo Road, The Rake's Progress*), op. cit.

Peter Glenville

HAALA, Erika, *Der Defangene: Von der Grenzen der wider Standkraft* in *Filmanalysen,* No. 1, Altenberg, 1961.

Bob Godfrey

RIDER, David, *The See-It-Yourself Cartoon Kit* in *Films and Filming,* August 1962.

RIDER, David, *Biography* in *Films and Filming,* January 1964.

Val Guest

KAUFMAN, Stanley, (*Expresso Bongo*) in *A World on Film,* Harper & Row, 1966.

John Guillermin

GEURIF, Francois, *John Guillermin, L'Homme à tout faire* in *Positif,* No. 99, November 1968.

Alec Guinness

MCVAY, Douglas, *Alec Guinness* in *Films and Filming,* May 1961.

Halas and Batchelor

WEINBERG, Herman G., *Animal Farm* in *Film Culture*, No. 2, March/April 1955.

Robert Hamer

ANSTEY and eds (*Kind Hearts and Coronets*), op. cit.

ROTHA, Paul, *The Scapegoat* in *Films and Filming*, September 1969.

STANBROOK, Alan, *Great Films of the Century: Kind Hearts and Coronets* in *Films and Filming*, April 1964.

Trevor Howard

WHITEHALL, Richard, *Gallery of Great Artists No. 2 – Trevor Howard* in *Films and Filming*, February 1961.

Ken Hughes

KAUFMAN, Stanley, in *A World on Film*, Harper & Row, 1966.

Brian Desmond Hurst

AGATE, James, *Heroes of Arnheim* and *Theirs Is The Glory* in *Around Cinemas: Second Series*, Home & Van Thal, 1946.

Pat Jackson

AGEE (*Western Approaches*), op. cit.

WINNINGTON (*Western Approaches*), op. cit.

Humphrey Jennings

ANDERSON, Lindsay, CALLENBACH, Ernest, MERRALL, James, NOXON, Gerald, SANSOM, William, *Special Feature: Humphrey Jennings* in *Film Quarterly*, Winter 1962.

RHODE, Eric, *Humphrey Jennings* in *Tower of Babel*, Weidenfeld & Nicolson, 1966.

STRICK, Philip, *Great Films of the Century No. 11 – Fires Were Started* in *Films and Filming*, May 1961.

Anthony Kimmins

WINNINGTON (*Mine Own Executioner*), op. cit.

Frank Lauder

ANSTEY and eds (*The Happiest Days of Your Life*), op. cit.

Philip Leacock

BAKER, Peter G., *Reach for Glory* in *Films and Filming*, November 1962.

GILCHRIST, John, *Escapade* in *Film Culture*, No. 12, 1957.

David Lean

AGEE (*In Which We Serve, Brief Encounter, Great Expectations*), op. cit.

ANSTEY and eds (*The Passionate Friends*), op. cit.

BOURGEOIS, Jacques, *Renouvellement de la tranche de vie* (*Brief Encounter*) in *La Revue du cinéma*, No. 3, December 1964.

ELLINS, Stanley, *Mr. Dickens and Mr. Pichel* in *Hollywood Quarterly*, Fall 1947.

FENIN, George, *Bridge on the River Kwai* in *Film Culture*, No. 17, February 1958.

LANDSBERGIS, A., *Summertime* in *Film Culture*, No. 4, Summer 1955.

MCVAY, Douglas, *Lean – Lover of Life* in *Films and Filming*, August 1959.

PICHEL, Irving, *This Happy Breed and Great Expectations* in *Hollywood Quarterly*, July 1947.

WINNINGTON (*Brief Encounter, Great Expectations*), op. cit.

Jack Lee

WINNINGTON (*Children on Trial, Woman in the Hall*), op. cit.

J. Lee Thompson

MOSER, Norman C., *Tiger Bay* in *Film Quarterly*, Summer 1960.

Joseph Losey

BERNARD, Marc, FABRE, Michel, MACDONALD, Richard, MOURLET, Michel, RISSIENT, Pierre, SERGUINE, Jacques, *Joseph Losey* in *Cahiers du cinéma*, No. 111, September 1960.

CAMERON, Ian, PERKINS, V. F., SHIVAS, Mark, *Joseph Losey* in *Oxford Opinion*, February 1961.

DURGNAT, Raymond, *Losey – Puritan Maids* in *Films and Filming*, May 1966.

TOURNES, Andrée, *Les Damnés, Conte Philosophique* in *Jeune cinéma*, No. 13, 1966.

WOOD, Robin, *The Criminal* in *Motion*, No. 4, February 1963.

David Macdonald

AGEE (*Desert Victory*), op. cit.

ANSTEY and eds (*Christopher Columbus*), op. cit.

Alexander Mackendrick

RITTGERS, Carol, *The Ladykillers* in *Film Culture*, No. 8, 1956.

Bernard Miles

ANSTEY and eds (*A Chance of a Lifetime*), op. cit.

John Moxey

DURGNAT, Raymond, *Lettre d'Angleterre: City of the Dead* in *Midi-Minuit Fantastique*, No. 10-11, Winter 1964-5.

Laurence Oliver

AGEE (*Henry V, Hamlet*), op. cit.

DIETHER, Jack, *Richard III, The Preservation of a Film* in *The Quarterly of Film Radio and Television*, Spring 1957.

JOHNSON, Ian, *Merely Players* in *Films and Filming*, April 1964.

LEYDA, Jay, *Richard III: The Evil That Men Do* in *Film Culture*, No. 7, 1956.

MACGOWAN, Kenneth, *Summer Films Imported and Domestic* in *Hollywood Quarterly*, October 1946.

PHILLIPS, James E., *By William Shakespeare With Additional Dialogue By*, in *Quarterly of Film Radio and Television*, Spring 1951.

PHILLIPS, James E., and SCHEIN, Harry, *Richard III: Two Views* in *Quarterly of Film Radio and Television*, Spring 1957.

RICHARDSON, Tony, *London Letter* (on *Richard III*) in *Film Culture*, No. 8, 1956.

ROBSON (*Henry V*), op. cit.

WINNINGTON (*Hamlet*), op. cit.

Gabriel Pascal

AGATE, James, *The Lost Million* (*Caesar and Cleopatra*) in *Around Cinemas: Second Series*, Home & Van Thal, 1946.

AGEE (*Caesar and Cleopatra*), op. cit.

Ronald Neame

TYLER, Parker, *Megalomaniascope and the Horse's Mouth* in *Sex Psyche and Etcetera in the Film*, Horizon, 1949.

WHITEHALL, Richard, *Tunes of Glory* in *Films and Filming*, December 1960.

Leslie Norman

BAKER, Peter G., *Summer of the Seventeenth Doll* in *Films and Filming*, March 1960.

JEUNE, C. A., *The Long and the Short and the Tall* in *Films and Filming*, March 1961.

Michael Powell

ANSTEY and eds (*The Small Back Room*), op. cit.

JOHNSON, Ian, *Peepshow, A Pin to See the* in *Motion*, No. 4, February 1963.

LEFEBRE, Raymond, PRAYER, Jacques, ROMER, Jean-Claude, TAVERNIER, Bertrand, *Dossier Michael Powell* in *Midi-Minuit Fantastique*, No. 20, October 1968.

ROBSON (*A Matter of Life and Death*), op. cit.

WINNINGTON (*A Canterbury Tale, A Matter of Life and Death*), op. cit.

Carol Reed

AGEE (*Odd Man Out*), op. cit.

ANSTEY and eds (*The Third Man*), op. cit.

ARCHER, Eugene, *A Kid for Two Farthings: Mythology of London* in *Film Culture*, No. 8, 1965.

HADSELL, John, *Odd Man Out* in *Classics of the Film*, Wisconsin University Press, 1965.

JOHNSON, Albert, *The Key* in *Film Quarterly*, Fall 1958.

POLONSKY, Abraham, *Odd Man Out and Monsieur Verdoux* in *Hollywood Quarterly*, July 1947.

ROBINSON, David, *Our Man in Havana* in *Films and Filming*, February 1960.

SARRIS, Andrew, *Carol Reed in the Context of His Time* in *Film Culture*, No. 10-11, 1956-7.

TYLER, Parker, *The Artist Portrayed and Betrayed (Odd Man Out)* in *The Three Faces of Film*, Yoseloff, 1960.

WHITEHALL, Richard, *Great Films of the Century No. 16: The Stars Look Down* in *Films and Filming*, January 1962.

Wesley Ruggles

WINNINGTON (*London Town*), op. cit.

Margaret Rutherford

ROBIN, Ladislas, *Margaret Rutherford* in *L'Age du cinéma*, No. 1, March 1961.

Steve Sekely

DURGNAT, Raymond, *Lettre d'Angleterre: Day of the Triffids* in *Midi-Minuit Fantastique*, No. 7, September 1963.

Peter Sellers

LETNEE, Kenneth J., *The Films of Peter Sellers* in *Hollywood Quarterly*, Fall 1960.

MCVAY, Douglas, *One Man Band* in *Films and Filming*, May 1963.

Anthony Simmons

LASSALLY, Walter, *Making Bow Bells* in *Films and Filming*, December 1954.

Barbara Steele

CAEN, Michel, ROMER, Jean-Claude, *Barbara Steele* in *Midi-Minuit Fantastique*, No. 17, June 1967.

DURGNAT, Raymond, *Barbara Steele* in *Motion*, No. 4, February 1963.

Peter Ustinov

KAEL, Pauline, *Billy Budd* in *I Lost it at the Movies*, Little Brown, 1965.

USTINOV, Peter, *Art and Artlessness* in *Films and Filming*, October 1968.

Harry Watt

WINNINGTON (*The Overlanders*), op. cit.

Herbert Wilcox

AGATE, James, *Fraternity Square* (*I Live in Grosvenor Square*) in *Around Cinema: Second Series,* Howe & Van Thal, 1946.

WINNINGTON (*Spring in Park Lane*), op. cit.

Richard Williams

WILLIAMS, Richard, *Animation and the Little Island* in *Sight and Sound,* Autumn 1958.

Terence Young

ANSTEY and eds (*They Were Not Divided*), op. cit.

DURGNAT, Raymond, *James Fleming contre Ian Bond ou The Man With the Golden Eye* in *Midi-Minuit Fantastique,* No. 12, May 1965.

Various

AGEE (*Dead of Night*), op. cit.

ANSTEY and eds (*Trio*), op. cit.

BOURGEOIS, Jacques, *Au coeur de la nuit* (*Dead of Night*) in *La Revue du cinéma,* No. 1, October 1946.

BULLOUGH, John, *The Goons in the Case of the Mukkinese Battlehorn* in *Film,* No. 11, January/February 1957.

TYLER, Parker, *Film Form and Ritual as Reality* (*Dead of Night*) in *The Three Faces of Film,* Yoseloff, 1960.

Screenplays

Billy Budd, Extract in *Films and Filming,* January 1962.

Brief Encounter in MANVELL, Roger, ed., *Three British Screenplays,* Methuen, 1950.

Encore (with original stories), Heinemann, 1951.

Kind Hearts and Coronets (in French as *Noblesse Oblige*) in *L'Avant-scène cinéma,* No. 18, 1962.

Odd Man Out in MANVELL, op. cit.

The Prisoner, Extract (in German) in *Filmanalysen,* No. 1, Altenberg, 1961.

Quartet (with original stories), Heinemann, 1948.

Reach for Glory, Extract in *Films and Filming,* June 1962.

Scott of the Antarctic in MANVELL, op. cit.

Secret People inaANDERSON, Lindsay, *Making a Film,* Allen & Unwin, 1952.

Trio (with original stories), Heinemann, 1950.

Filmography

D = Director, P = Producer, S = Screenplay (including adaptation, additional dialogue, or other writing credit), Ex = based on an original work by, PC = Production company, R = First released by, W = With (leading actors only).

Across the Bridge, 1957, D, Ken Annakin, P, John Stafford, S, Guy Elmes, Denis Freeman-ex Graham Greene, PC, R, Rank, W, Rod Steiger, David Knight, Marla Landi, Bernard Lee, Bill Nagy 203

Albert, R.N., 1953, D, Lewis Gilbert, P, Daniel M. Angel, S, Vernon Harris, Guy Morgan-ex Morgan, Edward Sammis, PC, Dial, R, Eros, W, Anthony Steel, Jack Warner, Robert Beatty 161

Alfie, 1965, D, P, Lewis Gilbert, S, Ex, Bill Naughton, PC, Sheldrake, R, Paramount, W, Michael Caine, Shelley Winters, Millicent Martin, Julia Foster, Jane Asher, Vivien Merchant, Eleanor Bron, Denholm Elliott 241

All Night Long, 1962, D, Basil Dearden, P, Michael Relph, S, Nel King, Peter Achilles, PC, Bob Roberts, R, Rank, W, Patrick McGoohan, Marti Stevens, Betsy Blair, Keith Michell, Richard Harris, Bernard Braden 130

All over the Town, 1948, D, Derek Twist, S, Twist, Michael Gordon, Inez Holden-ex R. F. Delderfield, PC, Wessex, R, G.F.D., W, Norman Wooland, Sarah Churchill, Cyril Cusack 39, 153–4

And Women Shall Weep, 1959, D, John Lemont, P, Norman Williams, S, Leigh Vance & Lemont, PC, Alliance-Ethiro, R, Rank, W, Ruth Dunning, Claire Gordon, Max Butterfield, Gillian Vaughan, Richard O'Sullivan 170

Angel Who Pawned Her Harp, The, 1953, D, Alan Bromly, P, Sidney Cole, S, Charles Terrot & Cole-ex Terrot, PC, Group 3, R, British Lion, W, Diane Cilento, Felix Aylmer, voice of Robert Eddison 66

Angry Hills, The, 1959, D, Robert Aldrich P, Raymond Stross, S, A. I. Bezzerides-ex Leon Uris, PC, Raymond Stross, R, M.G.M., W, Robert Mitchum, Gia Scala, Stanley Baker, Donald Wolfit 292

Diana Morgan, Roland Pertwee, T. E. B. Clarke-ex Denis Ogden, PC, Ealing, W, Françoise Rosay, Glynis Johns, Tom Walls, Mervyn Johns, Alfred Drayton 21, 125

Hamlet, 1948, D, P, Laurence Olivier, S, Alan Dent-ex William Shakespeare, PC, Two Cities, R, G.F.D., W, Laurence Olivier, Eileen Herlie, Jean Simmons, Terence Morgan, Basil Sydney, Peter Cushing, Stanley Holloway, Felix Aylmer 137, 138

Hand in Hand, 1960, D, Philip Leacock, P, Helen Winston, S, Diana Morgan-ex Sidney Harmon, Leopold Atlas, P, Helen Winston, R, Warner-Pathe, W, John Gregson, Sybil Thorndike, Finlay Currie, Philip Needs, Loretta Parry 120

Happiest Days of Your Life, The, 1950, D, Frank Launder, P, Sidney Gilliat, Launder, S, Launder & John Dighton-ex Dighton, PC, Individual (Gilliat-Launder), R, British Lion, W, Alastair Sim, Margaret Rutherford, Joyce Grenfell, Edward Rigby 142, 180, 195, 290

Heart of the Matter, The, 1953, D, George More O'Ferrall, P, Ian Dalrymple, S, Dalrymple, Lesley Storm-ex Graham Greene, PC, London Films, R, British Lion, W, Trevor Howard, Elisabeth Allan, Maria Schell, Denholm Elliott, Peter Finch, Michael Hordern 202

Heavens Above!, 1963, D, P, John and Roy Boulting, S, Frank Harvey, John Boulting-ex Malcolm Muggeridge, PC, Charter, R, British Lion, W, Peter Sellers, Cecil Parker, Isabel Jeans, Eric Sykes, Bernard Miles, Malcolm Muggeridge 39, 62, 124

Hell Drivers, 1957, D, Cy Endfield, P, Benjamin Fisz, S, John Kruse, Endfield-ex Kruse, PC, Aqua, R, JARFID, W, Stanley Baker, Herbert Lom, Peggy Cummins, Alfie Bass, Patrick McGoohan 46, 122, 123, 125, 293

Hell Is a City, 1959, D, Val Guest, P, Michael Carreras, S, Guest-ex Maurice Procter, PC, Hammer, R, Warner-Pathe, W, Stanley Baker, Donald Pleasence, Maxine Audley, Billie Whitelaw, Joseph Tomelty 165

Hellfire Club, The, 1960, D, P, Robert S. Baker, Monty Berman, S, Jimmy Sangster, Leon Griffiths-ex Sangster, PC, New World, S, Regal International, W, Keith Michell, Peter Arne, Adrienne Corri, Kai Fischer, Peter Cushing 133, *235*, 262

Henry V, 1944, D, P, Laurence Olivier, S, Alan Dent-ex William Shakespeare, PC, Two Cities, R, Eagle-Lion, W, Laurence Olivier, Renee Asherson, Leslie Banks, Robert Newton, Max Adrian 135–7, 138

Here Come the Huggetts, 1948, D, Ken Annakin, P, Betty Box, S, Mabel & Denis Constanduros, Peter Rogers, PC, Gainsborough, R, G.F.D., W, Jack Warner, Kathleen Harrison, Jane Hylton, Susan Shaw, Petula Clark 53

High Bright Sun, The, 1964, D, Ralph Thomas, P, Betty Box, S, Ex, Ian Stuart Black, PC, Box-Thomas, R, Rank, W, Dirk Bogarde, George Chakiris, Susan Strasberg, Denholm Elliott 129, 204

High Flight, 1957, D, John Gilling, P, Phil C. Samuel, S, Joseph Landon, Ken Hughes, John Gilling-ex Jack Davies, PC, Warwick, R, Columbia, W, Ray Milland, Kenneth Haigh, Bernard Lee, Anthony Newley 100

I See a Dark Stranger, 1946, D, Frank Launder, P, Launder, Sidney Gilliat, S, Launder, Gilliat, Liam Redmond-ex Launder, Wolfgang Wilhelm, PC, Individual, R, G.F.D., W, Deborah Kerr, Trevor Howard, Raymond Huntley 290

It Always Rains on Sunday, 1947, D, Robert Hamer, P, Michael Balcon, S, Angus MacPhail, Cornelius, Hamer-ex Arthur La Bern, PC, Ealing, R, G.F.D., W, Googie Withers, Jack Warner, John McCallum, Susan Shaw, Patricia Plunkett, Alfie Bass 59, 144, 244

It Happened Here, 1963, D, P, S, Kevin Brownlow, Andrew Mollo-ex Brownlow, PC, Rath Films, R, United Artists, W, Pauline Murray, Sebastian Shaw, Fiona Leland, Honor Fearson, Peter Dineley 90

It's Great To Be Young, 1956, D, Cyril Frankel, P, Victor Skutezky, S, Ex, Ted Willis, PC, Marble Arch, R, Associated British Pathe, W, John Mills, Cecil Parker, Jeremy Spenser 68, 83

It's Hard to Be Good, 1948, D, P, S, Jeffrey Dell, PC, Two Cities, R, G.F.D., W, Anne Crawford, Jimmy Hanley, Raymond Huntley 209

It's That Man Again, 1943, D, Walter Forde, P, Edward Black, S, Howard Irving Young, Ted Kavanagh, PC, Gainsborough, R, G.F.D., W, Tommy Handley, Greta Gynt, Jack Train and the I.T.M.A. Company 168–9

Jack the Ripper, 1958, D, P, Robert S. Baker, Monty Berman, S, Jimmy Sangster-ex Peter Hammond, Colin Craig, PC, Mid-Century, R, Regal International, W, Lee Patterson, Eddie Byrne, Betty McDowall, George Rose 262

Jacqueline, 1956, D, Roy Baker, P, George H. Brown, S, Patrick Kirwan, Liam O'Flaherty, Patrick Campbell, Catherine Cookson-ex Cookson, PC, Rank, R, JARFID, W, John Gregson, Kathleen Ryan, Cyril Cusack 67

Jason and the Argonauts, 1963, D, Don Chaffey, P, Charles H. Schneer, S, Jan Read, Beverley Cross, PC, Morningside-Worldwide, R, British Lion-Columbia, W, Todd Armstrong, Nancy Kovack, Gary Raymond, Honor Blackman, Nigel Green 274

Jazz Boat, 1959, D, Ken Hughes, P, Harold Huth, S, Hughes, John Antrobus-ex Rex Rienits, PC, Warwick, R, Columbia, W, Anthony Newley, Anne Aubrey, Lionel Jeffries, David Lodge 78

Jigsaw, 1961, D, P, S, Val Guest-ex Hillary Waugh, PC, Figaro, R, BLC-Britannia, W, Jack Warner, Ronald Lewis, Yolande Donlan, Michael Goodliffe, John Le Mesurier, Moira Redmond 164

Johnny Frenchman, 1945, D, Charles Frend, P, Michael Balcon, S, T. E. B. Clarke, PC, Ealing Studios, R, Eagle-Lion, W, Françoise Rosay, Tom Walls, Patricia Roc 125

Josephine and Men, 1955, D, Roy Boulting, P, John Boulting, S, Nigel Balchin, Frank Harvey, Roy Boulting-ex Balchin, PC, Charter, R, British Lion, W, Glynis Johns, Jack Buchanan, Donald Sinden, Peter Finch, Heather Thatcher, Ronald Squire 290

Lord of the Flies, 1963, D, S, Peter Brook-ex William Golding, P, Lewis M. Allen, PC, Allen Hodgdon/Two Arts, R, BLC/British Lion, W, James Aubrey, Tom Chapin, Hugh Edwards, Roger Elwin, Tom Gaman 205

Love Lottery, The, 1953, D, Charles Crichton, P, Monja Danischewsky, S, Harry Kurnitz, Danischewsky-ex Charles Neilson Gattey, Zelma Bramley-Moore, PC, Ealing-Michael Balcon, R, G.F.D., W, David Niven, Peggy Cummins, Anne Vernon, Herbert Lom 314*n*

Love Match, The, 1954, D, David Paltenghi, P, Maclean Rogers, S, Geoffrey Orme, Glenn Melvyn-ex Melvyn, PC, Group 3-Beaconsfield, R, British Lion, W, Arthur Askey, Glenn Melvyn, Thora Hird, Shirley Eaton

Love Me, Love Me, Love Me, 1962, D, P, Richard Williams, S, Stan Hayward, PC, Richard Williams, R, British Lion 63

Love on the Dole, 1941, D, P, John Baxter, S, Walter Greenwood, Barbara K. Emary, Rollo Gamble-ex Ronald Gow-ex Greenwood, PC, British National, R, Anglo-American, W, Deborah Kerr, Clifford Evans 57

Loves of Joanna Godden, The, 1947, D, Charles Frend, P, Michael Balcon, S, H. E. Bates, Angus MacPhail-ex Sheila Kaye-Smith, PC, Ealing, R, G.F.D., W, Googie Withers, John McCallum, Jean Kent 37

L-Shaped Room, The, 1962, D, S, Bryan Forbes-ex Lynne Reid Banks, P, James Woolf, Richard Attenborough, PC, Romulus, R, British Lion, W, Leslie Caron, Tom Bell, Brock Peters, Cicely Courtneidge, Bernard Lee 2, 205–6

Lucky Jim, 1957, D, John Boulting, P, Roy Boulting, S, Patrick Campbell, Jeffrey Dell-ex Kingsley Amis, PC, Charter, R, British Lion, W, Ian Carmichael, Terry-Thomas, Hugh Griffith, Sharon Acker 39, 194

Madeleine, 1950, D, David Lean, P, Stanley Haynes, S, Nicholas Phipps, Haynes, PC, Cineguild-Pinewood, R, G.F.D., W, Ann Todd, Ivan Desny, Norman Wooland, Elizabeth Sellars 223

Madonna of the Seven Moons, 1944, D, Arthur Crabtree, P, R. J. Minney, S, Roland Pertwee-ex Margery Lawrence, PC, Gainsborough, R, Eagle-Lion, W, Phyllis Calvert, Stewart Granger, Patricia Roc, Dulcie Gray, Jean Kent 260

'Maggie', The, 1954, D, Alexander Mackendrick, P, Michael Truman, W, William Rose, PC, Ealing, R, G.F.D., W, Paul Douglas, Alex Mackenzie, James Copeland, Abe Barker 19

Magic Box, The, 1951, D, John Boulting, P, Ronald Neame, S, Eric Ambler-ex Ray Allister, PC, Festival Film Productions, R, British Lion, W, Robert Donat, Maria Schell, Richard Attenborough, Laurence Olivier, Michael Redgrave, Eric Portman, Margaret Rutherford, Glynis Johns 18, 19

Major Barbara, 1941, D, P, Gabriel Pascal, S, Ex, George Bernard Shaw, PC, Gabriel Pascal, R, G.F.D., W, Wendy Hiller, Rex Harrison, Robert Morley, Robert Newton, Emlyn Williams, Sybil Thorndike, Deborah Kerr 32

Next of Kin, The, 1942, D, Thorold Dickinson, P, Michael Balcon, S, Dickinson, Basil Bartlett, Angus MacPhail, John Dighton, PC, Ealing & Directorate of Army Kinematography, R, United Artists, W, Jack Hawkins, Mervyn Johns, Stephen Murray *248, 276*

Next to No Time!, 1957, D, S, Henry Cornelius-ex Paul Gallico, P, Albert Fennell, PC, Montpelier-Henry Cornelius, R, British Lion, W, Kenneth More, Betsy Drake, Bessie Love, Roland Culver, Patrick Barr *45*

Nice Time, 1957, D, S, Claude Goretta, Alain Tanner, PC, British Film Institute Experimental Film Fund, R, Curzon *156*

Night and the City, 1950, D, Jules Dassin, P, Samuel G. Engel, S, Jo Eisinger-ex Gerald Kersh, PC, R, 20th Century-Fox, W, Richard Widmark, Gene Tierney, Googie Withers, Hugh Marlowe, Herbert Lom *293*

Night Mail, 1936, D, Basil Wright, Harry Watt, P, John Grierson, S, Watt, Wright, R, ABFD, W. H. Auden, PC, G.P.O. Film Unit *145, 146, 149*

Night My Number Came Up, The, 1955, D, Leslie Norman, P, Michael Balcon, S, R. C. Sherriff-ex Victor Goddard, PC, Ealing, R, G.F.D., W, Michael Redgrave, Alexander Knox, Sheila Sim, Denholm Elliott, Michael Hordern *30, 125, 264*

Night Must Fall, 1964, D, Karel Reisz, P, Albert Finney, Karel Reisz, S, Clive Exton-ex Emlyn Williams, PC, R, M.G.M., W, Albert Finney, Mona Washbourne, Sheila Hancock, Susan Hampshire *264*

Night of the Demon, 1957, D, Jacques Tourneur, P, Frank Bevis, S, Charles Bennett, Hal. E. Chester-ex M. R. James, PC, Sabre, R, Columbia, W, Dana Andrews, Peggy Cummins, Niall MacGinnis, Athene Seyler, Maurice Denham *265*

Night of the Eagle, 1962, D, Sidney Hayers, P, Albert Fennell, S, Charles Beaumont, Richard Matheson, George Baxt-ex Fritz Leiber, PC, Independent Artists, R, Anglo-Amalgamated, S, Peter Wyngarde, Margaret Johnston, Anthony Nicholls, Colin Gordon, Janet Blair *265*

Night to Remember, A, 1958, D, Roy Baker, P, William MacQuitty, S, Eric Ambler-ex Walter Lord, PC, R, Rank, W, Kenneth More, Ronald Allen, David McCallum, Michael Goodliffe, George Rose, Honor Blackman *22, 182, 200, 288*

Night without Sleep, 1952, U.S.A., D, Roy Baker, P, Robert Bassler, S, Frank Partos, Elick Moll-ex Moll, PC, R, 20th Century-Fox, W, Linda Darnell, Gary Merrill, Hildegarde Neff *287*

Nine Men, 1942, D, Harry Watt, P, Michael Balcon, S, Watt-ex Gerald Kersh, PC, Ealing, R, United Artists, W, Jack Lambert, Gordon Jackson, Frederick Piper, Grant Sutherland, Bill Blewett *119, 129, 152*

No Love for Johnnie, 1960, D, Ralph Thomas, P, Betty Box, S, Nicholas Phipps, Mordecai Richler-ex Wilfred Fienburgh, PC, Five Star, R, Rank, W, Peter Finch, Stanley Holloway, Mary Peach, Donald Pleasence *70, 82–3*

No Resting Place, 1950, D, Paul Rotha, P, Colin Lesslie, S, Rotha, Lesslie, Michael

Sahara, 1943, U.S.A., D, Zoltan Korda, P, Harry Cohn, S, Zoltan Korda, William Cameron Menzies, James O'Hanlon-ex Philip MacDonald-ex Russian Film *The 13*, PC, R, Columbia, W, Humphrey Bogart, Lloyd Bridges, Rex Ingram 129–30

Sailor Beware, 1956, D, Gordon Parry, P, Jack Clayton, S, Ex, Philip King & Falkland L. Cary, PC, Romulus-Remus, R, Independent-British Lion, W, Peggy Mount, Cyril Smith, Shirley Eaton, Ronald Lewis 63, 120, 158, *231*

Sammy Going South, 1963, D, Alexander Mackendrick, P, Hal Mason, S, Denis Cannan-ex W. H. Canaway, PC, Greatshows-Michael Balcon, R, M.G.M., W, Edward G. Robinson, Fergus McClelland, Constance Cummings, Harry H. Corbett 178, 179

San Demetrio London, 1943, D, Charles Frend, P, Michael Balcon, S, Robert Hamer, Frend, F. Tennyson Jesse, PC, R, Ealing, W, Walter Fitzgerald, Mervyn Johns, Robert Beatty, Gordon Jackson 100, 149, 152

Sanders of the River, 1935, D, Zoltan Korda, P, Alexander Korda, S, Lajos Biro, Jeffrey Dell-ex Edgar Wallace, PC, London Films, R, United Artists, W, Leslie Banks, Paul Robeson, Nina Mae McKinney 93

Sapphire, 1959, D, Basil Dearden, P, Michael Relph, S, Janet Green, Lukas Heller, PC, Artna, R, Rank, W, Nigel Patrick, Michael Craig, Yvonne Mitchell, Paul Massie, Bernard Miles 72, 76, *77*, 77, 130, 194, 285, 287

Saraband for Dead Lovers, 1948, D, Basil Dearden, P, Michael Balcon, S, John Dighton, Alexander Mackendrick-ex Helen Simpson, PC, Ealing, R, G.F.D., W, Stewart Granger, Joan Greenwood, Flora Robson, Françoise Rosay, Anthony Quayle 213, 260

Satellite in the Sky, 1956, D, Paul Dickson, P, Edward J. & Harry Lee Danziger, S, John Mather, J. T. McIntosh, Edith Dell, PC, Tridelta, R, Warner Brothers, W, Kieron Moore, Lois Maxwell, Donald Wolfit, Bryan Forbes, Jimmy Hanley 152

Saturday Night and Sunday Morning, 1960, D, Karel Reisz, P, Tony Richardson, S, Ex, Alan Sillitoe, PC, Woodfall, R, British Lion-Bryanston, W, Albert Finney, Shirley Anne Field, Rachel Roberts, Norman Rossington 53–4

Scapegoat, The, 1958, D, Robert Hamer, P, Michael Balcon, S, Hamer, Gore Vidal-ex Daphne du Maurier, PC, du Maurier-Guinness, R, M.G.M., W, Alec Guinness, Bette Davis, Nicole Maurey, Irene Worth, Pamela Brown, Peter Bull 144

School for Scoundrels, 1959, D, Robert Hamer, P, Hal E. Chester, S, Chester, Patricia Moyes-ex Stephen Potter, PC, Guardsman-Associated British, R, Associated British-Pathe, W, Ian Carmichael, Terry-Thomas, Alastair Sim, Janette Scott, Dennis Price 196

School for Secrets, 1946, D, S, Peter Ustinov, P, Ustinov, George H. Brown, PC, Two Cities, R, G.F.D., W, Ralph Richardson, Raymond Huntley, Richard Attenborough, Marjorie Rhodes 142

Scott of the Antarctic, 1948, D, Charles Frend, P, Michael Balcon, S, Walter Meade, Ivor Montagu, Mary Hayley Bell, PC, Ealing, R, G.F.D., W, John Mills, Derek Bond, Harold Warrender, James Robertson Justice 18, 19

Index

Page numbers in **bold** indicate detailed analysis; those in *italic* denote illustrations.
n = endnote.

List of Illustrations

While considerable effort has been made to correctly identify the copyright holders, this has not been possible in all cases. We apologise for any apparent negligence and any omissions or corrections brought to our attention will be remedied in any future editions.

The Man in the White Suit, © Ealing Studios Ltd; *Girls at Sea*, Associated British Picture Corporation; *Tamahine*, Associated British Picture Corporation; *The 39 Steps*, Gaumont-British Picture Corporation; *Sabotage*, Gaumont-British Picture Corporation; *The Thief of Bagdad*, © Alexander Korda Films, Inc.; *Room at the Top*, © Remus Films Ltd; *The Way to the Stars*, Two Cities Films/United Artists; *The Battle of the Sexes*, © Prometheus Film Productions; *How I Won the War*, Petersham Films Ltd; *The Rake's Progress*, Individual Pictures/Independent Producers; *Kind Hearts and Coronets*, Ealing Studios; *Sparrows Can't Sing*, Carthage/Elstree Distributors/Warner-Pathé Distributors; *Saturday Night and Sunday Morning*, © Woodfall Film Productions; *The Family Way*, Jambox; *Once a Jolly Swagman*, © Independent Producers Ltd; *Millions Like Us*, Gainsborough Pictures; *The Loneliness of the Long Distance Runner*, © Woodfall Film Productions Ltd; *This Sporting Life*, Independent Artists; *Poor Cow*, © Fenchurch Films Ltd; *Flame in the Streets*, The Rank Organisation Film Productions Ltd; *Sapphire*, Artna Films; *Miracle in Soho*, © The Rank Organisation Film Productions Ltd; *The Angry Silence*, © Beaver Films; *Blow-Up*, © Metro-Goldwyn-Mayer, Inc.; *Tiger in the Smoke*, Leslie Parkyn Productions/Rank Film Productions; *Great Expectations*, Cineguild, Independent Producers; *The Browning Version*, Javelin Films; *For Them That Trespass*, Associated British Picture Corporation/Associated British Pathé; *Time without Pity*, Harlequin Productions; *Reach for Glory*, Blazer Films; *A Matter of Life and Death*, Archers Film Productions/Independent Producers/The Rank Organisation; *Live Now Pay Later*, Woodlands Productions; *Passage Home*, © Group Film Productions Ltd; *I'm All Right Jack*, Charter Film Productions; *I Believe in You*, Ealing Studios; *The Millionairess*, Twentieth Century-Fox Film Corporation; *The Damned*, © Swallow Productions Ltd; *Nothing But the Best*, © Domino Productions; *Momma Don't Allow*, British Film Institute Film Fund; *The Entertainer*, Woodfall Film Productions/Holly Productions/British Lion Films/Bryanston Films; *Coal Face*, EMPO, GPO Film Unit; *Housing Problems*, British Commercial Gas Association; *Thursday's Children*, Morse Films/World Wide Pictures; *H.M.S. Defiant*, © G.W. Films Limited; *Blackmail*, British International Pictures; *They Made Me a Fugitive*, Shipman, A.R./Warner Bros. Pictures Ltd; *The Citadel*, © Loew's Incorporated; *Odd Man Out*, Two Cities Films/General Film Distributors; *Old Mother Riley Headmistress*, Harry Reynolds Productions Ltd/Renown Pictures Corporation; *The Belles of St. Trinians*, © British Lion Film Corporation Ltd; *Guns at Batasi*, © Twentieth Century-Fox Film Corporation Ltd; *Sailor Beware*, © Remus Films Ltd; *Woman in a Dressing Gown*, Godwin-Willis Productions/Associated British Picture Corporation; *Knave of Hearts*, Transcontinental Film Productions; *Secret People*, Ealing Studios; *Yesterday's Enemy*, Hammer Film Productions; *Idol of Paris*, Premier Productions; *The Tales of Hoffmann*, London Film Productions/Michael Powell & Emeric Pressburger Productions/British Lion Film Corporation; *Our Mother's House*, © Metro-Goldwyn-Mayer, Inc.; *The Hellfire Club*, © New World Pictures Ltd; *Dracula*, © Hammer Film Productions; *The Stranglers of Bombay*, © Hammer Film Productions/© Columbia; *Dead of Night*, © Ealing Studios Ltd; *The Next of Kin*, Ealing Studios/The Directorate of Army Kinematography; *Black Narcissus*, © Independent Producers Ltd; *Old Bones of the River*, Gainsborough Pictures; *Beat Girl*, © Willoughby Film Productions Ltd; *The Brides of Dracula*, © Hotspur Films Ltd; *Guns of Darkness*, © Cavalcade Films Ltd; *The Queen of Spades*, World Screen Plays/Associated British Picture Corporation; *The Gypsy and the Gentleman*, © The Rank Organisation Film Productions Ltd; *The Criminal*, © Merton Park Studios.